# PLEISTOCENE GEOLOGY AND BIOLOGY

with especial reference to the British Isles

# PLEISTOCENE GEOLOGY
# AND BIOLOGY

with especial reference to the British Isles

R. G. WEST

LONGMANS

LONGMANS, GREEN AND CO LTD
London and Harlow
*Associated companies, branches and representatives*
*throughout the world*

© *Longmans, Green & Co Ltd 1968*
*First published 1969*
*Second impression 1969*

SBN 582 44851 4

*Set in 10 on 11 pt Times new Roman*
*and printed in Great Britain by*
*Butler & Tanner Ltd, Frome and London*

# PREFACE

PLEISTOCENE studies are concerned with the reconstruction of conditions of environment and life in the immediate past, and a number of sciences are thereby involved. The geologist studies the chronology, stratigraphy and sediments of the Pleistocene, the palaeontologist and ecologist the record of fossil plants and animals. The geographer is concerned with the history of landforms in terms of the physical events of the Pleistocene, and the archaeologist with the history of man. The climatologist is interested in the climatic changes which are characteristic of the Pleistocene and which are still proceeding at present, and the glaciologist is interested in problems of ice advance and retreat.

It is important that the student in any one of these fields of interest should have a working knowledge of the principles involved in other fields, and in writing this book I have had the aim of providing a general account of various aspects of Pleistocene studies, suitable for use by third-year undergraduates, and by more advanced students, in the subjects of geology, biology, geography and archaeology. As well as the theoretical material, I have tried to include methods of investigation used in Pleistocene studies, as an understanding of field and laboratory work is very necessary in the study of the Pleistocene.

The area I have considered is restricted mainly to the glaciated and periglacial parts of north-west Europe, and the two final chapters deal specifically with the Pleistocene of the British Isles. In these chapters I have aimed to outline the present state of knowledge and the problems which await solution.

The reader will note that limited reference is made to Pleistocene stratigraphy outside the British Isles, to archaeology, and to various aspects of geology, such as marine and cave geology. These are subjects which are already well served by textbooks, and I have not intended this book to be encyclopaedic. Rather, I hope it will be a useful handbook to those interested in the Pleistocene of the British Isles.

Finally, I must thank my colleagues for their invaluable help and advice while writing the book. In particular, those who have helped me on subjects outside my direct experience—Dr J. M. Coles, Dr

B. M. Funnell, Dr K. A. Joysey, Dr H. H. Lamb, Dr V. R. Switsur and Dr E. H. Willis. I am also indebted to Dr F. A. Hibbert for much help with the manuscript, to Dr J. K. St Joseph for air photographs from the Cambridge University Collection and to Mr B. W. Sparks and Professor F. W. Shotton for photographs.

# ACKNOWLEDGMENTS

We are grateful to the following for permission to reproduce illustrations:

The Alberta Society of Petroleum Geologists for fig. 8.4c; *American Journal of Science*: fig. 9.5; *Biuletyn Periglacjalny*: fig. 5.16; Blackwell Scientific Publications Ltd: figs. 7.6, 13.10; British Association for the Advancement of Science: figs. 13.20, 13.21; Cambridge University Press: figs. 8.11a, 13.3, 13.6, 13.11; J. W. Edwards (Publishers), Inc: fig. 5.5; Ferd, Dümmler Verlag, Bonn: fig. 5.20; The Geological Association: figs. 11.5, 12.9; The Geological Society: fig. 3.4; The Geological Society of America: figs. 3.5, 5.4, 13.16; Geologische Dienst: fig. 8.7; Geologie en Mijnbouw: fig. 13.2; Geologisch-Mineralogisch Instituut, Leiden: fig. 5.17; Geological Survey of Finland: plates 3, 4a, 4b; Macmillan & Co. Ltd: fig. 3.9; *Nature*: fig. 12.13; Dr Sissons and Oliver & Boyd Ltd: fig. 12.22; The Royal Geographical Society: fig. 10.10; The Royal Meteorological Society: fig. 10.12; The Royal Society of Edinburgh: fig. 13.15; The Royal Scottish Geographical Society: fig. 3.14; The Royal Society: figs. 7.4, 13.12, 13.13, 13.14, 13.17; Smithsonian Press: fig. 9.3; Sveriges Geologiska Undersökning: fig. 5.1; John Wiley & Sons, Inc: figs. 8.4a, 8.9, 8.10.

# CONTENTS

# LIST OF TEXT FIGURES

# PLATES

between pp. 162–3

# CHAPTER 1

# THE PLEISTOCENE

THE Pleistocene covers the most recent part of geological time, the last two million years or so. The term was coined by Charles Lyell in 1839 to include the recent strata containing molluscan faunas with more than seventy per cent of living species. A few years later, in 1846, Edward Forbes modified the use of the term to make it equivalent to the Glacial Epoch. This definition has remained generally in use. It recognises that the distinctive character of the Pleistocene is the occurrence of repeated extensions of the world's ice fields, on a scale which is recorded only a few times before in the earth's geological history.

The Pleistocene is of the greatest interest to the geologist and biologist. It is young enough for the sequences of rocks, faunas and floras to be preserved in great detail. Because ice sheets and valley glaciers still exist, we are able to interpret the phenomena of Pleistocene glaciation in terms of observations of present glacial phenomena. Similarly with the plants and animals; many of the Pleistocene species are still living, and we are able to interpret past conditions of vegetation and fauna, and so climate and environment, in terms of the properties of living species. We can obtain a record of the origin of the present patterns of distribution of living species, including man, whose evolution in the Pleistocene is well documented by the record in Pleistocene deposits of flint tools, and, less frequently, bones.

The climatic changes of the Pleistocene are largely responsible for the appearance of our present landscape. In the highlands erosion by glaciers has moulded the landforms, while in the lowlands a mantle of glacial and periglacial deposits covers much of the country. In the river valleys, terraces have been formed in response to changes of sea-level and to changes of velocity and load caused by climatic and vegetational changes.

There is no reason to suppose that the climatic conditions which lead to repeated glaciations in the Pleistocene have ceased and it is probable that we are now living in a temperate interglacial period.

1

The cause of the climatic changes remains very much unknown, though there are a number of hypotheses. A great deal of information is available about the results of climatic changes in geological and biological terms, but much remains to be discovered of the facts of the Pleistocene before any of the hypotheses can be considered proven.

From the economic point of view, the wide distribution of Pleistocene deposits makes them important in matters of land use, water supply, and as a prime source for sand and gravel for the constructional industries. But even this economic importance has not been conducive to detailed mapping studies of the Pleistocene in Britain, and up to recently, apart from the nineteenth-century pioneers such as Prestwich and Clement Reid, there has been no great tradition of Pleistocene geological research as there has been in the other heavily glaciated countries of northern Europe.

### *'Drift' and the origin of the glacial theory*[1]

A distinction made by geologists in the beginning of the nineteenth century was between underlying solid rocks, usually of regular and orderly arrangement, and the irregular beds of such unconsolidated deposits as sand and gravel, which lay scattered about the surface. These superficial deposits were frequently found to contain rock fragments (erratics) foreign to the local underlying solid rocks, and they became known as 'drift', with the implication that they had drifted into their present position by the action of flood-waters.

The widespread occurrence of the drift was taken by many to be the result of the Biblical flood or deluge. This 'Diluvial Theory' of the origin of the drift was brought forward by such geologists as William Buckland and Adam Sedgwick, during the eighteen-twenties. At this time Mantell divided the drift into an older part, named the Diluvium, formed by processes no longer operative, and a younger part, the Alluvium, formed by processes still operative (e.g. aggradation in rivers). These terms still persist, especially in Germany, and in general signify Pleistocene and Holocene respectively.

With the increase in polar exploration in the early nineteenth century, it became easier to visualise the agency of floating ice as a conveyor of drift, and the Diluvial Theory was to some extent replaced by a theory postulating the carriage of the drift to its resting place by floating ice. Charles Lyell and Roderick Murchison were amongst the early supporters of this theory. Once this view was accepted, the discovery of drift at high level, for example on Moel Tryfan in north Wales at 1400 feet, implied a time of considerable submergence, during which floating ice deposited the drift. Such a submergence, then known as the Great Submergence, was accepted by some protagonists of the Floating Ice Theory.

At about the same time, in the eighteen-twenties and thirties, several continental geologists had been trying to explain the presence of large erratic boulders in Switzerland. The names of J. P. Perraudin, J. Venetz, J. de Charpentier and L. Agassiz are associated with the attribution of the movement of these erratic blocks to glacier ice, and so with the origin of the Glacial Theory of the origin of the drift. It was supposed that the former extent of glaciers was far greater and during this great expansion of the glaciers the erratic blocks had been carried to the areas where, on the melting of the ice, they were deposited.

Agassiz introduced his ideas on the transport of the drift by glacier ice to Britain in 1840. He soon convinced Buckland and others of the ability of the Glacial Theory to explain the origin of the drift, but general acceptance of the theory was slow, and it was not until the eighteen-sixties and seventies that the majority of geologists came to regard land-ice, not floating ice, as the agency of transport of the drift.

Stratigraphical studies of the drift started in the eighteen-fifties, and revealed evidence for more than one great expansion of former ice sheets and glaciers. The idea of multiple glaciation in the Pleistocene became accepted by most geologists in the latter half of the nineteenth century. In 1877, four glaciations were recognised by Geikie in East Anglia, and in 1909, four by Penck and Brückner in the Alps, and the same number of glaciations was subsequently recognised in other parts of the world. But more recently evidence has been obtained for six or more cold periods, each separated by temperate stages. Much of this evidence for climatic change has come from biological studies of Pleistocene deposits, as well as from geological evidence.

## Use of the term 'Pleistocene'

In this book I have used Pleistocene in the original sense of Lyell, making it include a segment of time up to the present day, and thus avoiding the terms Holocene, Recent or Post-glacial. The reasons for so doing are given in Chapter Eleven, on the subdivision of the Pleistocene.

## The general nature of Pleistocene deposition and erosion

During the temperate intervals of the Pleistocene we may envisage a landscape similar to our landscape at present, but largely forested.

B

The main depositional processes were as now: the filling of river valleys, especially seaward, by alluvium (peat, silt and clay), down-cutting by rivers in upland areas, the accumulation of beaches and other marine sediments, the filling of lakes with lake sediments, the adjustment of unstable slopes by downwash, and the growth of peat on raised and blanket bogs. The deposits ('non-glacial') formed by these processes in former temperate intervals can now be seen buried beneath glacial deposits of subsequent glaciations.

During the glaciations a greatly different system of erosion and deposition is found. The advance of the ice sheets scoured and eroded the uplands and parts of the adjacent lowlands. Where the ice became slow-moving or ceased movement, it deposited the load of rock debris picked up further upstream, and so extensive sheets of glacial deposits are found in the distal areas of the ice advance. Outside the areas of glaciation, in the so-called periglacial areas, the cold climate caused the formation of solifluction deposits, of loess, and of types of patterned ground now characteristic of arctic regions. The landscape here was clothed with open vegetation of northern type.

A third category of features includes the river terrace systems, formed by fluctuating conditions of erosion and aggradation, con-sequent on changes of sea-level, and on climatic and vegetational changes. Their formation continued throughout the periglacial and temperate periods.

The landscapes formed by all these processes are the background against which we must consider the geology and biology of the Pleistocene.

## REFERENCE

1 NORTH, F. J. 1943. 'Centenary of the glacial theory', *Proc. Geol. Ass. London*, **54,** 1–28.

# CHAPTER 2

# ICE AND GLACIERS

*Glaciers*

GLACIAL ice is found above surface in the form of glaciers and ice sheets and is distinct from the ground ice which forms below surface in regions of frozen ground. Glacial ice develops where accumulation of snow exceeds loss by wastage, and at present it covers some ten per cent of the world's land surface.

The development of the gross form taken by glacial ice (fig. 2.1) depends on the climate and the landforms. In a mountain region whose altitude exceeds the regional snow line (i.e. the limit to which perpetual snow descends), glaciers will tend to form in corries and valleys (plate 1). If the glacier system is extensive there will be main and tributary glaciers. If the main valley glaciers flow down on to the lower foreland regions they will form radiating piedmont glaciers.

If the climate is sufficiently favourable for glacier formation, the bulk of ice grows, becomes independent of the landforms, and buries them. Thus an ice cap may form and grow to become an ice sheet (plate 2). Examples of ice sheets are the great continental ice sheets of Greenland and Antarctica. Such ice sheets may marginally impinge on a mountain system and have outlets through their valleys, so that these outlet glaciers resemble valley glaciers.

*Formation of ice*

Snow after falling suffers compaction, crushing, melting and re-crystallisation, and these processes result in loss of porosity and permeability and increase in grain size, density and hardness till ice is formed from the snow. Thus new snow flakes, density about 0·1, after a few days become what is known as old snow, which has a granular structure and greater density. This becomes converted to firn with a density of 0·3 and greater. Further compaction and recrystallisation leads to the production of ice, impermeable and with a density greater than 0·8. This ice may start flowing under gravity and by plastic deformation becomes glacier ice.

5

*Fig. 2.1* Surface contours and outline of ice of various types of glacier (after Ahlmann).

a. Corrie glacier. Sonntag Kees, the Alps (lat. 47°07′ N, long. 12°18′ E).
b. Valley glacier. Vedretto del Forno, the Alps (lat. 46°19′ N, long. 9°43′ E).
c. Piedmont glacier. Murray Glacier, Spitsbergen (lat. 78°44′ N, long. 11° E). Note the expanded lobate terminal area.
d. Glacier cap or small ice sheet. Hardanger, Norway (lat. 60°32′ N, long. 7°25′ E).
e. The Vatnajökull ice sheet in Iceland. There is a central domed plateau with steeper draining glaciers of various shape at the margin.

(e)

Dyngju Glacier

Brúar Glacier

Norðlingalægð

Breiðamerkur Glacier

Skeiðarár Glacier

Skaftár Glacier

1600 m

1500 m

1000 m

18°

17°

16°

64°30'

64°

64°30'

64°

km
m

40

25

20

Fig. 2.2

a. Section down centre line of a valley glacier, showing regions of accumulation and ablation, and relative rates of flow in vertical and lateral section over a period of two years. The two vertical lined areas show surplus of accumulation on left and wastage of ice on right.

b. Section down centre line of a valley glacier, showing relation of crevassing to bedrock. Concentration of drainage may occur in bergschrund and crevasse areas, giving kames on down-melting. Shearplane moraines may form at the terminus on down-melting or push-moraines if readvance occurs.

c. Section through an ice sheet. To the left the ice terminus is in a relatively horizontal area; to the right the ice drains through a col in a ridge and takes the form of an outlet valley glacier.

*Morphology of glaciers*

The firn limit (limit of annual snow blanket at the glacier surface at the end of a melting season) on a glacier divides off the upper zone of accumulation of ice from a lower zone of ablation (wastage) of ice (fig. 2.2). At the headward end of a glacier there is usually a deep, near vertical, crevice, the bergschrund, dividing the ice from the confining rock. The surface of a glacier down its length is very variable and is dependent on the rate of flow and the slope of the subglacial floor. If the subglacial floor is stepped an ice fall will be formed. Crevasses are produced in the ice when stretching, resulting from differential flow rates, overcomes the breaking strength of the ice. Longitudinal stretching, resulting from an increase in slope of the floor, forms transverse crevasses; lateral stretching, from a widening of the ice stream, causes longitudinal crevasses; oblique crevasses are due to shear against side walls, and radial crevasses the result of the type of glacier expansion seen in piedmont glaciers. Crevasses are important to the glacial geologist for they concentrate drainage and thus localise deposition of sediment by the drained meltwaters.

The terminus of a glacier may be sloping or steep. A gentle slope results from considerable ablation and consequent thawing of the ice. In a rapidly advancing glacier the edge may be much steeper, and in one ending in standing water, the edge may form a vertical cliff which calves off icebergs. The end- and side-moraines associated with glaciers are considered in the next chapter.

Within the ice itself, deformation and flow result in the formation of features important to the glacial geologist. Thrust planes may be formed near the snout of the glacier, resulting from movement of active ice over basal, immobile, or slower moving ice. Folding may be present and seems to be especially characteristic of areas of compressive flow where the ice becomes thicker. Two characters of banding which appear less important to the glacial geologist are foliation of ice, apparent from differences in the size and arrangement of ice crystals, and ogives, curved alternating light and dark bands or swalls or swells appearing on the surfaces of or within glaciers below ice falls.

*Cold and warm glaciers*

Two types of glacier have been distinguished, cold (or polar) and warm (or temperate) (fig. 2.3). They are not clear-cut divisions for one part of a glacier may be of one type and another part the other.

In cold glaciers, negative temperatures prevail throughout the ice. The base may be frozen or at melting point. There is little melting and melt-water occurs only on the surface. Such glaciers occur in high latitudes. At the prevalent low temperatures, they do not flow as easily as warm glaciers.

In warm glaciers, the ice at a particular depth is at or within 1°C of its pressure melting point at that depth. The surface layers in winter may have negative temperatures. Ablation results in melting and

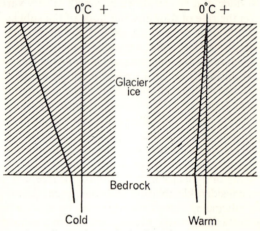

*Fig. 2.3* Thermal gradients through the ice of a cold (polar) and a warm (temperate) glacier. At the base of the warm glacier melting will occur because the earth's heat cannot be conducted upwards on the reversed gradient established by the pressure melting temperature (after Sharp).

melt-water is present at the base and at other levels of the glacier. The ice of a warm glacier can be deformed more easily, and flow is relatively faster than in cold glaciers. Warm glaciers are those of highlands in middle and low latitudes, especially in maritime regions.

Because of differences in flow and melt-water formation, cold and warm glaciers probably differ in the nature and degree of erosion and drift transport they cause. Though the differences may not yet be distinguishable from studies of the deposits and landforms left by Pleistocene glaciers, they should be borne in mind when comparing ice work at the present day by cold and warm glaciers. For example, the cold marginal parts of an ice sheet may be effective in picking up drift by a basal freezing-in process,[2] and the marginal part of a warm glacier in a maritime climate may release much flow till by surface melting. In all probability, the Pleistocene ice sheets were predominantly cold except for southern areas, especially those with a maritime climate.

*Movement of ice*

The movement of ice increases with increase of gradient, of thickness and of positive economy. The maximum rate of flow is found near the firn limit because here the quantity of ice passing at a given cross-section is greater, by the increase of accumulation, than that passing at a given point further upstream, and, because of ablation, more than that passing at a given point downstream.

In a valley glacier the horizontal and vertical velocity profiles are generally like that shown in fig. 2.2a. Speeds of greater than 100 feet a day are known from outlet glaciers of the Greenland ice sheet, but many glaciers only move at the rate of a few feet per day. Besides these regular flows, irregular surges occur where the flow velocity increases by as much as a hundred times over a short period. Such surges have been recorded from valley glaciers and smaller ice sheets. The cause of such surges is not fully understood. They are clearly due to some type of instability associated with glacier flow. Such instability could, for example, result from basal warming of a previously cold glacier base, which could initiate rapid sliding of the glacier ice. Such readjustments and surges may be of importance in glacial geology, as they may lead to successive ice advances in different directions.

In general, two modes of glacier flow occur. The first is extending flow, in which the glacier surface is stretching along the flow line, partly to compensate for surface accumulation and to adjust to a decreasing thickness downstream. The second mode is compressive flow, which is the converse of the above and is normally due to the effects of ablation and increasing thickness downstream.

Various processes have been put forward to explain ice flow. Mass movement of ice over the subglacial floor takes place by basal sliding and by internal deformation or shear throughout the ice mass. Basal sliding appears to be confined mainly to situations where the bedrock contact is at the pressure melting point. Internal shear takes place at all temperatures, and increases towards the bed of the glacier. Such internal deformation within the ice is explained by intra-granular adjustments within each ice crystal and by progressive recrystallisation within the ice mass. Regelation of ice is important in the process of basal sliding.

*Accumulation and ablation*

Glaciers gain ice by accumulation (or nourishment) and lose it by ablation (or wastage).

Accumulation results from snow, frost, hail and freezing rain falling above the snow line in the area of the glacier's nourishment. Drifted and avalanched snow may add to the quantity. Much of the precipitation is in the form of snow, mainly caused by ascent of warm moist air into cooling temperatures over mountain regions. Because of the nature of the nourishment, in most regions winter temperatures are of prime importance in determining the rate of accumulation (fig. 2.4a).

Fig. 2.4

a. The yearly course of accumulation and ablation in a glacier. If the glacier has a positive economy the area enclosed by the accumulation curve will be greater than that enclosed by the ablation curve, and vice-versa if there is a negative economy (after Sharp).

b. Economy of the Hoffell glacier at the east side of the Vatnajökull ice sheet in Iceland. The curves show average accumulation and ablation at successive heights over the period 1935–8 (after Ahlmann).

The area of ablation extends from the glacier terminus upwards to the firn limit of the glacier. Ablation by melting occurs partly through direct radiation of the sun. This effect is reduced by reflection from the snow's surface; it is important in high latitude cold glaciers. Evaporation and deflation of snow are also active as ablation agents in cold glaciers. Conduction, condensation and convection of heat from the atmosphere are important in causing ablation by melting of temperate glaciers in lower latitudes, especially in maritime climates.

They result in greater ablation than that caused by radiation. Heat is lost to the ice from warm moist air rising over the glacier's surface. Cooling of the air in contact with the ice results in condensation and the heat liberated by condensation adds to the degree of ablation. If the ice is covered by a thin drift layer ablation may be increased because more heat is absorbed by radiation, but if the drift cover is thick, heat conduction will be slow and reduced ablation will result.

In addition to loss of ice by melting, evaporation and deflation, mass wastage may occur through calving of icebergs from an ice front meeting standing water. Calving results both from buoyant ice breaking off from submerged parts of the ice cliff and from ice masses falling downslope from above the waterline.

The processes of ablation are largely summer activities (fig. 2.4a), so that the degree of ablation in most regions is chiefly determined by summer temperatures, except where calving is dominant.

## The balance between accumulation and ablation

The position and movement of the margins reflect the ratio of accumulation to ablation over an appropriate period. If the volume of ice gained by accumulation is greater than that lost by ablation (giving a positive economy), the ice front will advance. If ablation is greater than accumulation (giving a negative economy), the ice will thin and as a result there will be a recession of the ice front (fig. 2.4a). Flow may continue as recession occurs, except where the accumulation drops to such a value that flow halts and mass stagnation occurs. If accumulation balances ablation a standstill of the ice front occurs, but owing to short and long term climatic fluctuation such a situation is probably never realised for any length of time.

Warm glaciers are sensitive to changes of summer temperature, which cause changes in the ablation rate and are thus important in determining whether a glacier's economy will be a positive or negative one.

The term regimen has been used to describe the activity of a glacier taken as a unit, including the balance between accumulation and ablation (economy), the amount of accumulation and ablation (and thus the effective climatic factors) (fig. 2.4b) and the rate of flow.

Cold glaciers in regions with a continental climate at high latitudes (e.g. the glaciers of Antarctica and northern Greenland) characteristically have low rates of accumulation and low ablation. They have an inactive regimen, with relatively slow rates of flow. The warm glaciers of highlands in middle and low latitudes (e.g. those of Norway) have much higher rates of accumulation and ablation and are said to have an active regimen (fig. 2.4b). The Greenland ice sheet varies between these two. In the southerly part near the coast, precipitation is higher, and accumulation greater than in the interior. In the southern coastal areas the regimen is much more active, with considerable rates of flow, than in the interior and the north, where flow may be very small. The differing regimens are of interest to the glacial geologist, for the activities of ice resulting in geological features depend on rates of flow and the amount of melt-water.

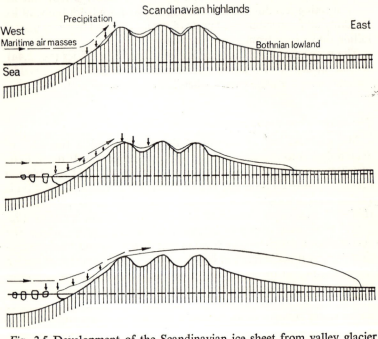

*Fig. 2.5* Development of the Scandinavian ice sheet from valley glacier stage to piedmont stage to ice sheet (after Flint).

### Continental ice sheets

The characters of valley glaciers, their development, rapidity of flow and nourishment have been considered already in the course of the chapter. Continental ice sheets are of equal interest to the glacial geologist for mostly it is the Pleistocene equivalents of these that left the landforms and deposits which he studies. The best-known ice sheet is that of Greenland and many of the following observations are based on evidence from it. Apart from emergent mountains (nunataks) an ice sheet completely buries the landscape so no trace of the original relief is left. Presumably ice sheets develop from valley glaciers which extend to form piedmont glaciers which themselves grow and coalesce to form the sheet.

The development of the Scandinavian ice sheet is shown in fig. 2.5. The result in section is an ice dome with low surface gradient. Ice sheets have not been so well studied as valley glaciers and the distribution of movement within one is not well known. It probably

*Fig.* 2.6 Surface profiles of various small ice caps, in sections where ice rests on an approximately horizontal bed, and at two places at the edge of the Greenland ice sheet, at sections where the ice lies generally within ±500 m of sea-level (after Robin).

follows the pattern shown in fig. 2.2c, with a slowly subsiding or very slow flowing centre, with flow increasing laterally. This is because nourishment tends to be greatest on the flanks where precipitation is greatest, compared with the drier conditions at higher altitudes near the centre. The low surface gradient is associated with greater ice thickness. Differential flow rates, perhaps related to regions of different accumulation rate and to differences in subglacial gradient occur within the ice sheet. The greatest rates of flow will be near the firn limit, as already mentioned, and if this is near the margin as with the Greenland ice sheet, maximum flow and thus ice work will occur near the margin. As the ice sheet grows this area of maximum ice

*Fig. 2.7*

a. Estimated surface contours of the Scandinavian ice sheet in Late Weichselian time (zone III) (after Robin).

b. Estimated profile across the Scandinavian ice sheet in Late Weichselian time (zone III). Estimated positions of ice and bedrock surfaces allowing for isostatic downwarping are also shown (after Robin).

work will move outwards. As with valley glaciers, shearplanes will tend to develop at the margin, and perhaps further upstream if the relief is unfavourable to the advance of the ice.

The surface contours of Pleistocene ice sheets have been reconstructed on the basis of profiles of present-day ice sheets, which show a certain regularity of profile in spite of differences in accumulation rate; such regularity has in fact been predicted from studies of the properties of ice.[1] Examples of profiles are shown in fig. 2.6, and an example of a reconstruction of the Scandinavian ice sheet in Late Weichselian times is shown in fig. 2.7.

It is unlikely that the balance between accumulation and ablation allowed very long standstills at the margin of an ice sheet. The economy would be very sensitive to climatic change particularly near the southern margins. Shrinkage of an ice sheet takes place primarily by recession through thinning and slower flow, though stagnation *in situ* is likely to occur later. During the course of shrinkage and disappearance small ice caps or valley glaciers will be left on highlands if net accumulation remains in these areas. These may readvance if the accumulation balance increases again. If there is complete stagnation the ice sheet thins and masses of ice become separated by the emergent subglacial landforms, and the ice may survive longest in the basins and valleys.

## REFERENCES*

AHLMANN, H. W. 1948. *Glaciological research on the north Atlantic coasts.* Royal Geographical Society Research Series, No. 1.

FLINT, R. F. 1957. *Glacial and Pleistocene Geology.* New York: Wiley.

SHARP, R. P. 1960. *Glaciers.* Eugene: Oregon State System of Higher Education.

SHUMSKII, P. A. 1964. *Principles of structural glaciology.* New York: Dover.

1. ROBIN, G. DE Q. 1964. 'Glaciology', *Endeavour*, **23**, 102–7.

2. WEERTMAN, J. 1961. 'Mechanism for the formation of inner moraines found near the edge of cold ice caps and ice sheets', *J. Glaciology*, **3**, 965–78.

* In the bibliography to each chapter, general references precede the numbered specific references.

# CHAPTER 3

# GLACIAL GEOLOGY

### Glacial erosion and deposition

THE erosional and depositional activities of ice in advance and retreat are generalised in fig. 3.1. Distinct zones of activity may usually be recognised. First an area of erosion, nearest to the centre of dispersion of the ice; secondly, an area of deposition of the drift where the load of debris picked up earlier by the eroding ice is deposited; then a zone of end-moraine formation which marks the termination of the ice, and finally a zone of proglacial deposition associated with melt-waters.

a

b

*Fig. 3.1* Features associated with ice standstill and retreat.

a. Ice margin near maximum. Zones of basal, marginal and proglacial deposition are distinguished.

b. After retreat. Hummocky moraines of till and ice-contact deposits have been formed.

18

Thus in a region which has recently suffered glaciation, the inner zone may be recognised by a bare bedrock surface, with a mantle of drift absent or very thin, the next zone by the presence of large sheets of till in the form of ground-moraine, and the outer zones by the presence of end-moraine and ice-contact features running into outwash.

In such a setting we can proceed to describe the various glacial deposits, the form taken by them, and then features resulting from glacial erosion.

### Glacial deposits

The history of glaciation is largely based on studies of glacial deposits and of the landforms resulting from accumulation of these deposits and from erosion by glacial ice. The deposits and their land-forms are very variable and in order to be able to interpret them in terms of glacial history a good understanding of their origin is necessary. Glacial deposits may be classified according to their con-stituent sediments or according to the form these deposits take. For the classification of the sediments of the drift the degree of stratifica-tion, i.e. the part which water has played in their deposition, is the most important criterion. Thus we have the extremes of till—an unsorted and unstratified deposit formed directly from the ice with-out the intervention of water-sorting, and of the outwash sediments —those carried forward from the ice by melt-water and then de-posited with sorting and stratification. Between these two extremes we have ice-contact stratified deposits, formed near to the ice, but washed to some degree by melt-water. These subdivisions are con-venient for describing glacial deposits, but, of course, all grades are possible between them and they cannot be considered as clear-cut entities.

The same may be said of the categories depending on the form taken by the glacial deposits. Here again we have three main sub-divisions. First are those constructional landforms built up by the direct action of the ice, moraine, usually composed of till. The moraine may be ground-moraine (that forming the generally low-relief landscape to the interior of the ice margin), or lateral moraine or end-moraine, according to its position in relation to the ice front. The second group is of ice-contact features which consist predom-inantly of ice-contact deposits, but which may also contain some till. Such features are usually formed by deposition from melt-water in close contact with ice. The last group is of features associated with proglacial sediments; for example, outwash plains and valley trains.

c

The classification may be summarised as follows:
Sediment 1. Unstratified. e.g. till.
         2. Stratified. a. Ice-contact deposits.
                       b. Proglacial deposits; e.g. outwash sand
                          and gravel, varved clays.
Landform 1. Moraines; e.g. ground-moraine, end-moraine.
         2. Ice-contact features; e.g. kames, eskers.
         3. Proglacial features; e.g. outwash plains, valley
            trains.

## SEDIMENTS

*Till*

Eroding ice picks up all shapes and sizes of rocks as it advances over bedrock, as well as the rock flour resulting from glacial abrasion. The deposits laid down directly by ice have hardly suffered much sorting action by water and consequently they have a characteristically unsorted and unstratified appearance, all size grades from clay to boulders being mixed together in the deposit, with the softer erratics (e.g. chalk) being clearly striated. A mechanical analysis of till is shown in fig. 5.2. Different size grades may predominate in different tills; for example, the matrix is very largely clayey in the kind of till known as boulder clay.

Various types of till can be distinguished. Lodgement till is laid down at the base of glacial ice, during the melting of debris-rich ice. This till will be lodged during ice advance as the load of debris increases and pressure-melting occurs. Another type is ablation till, formed at the surface or within ice by ablation of debris-rich ice, and, in valley glaciers, by the accumulation of surface material (superglacial till) derived in part from the surrounding land surfaces. In ablation till the fine sediment grades are sometimes absent, having been removed by surface melt-water streams. In the course of ablation near margins of glacial ice, silty or clayey till may become heavily charged with water and flow. Such flow tills are commonly seen in melting end-moraine areas. They will have the appearance of till, but will have been subject to solifluction.

Tills are characterised by the provenance of their contained erratic stones and matrix, and by the orientation of the stones. If the source of a particular rock-type found in the till is known, the direction of the movement which carried the erratic from its source will be apparent. In a region which has undergone multiple glaciation this direct interpretation may not apply, because erratics of an earlier glaciation may be redirected by a later one.

Where a rock source is sufficiently well known, it may be possible to map a boulder train, a spread of a particular erratic fanning out from the source rock (fig. 3.2), e.g. the boulder train of Ailsa Craig in the Irish Sea area.

The numerical analysis of erratic types in a till is sometimes used to characterise particular tills. For example, in Denmark the ratio

*Fig. 3.2* Distribution of some erratics by ice in north-west Europe.

    A. Ailsa Craig riebeckite-eurite.
    B. Oslo rhomb-porphyry.
    C. Dala porphyries.
    D. Viipuri Rapakivi granites.
    southern ice limit.

between flints and eruptive and crystalline rocks has been used to characterise different till sheets.[10]

The matrix of a till also gives evidence of the direction of ice movement. Ice moving east in East Anglia picked up the dark blue

Mesozoic clays of the Midlands and it is this clay which forms an important part of the till matrix and gives a blue colour to some of the chalky boulder clays of this area. Likewise, the matrix of a till deposited from ice which passes over wide outcrops of sandstone will be sandy.

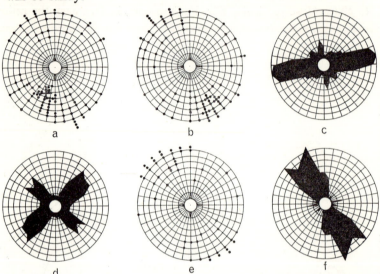

*Fig. 3.3* Stone orientation diagrams. a, b, e. Dip diagrams. Each dot represents one stone; the direction of the long axis is shown by the direction of the radius on which the dot lies (north at the top), and dip by the distance of the dot from the outermost circle of the diagram, the concentric circles indicating 10° intervals of dip, 0° on the outermost circle, 80° on the innermost.

a. In talus of a till slope at Sporle, Norfolk, the cross marking the angle and direction of slope of the talus surface.

b. In the parent Gipping Till at the same section.

e. In Norwich Brickearth at Scratby, Norfolk.

c, d, f. Rose diagrams showing the directions in 10° classes of the long axes of stones in a till count. The number of stones in each class is shown by the distance of each peak from the innermost circle, each circle representing one stone in c and d, half a stone in f, with half the number of stones in each class being placed on opposite sides of the centre of the diagram.

c. In Lowestoft till at Scratby, Norfolk. The same cliff section as e and f.

d. In till band in ice, Brageneset, Nordaustlandet, Spitsbergen.

f. In Norwich Brickearth at Scratby, Norfolk; the rose diagram corresponding to the dip diagram e.

The orientation of stones within a till may also give important evidence of direction of ice movement. The striae on an erratic from till are often parallel to the long axis of the erratic, indicating that ice movement is in a direction parallel to the long axis. Such long-axis orientation has also been observed in tills in ice, and it results from the tendency of elongated stones to lodge in till with their long axes parallel to the direction of ice flow.[1, 4] If, therefore, we take a sample of a hundred stones, for convenience not smaller than 2 cm size, from a till and measure the orientation of their long axes, the preferred orientation will give the direction of movement of the ice which deposited the till.[1, 6, 8, 14] The measurements are simply made with a compass as the stones are excavated from a limited area of the exposure of the till, and the results are plotted on a rose diagram, as shown in fig. 3.3. The dip of the long axes can be measured at the same time. If there is a preferred dip, then it is possible that the deposit is a solifluction one rather than a till (fig. 3.3a). Care should be taken to choose till exposures unaffected by weathering and undeformed by cryoturbation or by subsequent ice movement.[9] The exposures should be in areas of relatively flat landscape; if there is much bedrock relief, ice flow directions may be locally varied by it. Any interpretation of regional ice flow directions must be based on a large number of measurements over the whole region. Interpretations of the ice flow of different glaciations by measurements of a number of successive till sheets is shown in fig. 3.4.

Thin-section studies of tills show that there may be a preferred orientation of small fragments, and the fabric pattern resulting has been found in many examples to be similar to the macrofabric pattern. The microfabric is studied in the laboratory using thin-sections from small blocks of oriented till obtained in the field.[11]

Though till is usually structureless to the naked eye, it sometimes shows banding, lamination or contortion (plate 15b). These may be the result of structures present in the till-rich ice which deposited the till. Banding may be caused by alternate layers of coarse and fine-grained till, and lamination by deposition of till from shear-planes in ice. Such shearplanes may contain till of rather different constitution, say more chalky, and the result, on the melting of the ice, will be the formation of chalk-rich till laminations in the till. Contortions in till may result from melting-out of contorted ice such as is nowadays seen at the margins of advancing glaciers, especially in push-moraines, or from shoving or drag by overriding ice after deposition, or by slumping of water-rich till after deposition (flow till). These possibilities should be borne in mind when studying till, especially till fabric, as they will affect stone orientation. In

*Fig. 3.4* Map showing directions of preferred orientations in East Anglia. Where there are two tills in one section the lower passes beneath the circle marking the site.

particular, in shearplane or narrow-band tills preferred orientations may be transverse (fig. 3.3d).[4]

The relation of till to underlying beds is various. The contact may be a plane of erosion, or the till may rest on lower sediments with no sign of disturbance, or there may be folding and faulting of the lower sediments. Deformation results from the action of drag and push on weak incompetent beds below. If, on the other hand, deposition is dominant, the lower beds may not show deformation.

*Fig. 3.5* Directional data on the Lake Chamberlain glaciation, southern Connecticut; azimuths of three parameters (Flint 1961).

A. Probable directions of transport of rock types in the Lake Chamberlain Till. Data derived from 103 of 108 stones collected from the till at the type locality (5 were eliminated as not diagnostic of direction of transport). In plotting the diagram only the area north of the collection locality was considered. Radial lines drawn from locality of collection embrace limits of outcrop area of each rock type; length of line indicates distance to nearest outcrop, regardless of size.
B. Orientation diagram, Lake Chamberlain Till, type locality. Of 107 stones collected, 20 were first eliminated by inspection, because they are essentially equidimensional or have vertical long axes. Dashed line shows median orientation of the principal mode.
C. Directions of striations on bedrock immediately underlying Lake Chamberlain Till at the type locality. All lie within a range of 6°. Lengths of lines have no significance.

As examples of the scope of till studies and interpretation, the papers of Flint[3] and Dreimanis and Reavely[2] are cited. Fig. 3.5 shows the properties of a till in Connecticut studied by Flint.[3]

## Ice-contact deposits

The characters of ice-contact stratified drift, intermediate between the unsorted till and well-stratified and sorted outwash, arise from the rapid changes in the processes of sedimentation which occur near melting ice. There are frequent marked and sudden changes in the grain size and sorting of the sediments, boulders being inter-bedded with sand, for example, and there may commonly be inter-calations of till (plate 14b). The sediments are often built up against walls of ice, and when this melts, they will be deformed by slumping at the place of ice-contact. Deformation may also be caused by ice-push as well as ice-collapse.

## Proglacial deposits

Melt-waters carry outwash from the ice front. The sediment deposited from the melt-waters depends on the marginal landscape. If it slopes steeply away, no outwash may be deposited as the speed of the melt-water is sufficient to carry the load and perhaps cause erosion of melt-water channels as well. If the slope is gentle, sedi-ments may be deposited above the local standing water level to form sheets or bands of outwash. Such glacio-fluvial deposits are supra-aqueous. Or the outwash may be discharged into an ice-marginal lake to form glacio-lacustrine deposits or into the sea to form glacio-marine deposits. In all these instances sorting occurs and the stratifi-cation of the sediments is far more regular than with the ice-contact sediments.

The grain size deposited at any one place depends initially on the outwash load, whether it is rich in gravel, sand, silt or clay, and secondly on the distance of the place from the immediate melt-water source. Thus the coarsest grades are deposited near the source, the finest further downstream. In the case of the supra-aqueous deposits (fig. 3.6a), the coarser materials build up fans with a characteristic channelling such as would be formed by deposition from streams, while the finest grades are carried downstream and may be deposited only when they reach standing water, perhaps the sea. With sub-aqueous deposition (fig. 3.6b), deltas showing more regular sedi-mentation are built up by the coarser parts of the load shed by the melt-water, and the finer grades pass into suspension and are deposited distally to the deltas. Rafting of coarse material contained in ice into lake or sea may, however, introduce coarse unsorted or sorted grades into the finer sediments, and the grounding of icebergs may result in deformation of sediments. The wave action in such lakes will re-sort the marginal deposits to produce coarse beach sediments and finer offshore sediments. The finest sediments will be deposited in the deeper water.

It is in proglacial standing water that the laminated clays known as varved clays are formed (plate 3, fig. 3.7). During the summer melt the finer grades are delivered into proglacial lakes, the particles here precipitating in order of their size, the coarsest first. At the onset of winter melting may cease and during this season the finest particles precipitate. The increase of melting in the next summer again introduces abruptly the coarsest grades into the sediment. The result is a sharp winter-to-summer transition and a gradual summer-to-winter one, the sediment between the sharp dividing lines represents one

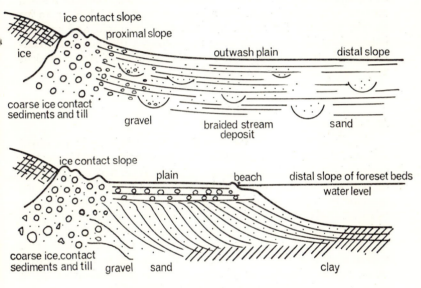

*Fig. 3.6* Proglacial land forms and deposits.
    a. Section through an outwash plain.
    b. Section through a marginal delta.

year's sedimentation, known as a varve (plate 3). Varves in freshwater have the clear-cut distinction just described and they are called diatactic varves (plate 4a). Where the water is saline, however, the dividing line between the varves is not so sharp, because flocculation of the finer particles caused by the presence of electrolytes enables these finer particles to precipitate soon after their arrival in the water body, and thus the distinction at the winter to summer change is not so sharp (plate 4b). Such a varve is named symmict. The annual deposition of varves, either diatactic or symmict, enables them to be used as valuable indicators of the passing of time.

*The quantities of till and stratified drift*

The amount of different glacial sediments produced by an ice sheet or valley glacier varies greatly. Thickness of deposit bears a close relation to mode of advance and retreat; time is normally a subordinate negligible factor. A great thickness of till can be deposited in a short time if ice is carrying a large load of debris, or conversely, an ice advance may leave little or no till if the ice is clean. The quantity of stratified drift produced will vary according to the mode of melting of the ice. A down-melting *in situ* may produce a small amount of stratified drift, but a large amount of till.[5] Near an ice margin reaching far south, ablation may be rapid and may be balanced by ice advance leading to prolonged production of meltwater and stratified deposits. Here the amount of stratified drift may greatly exceed the amount of till.

## LANDFORMS

*Morainic forms*

Moraine is the term for constructional forms built up by the direct action of the glacial ice. Deposits of lodgement till formed in the belt of deposition behind end-moraines of the ice front may take the form of gently undulating or flat plains, known as till plains or ground-moraine flats. The morainic forms of the interior may be of greater relief than this, and many irregularities can be introduced during the disintegration of the ice well behind the ice front. Such disintegration will produce forms, mainly of till but with some stratified drift, which are either linear and directionally related to the ice movement, representing fillings of crevasses or accumulations of till in thrust planes in the ice (the so-called washboard forms), or are distributed more irregularly and form hummocky moraine areas and kettles (plate 5a). These last forms are deposited on the final down-melting of the ice and are not related to the original oriented features of the ice sheet, as are the former.

A special depositional form found in the lodgement zone behind the end-moraines is the drumlin (fig. 3.12, plate 5b). Ideally, drumlins are streamlined, oval, asymmetrical hills, varying greatly in size and shape, from about 100 to 2000 yards long, 50 to 500 yards wide, and 20 to 200 feet high. They have their long axes parallel to the general direction of the ice flow in the region, and with steepest (stoss) sides upstream and gentlest (lee) downstream. Drumlins usually occur not singly but in fields of hundreds and thousands. Their appearance in the mass gives rise to the 'basket of eggs' landscape.

Lodgement till is the main constituent of drumlins, though sorted and stratified drift are sometimes found in them. The till usually shows a preferred orientation of long axes of stones parallel to the long axis of the drumlin. The predominance of till, together with the fact that drumlins are found in the zone of deposition immediately behind end-moraines, indicates that they were formed by actively advancing ice. The production of drumlins, instead of a till plain, is generally thought to be caused by increased lodgement of till on to obstacles, such as rock bosses (often found as cores in drumlins), immovable patches of basal drift in the ice, or overridden moraines, the result being streamlined hillocks with long axes parallel to the flow of the ice.

## End-moraines

Where the ice edge has stayed stationary for any length of time a series of deposits, mainly till and ice-contact sediments, is accumulated at the edge. The presence of an end-moraine therefore indicates a balance between the rate of flow of ice forwards and the rate of ablation. The limit of a glaciation may not be marked by an end-moraine if de-glaciation immediately started when the advance finished. The hummocky form of end-moraines may distinguish them from the more subdued forms found inside and outside the end-moraine belt, but there is often difficulty in separating true end-moraine forms from those hummocky features left by disintegration of ice towards the interior of an ice sheet.

End-moraines are very diverse in form (fig. 3.7); this diversity results from the position of the ice front in relation to the landforms of the periglacial region, from the relative proportions of till and stratified drift produced, and from the length of time the ice front was stationary. A series of ice lobes may produce lobate end-moraines, with interlobate end-moraines formed where the lobes meet laterally. The morainic material may be piled into a series of ridges, parallel to the ice edge and made discontinuous by melt-water streams, or it may take the form of irregular hummocky topography full of small hillocks and enclosed lake basins. If the ice has pushed up a ridge of sediment in front of it a push-moraine is formed. Here the sediments will be contorted by the ice-push.

If the ice ends in a lake or in the sea the end-moraines are predominantly of stratified drift (fig. 3.6b) and take the form of delta deposits with a steep ice-contact slope and a slope of foreset beds distally to the ice. The deltas may be confluent to produce a long ridge parallel to the ice front or may be isolated.

The so-called recessional end-moraines mark short halts or re-advances in a general recession of an ice front. Their presence implies

(a) hummocky moraine · inner melting zone · glacier · push moraine

(b)

(c) margin of ice sheet · lake · lake ice

(d) ice · ice

(e) ice · rock

continued ice flow with much ablation, in contrast to the regional disintegration of an ice sheet resulting from stoppage of flow and increase of ablation. Again it may be difficult to separate recessional moraine landforms from general disintegration landforms, but the former characteristically show a linear arrangement corresponding to the position of the ice margin, absent in the latter.

The end-moraines of corrie and valley glaciers are often formed by girdles of fragmentary rubble, derived in part from the rock debris falling on the surface of the glacier from valley sides, and forming a block-moraine. These end-moraines often extend to the valley sides to link up with lateral moraines, formed as banks at the ice edge next to the confining valley slope (plate 1).

## Ice-contact forms

The two characteristic forms associated with ice-contact sediments are the ice-contact slope, marking the place where such sediments were built up against ice, and the kettle or kettle-hole (plate 5a), a depression resulting from the collapse of sediments by the melting of a block of ice buried in them. The blocks of ice are isolated from the main ice by areas of stagnation, or they may be bergs calved off the ice front, and they become buried by ice-contact drift or outwash deposited as the stagnation proceeds. Kettle-holes are very variable in size; most have a diameter from 20 to 500 yards and a depth of 15 to 100 feet. Most frequently they form lakes in enclosed

*Fig. 3.7* Various types of end-moraine.

a. Sketch of terminus of Usher Glacier, Spitsbergen, 1927 (after Gripp), about 4 kilometres wide, showing push-moraines.

b. Sections through terminus of Green Bay Glacier, Spitsbergen, 1927 (after Gripp). Push-moraine on the left, glacier to right; the basal sketch shows the emergence of a subglacial stream as a spring. All show till in shearplanes and basal till.

c. Sketch of hummocky end-moraine at the west margin of the Vestfonna ice sheet, Nordaustlandet, Spitsbergen, 1955. Much slumping of saturated till occurs here.

d. Interlobate moraine. In the re-entrant between two ice lobes a string of hummocky moraine and kames occurs, formed at a time when the lobes were more extensive (dashed line). Kames are shown formed at that time in the area of drainage concentration between the lobes.

e. Block-moraine. Section through terminus of a small valley glacier. Origin of part of the morainic debris may be by the sliding over ice of blocks of rock moved from the upper bed rock slopes by nivation. If the marginal feature is entirely of this origin then it is known as a protalus rampart.

hollows, but they may be dry or linked with an outside drainage system. Although kettle-holes are characteristically found in ice-contact sediments, they have been reported occasionally in till.

The most important constructional features formed against ice by ice-contact stratified sediments are eskers, kames and kame terraces (fig. 3.8, plate 6a). Deposits in former melt-water streams confined

a

b

*Fig. 3.8* Origin of various landforms built of ice-contact stratified sediments.

1. Kame terrace.
2. Ice-contact slope of terrace, with kettle-hole.
3. Crevasse-fillings.
4. Esker.
5. Kame.
6. Moulin kame with nucleus of till pushed up by ice pressure (marked by arrows).

by ice appear on the melting of the ice as the long sinuous ridges known as eskers (fig. 3.9). These ridges may range in height from 5 to 100 feet and may, with discontinuities, extend up to several miles. They are usually symmetrical in cross-section and the general direction of stream flow is indicated by the arrangement of the irregular stratification of the ice-contact sediments. It is thought that the streams in which eskers form are usually subglacial, but other theories of esker formation contend that in part the streams may be supra- or englacial, and that when the ice melts, the deposits are let down to form the ridges. Probably eskers of all these possible origins

*Fig. 3.9* Map of portion of the central plain of Ireland, embracing an area about 50 miles × 30 miles, and showing the distribution and trend of the eskers. The arrows show the direction of the ice motion where this is indicated by glacial striae, drumlins, or the transport of material (Wright 1937).

occur but the subglacial type appear to be more common. Some eskers are beaded; that is to say, they show regular expansions at intervals. It is supposed that the expansions are deltas formed in an extra-marginal lake at the edge of the ice by the emergent glacial streams, each delta marking a former standstill of the ice front, or are small kames formed by the issuing water at stages of retreat.

Eskers are generally found to be roughly parallel to the last direction of flow of the local ice. Thus in a valley lobe, they may follow the course of the valley. Or in a larger ice lobe which mantles a subglacial topography of some relief they may course uphill and over divides, as the flow of the subglacial water is dependent not on the subglacial topography but on hydrostatic pressures within the ice sheet.

It is evident from their mode of formation that eskers cannot occur during the advance of ice and they are therefore a sign of ice stagnation, being formed during the thinning and stagnation of the terminal zone of the ice, when melt-water was abundant.

---

*Fig. 3.10* The 'esker' at Blakeney, Norfolk.

a. Plan of 'esker', with approximate contours.
b. Long profile of 'esker'.
c. Cross-profiles of 'esker'.
d. Sketch of relation between gravel surface of
   'esker' and the till (pecked line) on which it rests.

The general slope of the 'esker' is towards the west, and its broad-topped east and west ends are almost level. If the ridge were a true subglacial esker it would be expected to show a more irregular crest roughly parallel to the subglacial floor (d), whereas the flat surfaces at the ends point to a more complex form in which crevasse filling played an important part. At the eastern end, where the feature is most marked, the 'esker' is parallel to nearby elongated kames which appear to be crevasse fillings, and the sharp angular bends in the ridge are consistent with its interpretation as a form due to melt-water drainage through a system of crevasses. The overall surface gradient indicates the north-westwards flow (back into stagnating ice). The bedding in the gravels indicates the same direction of drainage.

The development of the ridge is interpreted as follows. A crevasse, formed where stagnating ice was under tension on the brow of a ridge, was filled from the east by a westward-flowing stream. Fluvioglacial material built up until it formed the flat eastern end of the ridge and overtopped the divide to the west. Some erosion here is indicated by sections which show the gravel to rest in a channel cut in the marly boulder clay. Also the gravel is thin compared with the much greater thicknesses at either end, as is shown in the generalised profile (d). Over the divide the gravel built up on the down-slope in another crevasse system to form the considerable thickness shown at the north-west end.

**(a)**

Blakeney

100

75  N

50

100

75  100

125  New Barn

150

150  150

150

F  100

125

One mile horizontal for map and section

**(b)**

Section along regional slope slightly below esker

Quarried

Road  Road

150'

(A) (B)  Road  New Barn  (D)(E)  Pecked line shows  (F)  100'

Road  (C)  Pinnacle heights in quarries  50'

0'

**(c)**

S  (A)  N    S  (B)  N    S  N  (C)

S  N  S  .S  N

S  (D)  N  S  (E)  N  (F)

Scales in feet for cross profiles  20  10  0  50 100

**(d)**  N.W.  S.E.

D

Kame terraces are formed laterally to ice by streams running between the ice and a confining slope. On the melting of the ice, the terrace margin nearest the ice wall forms an ice-contact slope, marking the previous position of the ice. The terrace and its ice-contact slope may be pitted by kettle-holes. The regularity and length of kame terraces depend on the form of drainage of the stagnant ice. Usually kame terraces are not so regular or extended as normal terraces formed by incision of rivers in flood plains, but it may be difficult to separate the two types.

Kames are low isolated hills, usually with steep sides, formed of ice-contact stratified drift. Often they are in the form of short ridges. Kames are formed in crevasses, perforations in the ice (moulin kames) or depressions in stagnant ice, or they may be deposited at an ice edge by emergent melt-water streams; in all these instances, the melting of the ice leaves isolated mounds of ice-contact stratified drift. Sometimes the mounds tend to occur on the tops of rises in the subglacial floor, where the ice is thinner during down-melting, and where drainage evidently became concentrated. If a group of elongated kames forms a pattern related to possible crevasse patterns near the margin of an ice sheet, they are usually considered as crevasse-fillings. The surface of a crevasse-filling (fig. 3.10) will be graded to the surface or sub-surface melt-water drainage system, while in a subglacially formed esker, the surface is usually parallel to the subglacial floor. A stream depositing sediment in a crevasse may drain subglacially, so that an esker may be confluent with a crevasse-filling. Crevasse-fillings may also be partly formed from basal lodgement deposits squeezed up into the crevasse by ice pressure.

*Proglacial forms*

Outwash from an ice front may deposit a supra-aqueous outwash plain or fan, or, if there is a marginal lake or sea, a sub-aqueous delta. These, of course, merge with the end-moraine forms already described. Each of the two categories, the supra-aqueous and sub-aqueous, has a characteristic form (fig. 3.6). The outwash plain has a steep ice-contact slope marking the position of the ice (the proximal margin). This slope may be pitted by kettle-holes. From this proximal edge, which is naturally the highest part of the plain, the surface slopes away gradually in the direction of drainage (the distal slope). Outwash plains vary in size, depending on the size of the streams contributing the outwash, the load of the outwash and the length of time of formation. A series of streams close together may form a series of joined outwash fans, which may coalesce to give a single large outwash plain, perhaps up to three or four miles long and a mile or more wide. Some outwash plains are pitted by kettle-holes. This indicates that an ice recession left blocks of ice later covered by outwash. The melting of the ice blocks led to the pitting. Outwash plains formed over areas not ice-covered shortly before will not be pitted.

The outwash deltas are of quite different form. They have a flatter surface formed from the topset beds, making a contrast with the steeper distal slope resulting from the inclination of the forest beds. There may be a wave-cut beach at the junction of the flat and the slope. As with the outwash plains the proximal side may be marked by an ice-contact slope, which may be pitted by kettle-holes.

Where outwash is confined to a valley, a valley train with rather a steeper gradient, e.g. 20 feet per mile, may be built up by aggradation of the load within a valley. Terraces may be later cut in the infilling, depending on later changes of the base-level of the proglacial stream. Difficulties of separating such terraces from kame-terraces have already been considered.

Under the heading of proglacial landforms there are also the beaches, terraces, bars and lake-clay flats associated with the filling by sediment of ice-marginal lakes or seas.

*Summary of the relation of deposition to ice advance and retreat*

The surface scheme of glacial deposits and forms shown in fig. 3.1a gives their arrangements at only one stage in a glaciation. The ice has advanced to that point and will recede from it. During the advance lodgement till is the chief deposit. During the standstill, till, ice-contact stratified drift and outwash are formed and till may be deposited under the ice by pressure-melting. During the recession and down-melting, till is deposited from the basal debris-rich ice, and ice-contact stratified drift and outwash are deposited over the previous deposits. Similarly, the till plain results from the advance, the end-moraine and outwash plains and deltas from the standstill and the kames and eskers appear during the recession and down-melting. The processes associated with advance, standstill, recession and down-melting will result in the formation of the sequence of glacial deposits and the distribution of landforms now present. Each process may be of different magnitude in different glaciations, so that much diversity is to be expected in landforms and sequences of deposits.

EROSION

Both ice and melt-water action give rise to erosional features associated with glaciation. We shall first consider the processes concerned
in erosion and then describe the effects on the landforms.

*Processes*

Chemical forms of erosion are of little or no significance or importance, because of the prevailing low temperatures, but mechnical
processes are important. Removal of bedrock by plucking or quarrying will result from pressures such as friction and drag exerted by
the ice during flow, especially in well-jointed rocks. In temperate
glaciers (and possibly in continental ice sheets developing in
temperate regions during the Pleistocene) the ice is at or very near
the pressure melting-point at any depth, and water is present throughout. Any release of pressure will bring about freezing, so that water
in cracks in the subjacent bedrock may freeze and thaw. This will
assist in the quarrying action of the ice. Another possible process
is that a release of pressure on parts of the bedrock will allow
release of strains inherent in the rock with the result that cracks
occur and fragments are removed. It is also possible that large fragments of unconsolidated cubglacial sediment or rock may become
frozen to the base of the ise and are thus incorporated in the load.

These processes result in fairly large-scale removal of bedrock.
At the other end of the scale there is the important process of
abrasion of the bedrock by the load in the ice. Abrasion is mechanical
erosion on a small scale and leads to the production of 'rock flour'
which becomes incorporated in the load together with the larger
fragments derived by quarrying. Abrasion is the principal form of
erosion of frozen, and therefore unjointed, ground.

The process of nivation is also important in erosion. Nivation is
the breaking-up of near-surface rocks by freeze and thaw action and
the redistribution of the rubble down slope by such processes as
solifluction and melt-water flow.

*Small-scale effects*

These are the results of abrasion inscribed on the surfaces of the
subglacial floor and on rocks within the load. The inscriptions include
grooves, striae, and various sets of markings like chattermarks,
crescentic gouges and crescentic fractures.

The size of the linear forms depends on the size of the abrading
fragment held in the ice. Large grooves may be formed in soft

rocks, but in harder, but not too hard, rocks the fine lines of striae, up to about a foot long, are more common. They are usually best developed on the upstream (stoss) sides of rock bosses beneath the ice. Other processes involving flow and friction, e.g. grounding icebergs, solifluction, may produce striae, but the regional setting of the particular occurrence should make the origin clear. Polishing of rock surfaces is produced by multitudes of very fine striae etched by fine particles held in the ice.

*Fig. 3.11* Various small-scale abrasion marks.
    a. Chattermarks.
    b. Crescentic fractures or friction cracks.
    c. Crescentic gouge.
    d. Lunate fracture.

Sets of marks and gouges (fig. 3.11) are often found on the glaciated surfaces of hard brittle rocks. The sets are drawn out along the line of ice advance and may extend up to a foot or so, each mark being up to a few inches across. They may result from a series of impacts of stones in the ice load, giving chattermarks, or they may be crescentic in shape. Friction cracks or crescentic fractures are concave downstream, and are supposed to be formed when pressure forward of a stone in the ice load was relieved by cracking of the rock surface. A series of such cracks implies the action was repeated a number of times. Gouges concave downstream and upstream are also known. They appear to result from pressure producing cones of fracture. The exact method of production of these crescentic features is not clear. The orientation may depend on whether the fragment causing the effect is sliding or rolling.

The orientation of all these small-scale features gives two possible directions of ice flow, but it seems that there are no fool-proof criteria available yet for deciding which is the correct direction. Other evidence of ice movement must be taken into account. Usually the regional setting of their occurrence and the character of the till gives a decisive answer.

*Landforms associated with glacial erosion*

The characteristic forms resulting from mountain glaciation are the corrie (cirque, cwm), U-shaped valleys, hanging valleys, and rock steps in valleys. Continental glaciation by ice sheets produces regional basins of erosion, and a smoothed relatively driftless aspect to the land. There is of course no clear dividing line to the landforms produced by each, for valley glaciers may develop to piedmont glaciers, and to lowland ice sheets, and the ice of continental ice sheets may reach valley systems and so modify them.

Corries (plate 6b) are depressions, usually semi-circular or oblong, excavated in mountain slopes. They have steep back walls and often contain lakes. They arise by nivation in sheltered places where perennial snow (firn) accumulates, and are therefore most likely to form on north- and east-facing slopes where the snow suffers least ablation. Their distribution is also affected in some degree by rock structure, nivation being more rapid where the rocks are well jointed. Once the firn has settled in a chance hollow, nivation starts as a result of the daily melt and nightly freeze, and the hollow enlarges. If the firn is converted to ice, the ice may accumulate until flow starts, and then ice flow will increase the size of the corrie by abrasion and quarrying. Quarrying will be particularly active in the bergschrund next to the head wall of the corrie, where blocks will be loosened by freeze and thaw. Two types of corries have been distinguished, those produced by nivation, with a floor of debris, and those cleaned out to bedrock by flowing ice.

The lower limit of the accumulation of a bank of firn is the lower limit of the orographic (local) snow-line. Other conditions allowing, corries will therefore tend to develop close to the firn limit, and thus their altitude is an important clue to past changes of the snow-line.

Excavation of corries on mountain areas leads to the characteristic alpine landforms with sharp arrêtes, steep peaks and closely spaced deep corries.

*Fig. 3.12* Roches moutonnées, crag and tail, and drumlins. Directions of ice movement shown by arrows (after various authors).

a. Outlines of roches moutonnées (in long-section). The uppermost of the group of three has lee-side plucked, and is enlarged on the right, showing the relation of plucking to jointing. Where the rock is less well jointed, on the stoss-side of the enlarged section or in the two lower examples on the left, the rock surface is moulded by abrasion.

b. Rock steps resulting from variation in jointing of bedrock.

c. Crag and tail. Long-section and plan.

d. Drumlins. Long-section outlines on the left, plans and cross-section outlines on the right.

e. Transverse section through drumlin partially built of bedrock.

Hanging tributary valleys are also characteristic of mountain glaciation. They form as a result of the greater deepening and widening of the main valley by the larger main glacier compared with the smaller amount of erosion by the minor tributary glaciers. On the melting of the ice, the tributary valleys are left hanging, and become the sites of waterfalls.

The glaciated valley (plate 6b) is U-shaped, because the erosion by the glacier is spread to all parts of the valley floor and side submerged by ice. This contrasts with the V-shaped valley of river erosion, where the point of erosion is at the bottom, and where the slopes are subject to mass-wastage. Erosion by valley glaciers will also truncate spurs. The height reached by the ice up the valley sides may be marked by the trimline. Below this the rocks are smoothed and polished. Above it nivation has produced an irregular surface. The drowning of valleys deeply excavated by ice is one cause of the formation of fjords.

Rock steps (fig. 3.12) are also characteristic of the floors of glaciated valleys. Changes in gradient, and thus in the erosive power and quarrying action of the ice, and changes in prevalence of jointing of the bedrock, will produce steps in the rock floor.

Roches moutonnées (fig. 3.12) are asymmetrical bosses of rock characteristic of areas showing glaciated bedrock. The upstream side (stoss) is smoothed by abrasion, and the lee side is made irregular and steep by quarrying. If drift is deposited in the lee the form

*Fig. 3.13* Pleistocene glaciation of northern Europe, showing the highland zone (∥), the marginal drift covered zone (—) and the intervening lowland area now the Baltic.

becomes one of crag and tail and the outline may approximate to that of a drumlin. It is only a step away for deposition to replace erosion and for the crag to become the core of a drumlin.

A feature related to erosion by continental ice sheets is the occurrence of large basins between the zones of accumulation and deposition of drift. Such basins may coincide with outcrops of softer rocks. Examples are the Great Lakes of North America and the Baltic in Northern Europe (fig. 3.13). But such basin formation may also be associated with earth movements occurring near the edges of continental shields.

### Landforms associated with melt-waters

Melt-water carrying drift is an important erosive agent. Beneath the ice, drainage waters and their load may erode moulins (pot-holes) and subglacial channels (tunnel valleys). These last may also partly be formed from erosion by glacier tongues. Near the margin of the ice, especially on valley slopes, networks of channels (fig. 3.14) indicate the position of marginal, sub-marginal or subglacial drainage streams during deglaciation. Drainage of melt-water from marginal lakes leads to the formation of overflow channels. The margins of the

*Fig. 3.14* Melt-water channels on the southern side of Strath Allan, Perthshire. Dotted lines are kilometre grid squares (Sissons 1960–1).

later Scandinavian ice sheets in Europe are marked by wide drainage ways (Urstromtäler), often associated with dunes (fig. 5.3); they carried the melt-waters from the outwash plains west to the North Sea area.

*Erosion and transport of drift*

Various factors will affect the rate of erosion by ice and thus the size of the load of debris carried by the ice. The rate of movement of the ice, its weight and thickness, are important. So is the load carried by the ice. The debris is concentrated at the base of the ice, for this is where it is obtained from the bedrock, and therefore its abundance and character, whether hard or soft, will help to determine the degree of erosion. Most of the debris is acquired by quarrying and the degree of hardness and jointing of the bedrock as well as the landforms beneath the ice, will therefore also determine the rate of erosion.

With valley glaciers, erosion is much more spectacular than with ice sheets. Deep valleys are gouged out by quarrying and abrasion, the former being more important. The load carried by the ice is both basal, derived by erosion caused by the flowing ice, and superglacial. The superglacial drift is acquired by rock falls on to the surface of the glacier; the surface moraines so formed are drawn out as lines down the surface of the glacier, parallel to the direction of movement. They form the lateral moraines characteristic of valley glacier systems. The lateral moraines from tributary glaciers become medial moraines of a main glacier (fig. 3.15) and these medial moraines will extend down into the body of the main glacier, reflecting their origin in the lateral and basal load of the tributary.

With ice sheets the process of erosion and transport of drift are much more difficult to observe than with valley glaciers. Movement of the ice is most rapid nearer the edge of an ice sheet, while at the centre movement will be at a minimum. In the central parts of the area covered by an ice sheet, little erosion may occur and the pre-glacial weathering rind may be preserved. Erosion will be at a maximum nearer the margin and as the ice sheet grows the region of erosion will also move outwards. The load is principally basal, though englacial and superglacial drift may be derived by erosion from the rocks emerging through ice sheets and forming nunataks. The zonal arrangement of erosion, deposition, outwash referred to at the beginning of the chapter will be affected by the hardness of the bedrock and the region of erosion is also determined by this. Thus, the trough of erosion forming the Baltic Sea marks, roughly speaking, the boundary between hard rocks of Scandinavian and the younger soft rocks of the north German plain.

Though many individual rock types forming boulder trains are obviously transported great distances by ice, either by a single or successive ice advances, the bulk of the drift is transported less far, perhaps as little as a few miles. The evidence for this is the correspondence of the contact of the drift and the bedrock. Thus till may

*Fig. 3.15* Moraine emplacement in a valley glacier with tributary glaciers. The ice of glacier a with its basal moraine is superimposed on the ice of glacier b. Glaciers b and c are side by side, and d is inset into c. Medial and lateral moraines are present (after Sharp).

be deposited from the load soon after the debris has been acquired by the ice, depending on the rate of movement of the ice and the size of the load. Besides being carried forward at the base of the ice, the load may also be thrust up along shearplanes in the marginal zone of ice fractures, especially if the ice terminates against a slope. Drift may thus be carried up high above its place of origin. An example is the shelly drift carried up the slopes of north Wales by the Irish Sea ice to a height of 1400 feet O.D. at Moel Tryfan.

The vast quantities of glacial drift indicate that erosion by ice was very active. No rough calculations have been made as to the extent of erosion in Britain, but it has been estimated that if all the drift from Scandinavia found in Northern Europe were replaced, it would fill the Baltic and increase the height of Scandinavia's surface by around 80 feet.

# REFERENCES

FLINT, R. F. 1957. *Glacial and Pleistocene geology.* New York: Wiley.
THWAITES, F. T. 1959. *Outline of glacial geology.* Ann Arbor.
CHARLESWORTH, J. K. 1957. *The Quaternary Era.* London: Arnold.

1 DONNER, J. J. and WEST, R. G. 1956. 'The Quaternary geology of Brageneset, Nordaustlandet, Spitsbergen', *Norsk Polar-institutt Skrifter,* No. 109.
2 DREIMANIS, A. and REAVELY, G. H. 1953. 'Differentiation of the lower and the upper till along the north shore of Lake Erie', *J. Sedim. Petrology,* **23,** 238–59.
3 FLINT, R. F. 1961. 'Two tills in southern Connecticut', *Bull. Geol. Soc. Am.,* **72,** 1687–92.
4 GLEN, J. W., DONNER, J. J. and WEST, R. G. 1957. 'On the mechanism by which stones in till become oriented', *Am. J. Sci.,* **255,** 194–205.
5 GRAVENOR, C. P. and KUPSCH, W. O. 1959. 'Ice-disintegration features in Western Canada', *J. Geol.,* **67,** 48–64.
6 HARRISON, P. W. 1957. 'New technique for three-dimensional fabric analysis of till and englacial debris containing particles from 3 to 40 mm in size', *J. Geol.,* **65,** 98–105.
7 HOLMES, C. D. 1941. 'Till fabric'. *Bull. Geol. Soc. Am.,* **52,** 1299–1354.
8 LUNDQUIST, G. 1948. 'Blockens orientering i olika Jordarter', *Sver. Geol. Unders.,* Ser. C, No. 492 (Årsbok 42, No. 6).
9 MACCLINTOCK, P. and DREIMANIS, A. 1964. 'Reorientation of till fabric by overriding glacier in the St. Lawrence Valley', *Am. J. Science,* **262,** 133–42.
10 NORDMANN, V. 1928. 'Summary of the geology of Denmark', *Danm. Geol. Unders.,* V Raekke, No. 4.
11 OSTREY, R. C. and DEANE, R. E. 1963. 'Microfabric analyses of till', *Bull. Geol. Soc. Am.,* **74,** 165–8.
12 SAURAMO, M. 1923. 'Studies on the Quaternary varve sediments in southern Finland', *Comm. Geol. de Finlande Bull.,* No. 60.
13 SISSONS, J. B. 1960–1. 'Some aspects of glacial drainage channels in Britain', *Scot. Geogr. Mag.,* **76,** 131–46; **77,** 15–36.
14 WEST, R. G. and DONNER, J. J. 1956. 'The glaciations of East Anglia and the East Midlands; a differentiation based on stone-orientation measurements of the tills', *Q. J. Geol. Soc. Lond.,* **112,** 69–91.

# CHAPTER 4

# NON-GLACIAL SEDIMENTS
# AND STRATIGRAPHY

P LEISTOCENE sediments come under the geologist's heading of
'soft rocks'. They are usually unconsolidated and can readily be
broken up by hand. Two categories of sediment can be distinguished: inorganic, composed of mineral sediments, and biogenic,
composed of the products of plant and animal life.

The biogenic fraction can be divided into an organic component of
humus and decayed parts of plants and animals, and an inorganic of
diatom frustules, mollusc shells and sponge spicules. The term organic
is often loosely used in place of biogenic; but it is used here in the
stricter sense to denote the organic component of the biogenic
deposits. In the biogenic category it is convenient to include those
sediments which are a mixture of inorganic and biogenic matter.

The biogenic deposits are treated here at much greater length than
the inorganic. The latter, and their environments of deposition, are
described in the standard geological textbooks, but the former, of
great importance to the Pleistocene geologist, do not receive such
detailed treatment.

*Inorganic sediments*

The British Standard definitions for the size grades of the inorganic
fractions of sediments are given in table 4.1. There are many other
definitions of the different grades. As non-glacial sediments, the
coarser grades are found in sediments deposited by water of high
velocity in upland areas, or as beaches in coastal areas. They form a
more important component of the glacial sediments than of the non-
glacial sediments.

The degree of rounding of stones in river and glaciofluvial environments has been much studied.[1] It depends on a number of
factors including hardness of the stones and the extent to which they
have been subject to rolling, and may be a useful character to separate
sets of river or glaciofluvial gravels of different origin and history.

Electron-microscopic examination of quartz sand grains has indicated that certain surface features of the grains are a result of shaping in glacial, glaciofluvial, dune, beach and estuarine environments.[8]

The finer grades, sand, silt and clay, are most commonly associated with fluvial or estuarine deposition under conditions of low water velocity. Floodplain alluvium is mainly composed of such fine grades in varying proportions. The variation results from the differences in load and velocity of the water depositing the alluvium. The term 'brickearth' covers a wide variety of unconsolidated fine-grained sediments, but many brickearths are ancient alluvial deposits of Pleistocene rivers.

Under estuarine conditions, which can usually be determined palaeontologically, the finer grades again predominate, as a result of coagulation and flocculation of the fine particles brought about by fresh meeting saline water.

Chemical precipitates, such as calcareous tufas, vivianite (ferrous phosphate) and limonite (bog-iron) are sometimes found as Pleistocene deposits. The first are often important because of their richness in fossil molluscs.

*Table 4.1* Size grades of inorganic sediments

| | | Size of particle (mm) |
|---|---|---|
| Cobbles | | 200–60 |
| Gravel | coarse | 60–20 |
| | medium | 20–6 |
| | fine | 6–2 |
| Sand | coarse | 2·0–0·6 |
| | medium | 0·6–0·2 |
| | fine | 0·2–0·06 |
| Silt | coarse | 0·06–0·02 |
| | medium | 0·02–0·006 |
| | fine | 0·006–0·002 |
| Clay | | smaller than 0·002 |

*Biogenic sediments*

Biogenic sediments are commonly deposited during the non-glacial phases and therefore their study is very important for investigations of environmental history during these phases. There are a number of classifications of biogenic sediments; most useful are a genetic classification, explaining the origin of different types of biogenic deposit, and a descriptive classification for use in the field.

*A genetic classification.* Biogenic deposits form where plant (and, more rarely, animal) detritus is produced, and preserved from decay by the prevention of oxidation, usually because of the presence of water. For example, biogenic, chiefly organic, deposits will form in lake basins, as a result of the deposition of plant and animal skeletons (inorganic biogenic component) and of fine organic matter derived from the breakdown of aquatic plants, both large and microscopic; or peat forming plants will build up organic deposits in wet and rainy upland areas where the drainage is poor.

A biogenic deposit forms from the detritus of particular plant communities, and these plant communities are characteristic of particular environments. A genetic classification therefore takes into account the chief environmental factors which control the distribution of the plant communities forming the biogenic deposit (fig. 4.1).

Several criteria are used in a genetic classification:

1. Position of the deposit in relation to the free water surface or groundwater.

Limnic deposits (inorganic and biogenic) formed below low water level.
Telmatic deposits (usually chiefly organic) formed between low and high water levels.
Semi-terrestrial deposits (usually chiefly organic) formed at about high water level.
Terrestrial deposits (organic only) formed above high water level. Terrestrial organic deposits can form as a result of bad drainage, where ground water level is high. Such deposits have been termed soligenous. Or they may be formed as a result of high rainfall allowing plant communities to grow up beyond the influence of the ground water level. These are known as ombrogenous deposits.

2. Manner of deposition. Biogenic deposits are autochthonous (or sedentary) where the plant detritus is deposited where the plant is growing. Autochthonous biogenic, chiefly organic, deposits are called peats. The plant material is usually coarse and well-preserved, and identifiable to the peat-forming plants.

When the plant detritus is transported and then deposited, as in a lake, an allochthonous (or sedimentary) deposit is formed. Such deposits are often termed muds (in contrast to the geologist's definition of mud—an unconsolidated rock of clay grade). The plant material is usually finely divided and much of it is unidentifiable to particular species.

3. Supply of nutrients to the plant communities producing the deposits. With a rich supply of mineral nutrients, eutrophic conditions

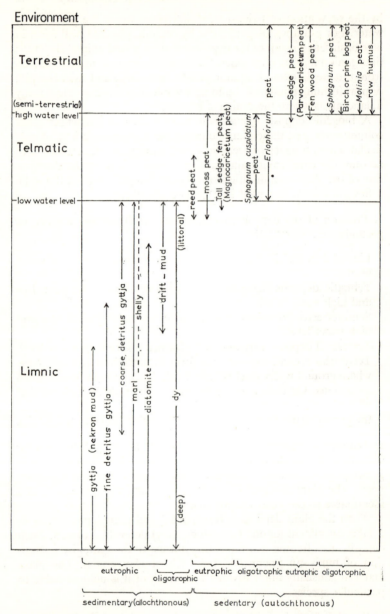

*Fig. 4.1* Relation between environment and types of sediment formed (after Lundquist).

are said to be present. They favour the growth of fen, and autoch- thonous fen peats are formed as a result. In open water under these conditions there is a rich aquatic flora and much plankton, and gyttja* (nekron mud) is formed as an allochthonous deposit.

With a poor supply of nutrients, oligotrophic conditions are pre- sent. Valley bogs are formed where water level is high in the low- lands, and raised and blanket bogs where the rainfall is sufficiently high. Acid bog peats are formed under these conditions. In open waters, there are poor crops of plankton and most organic deposition is of amorphous humus, called dy† (gel-mud).

4. Topographical and drainage conditions. Three categories of mire, each associated with particular peat types, were described by L. von Post.[10]

*Topogenous mires.* Topography is the determining factor and pro- duces water-holding basins. If such a mire is eutrophic, it is termed a fen. If oligotrophic, a valley bog.

*Ombrogenous mires.* The peat-forming plants (mostly *Sphagnum* mosses) are sustained by high rainfall, and are not dependent on ground water supply. The two main types of ombrogenous peats are those formed on raised bogs, where the *Sphagnum* peat grows in a massive dome above the ground water level in flat areas (plate 8), and blanket bog, which forms where the rainfall is high enough to allow the growth of the peat-forming plants even on slopes. As a result the peat completely blankets the landforms. Ombrogenous peats are of oligotrophic type, as their water supply is derived from the rainfall.

*Soligenous mires.* Peat formation occurs as a result of the concentra- tion of surface drainage. Topography is not so important, but there are all transitions to the topogenous type. The peats are usually of an oligotrophic type.

## The principal biogenic sediments

Fig. 4.1 gives the principal types of biogenic sediment and their relation to water level and to eutrophic or oligotrophic conditions.

---

* Originally the term gyttja was coined by H. von Post[9] to describe a copro- genous deposit formed by animals on and within a lake bottom, consisting of plant fragments, diatom frustules, quartz grains, pollen and spores. Its present day use has been changed and takes note primarily of the organic fraction.

† Originally the term dy was coined by H. von Post[9] to describe a gyttja (von Post's sense) mixed with unsaturated humic colloids. It is now usually used to describe a deposit of humus colloids.

In addition to the sediments described below chemical sediments such as calcareous tufas, vivianite and limonite sometimes occur. Naturally there are transitions between the principal types of sediment now described. The terms are applicable as a result of field inspection of sediments, but if necessary the identifications can be confirmed by laboratory analysis. The following arrangement is after Osvald.

A. *Sedimentary* (allochthonous deposits). These are all limnic.

*Gyttja* (nekron mud). Usually greenish, amorphous jelly, with a C/N (carbon/nitrogen) ratio lower than 10.[4] May be largely algal (*algal gyttja*), or mixed with calcium carbonate (*calcareous gyttja*, marl), or with clay (*clay gyttja*); the last can be moulded in the hand, unlike gyttja.

*Detritus gyttja* (detritus mud). This sediment contains small fragments of plants, and varies from fine to coarse depending on the depth of deposition. In the fine type (plate 9a), a deep water deposit, the plant remains are usually unidentifiable, but in the coarse type (plate 9b), formed in shallower water, the plant remains may be identifiable and usually include abundant fruits and seeds.

*Diatomite* (kieselgur). Rich in diatoms, usually mixed with gyttja or fine detritus gyttja.

*Drift mud* (drift peat). A shallow water sediment containing much drifted coarse plant material, including leaves and twigs. A fine grained component is lacking or small.

*Shell marl.* A gyttja or detritus gyttja rich in shells.

*Dy.* A dark brown sediment of amorphous humus colloids. The C/N ratio is greater than 10.[4]

B. *Sedentary* (autochthonous deposits). These are usually known as peats, and may be limnic, telmatic or terrestrial. The peats are named after the principal peat-forming plants found in the sediment.

1. *Limnic.* These peats are formed by plants growing in water and include such types as *Phragmites* peat (reed swamp peat), *Scirpus lacustris* peat and *Typha latifolia* peat.

2. *Telmatic.* Formed by plants growing between high and low water levels. The most important eutrophic types are:

*Cladium* peat. The reddish rhizomes of *Cladium* characterise this peat.

*Magnocaricetum* peat. Formed from the tall fen sedges.

Moss peat. Containing fen mosses such as *Amblystegium*.

Oligotrophic types include:

*Sphagnum cuspidatum* peat. This moss is common in pools on *Sphagnum* bogs.

*Eriophorum vaginatum* peat. Characterised by the shiny fibrous tussocks of *E. vaginatum*.

3. *Terrestrial*. Form above high water level, or at high water mark (semi-terrestrial). Eutrophic types are:

*Parvocaricetum* peat. Formed by the small sedges of terrestrial and semi-terrestrial habitats (plate 9c).

Fen-wood peat. Characterised by much wood, usually alder or birch.

Oligotrophic types are:

*Sphagnum* peat. Formed by hummock-forming species of *Sphagnum* (plate 9d).

*Sphagnum-Calluna* peat. Contains the black finely ridged twigs of *Calluna*.

Shrub bog peat. Contains the twigs of *Myrica*, *Vaccinium* and other shrubs found on bogs.

Birch bog peat. Contains birch twigs and leaves with *Sphagnum*.

*Eriophorum vaginatum* peat (see above).

*Scirpus caespitosus* peat. With the fibrous tussocks of *S. caespitosus*.

*Molinia* peat. With tussocks of the grass *Molinia coerulea*.

Raw humus. Sometimes develops to considerable depths in wet sandy heaths.

### A descriptive classification for field use

In the field it is necessary to describe organic sediments in as much detail as possible, yet without precise laboratory analysis. Troels-Smith has provided the most thorough system of field description, on which the following is based.

Three characters of the sediment must be observed, physical properties, components, and degree of humification.

A. *Physical properties*

1. *Colour*, whether uniform or mottled, whether changes colour on drying (change of colour on drying differentiates gyttja from dy; the former, green or brown when fresh, pales on drying, while the latter remains dark as it dries). Colour can be objectively described with the aid of the Munsell soil colour code. An impression of the colour of a sediment can be preserved by smearing some sediment on the page of a notebook.

2. *Structure*, whether granular, felted or fibrous.

3. *Nature of contact between different sediment types.* Important in interpretation of succession of sediments. May be sharp, irregular, or with a slow or rapid transition.

4. *Stratification*, whether homogeneous or stratified. If stratified, whether marked, or with alternating strata of different sediment types.

5. *Content of macrofossils*, plant or animal.

6. The following may be recorded on a 0 to 4 scale: *calcareousness*, by degree of fizz with 10 per cent HCl; *elasticity*, by squeezing; this deforms inorganic sediments, but organic sediments, especially peats, can recover their form after squeezing and thus have greater elasticity.

B. *Components.*
Apart from the inorganic fractions already described three categories of organic sediment may be distinguished. The latin terms in brackets are those suggested by Troels-Smith, and when abbreviated form his system of notation.

1. *Peat (Turfa).* Coarse macroscopic structure with large fragments of plants. Three main components are mosses (*T. bryophytica*), herbaceous plants (*T. herbacea*) and woody fragments (*T. lignosa*).

2. *Detritus (Detritus).* Small fragments of plants. Again three components can be distinguished: small fragments of wood (*D. lignosus*), small fragments of herbaceous plants (*D. herbosus*), and smaller fragments of size 2 mm to 0·1 mm of herbaceous and/or woody plants (*D. granosus*).

3. *Mud (Limus).* Fragments smaller than 0·1 mm, i.e. with microscopic structure only. The fragments may be organic, from plants or animals (*L. detrituosus*), or inorganic but biogenic, e.g. of diatom frustules (*L. siliceus organogenes*), or calcium carbonate or marl (*L. calcareus*).

C. *Humification.*
Humified components in organic deposits are soluble in dilute potassium hydroxide. The amount of humification may be measured in the field by adding a little sediment to a few ml of dilute KOH, and allowing some of the resulting liquid to be taken up on filter paper. The browner the liquid, the more highly humified is the sediment. A 0–4 scale of humification may be used. A similar scale may be used with von Post's squeezing method. Wet unhumified peat squeezed gives clear water. If the peat is humified amorphous humus can be squeezed out and colours the water, and the degree of humification may be assessed

by the amount of amorphous humus which can be squeezed through the fingers and by the darkness of the water.

In the field it may be difficult to distinguish some terrestrial and telmatic humified sediments from limnic sediments. This difficulty is dealt with in Troels-Smith's classification of the components by having two categories, humous substances (*Substantia humosa*) and humous mud (*Limus humosus*). The first indicates the presence of humified substances regardless of origin, the second is a dy.

Troels-Smith has put forward an elaborate system of notation for each of the above categories of component, for the physical properties of the sediments and for the degree of humification of the sediments, with the aim of providing concise descriptions of the sediments. Once the system is learned, there is no doubt that description is made easier. But in any case the outline of characters of sediments given above draws attention to the most important properties to be recorded in the field.

### Sediment symbols

Symbols customarily used for the commoner sediments are shown in fig. 4.2. In general, crossing lines indicate limnic sediments, vertical lines telmatic deposits and horizontal lines terrestrial deposits. In *Sphagnum* peats the closer the lines the higher the degree of humification indicated, and in gyttjas the closer the squares, the finer the sediment.

Troels-Smith (1955) has given an elaborate set of symbols, and sets of symbols have also been given by Jessen[5] and by Faegri & Iversen (1964).

### Redeposited sediments

Reworking and subsequent incorporation of older sediments into younger ones may occur in lake deposits as a result of changes of water level (fig. 4.3), by slumping of sediments on steep lake floors, or in a mire by slumping and erosion. Where the sediments are fairly compacted and clayey, the redeposited material may form a breccia (plate 7a). Careful observation of the sediments should reveal reworking, but in more organic or more sandy deposits, it is often very difficult or impossible to recognise. Other features may suggest erosion and the possibility of redeposition, e.g. an unconformity between two strata found in a line or borings, or a very sharp contact between two different sediments. The danger of redeposition is that the redeposited material contains fossils of two different ages, one from the

*Fig. 4.2* Sediment symbols commonly used.

*Fig. 4.3* Origin of redeposition in lake sediments.

a. Older (1) and younger (2) sediments in a lake basin.

b. The water level falls and erosion of 1 and 2 takes place at the margins. Redeposition of 1 and 2 takes place and forms 3, together with any contemporary lake sediments.

c. The water level rises to its previous level. The sediment 4 seals off the largely redeposited sediment 3. Sharp contacts occur between sediments 2 and 4, and 1 and 4. Below the contacts the surfaces of 1 and 2 may be reworked and hardened by drying out in the interval when the lake level was low.

redeposited material, the other contemporary with the redeposition. In clay-gyttja breccias, lumps of the redeposited material may be analysed separately, and the analyses may indicate their provenance. At the same time, in lake deposits redeposition is useful in giving evidence of the history of water levels.

### Laminated sediments

Laminations in biogenic limnic sediments are known from temperate stages of the Pleistocene (plates 4d, 7b). Light (summer) and dark (winter) layers alternate, the former being rich in calcium carbonate and the latter in organic matter. The precipitation of calcium carbonate in the summer is a result of removal of carbon dioxide and bicarbonate ions from the water by photosynthesis of aquatic plants. The annual origin of a pair of layers has also been demonstrated by studies of variation in the pollen and diatom contents between the light and dark layers.[11]

Such laminated sediments are found in deep lakes where, beneath the thermocline in an oxygen-poor environment, sediments are not disturbed because of the absence of a bottom fauna.

Other types of lamination may result from variations in diatom production or variations in the introduction of silt or clay into water bodies from streams draining into them.[2] In such examples studies of the environment of deposition and the detail of the laminations are necessary to draw conclusions about the periodicity of the laminations.

### Succession of non-glacial deposits

In any basin of non-glacial deposition, many types of sediment are usually found. The variety results from changes in the vegetation contributing the organic sediments and on the degree of subaerial denudation in the area of drainage contributing sediment to the basin. Both of these depend on the climatic conditions and on the water regime. A study of the succession of sediments will therefore reveal much of the environmental history of the times when the deposits were formed. The following are examples of successions and their interpretation. Illustrations of these successions are given in fig. 4.4.

A. *Solsö, Jutland.*[7] These deposits were formed in a lake basin in the ground moraine (till) A of the last but one glaciation in Denmark. The oldest sediment in the lake is a late-glacial grey clay (B) with the remains of arctic plants. The clay is probably derived from the washing of the local till. Then follows a brown sandy gyttja (C) formed during the temperate part of the last (Eemian) interglacial, when the surrounds were rich in vegetation and forested. A layer of grey-brown clay with some gyttja (D)

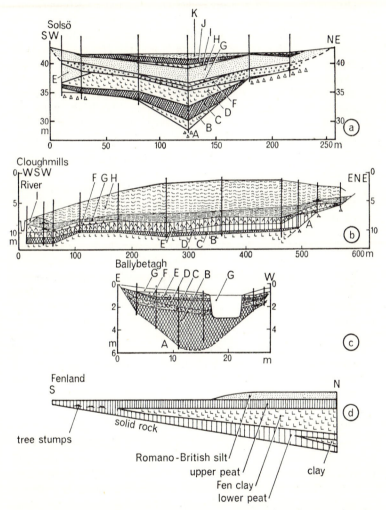

*Fig. 4.4* Four examples of sequences in non-glacial deposits. For descriptions see text.

a, Solsö, Jutland; b, Cloughmills, Co. Antrim, Ireland; c, Ballybetagh, near Dublin, Ireland; d, Fenland of East Anglia.

and a marginal sand (E) follows this. These sediments again contain an arctic flora. They are predominantly inorganic and were washed into the lake from the surrounding area, which was barely covered with vegetation, and thus subject to erosion in the cold climate. A grey sandy stony bed (F) follows and is best interpreted as a solifluction deposit at a time of severe climate. There is little sorting, which suggests the water level was low at this time. The grey clay G, the grey-brown sand H and the grey clay I are again limnic deposits formed under severe climatic conditions. The beds D to I cover the period of the last (Weichselian) glaciation. In the final layers J and K the sediments revert to an organic type, and they were formed during the temperate Flandrian, when the region was forested. J is a brown gyttja, and K a brown *Sphagnum* peat deposited as a bog grew over the surface of the lake.

B. *Cloughmills, Co. Antrim, N. Ireland.*[5] This is a section through a raised bog which developed over a lake. The grey limnic clay B is a late-glacial deposit and rests on a till A. An olive-brown algal gyttja (C) was then formed in the lake during the beginning of the temperate Flandrian. This is followed by a grey-brown *Phragmites* peat (D) and a *Phragmites*-wood peat (E), as the hydrosere developed with the lake becoming shallower and conditions changing from limnic to telmatic. This is succeeded by dark brown birch-wood peat (F) in the marginal parts of the basin of deposition, indicating the growth of birch wood over the previous sediments, as water level fell, and conditions became oligotrophic. Pine also grew at this time, as shown by the pine stumps recorded in the section in the wood peat F. Under ombrogenous conditions *Sphagnum* grew over the entire surface and a raised bog started to form. The dark brown *Sphagnum* peat G was deposited, and was humified in an interval of cessation of growth when pine again grew on the margins. The light brown fresh *Sphagnum* peat H was then formed after renewal of the bog growth. The sandy clay I is a flood deposit of the river.

C. *Ballybetagh, near Dublin.*[6] Here a series of late-glacial and post-glacial deposits is seen lying in a hollow in stony clay (A), probably reworked till. In this lake was deposited a light brown gyttja (B) during the interstadial conditions of zone II (Allerød) of the Late Weichselian, towards the end of the last (Weichselian) glaciation. During the colder zone III solifluction occurred and deposited in the lake a grey stony sand (C). During the subsequent temperate forested conditions of the Flandrian a light brown gyttja (D) was first deposited in the lake, then a thin layer of dark brown drift mud (E) when the water was shallow. Over this grew an alder-birch wood which formed the dark brown wood peat F. G is disturbed and recent peat covering the surface and filling peat diggings. The black mark in B on the right marks the position of a find of a skeleton of the Giant Irish deer.

D. *The Fenland of East Anglia.*[3] This schematic north-south section through the Fenland is about twenty-five miles long. The deposits vary in thickness from a few metres in the south to ten or more in the north. On the solid of the Fenland basin lies a series of temperate Flandrian deposits, both freshwater and brackish to marine. At the base lie freshwater peats, mostly telmatic (the lower peat). Freshwater deposition is interrupted by brackish to marine deposition as the sea-level rose in relation to the land. The wedges of blue-grey fen clay were formed as a result of the marine transgression. They are thickest on the seaward side. Regression of the sea-level resulted in an upper freshwater peat being formed. Finally, the Romano-British silt was deposited seawards as the upper peat was flooded.

## REFERENCES

BRITISH STANDARDS INSTITUTION. 1963. *Methods of testing soils for civil engineering purposes.* B.S. 1377: 1961.

DEEVEY, E. S. 1953. 'Palaeolimnology and climate', in *Climatic change,* ed. H. Shapley. Harvard University Press.

FAEGRI, K. and IVERSEN, J. 1964. *Textbook of modern pollen analysis.* 2nd edn. Oxford: Blackwell.

LUNDQUIST, G. 1927. Bodenablagerungen und Entwicklungstypen der Seen. *Die Binnengewasser,* **2.**

TROELS-SMITH, J. 1955. Characterization of unconsolidated sediments. *Danm. Geol. Unders.,* IV Raekke, **3,** No. 10.


1 BARSCH, H. and BRUNNER, H. 1963. 'Vergleichende untersuchungen zur morphometrischen analyse fluvialer gerölle', Report VIth International Congress of Quaternary, **3,** 21–38.

2 CALVERT, S. E. 1964. 'Factors affecting distribution of laminated diatomaceous sediments in Gulf of California', in *Marine geology of the Gulf of California—a Symposium.* Memoir No. 3, Amer. Assoc. Petrol. Geologists, 311–30.

3 GODWIN, H. 1940. 'Studies of the Post-glacial History of British Vegetation. III. Fenland pollen diagrams. IV. Post-glacial changes of relative land- and sea-level in the English Fenland', *Phil. Trans. R. Soc. Lond.,* B, **230,** 239–303.

4 HANSEN, K. 1959. 'Sediments from Danish lakes', *J. Sed. Petrol.,* **29,** 38–46.

5 JESSEN, K. 1949. 'Studies in late Quaternary deposits and flora-history of Ireland', *Proc. R. Irish Acad.*, **52**, B, 85–290.

6 JESSEN, K. and FARRINGTON, A. 1938. 'The bogs at Ballybetagh, near Dublin, with remarks on late-glacial conditions in Ireland'. *Proc. R. Irish Acad.*, **44**, B, 205–60.

7 JESSEN, K. and MILTHERS, V. 1928. 'Stratigraphical and palaeontological studies of interglacial fresh-water deposits in Jutland and north-west Germany', *Danm. Geol. Unders.*, II Raekke, No. 48.

8 KRINSLEY, D. H. and FUNNELL, B. M. 1965. 'Environmental history of quartz sand grains from the Lower and Middle Pleistocene of Norfolk, England, *Q. J. Geol. Soc. London*, **121**, 435–61.

9 POST, H. VON. 1862. 'Studier öfver nutidens koprogena jordbild-ningar, gyttja, dy, torf och mylla', *Kungl. Svenska Vetenskab. Akad. Handlingar*, **4**, 1–59.

10 POST, L. VON. 1926. 'Einige aufgaben der regionale moorforschung', *Sver. Geol. Unders.*, Ser. C, No. 337.

11 TIPPETT, R. 1964. 'An investigation into the nature of the layering of deep-water sediments in two eastern Ontario lakes', *Canadian J. Bot.*, **42**, 1693–1709.

# THE PERIGLACIAL ZONE

U NDER present-day conditions of climate in high latitudes and in mountain regions in lower latitudes frost action produces structures in the soils and solifluction (flow-earth) deposits. Likewise during the glacial stages of the Pleistocene the same processes occurred in the zone marginal to the advancing and retreating ice sheets. In addition, during the glacial stages, wind was responsible for the deposition of sands and silts in this marginal zone. All these processes have been grouped together under the term periglacial, signifying that they are characteristic of the climatic conditions of a zone around the ice sheets. The term is a useful one to name this group of processes and the climatic conditions associated with them, but it is necessary to remember that the processes may occur at the present time in arctic, sub-arctic or montane non-glaciated regions, and in the case of the aeolian sediments, also in climates warmer than these regions.

The periglacial features of the Pleistocene were formed in latitudes lower than those where similar features are now being formed, so that they are fossil relic features in the temperate regions. Each periglacial process occurs under particular conditions of soil, climate and drainage. Their study is therefore important for the interpretation of the environment in the regions around the ice sheets.

The principal periglacial effects can be divided into two. Those dependent on freezing and thawing in the soil induced by climatic conditions, including solifluction, structure in soil, and landforms resulting from the melting of frozen ground (thermokarst), and those dependent on wind or fluviatile action in sorting sediments (e.g. outwash deposits) produced at the margins of the ice sheet where little vegetation is present to bind the soil.

The study of periglacial features can be conveniently divided into the study of the deposits themselves, of ground ice, of the structures which result from frost action, and of the landforms produced by periglacial processes.

### DEPOSITS OF THE PERIGLACIAL ZONE

Periglacial sediments, as glacial sediments, can be divided into unsorted and sorted types. The sorting occurs through wind action to produce sediments of predominantly sand or silt grade, respectively cover-sands (flug-sand) and loess, or through fluviatile action in the periglacial region. Sorting as a result of freeze-thaw action has also been observed in the laboratory,[4] but it is not known how far this process is active in nature.

### Unsorted deposits

These are solifluction deposits (head, coombe rock, flow-earth) produced by the downslope movement of sediments saturated with water. Solifluction is not confined to periglacial regions. It occurs in andslips and under wet conditions in temperate and tropical regions.

*Fig. 5.1* Rose diagrams showing the orientation of long axes of stones in three solifluction deposits in Sweden. The arrows indicate direction of flow (Lundquist 1948).

But it is very common in periglacial regions, first because of the unconsolidated nature of most of the superficial sediments, and secondly because during the spring the frozen ground melts down from the surface, and the upper layers, being badly drained because of the impermeable frozen ground beneath, move down slope, even very shallow slopes of 2° to 5°.

The flowing motion produces a preferred orientation of the long axes of stones in the solifluction deposit parallel to the direction of flow,[11] with the dip of the long axes downslope. Fig. 5.1 shows the orientation of long axes of stones in some solifluction deposits.

Solifluction deposits may be difficult to distinguish from tills. Their local distribution as sheets on slopes, as lobes, fans and stone streams, the downslope orientation of the stones and the local pro-

venance of the stones may prove a deposit to be formed by solifluction. But where the landforms have changed considerably since deposition and where the deposit may have been derived from a glacial deposit and thus contain its erratics, it may be impossible to distinguish a till from a solifluction deposit.

A number of types of solifluction deposit have been distinguished. Massive solifluction leads to considerable thicknesses of deposit, often contorted and then known as turbulent solifluction. Solifluction on a smaller scale may appear to be laminar, with thin threads of sediment drawn out downslope. The intensity of solifluction depends on the slope, the nature of the source material and the frequency of freezing and thawing. Diurnal changes across the freezing point, such as occur in tropical mountains, produces solifluction on a smaller scale than that caused by the seasonal changes (often accompanied by shorter period changes) occurring in northern latitudes.

*Sorted deposits*
*Aeolian deposits.* That wind played an important part in the periglacial environment is shown by the wide distribution of wind-faceted stones (ventifacts, dreikanter) and wind-polished stones in the periglacial areas. The aeolian periglacial deposits are derived chiefly by deflation from areas of outwash, from surfaces of glacial deposits left freshly exposed by ice retreat, from the fine sediments deposited by proglacial rivers in the periglacial areas, and from frost-shattered rocks rich in sand and silt. The deflation may remove the finer fractions of sediments, leaving pavements of the coarser fractions, often with ventifacts.

Loess and cover-sands are two distinct types of aeolian deposit characterised by their grain size; loess is predominantly silt while cover-sands vary from fine to coarse sand. Mechanical analyses of typical examples are shown in fig. 5.2.

Loess is usually not stratified except where it has accumulated in wet depressions or ponds. The grains are mostly quartz, and the mineral content is naturally closely related to that of the sediments from which the loess originated by deflation. The grain size, though predominantly silt, may vary according to the distance of deposition from the deflation source. The more distant deposits have a finer grade. Loess, being aeolian, forms sheets of varying thickness which blanket the landforms. The thickness varies according to the closeness of the source and the direction of the prevailing wind. It may be so thin as to be hardly recognisable except by mechanical analyses,[18] or near the source it may form sheets up to fifty feet thick or more. Thick sections of loess show vertical cleavage and form steep cliffs.

*Fig. 5.2.* Cumulative frequency curves of different sediments. a, till; b, loess; c, cover-sand.

Unweathered loess is generally calcareous and effervesces with acid. Calcium carbonate may be segregated into nodules. A halt in deposition with or without climatic change results in soil formation with humus enrichment and loess sections showing such weathering horizons form the basis for Quaternary stratigraphy in many parts of central Europe (fig. 5.19). Unweathered loess may contain faunal remains including mammals and land and marsh shells. Plant remains are much scarcer as the conditions of deposition do not favour preservation.

Loess formation is not related to a very specific climatic environment; but its deposition in general, as shown by areas where it is now forming, requires a dry and windy climate, at least in the summer when melt-waters release much outwash and the ground is unfrozen. The fossil loess fauna indicates open conditions of vegetation such as now may be found in cold steppe regions. Similarly the distribution of Pleistocene loess in Europe (fig. 5.3), shows that it mainly accumulated in regions with a continental climate. The greatest thicknesses are associated with outwash sources in northern and central Eastern Europe. In the west the distribution becomes patchy. Presumably the oceanic climatic did not favour loess formation.

In Britain the brickearth common as a superficial deposit in the south and east is in many places loess,[20] and a loess fraction has been isolated from soils in places where loess is not apparent.[18]

*Fig. 5.3* Distribution of urstromtäler and loess in Europe (after Grahmann (1932) and Woldstedt).

Legend:
........ Urstromtäler
▬▬▬ limit of Weichselian glaciation
▬ ▬ ▬ limit of maximum glaciation
▨ loess

In the same way that loess blankets the landscape so does the coarser grade cover-sand. Investigations of this periglacial aeolian deposit originated in the Netherlands, where it is a common superficial deposit up to a few metres thick.[12, 27] In Europe it tends to occur between the loess belt and the limits of the Weichselian (Last) Glaciation. The mechanical analyses (fig. 5.2) indicate an aeolian origin of the sand, by deflation from unconsolidated glacial, proglacial and fluviatile deposits. The sand grains show the characteristic frosted surface of wind-blown grains, contrasted with the polished surface of water-worn grains.[3]

Cover-sands have a predominant grade of 105 to 210 $\mu$, though finer and coarser examples are known. They usually have a horizontal stratification, but may show sloping stratification related to accumulation as dunes or ridges. Alternating loamy (ill-sorted) and sandy (better-sorted) layers occur in cover-sands and these have been interpreted as being niveo-aeolian in origin, the loamy layers being transported by snow, the others by wind. Such alternating layers presently forming have been described from northern Europe.[23] Strings of pebbles in cover-sands have been interpreted as being deposited by wind during snow storms, following observations on the movement of fine gravel under such conditions. Snow meltwaters may also deposit coarser pebbly horizons with cross-bedding, associated with cover-sands. Such deposits have been termed niveofluviatile.

*Fluviatile deposits.* Sorted periglacial deposits are also produced by fluviatile action, for example sands and gravels deposited by summer snow melt-waters. Such fluviatile (or niveo-fluviatile) deposits may form spreads at the foot of erosional features or in the wide valleys which carry the melt-water floods of the spring. Such floods have been well described in Siberia by Haviland (1926). In the course of deposition rafts of frozen material may be incorporated, especially frozen peat beds cut from eroding river banks (fig. 13.5a). The rafts of organic material known as the Arctic Plant Bed in the terrace sands and gravels of the lower Lea Valley north-east of London originated in this way.

### PERMAFROST, SEASONAL FROZEN GROUND AND THE ACTIVE LAYER

Permafrost is the perennially frozen layer of the earth's surface. It is found where ground temperatures remain lower than 0°C over a period of years. Permafrost covers about twenty-two per cent of the

*Fig. 5.4* Extent of permafrost in the northern hemisphere (Black 1954).

land area of the northern hemisphere; its distribution is shown in fig. 5.4. The depth of permafrost reaches over 1000 feet in parts of Alaska and Siberia and where it is so thick reaches temperatures of −5°C to −12°C at depth. Where permafrost is discontinuous or sporadic, the thickness may be down to a few feet, with temperatures from above −1°C to −5°C. It is probable that present permafrost distribution is in part relic from past times of colder climate, as there

*Fig. 5.5* Sketch section through Siberia showing relative thicknesses of permafrost and active layer (Muller 1947).

is evidence of retreat and degradation of permafrost during the last hundred years in the northern hemisphere.

Outside the permafrost area, seasonal frozen ground may occur in climates with severe winters. The layer subject to annual freeze and thaw is called the active layer. Fig. 5.5 shows the relation between permafrost and active layer in Siberia. Many of the periglacial structures observed are associated with cryostatic pressures (pressures developed on freezing) in the saturated active layer as down-freezing takes place. The depth of the active layer depends on the extent of the temperature changes, the nature of the superficial soil and on the type of vegetation cover. At the base of the active layer, the temperature is equivalent to the mean annual temperature if the permafrost is in equilibrium with climate.

Table 5.1 shows the depth of the active layer at various latitudes in Siberia under different ground conditions.

*Table 5.1* Depths in metres of the active layer in Siberia
(from Müller 1947)

|  | Ground Conditions | | |
|  | Sandy | Clayey | Peaty |
|---|---|---|---|
| Coast of arctic ocean (continuous zone of permafrost) | 1·2–1·6 | 0·7–1·0 | 0·2–0·4 |
| At the latitude of Yakutsk (62° N) (discontinuous zone of permafrost) | 2·0–2·5 | 1·5–2·0 | ±0·5 |
| In area south of 55° N (southern part of discontinuous zone and sporadic zone of permafrost) | 3·0–4·0 | 1·8–2·5 | 0·7–1·0 |

The vegetation type and drainage is also of importance in controlling the depth of the active layer. For example, in Siberia, a terrace of saturated sandy clay, covered by 0·5 m peat with sparse larch shows an active layer of 0·5 to 0·8 m. Under similar conditions, but with grasses and broadleaf trees, there is an increased depth of active layer, 1·5 to 2·5 m, and a higher drier terrace with lichens, moss and pine shows a further increase to 2·5 to 3·5 m.


GROUND ICE

The effects of the growth of ground ice are seen in various fossil periglacial structures, and it is therefore necessary for the interpretation of these structures to know the possible origins of ground ice. Two types are important. The first occurs as a result of freezing of standing or running water; the second as a result of the freezing of water already held in sediments (segregation ice). The former type includes ice formed from spring waters (extruded ice), perhaps later buried by sediments, and ice formed by the annual freezing of meltwaters draining into contraction cracks in frozen ground. This latter has been called perennial vein ice and forms the foliated ice of ice-wedge networks. The second type, segregation ice, occurs as lenses or veins of ice formed by the segregation of ice when ground freezes, or is the result of freezing of water or liquefied sediment intruded under pressure along boundaries of impermeable deposits (injection ice). Today the most widespread ground ice is that of ice-wedge networks and segregation ice.

Segregation ice can develop in many different patterns, such as

| 1 | 7 | 13 |
| 2 | 8 | 14 |
| 3 | 9 | 15 |
| 4 | 10 | 16 |
| 5 | 11 | 17 |
| 6 | 12 | |

*Fig. 5.6* Sections of perennially frozen upper Pleistocene deposits in the Anadyr region, east Siberia (after Vtjurin 1964), showing types of ground ice in relation to sediment type.

a. Section through frozen till, Kanchalan estuary.
b. Section through frozen floodplain deposits of the river Kanchalan.

| *Sediments* | *Ground ice types* |
|---|---|
| 1. peat | 8. sublimation ice (crystallisation from water |
| 2. loam | vapour) |
| 3. sandy loam | 9. groups of ice-cemented stones |
| 4. peaty sand | 10. foliated ice of wedge |
| 5. gravel | 11–16. segregation ice of different textures |
| 6. till | 11. coarse reticulate |
| 7. limit of seasonal thaw | 12. partly foliated |
| | 13. irregular confused |
| | 14. horizontally foliated |
| | 15. incompletely foliated |
| | 16. reticulate-foliate |
| | 17. massive frozen sediment with pore ice |

foliar, reticulate, and irregular. Some of these types and the sediments in which they form are seen in fig. 5.6. On melting, signs of structure, e.g. lamination, will be left in the thawed sediment, and may be seen in some Pleistocene sediments.

The formation and melting of ground ice produces distortion and faulting in sediments, and characteristic land forms (thermokarst). These effects are considered later in relation to fossil periglacial structures and land forms.

### PERIGLACIAL STRUCTURES

Frost action working in the ground at high latitudes and altitudes produces patterned ground and isolated features. Some of these are seen as fossil structures, and as they are related to particular environmental conditions they can be valuable for the reconstruction of past environmental conditions. Present-day occurrences and processes will be described first and then fossil occurrences.

*Table 5.2* Types of patterned ground

| Pattern | Sorted(s) and non-sorted(ns) types | Remarks |
|---|---|---|
| 1. Circles | s  stone circles, debris islands<br>ns peat and tussock rings, spot medallions | isolated or grouped, circular or near circular features. The non-sorted types manifest in vegetation patterns. 1–10 m diameter |
| 2. Nets or hummock fields | s  patterns intermediate between 1s and 3s<br>ns earth hummocks, frost mounds, palsar; patterns intermediate between 1ns and 3ns | more closely spaced than 1, sizes similar |
| 3. Polygons | s  stone polygons<br>ns frost-crack and ice-wedge (tundra) polygons (plate 10b); tussock-birch heath polygons, desiccation polygons | patterns 1–10 m diameter, but non-sorted may be up to 100 m or more across. Non-sorted polygons manifest in vegetation patterns. Low centre (active growth) polygons, and raised centre (wedge degradation) polygons |
| 4. Steps | s  stone garlands<br>ns peat or turf terraces | on moderate slopes, and may form elongated polygonal patterns |
| 5. Stripes | s  stone stripes<br>ns vegetation stripes (plate 10a) | occur on slopes 2° or steeper, 1–10 m wide; non-sorted types manifest in vegetation patterns |

*Patterned ground*

Patterned ground is not confined to surfaces affected by frost; it is, for example, seen in the desiccation patterns of arid lands. But it is highly characteristic of arctic, sub-arctic and montane regions. Washburn[28] has produced a most useful descriptive classification of patterned ground. It is based on the shape of the pattern and the degree of sorting in the pattern. In general, the shape is related to the slope. On flat ground, circles, nets and polygons develop, on moderate slopes steps, and on steeper slopes stripes (plate 10a). The transition from polygon to stripe may be direct without steps. The magnitude of the patterns varies from $\frac{1}{2}$ m or even smaller, to 3 to 10 m. with a much greater size, up to tens of metres, with ice-wedge polygons. The size is related to the frequency of the freeze-thaw cycle, the availability of water and the severity of the climate. The smallest forms are found in montane regions, and the largest in continental arctic- or sub-arctic regions.

Table 5.2 indicates the variety of patterns; clear distinctions between the types are not always possible, as is to be expected with phenomena produced by a number of processes.

*Isolated structures*

In addition to those periglacial features organised into patterns, there are those which occur in an irregular or isolated fashion, such

*Fig. 5.7* Mounds resulting from frost action.
a. Pingo of Greenland type (after Müller 1959).
b. Pingo of Mackenzie type (after Müller 1959). 1–4 show stages of trapping of unfrozen saturated sediment by enveloping permafrost. 1. Lake and related unfrozen ground beneath. 2. Permafrost spreads as a result of lake shallowing and freezing of infill. 3. Hydrostatic pressure of water in unfrozen saturated sediments at depth causes bulging of ground. Ice begins to form as water is expelled upwards from the saturated ground beginning to freeze. 4. Envelopment by permafrost complete.
c. Hummock formed by local presence of segregation ice. Localisation may result from presence of sediment favouring segregation of ice (silt, clay), from thick peat cover and hydrology favouring total heat loss over the year (pals), or from degradation of widespread permafrost and ice-wedge systems leaving frozen ground nuclei in protected areas (thermokarst hummocks).
d. Formation of a mound as a result of seasonal freezing of a saturated terrace sand over impermeable rock. Arrows show direction of encroachment by permafrost and resulting upward hydrostatic pressure.

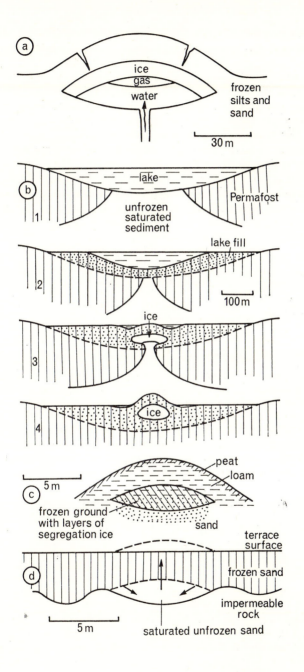

a

ice
gas
water

frozen
silts and
sand

30 m

b

lake

Permafost

1

unfrozen
saturated
sediment

lake fill

2

100 m

ice

3

ice

4

5 m

c

peat
loam

frozen ground
with layers of
segregation ice

sand

terrace
surface

d

frozen sand

impermeable
rock

5 m

saturated unfrozen sand

as frost mounds.[13] Their formation results from local peculiarities of drainage and sediment. With such local conditions, e.g. badly drained sand and silt, local ice lenses may develop in the permafrost or above it by segregation of ice, perhaps during the down freezing of the active layer, and on melting these produce horizontal veinlike structures or depressions in the ground. Freezing-down of the active layer in the autumn or the development of permafrost over water-bearing sediments may produce injections of saturated slower freezing clays or silts under pressure into frozen overlying coarser sediments (fig. 5.15).

A special form of frost mound resulting from the bulging-up of frozen ground under hydrostatic pressure from below is the hydrolaccolith. Here the pressure of water trapped between the freezing-down of the active layer or the enveloping permafrost above and

frozen ground      solifluction deposit      solifluction
                   and material freed from
                          melting ice                    pond

*Fig. 5.8* Decay of a frost mound. Slumping and solifluction degrade the raised mound as the ice melts. If the ice core is substantial and the water table high, a pond may be formed in the centre.

impermeable rocks or permafrost below causes the ground to swell and form mounds which in size may vary from a few metres across for annual mounds (mostly resulting from freezing-down of the active layer) to hundreds of metres for the perennial types. Typical structures are shown in fig. 5.7. The large perennial hydrolaccoliths are known as pingos,[14, 17] derived from the Eskimo for a large hillock.

The large pingos are of two types. The Greenland ('open system') type results from hydrostatic pressure of water moving upwards from under or in the permafrost and there freezing causing a conical swelling of the ground (fig. 5.7a); springs may be found in the crater at the top of the swelling. The Mackenzie ('closed system') type results from the hydrostatic pressure of water trapped between enveloping permafrost and permafrost already present at depth (fig. 5.7b). This type of pingo develops characteristically in lake basins.

Hydrolaccolith hillocks develop as outlined above and eventually a number of processes leads to their degradation. Loss of the covering sediment by solifluction, for example, leads to the melting of the ice mass by the penetration of summer warmth. If a spring is present in the crater, the outflowing water may breach the wall and degradation result. Fig. 5.8 portrays the degradation of a frost mound.[13]

*Causes of structure formation*

Very many hypotheses have been put forward to explain the origin of the structures already described.[28] Six main causes can be recognised:

1. The upward movement of stones by continued freezing and thawing (fig. 5.9). On freezing a fine-grained water-saturated sediment

*Fig. 5.9* Stone movement during freeze-thaw (Beskow 1930). 1–4 on freezing; 4–7 on thawing. The thin lines and vertically lined layers represent ground ice. The arrows between the black and outline small circles show the resulting movement of the centre of the stone, the outline circle giving the original position.

containing stones expands; embedded stones are thrust upwards. On thawing from the surface down the stone does not settle back to its original position because it will be held by its base in frozen sediment while thawed sediment collapses around it. The result is the tendency of stones to become oriented with their long axes vertical and finally thrust up out of the mass of sediment. In this way sorting of stones from such a sediment can occur.

2. Differential heaving produced by the effect of alternate freezing and thawing on sediments of different grain size. The finer sediments will expand more and thus low mounds or boils of fine sediment will rise to the surface. The amount of segregation ice formed will determine degree of heaving. Maximum segregation tends to occur in silts (fig. 5.6).

3. Pressure (cryostatic) effects such as those produced by down-freezing of the active layer in the autumn. The fine sediments will contain a greater amount of water and will stay unfrozen longer than the coarse sediments and relative movements between the fine or coarser sediments are liable to occur. Considerable hydrostatic forces will be exerted on the frozen sediment. Unfrozen sediment may be trapped between the down-freezing layer and the permafrost or other impermeable sediments. Liquid fine-grained sediments may then be injected upwards under heavy pressure as the sediments expand on freezing or a hydrolaccolith may be formed. Freezing of sediments may be delayed by the lowering of freezing point under pressure.

4. Contraction effects are of two kinds.
   a. On freezing water may be withdrawn to centres of ice formation and contraction of sediments will result. Desiccation cracks will be formed, which may later be filled with melt-water and ice-wedges may then start to form.
   b. Contraction may also be caused by the action of very low temperatures on frozen ground. Large tundra polygons are probably formed in this way.

5. The effect of peat and vegetational cover on the rapidity of freezing and thawing is important. A vegetation pattern may develop as soil structures develop and one will enhance the other.

   As an example of this type of effect we may take the formation of peat hummocks (palsar) which occur near the southern border of the permafrost region, e.g. northern Scandinavia. Frozen saturated peat has a higher thermal conductivity than saturated peat, which in turn has a higher thermal conductivity than dry peat. In the summer a surface layer of dry peat prevents the warming up of the soil, but in winter when the surface peat becomes wet and frozen, cold penetrates deeply. As a result, segregation ice forms on the peat and hummocks grow.

6. Solifluction. This has already been considered.

Usually it is not one of these effects that explains patterned ground, but a combination. For example, in stone circles, 1 will be important (and the sorting will be aided by eluviation of fines and gravity), in

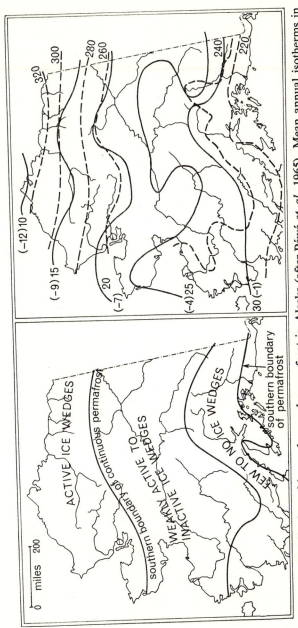

*Fig. 5.10* Distribution of ice-wedges and permafrost in Alaska (after Péwé *et al.* 1965). Mean annual isotherms in Fahrenheit and Centigrade (in brackets) are shown, also number of days in the year with freezing temperature.

stone stripes, 1 and 6, and in non-sorted polygons, 4 may be important but 1 weak. In palsar formation, 5 is important, and in hydrolaccoliths, 3.

### Relation of structures to permafrost and climate

The structures mentioned above are not all characteristic of areas where permafrost is present. Many occur under climates with seasonal or diurnal freeze-thaw changes. The following in particular

*Fig. 5.11* Schematic map of the distribution of underground perennial vein ice (mainly ice-wedges) in the U.S.S.R. (Shoezov 1959).

1. Area and southern limit of fossil and contemporary perennial vein ice.
2. Area and southern limit of fossil vein ice.
3. Southern limit of permafrost.
4. Regions with vein ice of considerable thickness.
5. Regions with vein ice of small thickness.
6. Sites where vein ice known from ground observation.
7. Sites where vein ice known from air observation.
8. Glaciers.

appear to be characteristic of permafrost areas: large sorted polygons, ice-wedge polygons, certain non-sorted circles and polygons (e.g. spotted tundra) and certain large sorted or non-sorted stripes. The distribution of ice-wedges in relation to temperature and permafrost in Alaska is shown in fig. 5.10, and in northern Eurasia in relation to permafrost in fig. 5.11.

The distribution in relation to climate of the structures is not known in detail.[26] In Eurasia it appears that large sorted structures are characteristic of high arctic and oceanic sub-arctic regions, e.g. Spitsbergen and the Scandinavian mountains respectively, while palsar and ice-wedge polygons are better developed in the more continental sub-arctic climates, where deep freezing takes place before much snow accumulates in winter.

The difficulty of climatic interpretation of periglacial features is that vegetation, soil type and drainage play such a large part in determining freeze-thaw effects, as has been already mentioned. Drainage is a particularly significant factor in determining freeze-thaw effects. Thus where seasonal freezing occurs, but not permafrost, the effects will be much more in evidence in badly-drained than well-drained ground. If permafrost is prevalent then freeze-thaw effects will be more widespread, occurring on both badly- and well-drained ground. Frost mounds are frequent in the boreal continental climate with deep summer thawing and thin permafrost, as seen in fig. 5.12, showing the distribution of mounds associated with injection ice in northern Eurasia. Mounds associated with seasonal freezing are also shown on this map.

*Fossil periglacial structures*

Many of the structures already described occur in the fossil state, that is, they occur in regions where climatic conditions no longer cause their formation. The following notes describe the most frequently found fossil structures and discuss their interpretation:

*Upright stones*, a result of process 1 above. Indicative of freeze/thaw but not necessarily permafrost.

*Involutions and injections.* In many vertical sections of Pleistocene deposits contorted structures appear in the superficial sediments. These are known as involutions. The contortions most often involve the interdigitation of lobes or flames of sediment of different grain size. The involutions may have a horizontal and vertical regularity making them appear closely related to structural surface patterns of the kind which develop in the active layer. Or they may be more

*Fig. 5.12* Schematic map of the distribution of mounds associated with injection ice in the U.S.S.R. (Shoezov 1959).

1. Arctic area, mounds not found.
2. Area with perennial (rarely seasonal) ice mounds, mainly by freezing of ground beneath lakes.
3. Area with perennial and seasonal ice mounds, mainly where springs occur.
4. Area with isolated seasonal mounds at spring outlets, outside the permafrost limit.
5. Groups of perennial ice mounds.
6. Isolated perennial ice mounds.
7. Groups of seasonal mounds.
8. Isolated seasonal mounds.
9. Southern limit of permafrost.
10. Boundaries of areas.

irregular and form flames which are probably the result of injection processes (fig. 5.15c). Various types of involution are shown in fig. 5.13. The contortions are chiefly the result of processes 2 and 3 above; where they occur on a slope they may be drawn out down-slope by solifluction.

1m

*Fig. 5.13* Various types of involution (a–d Sekyra 1961).

a. Injection of tongues of finer sediments (silt, clay) into overlying sand and gravel.

b. Frost pockets, frost kettles, or pillar involutions, with ascending tongues of finer sediments.

c. Irregular or amorphous involutions.

d. Festoons, with tongues of frost-shattered disintegrating rock rising into finer sediments.

e. Pocket involutions (finer sediments shaded).

f. Drip or plug involutions (finer sediments shaded).

G

Involutions and injections are not necessarily indicative of perma-frost conditions. They can be formed where the active layer overlies an impermeable sediment. Regular involutions should not be con-fused with load casts in water-laid deposits.[5, 6, 9] The geological context of the contortion should provide a distinction between the two.

*Ice-wedges.* When the ice of ice-wedge polygons melts, it will be re-placed by the collapse of adjacent sediments and by younger sedi-ments above it. The cast of the wedge may then be seen in vertical

*Fig. 5.14* Three types of ice-wedges in vertical section (Shoezov 1959). a, epigenetic wedge; b, epigenetic wedge showing renewed growth; c, syngenetic wedge.
1. annual layering of the ice in the wedges.
2. frozen ground, stratified.
3. active layer.

section (plate 14a, fig. 5.19) or in horizontal view (plate 10b). The sediment in or near the apparent cast may be faulted, through collapse of blocks of sediment, or it may be contorted, either as a result of collapse or partly because of earlier distortions resulting from the growth of the ice-wedge.

Ice-wedges may be epigenetic, penetrating the ground to form a wedge, or they may be syngenetic, growing vertically up as sediment accrues. Three types of wedge known from present-day observation are shown in fig. 5.14. Whether the epigenetic and syngenetic type can be distinguished in the fossil state it is difficult to say, but the syngenetic types have more parallel sides and blunter bases, and these properties may be preserved in the fossil state. The importance of the difference is that syngenetic wedges imply a long period of permafrost while sediment builds up, while epigenetic wedges give evidence for a period of permafrost at the particular horizon marked by their upper limit.

Fossil ice-wedges are of particular importance in periglacial stratigraphy; they form in frozen ground and are thus indicators of the past existence of permafrost. The size of ice-wedges is a function of age, as annual growth occurs. Their depth indicates the minimum permafrost depth, as they can only grow in frozen ground. The sediment penetrated by the wedge will be of importance for climatic interpretation. For example in the continuous permafrost zone in Alaska active wedges occur in sand gravel and silt, but in the discontinuous zone they are confined to silt. However, small thin cracks containing ice can occur as a result of contraction of seasonally freezing ground,[29] so that care should be taken about the interpretation of crack structures and their relation to permafrost.

*Polygons and stripes.* These have been recognised in vertical section and also in surface view. Sections showing these structures are not very common; examples are shown in fig. 5.15. Surface expression of polygons and stripes is best seen in aerial photographs, where the distribution of vegetation, dependent on soil differences resulting from the structures, clearly reveals the nature of the patterns. Such patterns are widely distributed in the Breckland of East Anglia (plate 10a).[30, 31] Small scale polygons and stripes do not necessarily indicate permafrost, but the large ones do. In some cases, e.g. tussock-birch heath polygons, it appears that the depth of the active layer is marked by the depth of disturbance of the soil, so that the depth of the active layer at the time of formation of the similar fossil structure may be estimated.

*Frost mounds.* The surface form taken by decayed frost mounds is mentioned later, but occasionally such structures are seen in section but not at the surface.[13] The presence of frost mound does not necessarily indicate permafrost. Small mounds (a few metres across) are usually annual and may develop by freezing down towards an impermeable unfrozen layer. The larger ones (pingos) are probably perennial and may then be associated with permafrost.

*Faulting* in superficial sands and gravels has been associated with tensions induced by the cooling of frozen ground in winter.[25]

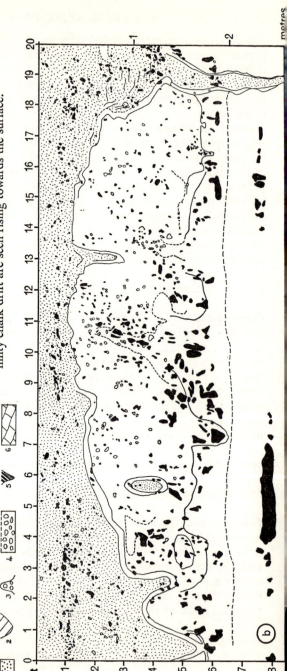

*Fig. 5.15* Three sections showing periglacial structures.

a. Stone network in section in north Germany (Wortmann 1956). 1, cover-sand; 2, loam; 3, stone pillars; 4, basal limestone rubble; 5, loam and limestone in fissures; 6, limestone (Turonian).

b. Non-sorted stripes in section in East Anglia (Watt, Perrin and West 1966). An aerial view of such stripes as these is shown in Plate 10a. Chalky drift overlies *in situ* Chalk. The stippled areas are sand and sandy soil. The more intense stippling in the middle indicates the presence of calcium carbonate. The parallel lines at the base of the stippled layer and the single lines within it indicate zones with clay enrichment. Flints are shown black, and erratics shown open. Injections of very flinty chalk drift are seen rising towards the surface.

0    2m

a ▭   b ▨   c ▥   d ▤   e ▦   f ▨   g ▨

c. Section showing injections of clay into overlying silts and sands near Warsaw (Makowska 1961). The relations of the injected clay and basin deposits suggest injection and deposition of the latter alternated. a, varved clays; b, injected clay; c, clay; d, silt; e, sand; f, sand with clay-balls; g, talus.

*Landforms*

Summer melt-water, solifluction and wind produce characteristic landforms, both constructional and erosional, in the periglacial region. The prevalence of solifluction will lead to a smoothed landscape. Such a landscape, smoothed, say, during the last glaciation in a periglacial region, contrasts greatly with the fresh landforms of the last glaciation deposits. This contrast has led to the concept of older and newer drift,[8] the boundary between them marking the limit of the last glaciation. Hills become flat-topped and may show periglacial contortions in the upper part. Laterally solifluction deposits mantle the slope, becoming thicker on the lower slopes.

Constructional features arise by the action of wind, melt-water and solifluction. Sand-dunes were built up in the great 'Urstromtäler' of northern Europe, wide valleys draining the ice fronts, and they were also formed by the blanketing cover-sands. The directions of winds prevalent during dune formation has been inferred from the orientation of the dunes (fig. 5.16) and the bedding of the dune sands.[12] Although longitudinal and transverse dunes of Pleistocene age are known, most dunes in the periglacial region are U-shaped with their convex side facing downwind, and also their steeper side and steep dip of foreset beds also facing downwind. Dunes imply strong prevalent winds and an abundant source of sand, but they are not necessarily associated with dry conditions and a lack of vegetation, though these of course greatly favour dune formation.

Constructional features are also formed by the lobes of fluviatile sediments deposited by the summer melt-waters. Similarly, solifluction lobes may be formed, sometimes very coarse and forming stone streams.

Erosion features are formed by solifluction and snow melt-waters. In the periglacial region, the open vegetation, the sudden bursts of melt-water liberated in the spring, and the impermeable frozen ground, combine to make surface drainage an important erosive agent. Channels may be formed in fluviatile deposits, and valleys in areas of greater relief. These valleys are often now dry and cannot carry water because they are cut in permeable sands and gravels. During periglacial times the frozen ground held up percolation and surface drainage followed. The frozen ground need not have been perennial, though the size of many dry valleys suggests that it often was.

The upper ends of the valleys often form wide shallow hollows which probably originated by solifluction and were enlarged by melt-waters. Further down the valley the sides are steeper and the strength

*Fig. 5.16* Late Weichselian cover-sands in the central Netherlands (Maarleveld 1960).

a. Ridges of younger cover-sand I (older Dryas, Zone I). 1, rivers; 2, dune ridges; 3, push-moraines of Saale age.
b. Orientation of dunes. 1, ridges of younger cover-sand II (younger Dryas, Zone III); 2, ridges of younger cover-sand I (older Dryas, Zone I).

of the melt-waters seems to have prevented the degrading of slopes by solifluction. The valleys again become shallow and wider as they flatten out. Small flat hollows were also formed by solifluction at the angle of slope at the top of the valley sides. Such hollows presumably represent an early stage of valley formation.

*Fig. 5.17a* Map of ridge dissected by periglacial valleys near Dotmarsum, south-east Netherlands (van der Hammen 1951). The ridge is an ice-pushed feature of the Saale glacial stage, and the valley fills are Late Weichselian and Flandrian. The valleys were cut during the mid-Weichselian glacial stage. Contours at 5 m vertical interval.

The arrangement of periglacial valleys may often take on a radial form, valleys occurring at regular intervals at right angles to the face of the slope (fig. 5.17a).

In certain valleys, especially those trending north–south, the angle of slope of each side may differ, giving an asymmetrical cross-section. There are a number of causes of this asymmetry.[22] In the upper parts of the valleys where no fill is present and erosion is active, the south- and west-facing slopes may be shallower than those facing north and east, as they will be subject more to insolation and thus be more liable to solifluction as the soil warms in summer. On the other hand, in the lower parts of the valley insolation may produce more melt-water at the base of the south- and west-facing slopes, and the stream so formed may undercut the slope and make it steeper than those facing north and east.

Besides dry valleys, other valleys of 'older drift' areas, carrying small misfit streams and substantial fills of gravel and sand, may have been widened by periglacial conditions; such valleys are not usually found in newer drift areas. The spreads of gravel and sand were probably largely deposited by swiftly moving snow melt-waters during the spring thaw. An example of such a wide valley carrying sand and gravel and with a small present-day stream is the river Lea valley, tributary to the Thames, north-east of London.

Irregular landforms produced by the melting of ground-ice has been termed thermokarst. The melting of such ice produces thaw lakes, isolated or in groups. A special case are the walled depressions, perhaps infilled by sediments, formed by decayed pingos.[13]

*Fig. 5.17b* Transverse section through valleys showing cambering and bulging of strata.

## Valley-bulging and cambering

Superficial disturbances of rocks in the valleys of the East Midlands and southern England have been ascribed to the establishment and melting of permafrost. The disturbances take the form of cambering of strata into the valleys, the development of sags and gulls, and bulging at valley bottoms (fig. 5.17b). Such disturbances are associated with favourable hydrological conditions for the saturation of rocks and for their early freezing as permafrost develops, e.g. where aquifers rest on impermeable clays. As a result of freezing, ice formation in saturated clays results in expansion and bulging of the rocks near the valley floor. On melting, the bulged material is subject to removal by streams, and as a result of the disappearance of the ground ice collapse occurs, thus leading to sagging and cambering of the overlying more competent strata.

## Distribution and stratigraphy of periglacial deposits

Fig. 5.18 shows schematically the distribution of various periglacial effects across a north–south section in central Europe. It is evident

*Fig. 5.18* Scheme of periglacial conditions, structures, and deposits in Europe (after Sekyra 1961).

that changes in climatic regime will produce differing periglacial effects, so leading to a sequence of periglacial deposits. Thus sections of superficial deposits often show disturbances by frost action, i.e. involutions and casts of ice-wedges, intercalated in undisturbed sediments which may be aeolian, fluviatile or lacustrine in origin, perhaps containing plant and animal remains. Such sequences of periglacial deposits are very important for the study of climatic and

*Fig. 5.19* Sections through periglacial deposits with structures.
a. Loess-stratigraphy at Hrubieszow in eastern Poland (Mojski 1961). IG, interglacial; G, glacial; i–s, interstadial. Two permafrost periods and several times of involution formation are shown in the upper glacial stage.
   1. Fluviatile sands (Holstein interglacial).
   2. Loess, alluvial and with involutions at base. Chernozem soil developed at top (Eemian interglacial soil), disturbed by involutions.
   3. Loess, alluvial at the base, and disturbed by involutions and solifluction at the base. Brown earth soil at top (Weichselian interstadial soil).
   4. Loess, disturbed by solifluction at the base, and with ice-wedge casts near the base. Thin brown earth soil at the top (Weichselian interstadial soil?).
   5. Loess, disturbed by solifluction and involutions at the base and in the upper part. Ice-wedge casts in the lower part. Present soil, degraded chernozem, at the top.
b. Section at Topola in southern Poland (Klajnert 1961).
   1. Loess (Weichselian glacial).
   2. Humus-rich soil (Eemian interglacial).
   3. Limestone gravel, sand and silt (Eemian interglacial).
   4. Lacustrine silts and silty sands, with involutions and pierced by ice-wedge cast (Saale glacial).
   5. Fluviatile gravels (Holstein interglacial).

a                    b

environmental changes, for they give a sequence of periods of permafrost, involution formation, solifluction, aeolian sedimentation and interstadial conditions.

Fig. 5.19 shows two sections giving evidence of changes in periglacial regime.

The mapping of periglacial features is a means of reconstructing Pleistocene climates. The difficulty is the synchronisation of periglacial deposits and structures across a region. An approach to such a reconstruction for the Weichselian periglacial climate in northern Europe is shown in fig. 5.20.

*Fig. 5.20* Climatic provinces of the Weichselian glacial stage in northern Europe (Poser 1948). The differentiation into provinces is based on the areal distribution of ice-wedge casts, involutions, frost heaving, asymmetric valleys, and forest and steppe-tundra pollen spectra, and on the summer thaw depth indicated by involutions.

    I. Permafrost-tundra climate. Permafrost, little summer warmth.
        a. glacial-maritime province.
        b. province between the Scandinavian and Alpine ice. The coldest area, with the least summer thaw depth.
        c. glacial-continental province
   II. Permafrost-forest climate. Permafrost, warmer summers.
  III. Maritime-tundra climate. Transition between Ia and IV. Winters not cold enough for permafrost, little summer warmth.
  IV. Maritime forest climate.

## REFERENCES

*Biuletyn Peryglacjalny*, Lodz. Ed. J. Dylik.

HAVILAND, M. D. 1926. *Forest, steppe and tundra.* Cambridge University Press.

MULLER, S. W. 1947. *Permafrost or permanently frozen ground and related engineering problems.* Ann Arbor: Edwards Inc.

SHOEZOV, P. F. 1959. *Osnovy Geokriologij.* Part I. Akademia Nauk. S.S.S.R.

SHUMSKI, P. A. 1964. *Principles of structural glaciology.* New York: Dover Publications.

VTJURIN, B. I. 1964. *Kriogennoe stroenie chetvertichnyx otlozhnenij.* Akademia Nauk. S.S.S.R.

1 BESKOW, G. 1930. 'Erdfliessen und strukturböden', *Geol. Fören. Stockh. Förh.*, **52**, 622–38.

2 BLACK, R. F. 1954. 'Permafrost—A review', *Bull. Geol. Soc. America*, **65**, 839–56.

3 CAILLEUX, A. 1942. 'Les actions éoliennes périglaciaires en Europe', *Mem. Soc. géol. de France*, n.s. **21**, No. 46.

4 CORTE, A. 1963. 'Particle sorting by repeated freezing and thawing', *Science*, **142**, 499–501.

5 DZULYNSKI, S. and WALTON, E. K. 1963. 'Experimental production of sole markings', *Trans. Edinb. geol. Soc.*, **19**, 279–305.

6 EMERY, K. O. 1950. 'Contorted Pleistocene strata at Newport Beach, California', *J. Sedim. Petrology*, **20**, 111–15.

7 GRAHMANN, R. 1932. 'Der Lösz in Europa', *Mitt. Gesell. f. Erdkunde zu Leipzig* (1930–31), 5–24.

8 GRIPP, K. 1924. 'Über die äusserste Grenze der letzten Vereisung in nordwest Deutschland', *Mitt. geogr. Ges. Hamburg*, **36**, 161–245.

9 JARDINE, W. G. 1965. 'Note on a temporary exposure in central Glasgow of Quaternary sediments with slump and load structures', *Scottish J. geol.*, **1**, 221–4.

10 KLAJNERT, Z. 1961. 'Topola'. In Guide Book of excursion Baltic to Tatras, Part 2, vol. 2, VI Congress International Association of Quaternary Research, Warsaw, 95–6.

11 LUNDQUIST, G. 1948. 'Blockens orientering i olika jordarter', *Sver. geol. Unders.*, Årsbok **42** (C), no. 497.

12 MAARLEVELD, G. C. 1960. 'Wind directions and coversands in the Netherlands', *Biul. Peryglacjalny*, **8**, 49–58.

13 MAARLEVELD, G. C. 1965. 'Frost mounds', *Med. Geol. Stichting*, n.s. **17**, 1–16.

14 MACKAY, J. R. 1963. *The Mackenzie Delta, N.W.T.* Memoir No. 8. Geographical Branch, Mines and Technical Surveys, Canada.

15 MAKOWSKA, A. 1961. 'Diapir forms in varved clays at Baniocha near Warsaw', in *Prace o Plejstocenie Polski Srodkowej.* Ed. S. Z. Rozyckiego. P.A.N. Komitet Geologiczny, 159–76.

16 MOJSKI, J. E. 1961. 'Periglacial deposits and structures in the stratigraphy of the Quaternary in Poland', *Instytut Geologiczny (Warszawa)*,
*Prace*, **34**, 675–96.

17 MÜLLER, F. 1959. 'Beobachtungen über pingos', *Medd. om Grønland*,
**153**, No. 3.

18 PERRIN, R. M. S. 1956. 'Nature of "Chalk Heath" soils', *Nature*, **178**,
31.

19 PÉWÉ, T. L., HOPKINS, D. M. and GIDDINGS, J. L. 1965. 'The
Quaternary geology and archaeology of Alaska', in *The Quaternary of
the United States*, eds. Wright, H. E., and Frey, D. G. Princeton University Press.

20 PITCHER, W. S., SHEARMAN, D. J. and PUGH, D. C. 1954. 'The
loess of Pegwell Bay, Kent and its associated soils', *Geol. Mag.*, **91**,
308–14.

21 POSER, H. 1948. 'Boden- und Klimaverhältnisse in Mittel- und
Westeuropa während der Würmeiszeit', *Erdkunde*, **2**, 53–68.

22 POSER, H. and MÜLLER, T. 1951. 'Studien an der asymmetrischen
Tälern des Niederbayrischen Hügellandes', *Nachrichten der Akad.
Wiss. in Göttingen, Math.-Phys. Klasse*, 1951, 1–32.

23 SAMUELSSON, C. 1926. 'Studien über die Wirkungen des windes in
den kalten und Gemässigten Erdteilen', *Bull. Geol. Institute Upsala*,
**20**, 57–231.

24 SEKYRA, J. 1961. 'Periglacial phenomena', *Instytut Geologiczny*,
*(Warszawa)*, *Prace*, **34**, 99–107.

25 SHOTTON, F. W. 1965. 'Normal faulting in British Pleistocene deposits', *Q. J. Geol. Soc. Lond.*, **121**, 419–35.

26 TROLL, C. 1944. 'Strukturböden, solifluktion und frostklimate der
Erde', *Geol. Rundschau*, **34**, 545–694 (In English translation: U.S.
Army Snow, Ice and Permafrost Research Establishment, translation
No. 43, 1958).

27 VAN DER HAMMEN, T. 1951. 'Late-glacial flora and periglacial phenomena in the Netherlands', *Leidse Geol. Meded.*, **17**, 71–183.

28 WASHBURN, A. L. 1956. 'Classification of patterned ground and
review of suggested origins', *Bull. Geol. Soc. America*, **67**, 823–66.

29 WASHBURN, A. L., SMITH, D. D. and GODDARD, R. H. 1963. 'Frost
cracking in a middle-latitude climate', *Biul. Peryglacjalny*, **12**, 175–89.

30 WATT, A. S., PERRIN, R. M. S. and WEST, R. G. 1966. 'Patterned
ground in Breckland: structure and composition', *J. Ecol.*, **54**, 239–58.

31 WILLIAMS, R. B. G. 1964. 'Fossil patterned ground in Eastern England', *Biul. Peryglacjalny*, **14**, 337–49.

32 WORTMANN, H. 1956. 'Ein erstes sicheres Vorkommen von peri-
glazialem Steinnetzboden im Norddeutschen Flachland', *Eiszeitalter
u. Gegenwart*, **7**, 119–26.

# CHAPTER 6

# STRATIGRAPHICAL INVESTIGATIONS

THE history of the Pleistocene is based on the stratigraphy of the deposits. From the point of view of gross stratigraphy, the interpretation of a succession of deposits is not normally difficult. For example, two tills separated by a thick sand indicate two ice advances, each laying down a till, separated by a phase of ice retreat during which the sand was deposited; and the occurrence of a peat deposit with remains of temperate trees between two tills indicates a period of ice retreat with a temperate climate between two ice advances.

The finer details of stratigraphy are just as important as the gross stratigraphy, for they give the clue to important details of environmental history. Climatic changes, from, say, arctic to temperate, are known to have taken place during the deposition of a few tens of centimetres of sediment or less. All changes of sediment, both in structure and composition, have significance. This is especially evident in the study of biogenic deposits and periglacial deposits. With biogenic deposits it is necessary to link the changing sediments with the contained fossil flora and fauna, because only in this way can the most complete environmental analyses be obtained. Taking a single bulk sample from, say, an open peat section, may give an overall view of the fossils over the whole period during which the peat was laid down, but will say nothing about environmental changes during this time. Careful stratigraphical study followed by close sampling is necessary to show this. Similarly with the study of periglacial deposits. Alternating conditions of, say, frost-heaving, polygon formation and aeolian deposition of sand will only be revealed by careful stratigraphical work.

Stratigraphical investigations of Pleistocene deposits will include the study of open or excavated sections and of underground stratigraphy by boring. The methods and techniques associated with each of these will be treated in turn.

## SECTIONS

The study of open sections is far more satisfactory than that of bore-hole samples, in particular because Pleistocene sediments are apt to vary considerably over short distances and borehole records may give an unreliable picture of the whole sequence; for example, the non-sequences may not be apparent. The first step in studying a section is to clean the face thoroughly to produce a vertical section, or if verticality is not possible, as is often the case in a talus slope, to make a series of vertical sections separated by horizontal steps. The horizontal steps may also be useful in giving a three-dimensional view of any structures present in the sediments and this may be important for the interpretation of the structures, e.g. those of periglacial origin. The recording of a section is most complete if done by both drawing and photography. Carefully drawn records (e.g. fig. 5.15) are just as valuable as photographs, and drawing a section in detail invariably brings to notice detail which would escape casual examination and photography. The most suitable method is to mark out a grid of metre squares on the face to be studied, and the details of stratigraphy can then be drawn to a suitable scale. This will vary according to the section being studied, but a scale of 4 cm to a metre is often satisfactory.

Sampling from open sections is far safer than from boreholes. The risk of contamination is low if suitable precautions are taken to clean the face and the sampling instrument. The distance apart of samples will vary according to the section. A 5-cm interval is usually adequate, but it is best to take additional samples near contacts of different sediment types, as the change of sediment type may result from a significant environmental change. If the sediments are compacted and varying rapidly vertically, it is best to use a closer interval than 5 cm. In the laboratory, samples wider apart than this can be analysed first and, if necessary, the full closer sequence can then be done. The vertical position chosen to sample should show the most complete series of sediments possible, but it may be necessary to take subsidiary series in other places to make the sampling complete.

For pollen analysis samples a small spatula or penknife will be found most useful, with the sample of about 5 cc being placed in a glass or plastic tube about 5 cm × 2 cm, which is then labelled with the depth. For analysis of macroscopic plant and animal remains it is best to take a series of bulk samples, in the same place as the pollen samples, so that the whole column of sediment is represented in the samples. The relation of the macroanalyses to the microanalyses will then be beyond doubt.

It may be more convenient to take a monolith of the sediments back to the laboratory for study and sampling there. A convenient size of monolith is 15 cm wide and 15 cm deep and in segments about 40 to 50 cm long. Such may be obtained in the softer sediments (e.g. mud and peat) by hammering a metal box of these dimensions into the face with a sledge hammer after lining the box with polythene sheeting. The sediment column can then be stored until ready for study. The same method may be used with clays, e.g. varved clays, but here, if it is just the varving which is to be studied, a much smaller monolith may be all that is necessary.

A method of preserving a thin film of sediments has been developed for use with exposures of clays, sands and fine gravels. This is the lacquer method, described in Appendix 2. There are also methods of impregnating unconsolidated sediments so that their microscopic structure can be studied in thin section.[1]

## BORING

### *Methods*

No one sampling device can sample with the same degree of success in all sediments. Here we are concerned with sampling in relatively unconsolidated sediments varying from till to gravel to sand to biogenic deposits of one sort or another. There are samplers which work in each of these sediments, and the choice of a particular sampling tool will depend on the type of sediment to be cored, the depth to which it is necessary to go, the manpower required to work the tool, the ease of transport, and the cost. The most difficult problem encountered when boring in Pleistocene sediments is that of penetrating through loose wet sand. There is usually no alternative to casing the borehole in this event, and a rig is necessary to do this at depth. Thus hand-operated methods are usually stopped by such sediment.

It is essential to choose the sampling methods best fitted to the job in hand. Each site has its own characteristics in terms of sediment, depth of sediment, ease of approach and so on. The investigator should be prepared to adapt the methods to his own particular problem, bearing in mind that the chief features of a sampler should be simplicity, ease of operation, robustness and ease of repair. It is always best to carry a tool kit so that repairs can be made in the field.

It is not possible to give here a complete description of the many boring tools which have been used for investigation of Pleistocene stratigraphy. A good comprehensive account has been given by Wright, Livingstone and Cushing[10] to which reference should be

H

made for greater detail. The most useful and commonly used sampling devices are described below. The principal properties of each sampling method are summarised in table 6.1.

Three classes of boring methods concern us. The first, for use in lakes or in the sea, are the free-fall samplers attached to a cable. The second are hand-operated devices working with rods, used on water or land, and the third are the heavier boring devices, usually with rigs, for use on water or land. The second group are most commonly used and more attention will be given to this group than the others.

### Free-fall samplers

These are simple short lengths of tubing of 2 to 5 cm diameter. They are attached to a cable and penetrate after free-fall into sediment to a distance determined by the height of the fall, the weight of the sampler, the diameter of the tube and the thickness of its wall and the amount of friction between the sediment and the tube wall. Core retaining springs filled at the base of the tube help to keep the core safe as the sampler is surfaced. This type of sampler is useful for sediments in deep water, but the core obtained is short and of course the depth of sampling is limited to the amount of penetration at one free-fall.

### Hand-operated samplers

These are attached to a string of rigid rods rather than to wire and can be used on land or on water if it is shallow enough. The diameter and composition of the rods is determined by the cost, the strength they are required to be and the weight they can be for a given method of transport. Light weight alloy rods are most convenient when the sampler has to be man-carried, but where weight is not so important and cost is, standard water pipe can be used. The rods may be 1, 1½ or 2 m in length and they can be joined either by a male and female

*Fig. 6.1* Samplers
a. Hiller, with section in open position.
b. Russian, with sections in open (1) and closed (2) position.
c. Dachnowski.
d. Livingstone.
e. Punch.
f. Screw auger.
g. Jack for screw auger.

a  b  c  d

1
2

e  f  g

coupling held by a set-screw as in the standard Hiller sampler, or by a coupling enclosed by a sliding tube held in place by spring-loaded pins.[5] Simple mechanical aids have been used to assist penetration or withdrawal of hand-operated samplers, such as chain-hoists, car jacks working on mole-grips attached to the rods and other jacking devices such as the one described later working with a screw auger.

Hand-operated samplers take in cores from the side as with a Hiller, or at the base as in piston or percussion corers, or take samples by screw or other type of auger. The piston corers are of two types, those where the piston is retractable and those where the piston remains stationary as the corer is driven.

*Table 6.1* Comparison of some hand-operated samplers

| Type | Sample Length | Width | Deformation of sediment | Compression of sediment | Suitability for sediments Good for | Bad for |
|---|---|---|---|---|---|---|
| Hiller | 50 cm | 3 cm | much | none | peat, compact mud | loose organic sediment, inorganic sediment |
| Russian | 50 cm | 5 cm | none | none | peat, mud | loose organic sediment, inorganic sediment |
| Dachnowski | 30 cm | 5 cm | little | little | non-fibrous peat, mud | fibrous peat, loose organic sediment |
| Livingstone | 50 cm | 4 cm | little | some | non-fibrous peat, mud | fibrous peat, loose organic sediment, inorganic sediment |
| Punch | 50 cm | 6 cm | little | some | compact organic sediment, clay, silt, fine sand | fibrous peat, loose organic sediment |
| Screw auger | 25 cm | 4 cm | much | much | compact organic sediment, clay and silt | soft organic and inorganic sediment |
| Other augers | 10–30 cm | 5–10 cm | much | little | compact organic sediment, clay, silt, sand, gravel | soft organic and inorganic sediment |

*Hiller sampler* (fig. 6.1a). This sampler is the classical peat borer. It consists of a sampling chamber 50 cm long and about 3 cm diameter with a slit about 2 cm wide down one side. This is covered by a close-fitting outer tube with a similar sized slit bordered by a flange 2 or 3 cm wide set at a tangent. An inner removable liner of light alloy can be used inside the chamber, so that the whole core obtained can be removed and taken back to the laboratory.

The sampler is pushed down with a slight clockwise pressure in the closed position, i.e. with the outer tube covering the slit of the inner tube. On reaching the sampling depth the sampler is rotated anti-clockwise, the two slits coincide, and on further rotation (2 or 3 times) the flange forces sediment into the inner tube. Clockwise rotation closes off the inner tube again and the sampler is withdrawn with a slight clockwise pressure to keep it shut. The samples are taken with a clean spatula from the centre of the chamber after opening the sampler by anticlockwise rotation, and after scrupulous cleaning off of the exposed sediment surface. The advantages of a Hiller are these: it is easy to use, there is no compression of the sediments, and it takes reasonable samples in fibrous, mossy, or wood peat and in fairly stiff lake muds. The disadvantages are these: it distorts sediments as the flange forces them into the tube—thus microstructures are obscured, it is jammed by sand, it will not hold loose sediments such as watery muds, or penetrate very compact sediments, the samples are liable to contamination by sediment and water getting into the tube as the sampler descends or ascends, and it is difficult to thoroughly clean the inside except where water is freely available.

*Russian peat sampler* (Fig. 6.1b).[3] This sampler consists of a half-cylinder (shuttle) 50 cm long and 5 cm diameter, fixed to the sampler head, and which can be rotated at depth through 180° to retain a half-cylinder of peat against a central anchor plate. The shuttle rotates round this anchor-plate, which projects into the sediment on one side and thus remains stationary while the shuttle rotates. The half cylinder of peat obtained by rotating the shuttle is bisected lengthways by a fin-plate at right angles to the anchor plate. The advantage of this sampler over the Hiller is that sediment structures are preserved, the sampler is more easily cleaned, and the sample obtained can be easily removed and stored in polythene sheeting.

*Dachnowski sampler* (Fig. 6.1c). This is a piston corer with a re-tractable piston. It has a tube about 30 cm long and 5 cm diameter, with a piston attached to the end of the rod bearing the tube. The sampler is lowered with the piston in position at the end of the tube. When the sampling depth is reached, the piston is raised to the top of the tube by withdrawing the rods till it is held in this position by a spring catch on the rod engaging a collar at the upper end of the tube, or by giving the rods a half-twist and engaging splines cut in the rod, and working in grooves at the top of the tube, against the top of the tube. The sampler is then pushed down the length of the tube and a core is taken. After raising, the core is extruded by pushing back the piston, and can either be sampled on the spot or taken back to the laboratory. The advantages of a Dachnowski sampler are that it is a simple design, light and easy to use, penetrates well in fairly stiff fine-grained sediments and takes undisturbed cores. Its disadvantages are that it will not retain loose sediments though core-retaining springs if fitted will help, it may be jammed by sand, it is liable to contamination from sediment and water leaking in through the top, it will take only a short sample, and compression of sediments is liable to occur.

*Livingstone sampler* (Fig. 6.1d).[6] In this type of piston sampler, the piston is held stationary while the coring tube is driven. Thus hydrostatic pressure above the core is eliminated and entry of unwanted sediment into the upper part of the tube before sampling is prevented. A core up to a metre or more can be taken at one drive, the limit being set by the friction of the sediment sample with the corer wall, increasing as penetration increases.

There are many types of this sampler.[10] Basically the sampler consists of a removable tube about a metre long and 4 cm wide fixed by screws to a head. The piston consists of two rubber stoppers on a threaded bolt, and the fit to the tube, which is critical, can be adjusted by tightening or loosening nuts bearing on the stoppers. The piston is held in the base of the tube by spring-loaded pins, and is attached to a wire running to the surface. The sampler is pushed to the required depth, the wire is then fixed firmly by mole-grips, and the sampler is driven down for the length of the tube past the stationary piston. The sampler is then raised and the core either extruded or removed in its tube back to the laboratory after corking the ends. A new tube is easily fitted and the operation repeated. A modification[9] makes the basal rod pass through the head and bear against the piston in its basal position, thus preventing unwanted movement of the piston while the sampler is being lowered. On reaching the required depth the rods are raised and the base of the basal rod returns to its normal position near the head where it is held by a spring catch working on a collar. The piston is held in position by a wire and the sampler is then driven down to take the sample. This sampler is more robust than the original and may be driven through compact sediments with a hammer. The hammering may result in more deformation of the core than usual.

A 10 cm diameter corer of Livingstone type[2,7] has been used to raise larger cores for macrofossil analysis and radiocarbon samples. In this modification the piston is held in position not by a wire but by a string of rods working inside the main rods. Mechanical aids, such as the use of chain hoist and a lightweight rig, are usually necessary to drive and raise the sampler. Cores 1·5 m long have been obtained using this sampler.

The advantages of a Livingstone sampler are these: it takes long cores, the cores can be taken in rapid succession once the field technique is mastered, the sediments are not or little deformed except perhaps at the base of each core where friction may be great at the end of a sampling drive, it is ideal for lake sediments which are not too compact or contain too much coarse inorganic sediment, and it can be easily used from a boat through casing (10 cm piping). Its disadvantages are that it will not sample coarse fibrous material which tends to become jammed in the mouth of the tube, the sediments are liable to be compressed, and if the sediments are very loose they may not be recovered. The last is unlikely with a long core as the friction is enough to hold the core. Loss can be prevented by pumping air down an air line to the base of the sampler and keeping pressure up as the sampler is withdrawn,[7] or by the use of a core retaining device fitted to the corer shoe. The most convenient of such devices for loose sediments is a flap valve cut from a cylinder of such a size that it fits closely in the side of the shoe, and shaped so that it closes the cylinder when it is forced down by the weight of sediment.

*Punch sampler* (Fig. 6.1e). This sampler was devised to take cores 6 cm in diameter and 50 cm long in compacted sediments containing much inorganic sediment. The tube is split into two lengthways and the two halves are held together by insertion at each end into the head and the shoe. Bolts run from the shoe to the head just inside the core tube so that the whole assembly can be bolted tight. The sampler is driven by sledgehammer working on a striking platform at the top. It can be raised by the jacking system shown in fig. 6.1g. The core obtained can be removed by slackening the bolts and removing one side of the tube. Good recovery of sediments has been obtained from interglacial deposits with this sampler, but compression and some deformation occur during sampling. It will not raise cores of uncompacted wet sediment.

*Screw sampler* (Fig. 6.1f). A single-spiral shipwright's auger has been successfully used to sample compacted clays and clay-muds. The diameter should be from 3 to 5 cm and the length about 40 cm. Such an auger can be screwed down through clays or clay-muds about 25 cm at a time. This depth of sediment will usually fill the auger. The samples taken from the filled auger should be from the centre of the spaces between the spiral, and the outer sediments and those touching the spiral should be removed before taking them. Naturally much deformation occurs with this sampler, but it does enable samples to be taken in deposits which could not be worked by hand with other types of sampler. Several metres can be penetrated by one man un-aided, though the work is slow, but if wet loose sediments are met, the method fails, as samples will be washed out by raising the auger.

*Other auger samplers*. Any type of post-hole or bucket auger will take disturbed samples if the sediments are compact enough, but the process of augering breaks up the sediments and samples for analysis should only be taken from unbroken lumps of material coming up in the auger. Thus it will not usually be possible with these types of auger to take samples at close intervals.

### Heavier sampling devices

These samplers are costly to run, more difficult to transport, and require more than one man to operate. They include commercial drilling rigs and other rigs especially designed for specific problems. Of the commercial rigs, the standard 4 inch (10 cm) percussion system with core samplers, as used by soil mechanics investigators, are very useful in compacted sediments, especially in the older Pleistocene deposits where gravel or till has to be penetrated before sampling of organic sediment can take place. A special type of sampler using a metal foil liner extruded from the base of the sampler as it is driven down has been used to take continuous cores in varved clays.[4] The foil effectively reduces the friction between the sediment and sampler wall, so it is possible to take cores of up to 20 m long.

Rotary coring devices are less useful except in compact sediments and usually the thickness of a deposit does not merit the setting up of such expensive rigs. If they are used, however, great care should be taken that any drilling mud used is free of microfossils.

Two other types of sampler are available for use on water. One is the Kullenberg sampler, famous for its use in raising cores up to 20 m long in deep water. The sampler is of a stationary piston type, weighted, and it is lowered till a few metres from the sediment surface when it is released and the piston held stationary. In deep water mechanical aids are necessary to control and effect the lowering and raising of the sampler. The other type of sampler for use in water is the Mackereth sampler.[8] This is easier to use than the previous one, takes a single core up to about 8 m, and can be worked by two men in a boat. The sampler is of the stationary piston type. It is lowered by rope to the surface of the sediment, and then driven down by compressed air supplied by an air line. The reaction is provided by a drum anchored to the bottom hydrostatically. The sampler is then raised by pumping air into the anchor drum, which rises carrying the sampler with it.

## Field operations

In the investigation of extensive fossiliferous deposits, e.g. those of a lake, a raised bog or an interglacial deposit, it is first necessary to carry out a programme of boring to determine the extent and stratigraphy of the deposits. In order to get a profile across the deposit lines of boreholes should be made and the stratigraphy of the whole reconstructed, as shown in fig. 4.4. Once the stratigraphy is clear the best site for detailed sampling can be chosen where the deposits are most completely preserved and thickest. In a lake deposit this is usually near the centre. Near the edge fluctuations of water level may cause periods of erosion and non-deposition, and then the record of sedimentation will be incomplete. In boring in sediments of lakes still existing, a recording echo-sounder may help to locate the most suitable place for boring, as there will be reflections from the sediment/water interface and from denser layers within the sediment.

On a land surface it is necessary to level the tops of the boreholes to obtain a satisfactory profile. A simple highway level is quite accurate enough for this task. In boring in a lake the water line is obviously a good datum point. The difficulty here is the erection of a stationary boring platform. The borers can be operated from a boat or, more conveniently, from a platform erected between two boats or two inflatable rafts. These must be securely anchored by at least three anchors. If the boring can be done while the lake is frozen, it is much easier to work through the ice than from boats.

In boring to obtain samples for analysis it is of prime importance to secure completely pure uncontaminated samples. Some samplers are more liable to lead to contamination than others, as discussed in the descriptions of the various sampling devices. A few general rules apply to all the devices. Ideally, the boring should be done on a day and a time of year when pollen production and dispersal are low or absent and when the weather is dry. Notes on the local vegetation should be made at the time of boring so if any contamination by recent pollen arises, it may be related to local conditions. The sampling device should be thoroughly cleaned by washing between each sample being taken. If possible samples should be taken alternately at successive depths in two closely adjacent boreholes, to lessen the risk of carrying material down the borehole and to prevent disturbance of the sediments where one sample ends and the next begins. When boring from land surfaces, a sod should first be removed from the top soil, and the first samples taken from this. Then the boring is carried out, sampling alternately from two holes. The sampler should be pushed down (except of course where augering is concerned) rather than screwing it in, so keeping the hole as clean as possible, and in soft deposits where sinking of the sampler may occur under its own weight, care should be taken to prevent any error in determining the sampling depth.

The actual taking of samples from different types of sampler has already been mentioned, and the same general rules about the distance between samples apply as to sampling from open sections. Samples (about 5 cc) from microanalysis are taken with a clean spatula or penknife, put in plastic or glass tubes, and their depth clearly marked on the tube.

Before the sampling is made it is best to describe the sediment in the sampler in as much detail as is possible in the field. The samples are then taken, either in the field or in the laboratory if the core can be transported home; the sediment is then removed from the sampler and if macrosamples are required, placed in a polythene bag. Further useful notes can often be made from the sediments after examination of hand specimens after removal from the sampler, e.g. the nature of any macrofossils present, or the degree of humification.

## SAMPLES AND STORAGE

Back in the laboratory, it is necessary to seal the microfossil samples with paraffin wax. Both these and the macrofossil samples should be kept damp and at a low temperature. Damp samples are far more easy to work and the low temperature reduces any chemical changes tending to occur.

# REFERENCES

FAEGRI, K. and IVERSEN, J. 1964. *Textbook of Modern Pollen Analysis.* 2nd edn. Oxford: Blackwell.

1 CATT, J. A. and ROBINSON, P. C. 1961. 'The preparation of thin sections of clays', *Geol. Mag.*, **98,** 511–14.

2 CUSHING, E. J. and WRIGHT, H. E. 1965. 'Hand-operated piston corers for lake sediments', *Ecology,* **46,** 380–4.

3 JOWSEY, P. C. 1966. 'An improved peat sampler', *New Phytol.,* **65,** 245–8.

4 KJELLMAN, W., KALLSTENIUS, T. and WAGNER, O. 1950. 'Soil sampler with metal foils: device for taking undisturbed samples of very great length', *Royal Swedish Geotechnical Institute,* Proc., No. 1. 75 pp.

5 LICHTWARDT, R. W. 1952. 'A new light-weight shaft for peat samplers', *Palaeobotanist,* **1,** 317–18.

6 LIVINGSTONE, D. A. 1955. 'A light-weight piston sampler for lake deposits', *Ecology,* **36,** 137–9.

7 SEROTA, S. and JENNINGS, R. A. 1957. 'Undisturbed sampling techniques for sands and very soft clays', *Proc. IV Int. Conference on soil mechanics and foundation engineering,* **1,** 245–8.

8 SMITH, A. J. 1959. 'Description of the Mackereth portable core sampler', *J. Sed. Petrol.,* **29,** 246–50.

9 VALLENTYNE, J. R. 1955. 'A modification of the Livingston piston sampler for lake deposits', *Ecology,* **36,** 139–41.

10 WRIGHT, H. E., LIVINGSTONE, D. A. and CUSHING, E. J. 1965. 'Coring devices for lake sediments', in *Handbook of palaeontological techniques,* eds. B. Kummel and D. M. Raup. San Francisco: Freeman.

# CHAPTER 7

# BIOLOGICAL INVESTIGATIONS

THE study of stratigraphy and of sediments leads to the reconstruction of the history of the geological environment, while the study of plant and animal remains leads to the reconstruction of the history of vegetation, flora and fauna. As life is intimately related to and dependent upon environment, so the knowledge of plant and animal remains leads also to reconstructions of climate and other factors of the environment, such as soils or the salinity of water.

Both geological and biological studies are necessary towards the building of the history of the Pleistocene. Each provides information which is complementary, and in particular circumstances one may provide much more information than the other. For example, in the study of the glacial stages evidence from the glacial deposits will give information about the distribution and movement of ice and the processes of its melting, but little climatic detail will emerge. On the other hand, the study of plant and animal remains from sediments formed in a periglacial area during a glacial stage will tell much about conditions of life and climate during the glacial stage.

The Pleistocene is characterised by climatic change and detail of climatic change can be deduced from biological studies. For this reason such studies become very important in the investigation of the Pleistocene. Reconstructions of past climatic change from fossils depend on how much is known of the ecology and distribution of the species found as fossils. In the Pleistocene many of the fossils are closely allied to or appear identical to present species, so that valuable reconstructions of past plant and animal life and climate can be made.

Many groups of animals and plants are found fossil with their harder parts preserved. Two broad categories of remains can be made, the macroscopic fossils or macrofossils, large enough to collect and study by naked eye or under low magnifications, and microscopic fossils or microfossils, which need special methods for extraction and a high-power microscope for observation.

Taking the plants first, the most common identifiable macrofossils are seeds, fruits, leaves, and wood fragments. The plant microfossils comprise the pollen grains of higher plants, the spores of lower plants, less commonly leaf hairs and epidermis, and the skeletons of diatoms and desmids. Among animals, macrofossils include the skeletal remains of vertebrates, the shells of molluscs, and the exoskeletons of insects and crustaceans, especially cladocerans and ostracods. The microfossils include rhizopods and foraminifers.

Each of these groups of organisms has advantages and limitations when used as evidence for environmental conditions, and it will be useful to discuss each group on its own.

*Plant macrofossils*[4, 5] (plate 11). These are mostly derived from plants growing locally near the site of deposition. In autochthonous deposits, the plants will be growing at the place they are found fossil; in allochthonous deposits they may be more distantly derived by, say, running water or solifluction. Plant remains from different plant communities will collect in allochthonous deposits and it may be difficult to separate them into the communities from which they originated, but the broad categories of community and thus environment, e.g. aquatic, marsh, woodland, are usually evident. Plant macrofossils are thus good indicators of local environment and vegetation.

*Plant microfossils*[10, 11] (plate 12). Pollen grains and spores in sediments mostly come from the air by fall-out (pollen-rain) and they are thus derived from the regional and local vegetation. Regional and local vegetational changes produced by climatic, edaphic or biotic changes cause changes in the pollen-rain and thus in the microfossils incorporated in sediments. Other plant microfossils, e.g. diatom[23] and desmid skeletons, originate in the water-body depositing sediment and as the populations of these in lakes is dependent on nutrients in the water as well as on climatic changes, they give information on conditions within the water-body.

*Vertebrates.*[9, 35] Remains of vertebrates are not so common as are other animal remains, except perhaps in cave deposits, where they may be abundant.[6] Autochthonous fossils include fish, amphibian and rodent remains of lake deposits, whereas allochthonous vertebrate faunas may be found in sands and gravels, and in cave deposits where animal bones may be accumulated by carnivores. Valuable evidence of both climate and environment may be established from studies of vertebrates, as their present-day ecology and distribution is usually rather well-known, e.g. the climatic indications of cold conditions given by the presence of lemmings and reindeer, and the open vegetational conditions indicated by horse. On the other hand, many important Pleistocene vertebrate species are extinct, e.g. species of elephant and rhinoceros, and these are more difficult to use in palaeoecological reconstructions. Another difficulty is caused by the robustness of vertebrate remains, which may lead to their redeposition in sediments much younger than the time of original entombment.

*Molluscs*[21, 27] (plate 16). Molluscs, especially the non-marine molluscs, have been successfully used to bring out details of climate and local ecology. The freshwater molluscs give indications of water conditions and salinity. The marine molluscs have been less well studied and their ecological interpretation is more difficult, mainly because of lack of detailed knowledge of the present-day ecology, but also because many species are extinct, especially in the early Pleistocene.

*Insects*[8, 24] (plate 16), *and crustaceans*. [13] Fossil insects also give good indications of climate and environment. Many have a narrow feeding range of plants and are associated with particular plant communities so their presence can be used to demonstrate the existence of such communities. Fossil crustaceans, especially cladocerans and ostracods, are often abundant in lake sediments, and besides climatic indications which the species may give, they also are useful in providing information on water conditions and nutrients, and the productivity of lakes in the past.

*Microscopic animals.* Foraminifera[12] are important in providing local and regional climatic information and their tests are the chief source of material for palaeotemperature determinations by the oxygen isotope method. They may also indicate local conditions of salinity and water-depth. Rhizopods[13] are found in bog and lake deposits, and are useful indicators in bogs of changing hydrological conditions, as the abundance of certain species appears to be related to the wetness of the bog surface.

### Preservation of Fossils

Most Pleistocene fossils are the harder parts of the animals or plants, having the same composition in the fossil state as when they were originally formed. There are exceptions, such as the mineralised bones of the lower Pleistocene (e.g. the black bones of the Netherlands Scheldt, which contain a large amount of cryptocrystalline pyrites). Usually little compression has occurred, so that the fossils are of the same dimensions as the harder parts of the living organism. An exception here is wood which is often found to be compressed and is difficult to identify in older Pleistocene deposits.

Impressions of fossilised plants may be found in sandstones, tufas and cave stalagmites. Here the original organism has disappeared, leaving its form impressed as a cast on the surface of the sediment in which it was buried.

Preservation is best where the fossils have remained under anaerobic and unleached conditions. Oxidation will quickly lead to destruction of fossils, particularly plant fossils, while leaching will dissolve calcareous fossils. Where some oxidation and some leaching has gone on, there may be differential destruction of fossils of different species and this may confuse the interpretation of fossil lists. Fossils are best preserved in unweathered fine-grained marine or freshwater sediments, or in terrestrial deposits which remain waterlogged. Where the grain size of the sediment is larger, percolation and oxidation may quickly destroy fossils.

## Primary and Derived Fossils

It is obviously necessary to know whether a fossil is in its primary position or has been derived from an older sediment and redeposited. Redeposition will result from reworking of an older deposit, say under conditions of fluctuating water-levels. It is particularly obvious in the case of large mammalian fossils such as teeth and bones, which may first be deposited in gravels, and then reworked as the gravels became subject to processes of erosion. But similar events can occur with microscopic fossils,[15, 20] such as pollen grains, as in the case of fossils introduced into till by ice action, then carried into lake deposits by streams draining the till surface during a subsequent warmer period. Both with micro- and macro-fossils it may be difficult to separate primary from derived fossils. The best clues are to be found in considering the sedimentary environment, that is, whether it is likely that the processes of sedimentation will be liable to cause derivation. Thus in autochthonous and pure biogenic deposits, little or no derivation is to be expected, but in inorganic sediments it may occur if the parent material from which the sediment is derived is fossiliferous.

Chemical methods, such as fluorine determinations of bones, may also reveal derivation. In a particular fauna preserved under the same conditions the fluorine content will be similar in different bones. An older bone which has been subject to a different history of fossilisation will have a different fluorine content.

*Fig. 7.1* Frequencies of ecological groups of freshwater molluscs in the late Ipswichian silty marls forming a river terrace at Histon Road, Cambridge. Dots are used where numbers are scarcely adequate for analysis. The relative changes in the groups are a key to the changing aquatic environment. The depth of sediment

*Qualitative and Quantitative Analyses*

A qualitative analysis of fossils from a particular sediment will give a list of species represented, while a quantitative analysis will give frequencies of each species. In some instances the presence of a particular species, e.g. that of a plant or animal characteristically

*Table 7.1* Ecological groups of molluscs used as a basis for environment analysis in central Europe (after Lozek 1965)

| | Ecological Groups | | Index Molluscs |
|---|---|---|---|
| **A** Woodland Species | 1 Closed forest<br><br>2 Woodland-Scrub (→ Timbered Steppe)<br><br>3 Moist woodland | | *Acicula, Aegopis, Ruthenica Bradybaena fruticum Cepaea hortensis Perforatella bidentata Pseudalinda turgida* |
| **B** Grassland Species | 4 Steppe—xerothermic rocks<br><br>5 Open country (in general) | | *Chondrula, Abida, Helicopsis, Cecilioides Pupilla muscorum Vallonia pulchella* |
| **C** Indifferent Species | 6<br>7<br>8 | woodland → grassland ←   dry medium (+ indifferent) damp | *Cochlicopa lubricella Cochlicopa lubrica Euconulus fulvus Vertigo substriata* |
| **D** Aquatic and marsh species | 9 Marshes—very moist habitats<br><br>10 Water (in general) | | *Vertigo antivertigo, Oxyloma, Carychium minimum Lymnaea, Viviparus, Unio, Pisidium* |

arctic, will give information on local climatic and environmental conditions. If, however, the relative frequencies of the different species are known, we may be in a position to make much closer reconstructions of past plant and animal life. Thus the difference between qualitative and quantitative analysis is analogous to the difference between a simple plant list from a plant community and a detailed plant-sociological description of the same community.

Before undertaking frequency analyses, it is worthwhile considering their significance. The main question is to what extent an

I

assemblage of fossils from a given horizon represents a random sample of local or regional life. With pollen and foraminifers the fall-out from the air and from the sea respectively make them well suited for frequency analyses, as the counts of different species are related to the regional living communities which gave rise to the

*Fig. 7.2* Frequencies of distribution (climatic) groups of molluscs in the Histon Road interglacial deposit (see fig. 7.1) (Sparks and West 1959).

A. species reaching to or almost to the Arctic Circle in Sweden.
B. species reaching approximately 63° N in Sweden.
C. species reaching approximately 60°–61° N in Sweden.
D. species found only in the very south of Scandinavia or confined to the European mainland.

fossils. With larger fossils, however, local effects may predominate, and quantitative analyses will give information on the types of community found locally. For example, in the case of freshwater and land molluscs, the frequencies of the different groups of molluscs requiring running water, marsh or dry land conditions, will give information on the local habitats present near the scene of deposition (fig. 7.1, table 7.1). Beetle remains and macroscopic plant remains have a similar type of significance. With even larger fossils, such as those of vertebrates, the frequency of fossils represented must be carefully considered, as it cannot be said that in any particular environment of deposition, e.g. a bog or a cave, the vertebrate skeletons are representative of regional or even local faunas. In the case of bogs, only those animals large enough to sink in and be trapped may be represented and in the case of caves the list of larger mammals may represent a hyaena's choice of food.

As well as considering the analyses from an environmental point of view, we have also to consider their use as indicators of climate. Qualitative studies will give an idea of climate, and may be preferred

*Table 7.2* Analysis of plant-geographical categories in the list of macroscopic plant remains from interglacial deposits at Bobbitshole, Ipswich (West 1957)

The figures give the number of species (or genera) in each category in each zone; figures in parentheses are the percentages of the zone totals in each category.

| Zone | 1 | 2 | 3 | 4 | 5 | 6 | Zone total |
|------|---|---|---|---|---|---|------------|
| | | | *Category* | | | | |
| f | — | 13(25) | 8(15) | 8(15) | 19(37) | 4(8) | 52 |
| e | — | 12(32) | 7(18) | 6(16) | 12(32) | 1(3) | 38 |
| d | 1(5) | 5(25) | 3(15) | 5(25) | 5(25) | 1(5) | 20 |
| c | — | 4(50) | 1(13) | 2(25) | 1(13) | — | 8 |
| b–c transition | 1(14) | 2(28) | — | 3(42) | 1(14) | — | 7 |

Definition of categories:

1. Arctic-alpine plants.
2. Plants distributed throughout Scandinavia.
3. Plants with northern limits in Scandinavia near the Arctic Circle.
4. Plants with northern limits in Scandinavia about midway between those in categories 3 and 5.
5. Plants with northern limits in the south of Scandinavia.
6. Plants with northern limits in north-west Europe south of Scandinavia.

in some instances, but quantitative lists are here again important, for it is the frequencies of plants or animals which require particular climatic conditions which will give the most information about climate (fig. 7.2, table 7.2). For example, rare warmth-loving plants may be found with an abundance of cold-loving plants. In a plain list of species their occurrence together might be problematical in the interpretation of climate, but when their relative frequencies are known, the interpretation may be easier.

### Choice of site

It is important to choose the best site available for the particular investigation in hand. For studies of regional vegetational change the centre of a large lake or bog may be most suitable, but for more detailed studies of local conditions of plant and animal life, marginal areas or small lakes or bogs may be best.

### Obtaining the data

In the collection of sediments for the extraction of fossils, it is all-important to know the exact provenance of the sample and the thickness of sediment it covers. An analysis of a bulk sample whose exact provenance at a site is unknown is not of much use in the reconstruction of past climates and environments. The sample should be large enough (say a kilogram) to provide material for the analysis of various groups of organisms, as it is also important that analyses of these different groups come from the same sediments. In this way a combined picture of the environment at the time the sediment was deposited can be built up.

While the recovery of large vertebrate fossils requires no special techniques, the extraction of smaller fossils depends on the use of a variety of techniques and processes, of which the most important are described in Appendix 1.

### Identification[26]

Identification of fossils must be by comparison with collections of reference material, e.g. slides of pollen of living species, shells of modern species of molluscs. It may be necessary to treat reference material (e.g. seeds, by boiling in sodium hydroxide for a short time) to bring it to a similar state of appearance as the fossils. It is obviously important to have reference collections in which the species are known to be correctly determined. Identification of a fossil may be limited because of the present unsatisfactory state of the taxonomy of the nearest living species.

Morphological similarities between fossil and type, such as shape, size, and surface patterns are the most certain guide to identity (plates 11, 12). Size-frequency analyses are also used when there is general morphological similarity, but difference in size between closely related species. For example, two species of the spruce, *Picea abies* and *P. omorica-type* have been separated on the basis of size differences (fig. 7.3).[3] However, the interpretation of size differences

*Fig. 7.3* Size frequency distribution of the height of the air sacs of fossil *Picea* pollen grains from late Eemian and early Weichselian deposits in Denmark. Mean size of same parameter of recent pollen grains of *P. omorica* (a), and *P. abies* (b) (after Andersen 1961). The curves indicate that the two species of *Picea* are present fossil.

has to be done with care, for different methods of preservation in sediments, different histories since incorporation in sediments, and different methods of fossil preparation (e.g. in making-up pollen slides) may all lead to size variation in the one species.

### Presentation of data

The data can be presented as qualitative lists of species, as lists of species with subjective estimates of frequency, as lists of species with

*Fig. 7.4* Pollen diagram from freshwater and estuarine sediments of Late Gipping and Ipswichian age. The basis for calculating the percentages is the total tree pollen. Proportions of the various categories of pollen and spores are shown on the right. Sediments: 1, freshwater silt and clay; 2, detritus mud with wood; 3, estuarine grey silty clay; 4, estuarine brown-grey silty clay.

absolute numbers of fossils found, or in the form of frequency diagrams. Frequency diagrams may be histograms (figs. 7.1 and 7.2), or the percentage frequencies may be used to form curves as in the familiar pollen diagram (fig. 7.4). In a series of analyses from a column of sediment, there is much to be said for the percentage frequencies at each level (e.g. the pollen spectrum at that level) being kept separate, the thickness of the line representing the thickness of sediment sampled at each level. Where large numbers of species are concerned it may be more convenient to group the species into ecological or

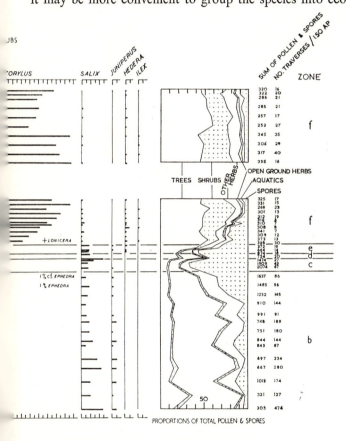

climatic groups, and then graph the frequencies of these groups (fig. 7.2).

There are a variety of ways in which pollen data can be presented in graphical form, depending on the sum of pollen used as a base for the calculation of pollen frequency percentages.[34] A pollen diagram is used primarily as a means of investigating regional vegetational

KENTMERE A.

*Fig.* 7.5 Pollen diagram through Late Weichselian and Early Flandrian lake sediments at Kentmere, Westmorland. The basis for calculating the percentages is the sum of pollen types in category A (tree pollen) and B (anemophilous terrestrial herbs). Category C contains other herbs, probably local and marsh species, and spores (Walker 1955).

change, and therefore the base of the percentage calculation should be related to the regional vegetation. The pollen sum in a forested area may be the tree pollen only, pollen of non-trees being expressed as a percentage of total tree pollen (fig. 7.4). The significant changes in forest composition over a period of time are thus clearly expressed. A second type of diagram (fig. 7.5), used where there is much non-tree pollen, uses as a pollen sum the total pollen of terrestrial plants. The difficulty here is recognising which pollen types are of terrestrial and regional origin and which are derived from local communities in the bog or around the lake from which the sediments are taken. Whatever the pollen sum used, it is important to state clearly in the diagram how it is constructed, and to give all the factual data without any element of interpretation, so that the reader can understand what the curves represent, and will be able to draw his own conclusions from the data provided.

Likewise, in quantitative lists of other organisms, the nature of the individual counted (fragments of shell, apex of shell, elytra of beetle, head of beetle) should be mentioned, again so that the reader can draw his own conclusions about the significance of the counts.

## Interpretation of data[27, 33]

The present is the key to the past in the use of the fossil record for reconstructions of plant and animal life, environments and climates. A knowledge both of taxonomy for the identification of species, and ecology for the interpretation of the fossil record, is essential. It is lack of knowledge of both these aspects which limit our interpretations. Lack of knowledge of taxonomy of plants and animals limits the success of our identifications, and lack of knowledge of the ecology of living plants and animals limits our reconstructions. We also suffer a lack of knowledge about the relation between living assemblages and the fossil assemblages likely to result from them.

In making deductions from lists of fossils it has to be assumed that in the past vegetation and fauna have been related to climate and topography as they are at the present day. There is ample support for this in the fact that reconstructions based on plant and on animal life are not at odds with one another. However, there is the possibility that some species have changed their ecological requirements while the morphology of their parts found fossil have not changed. For example, the gastropod *Potamopyrgus jenkinsi* appears to have spread from brackish to freshwater in the last hundred years. Taking an assemblage as a whole, however, if the species present point to similar conditions of environment and climate, there is no reason to suppose that ecological requirements of the species have significantly changed since the time of their fossilisation. It is thus safer to use assemblage rather than individual species as indicators of past conditions.

## Climatic deductions

The fossil assemblage gives a clear indication of the general climatic type, e.g. temperate or arctic, oceanic or continental. It may appear very similar to particular assemblages seen today, and then it may be possible to infer more detailed climatic conditions. As an example of such a type of interpretation, we can refer to the inter-stadial deposits in the Weichselian (last) glaciation at Chelford in Cheshire,[25] where pollen spectra from biogenic muds were very similar to the pollen rain in the *Betula-Pinus-Picea* forest of northern Finland.[1] Some approximations to the climate of the Chelford area during the deposition of the interstadial organic mud may be given by the climate of the area of distribution of this type of forest in northern Finland, with an annual rainfall of 400 to 700 mm, annual temperature amplitude 20° to 27°C, mean temperature of coldest month (February) −10° to −15°C, and that for the warmest month (July) 16° to 12°C. Of course, there is the assumption here that in each of the compared areas the vegetation was in equilibrium with the climate. This interpretation on the basis of the plants is supported by deductions of similar climatic conditions based on the study of the insect fauna of the same deposits.[7]

To proceed with climatic deductions more detailed than this, it is necessary to rely on present knowledge of the distribution of species, of the factors which determine this distribution, and of ecological behaviour. Where the factors are known to some extent, then it may be possible to make more detailed deductions about climate from the fossil occurrence of the species. For example, Iversen's detailed work[17, 19] on *Viscum*, *Hedera* and *Ilex* makes these genera particularly valuable as climatic indicators. The difficulty is that present distribution is not necessarily determined only by present climate. Historical factors, competition and edaphic factors will also effect the distribution, in ways often unknown. There is also the possibility, mentioned before, that the ecological tolerance of particular species may have changed, whilst the morphology of the part of the plant identified as a fossil remains unchanged. It would be rather surprising if some selection of biotypes had not taken place during the many migrations enforced by the repeated climatic changes of the Pleistocene.

There are some fossil assemblages which give contradictory climatic indications, for example, mixtures of cold- and warm-indicating species. Excluding the possibility that the mixture results from secondary deposition of fossils, there are a number of other possible explanations for such mixtures. It may be that under conditions of changing climate certain groups of organisms may migrate faster than others—e.g. water plants faster than land plants. We may then find a mixture of thermophilous water plants and boreal forest trees. It seems reasonable to expect that during the Pleistocene there was a lag between the changes of climate and the distributional responses of the different groups of plants and animals.

Another explanation of such anomalies is to assume that there is much microclimatic variation leading to admixture of fossilised organisms of different climatic or ecological requirements. Or there is the possibility that past Pleistocene climates (such as those of the present temperate zone during a time of maximum glaciation) may be different from any of the zonal climates of today. Thus the presence of thermophilous aquatic plants during past cold periods in the present temperate zone has been explained by the warming effect of the sun on water-bodies at these lower latitudes.

A last possibility would be that there has been a change in climatic tolerance of some of the species involved, and that the fossil taxon is now extinct. Such a change in tolerance, in a climatic or a wider ecological sense, might be demonstrated by the repeated finding of a particular species in association with other species which do not associate with it at the present day.

### Evidence of local and regional conditions of life

Some categories of fossils give evidence of local environmental conditions, others of regional conditions, as already mentioned. Microfossils, such as pollen, spores and foraminifers provide information of regional and local conditions, as they are derived from a wide source area. Larger organisms, such as molluscs and plant macrofossils, provide information on more local conditions, as their remains are usually not distributed far from their source. Two examples can be quoted to show the value of micro- and macro-analyses in the interpretation of phenomena as being of local or regional significance.

In fig. 7.6, it is seen that Cyperaceae macroscopic remains increase in quantity towards the top of the succession of lake sediments analysed. This change was accompanied by rising percentages of Cyperaceae pollen in the pollen diagram from the same sequence, most of which is therefore probably derived from local aquatic and marsh species of Cyperaceae, and does not reflect a regional change of vegetation.

The other example, also palaeobotanical, is taken from the vegetational history of the middle part, zone f, of the Ipswichian (last) interglacial in south-east England. In a number of pollen diagrams through zone f, *Alnus* pollen is very scarce, usually 1 to 5 per cent of the total tree pollen. The deposits concerned were formed in lakes or slowly-flowing rivers or streams. This scarcity of *Alnus* might suggest that the tree was absent or rare in the regional vegetation and in the local swamp communities bordering the sites of deposition. But at some levels on a zone f riverine deposit at Wretton, Norfolk, *A. glutinosa* fruits have been found abundantly and at the same levels *Alnus* pollen is sixty per cent of the total tree pollen. It seems that communities with *Alnus* were not widespread in this interglacial and that only locally do they contribute to the pollen rain. In the Flandrian (post-glacial) on the other hand, *Alnus* pollen becomes frequent throughout southern England at the beginning of the Atlantic, zone VII, though in a few diagrams it appears earlier. It appears that locally distributed communities with *Alnus* became widespread as a result of climatic changes occurring near the zone VI/VII boundary.

The macrofossils alone, both plant and animal, are useful in building up a picture of a changing local environment, as shown in fig. 7.6, which portrays the change from open water to reed swamp to

*Fig. 7.6* Diagram of the changing frequency of various macroscopic remains in the Ipswichian interglacial deposits at Bobbitshole near Ipswich. Aquatics to the left, reedswamp species in the centre and marsh plants to the right. The sequence of changes of the plant remains indicates change from open water to reedswamp to marsh, corresponding to the change in sediment from clay-mud to mottled alluvial clay (West 1957).

marsh vegetation, and fig. 7.7 which shows a change from freshwater to brackish water conditions as indicated by molluscs.

The microfossils are usually most useful for regional changes, as indicated in a typical pollen diagram. But in some cases, with very detailed pollen diagrams, it is possible to indicate the plant communities involved in the changes, as for example shown by Iversen[16, 19] in his studies of the phases of deforestation associated with Neolithic cultures in Denmark.

In interpretation we should also be aware of the possibility that past communities are not necessarily represented today. For example, it has been considered by some that under the stress of climatic change vegetational zones and even plant communities have migrated as a whole, e.g. the southward movement of vegetational zones in Europe during the Weichselian (last) glaciation. But floral lists from deposits of this age show mixtures of floristic elements, such as thermophilous water plants, tundra plants, steppe plants,

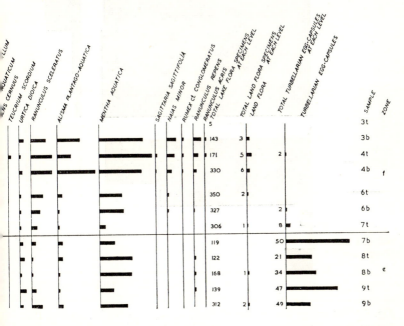

0  5  10   20   30   40   50   per cent of total specimens in lake flora at each level
        scale

alpine plants, dune plants and weeds. It seems that these grew in the same area at the same time. This is a clear indication that past vegetation types are not necessarily in existence today. A similar demonstration follows from a study of Russian periglacial floras,[14] which indicates new combinations of vegetational units, not found in the present vegetational zones (fig. 7.8).

Similar changes have been demonstrated in faunas, such as a mixture of arctic (e.g. lemming) and steppe (e.g. jerboa) species of rodents in cold Pleistocene faunas.[35]

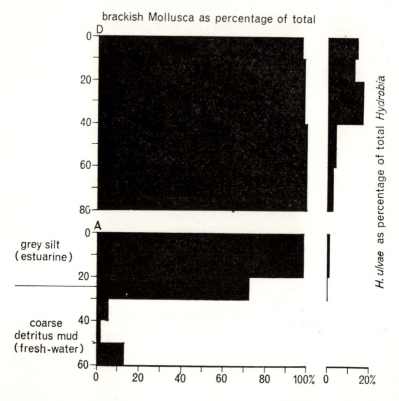

*Fig. 7.7* Percentage frequencies of *Hydrobia ventrosa* and *H. ulvae* at the change from freshwater to estuarine deposition during the Ipswichian interglacial at Selsey, Sussex. *H. ventrosa* prefers less saline water than *H. ulvae*. The pollen diagram from this deposit is shown in fig. 7.4 (after West and Sparks 1960).

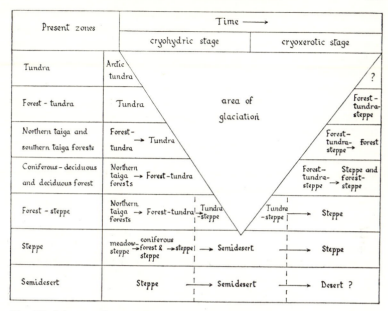

| Present zones | Time ⟶ | | |
|---|---|---|---|
| | cryohydric stage | | cryoxerotic stage |
| Tundra | Arctic tundra | area of glaciation | ? |
| Forest - tundra | Tundra | | Forest-tundra-steppe |
| Northern taiga and southern taiga forests | Forest-tundra ⟶ Tundra | | Forest-tundra-steppe ⟶ forest |
| Coniferous - deciduous and deciduous forest | Northern taiga ⟶ Forest-tundra forests | | Forest-tundra-steppe ⟶ Steppe and forest-steppe |
| Forest - steppe | Northern taiga ⟶ Forest-tundra forests → Tundra-steppe | Tundra-steppe ⟶ Steppe | |
| Steppe | meadow-steppe → coniferous forest & steppe → steppe ⟶ Semidesert | ⟶ Steppe | |
| Semidesert | Steppe ⟶ Semidesert | ⟶ Desert ? | |

*Fig. 7.8* Scheme of vegetational change in the Russian Plain at the time of maximum glaciation (after Grichuk and Grichuk 1960).

## Interpretation of pollen diagrams [11]

Pollen diagrams form such an important part of Pleistocene research that it is necessary to consider their interpretation separately. The results of pollen analysis are presented in curves or histograms showing the percentage frequency of the different pollen and spore types at successive levels (figs. 7.4 and 7.5), the base for the percentage being the total pollen, the total tree pollen or some other total preferred by the pollen analyst. Each analysis (pollen spectrum) is a count of a sample of the total pollen rain over the time in which the thickness of sediment sampled was deposited, except that there may be selective decay of certain pollen types after deposition (e.g. *Quercus* pollen is susceptible to, and *Pinus* is resistant to, weathering), and selective transport before incorporation into the sediment[22] (e.g. marine deposits often show over-representation of winged pollen grains of conifers).

The difficulty in the interpretation of pollen diagrams results from not knowing the relation between the pollen rain and the surrounding types of vegetation. Each plant community will contribute pollen to the pollen rain, the amount depending on the pollen production of each species in the community, the frequency of each species in the community, the size of the area covered by each community, and also on the structure of each community, important when considering the processes of the movement of pollen from the community into the atmosphere.[30]

The pollen production varies from species to species, so that low pollen producers, such as insect-pollinated species like *Acer*, may be little represented, even though frequent, while great pollen producers like the wind-pollinated *Pinus* may be very much over-represented in pollen analyses. Thus in interpreting pollen spectra it is important to remember that absence or low frequencies of pollen do not necessarily mean absence or rarity of a tree, and the converse. Also where tree cover is low and non-tree pollen frequent, tree pollen types having an ability to travel far, e.g. the winged *Pinus* grain, may be well represented because of long-distance transport.

In the absence of detailed studies of the relation between plant communities and the pollen rain they produce, during a study of vegetational history of a particular area it is wise to take recent samples from moss-polsters or surface muds of lakes, and consider their pollen content in relation to the make-up of the vegetation surrounding each sampling site. Some insight is then gained into the origin of the pollen rain in the area.

In any pollen diagram it is important to include the stratigraphy of the sediments, because the sediment will tell the reader the type of environment which received the pollen rain, and thus aid the interpretation. For example, the presence of raised bog peats will suggest the local origin of pollen types liable to be derived from the bog communities.

The stratigraphy will also indicate whether changes in the curves are of local or regional origin. Thus a hydrosere may be indicated in the sediment by a change from lake sediments to fen peats, then to raised bog peats. Maxima of *Alnus* or *Betula* pollen may be associated with the formation of wood peat at the fen stage rather than indicate any climatic change. If the course of the pollen curves is independent of sediment change they are probably of regional origin, and may then be governed by regional plant succession, resulting from climatic change, or merely from succession following competition after arrival and spreading of the species in the area without any specific climatic change.[19] It is important to bear these possibilities in mind when interpreting pollen curves. Synchroneity of changes over a wide area may indicate a climatic origin for the change, while trends such as one particular tree appearing later the further north the site may indicate that the time of arrival and spread of the species is important. Edaphic change, such as regional podsolisation of soils,[18] would be indicated by the increased frequency of heath plant pollen types.

A pollen zone is essentially an assemblage of particular pollen types, and should be named after the dominant pollen types. It should have a regional distribution, and so zonation should be based on diagrams where very local effects are excluded or at a minimum, as in the centre of a large lake basin. The zones are best based on so-called standard pollen diagrams.[2] The question of zonation in relation to stratigraphy is considered in a later chapter.

On the question of correlation between pollen diagrams over wide areas, it is essential to remember that similar climatic changes will have different effects on vegetation according to latitude and longitude. Possible effects of synchronous changes are illustrated in fig. 7.9.

*Fig. 7.9* Parallelism of climatic and vegetational change in north-west Europe. The curves show the course of vegetational change, as deduced from pollen analysis of sediments at the latitudes or altitudes corresponding to the named vegetational zones. In curve b, from a sub-arctic area, the oscillations are difficult to detect. In curve c, from the boreal coniferous zone, the oscillations are recorded by interchange between tundra and sub-arctic birch, and finally to coniferous forest. In curve f, from the temperate zone, the same oscillations are recorded as interchange between boreal coniferous forest and temperate forest.

*The interglacial cycle*

As we have shown, biological investigations of the Pleistocene have resulted in the clear association of climatic change with changes in flora, fauna and soils. Some of the changes associated with the interglacial cycle of climatic amelioration are shown in fig. 7.10. These are the gross changes which are evident from studies of the flora and fauna. Minor fluctuations of climate and the detailed behaviour of

K

particular species and of communities are much more difficult to
define, though equally important from the biological point of view,
and much further study is required for their elucidation.

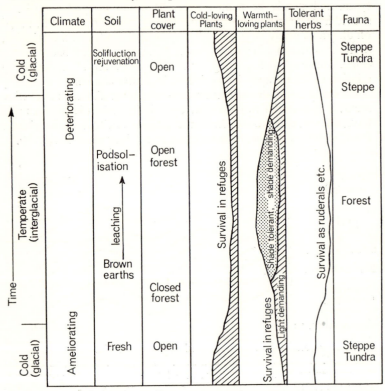

*Fig.7.10* A scheme of environmental and vegetational changes in temperate
north-west Europe during an oscillation from cold (glacial) to temperate
(interglacial) and back to cold (glacial).

## REFERENCES

1 AARIO, L. 1944. 'Über die pollenanalytischen methoden zur Unter-
suchung von Waldgrenzen', *Geol. Fören. Stockh. Förh.*, **66,** 337–54.
2 ANDERSEN, A. 1954. 'Two standard pollen diagrams from south
Jutland', *Danm. Geol. Unders.*, II Raekke, No. 80, 188–209.
3 ANDERSEN, S. T. 1961. 'Vegetation and its environment in Denmark
in the Early Weichselian Glacial', *Danm. Geol. Unders.*, II Raekke,
No. 75.
4 BEIJERINCK, W. 1947. *Zadenatlas der Nederlandsche Flora*. Wagenin-
gen: Veenman.

5 BERTSCH, K. 1941. *Früchte und Samen. Handbücher der praktischen vorgeschichtsforschung*, **1**. Stuttgart: Enke.

6 BORDES, F. and PRAT, F. 1965. 'Observations sur les faunes du Riss et du Würm I', *L'anthropologie*, **69**, 31–46.

7 COOPE, G. R. 1959. 'A Late Pleistocene insect fauna from Chelford, Cheshire', *Proc. R. Soc. London*, B, **151**, 70–86.

8 COOPE, G. R. 1961. 'On the study of glacial and interglacial insect faunas', *Proc. Linn. Soc. London*, **172**, (1959–60), 62–5.

9 CORNWALL, I. W. 1956. *Bones for the archaeologist*. London: Phoenix House.

10 ERDTMAN, G. 1943. *An introduction to pollen analysis*. Waltham, Mass.: Chronica Botanica.

11 FAEGRI, K. and IVERSEN, J. 1964. *Textbook of pollen analysis*. 2nd edn. Oxford: Blackwell.

12 FEYLING-HANSSEN, R. W. 1964. 'Foraminifera in late Quaternary deposits from the Oslofjord area', *Norges Geol. Unders.*, No. 225.

13 FREY, D. G. 1964. 'Remains of animals in Quaternary lake and bog sediments and their interpretation', *Arch. Hydrobiol. Beih.*, **2**, 1–114.

14 GRICHUK, M. P. and GRICHUK, V. P. 1960. 'O prilednikovoi rastitelnosti na territorii S.S.S.R', in *Periglacial phenomena of the U.S.S.R.* eds. Markov, K. K. and Popov, A. I. Moscow.

15 IVERSEN, J. 1936. 'Sekundäres pollen als Fehlerquelle', *Danm. Geol. Unders.*, IV Raekke, **2**, No. 15.

16 IVERSEN, J. 1941. 'Land occupation in Denmark's Stone Age', *Danm. Geol. Unders.*, II Raekke, No. 66.

17 IVERSEN, J. 1944. '*Viscum, Hedera* and *Ilex* as climate indicators', *Danm. Geol. Unders.*, IV Raekke, **3**, No. 6.

18 IVERSEN, J. 1958. 'The bearing of glacial and interglacial epochs on the formation and extinction of plant taxa', *Uppsala Universitets Årsskrift*, **6**, 210–15.

19 IVERSEN, J. 1960. 'Problems of the Early Post-glacial forest development in Denmark', *Danm. Geol. Unders.*, IV Raekke, **4**, No. 3.

20 LEROI-GOURHAN, A. 1965. 'Les analyses polliniques sur les sediments des grottes', *Bull. Assoc. française pour l'Etude du Quat.*, 1965, 145–52.

21 LOZEK, V. 1965. 'Problems of analysis of the Quaternary non-marine Molluscan fauna in Europe', *Geol. Soc. Amer. Special Paper* 84, 201–18.

22 MULLER, J. 1959. 'Palynology of recent Orinoco delta and shelf sediments', *Micropalaeontology*, **5**, 1–32.

23 ROUND, F. E. 1957. 'The Late-glacial and Post-glacial diatom succession in the Kentmere Valley deposit', *New Phytol.*, **56**, 98–126.

24 SHOTTON, F. W. 1965. 'Movements of Insect Populations in the British Pleistocene', *Geol. Soc. Amer. Special Paper* 84, 17–33.

25 SIMPSON, I. M. and WEST, R. G. 1958. 'On the stratigraphy and palaeobotany of a late-Pleistocene organic deposit at Chelford, Cheshire', *New Phytol.*, **57**, 239–50.

26 SMART, J. and TAYLOR, G. 1953. *Bibliography of key works for the*

*identification of the British Fauna and Flora.* 2nd edn. London: The Systematics Association.

27 SPARKS, B. W. 1961. 'The ecological interpretation of Quaternary non-marine Mollusca', *Proc. Linn. Soc. London*, **172**, (1959–60), 71–80.

28 SPARKS, B. W. and WEST, R. G. 1959. 'The palaeoecology of the Interglacial deposits at Histon Road, Cambridge', *Eiszeitalter und Gegenwart*, **10**, 123–43.

29 SPARKS, B. W. and WEST, R. G. 1960. 'Coastal interglacial deposits of the English Channel', *Phil. Trans. R. Soc. London*, B, **243**, 95–133.

30 TAUBER, H. 1965. 'Differential pollen dispersion and the interpretation of pollen diagrams', *Danm. Geol. Unders.*, II Raekke, No. 89.

31 WALKER, D. 1955. 'Studies in the Post-glacial history of British vegetation. XIV. Skelsmergh Tarn and Kentmere, Westmorland', *New Phytol.*, **54**, 222–54.

32 WEST, R. G. 1957. 'Interglacial deposits at Bobbitshole, Ipswich', *Phil. Trans. R. Soc. London*, B, **241**, 1–31.

33 WEST, R. G. 1964. 'Inter-relations of ecology and Quaternary palaeobotany', *J. Ecol.*, **52** (suppl.), 47–57.

34 WRIGHT, H. E. and PATTEN, H. L. 1963. 'The pollen sum', *Pollen et spores*, **5**, 445–50.

35 WRIGHT, W. B. 1937. *The Quaternary Ice Age.* London: Macmillan.

# CHAPTER 8

# LAND/SEA-LEVEL CHANGES

Iᴺ coastal areas around the world there is ample evidence of changes of ocean-level relative to land. Old shore-lines, such as those marked by raised beaches, are found at considerable heights above present sea-level, indicating former sea-levels higher than the present in relation to the land, while drowned valleys indicate flooding by a rise of sea-level relative to the land. It is necessary to use the term relative in this context, as there is no certainty that the effects are caused solely by rise or fall in sea-level or by rise or fall of land. Both may be involved in any changes to produce the net result seen today. Similar ancient shore-lines, resulting from the same type of causes, are also found around the inland waters.

The interest of the study of past sea-levels is twofold. It gives us an insight into the mechanisms which are now important in determining the sea-level relative to that of the land, mechanisms which must have operated over the whole of geological time. Secondly, land/sea-level changes are important in studying the movements of faunal and floristic elements in the past.

Changes in land/sea-level result from two principal causes. Local upwarping or downwarping of rocks and world-wide (eustatic) changes of sea-level. We shall discuss the role of each of these two in causing changes of relative land/sea-level.

## Local effects

These are upwarping or downwarping of limited areas of the earth's crust. The causes are structural changes of the earth's crust brought about by the deformation or displacement of rocks. A particular example is isostatic change, which is thought to result from adjustment in the balance between different parts of the crust, so that if for example a load of sediment is added in one area of ocean depression occurs concurrently in that area, while a corresponding rise will occur where the load of rock is being reduced by erosion.

135

Adjustment of levels by flowage of material deep in the earth follows until isostatic equilibrium is re-established (fig. 8.1).

A special case of isostasy, and one important in the present context, is where the load is of ice, and depression of the crust by deformation follows the build-up of an ice sheet (fig. 2.7b). On removal of the load during deglaciation, there is a slow recovery of the crust and an updoming of the land surface results. That the removal of ice load is indeed the cause of the isostatic adjustment which leads to updoming is suggested by the close relation between

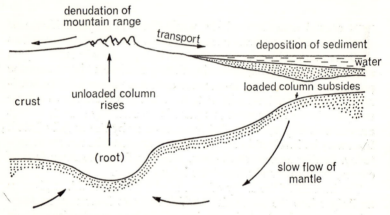

*Fig. 8.1* Diagram illustrating isostatic readjustment in response to denudation and deposition (after Holmes).

the limits of ice sheets and the limits of updoming in Scotland, Scandinavia and Canada, by the signs of uplift near the margins of presently glaciated areas (Greenland, Spitsbergen, Antarctica), by the concentric arrangement of isobases (lines joining points of equal uplift) in relation to the centre of dispersion of the ice, and by gravity anomalies indicating deficiencies of mass in formerly glaciated areas showing present uplift, e.g. Scandinavia and Canada. The amount of depression by ice load will depend on the density and thickness of the ice, the density of the material beneath and its rate of deformation. If we estimate as an approximation that the density of the flowing material is three times that of ice, the amount of depression will be a third the maximum thickness of the ice. Niskanen[18] has made some calculations regarding total crustal depression and thickness of the Scandinavian ice. He estimated 730 m of depression and 2650 m of ice. There appears to be a minimum ice load causing depression, as there is little evidence that the ice bodies of small glaciers produce an effect on the earth's crust. Thus there is evidence of such effects with ice caps greater than 500 km in diameter and with ice more than 1 km thick.[1]

An interesting question in relation to isostatic depression by ice load is whether there is a compensatory uplift in areas marginal to the ice sheet, or alternatively, a compensatory downwarping in marginal areas accompanying the uplift of a deglaciated area. Such has not yet been conclusively demonstrated, but there are indications as seen in the present downwarping of the southern margin of the Baltic shown in fig. 8.2.

The evidence for isostatic recovery after deglaciation comes from observations of heights of raised beaches. From these, isobases showing the form and degree of the uplift (fig. 8.10) can be drawn, with the zero isobase marking the outer limit of uplift. There has been much discussion over whether uplift is regular and the updoming simple, whether discontinuities occur in the rise, whether block uplift occurs, and whether hinge lines occur dividing areas of unequal rate of uplift. This last point is discussed later in relation to the Baltic area.

## Eustatic movements of sea-level[6]

Eustatic movements of sea-level can result from changes in the form of ocean basins and consequently the thickness of the oceans, from accumulation of sediments displacing sea-water, from displacement of sea-water by isostatic recovery or other sorts of uplift, and from changes in the temperature of sea-water causing volume changes. The last is of little significance; it has been estimated that a rise of 1°C would raise sea-level by 60 cm. The magnitude of the other factors in effecting movements of sea-level is unknown.

Besides these factors there is the glacial control of sea-level. The level of the oceans is related to the balance between the volume of water in the oceans, the amount of moisture in the atmosphere and the volume of water on the land surface. During a glaciation, atmospheric temperatures fall, and water accumulates on the land surface as a result of increased snowfall, reduced ablation in the summer, and freezing of water on and in the ground. Thus sea-level will fall because of the increase in water held on the land surface, principally in the form of ice. Conversely, when temperatures rise, the ice will start to melt, water will return to the oceans and sea-level will rise.

Various calculations have been made to estimate the amount of fall of sea-level during the glaciations, based on estimates of the volume of ice formed. They range from 80 to 150 m. This figure is not very different from figures obtained from geological evidence of lowered sea-levels.

It has also been estimated that the sea-level would rise by 40 to 60 m if all the world's ice were melted. But shore-lines of more than twice this height are known and while other effects than glacial control may be involved, such as local uplift, it appears that there is a general trend of overall eustatic change during the Pleistocene. This is indicated by the fact that shore-lines are progressively younger as they get lower. A number of explanations have been put forward to explain this, including marginal upwarping of continents and decrease of ocean level by build-up of Antarctic ice. But the cause is not yet clear.

Elucidation of the course of the eustatic changes in sea-level can only result from shore-line studies and radiocarbon dates of sub-merged peats and emerged marine sediments or organisms, in areas of supposed crustal stability, such as South Africa and Western Australia. The course of the Flandrian eustatic rise has been charted many times (e.g. fig. 8.7), but there are still doubtful points about the curves, such as whether the Flandrian seas have ever risen much above their present level, and when the present sea-level was reached. More dating studies are required in areas of crustal stability before the curve is acceptable.

### The Isokinetic Theory of W. B. Wright and the causes of shore-line displacement

W. B. Wright[25] in 1914, in considering the shore-lines of northern Europe, showed that a combination of isostatic recovery with a eustatic rise of sea-level gave an explanation of the Late Weichselian and Flandrian shore-lines. He suggested that shore-lines were formed as a result of sea-level standstills when rate of eustatic rise was the same as the rate of isostatic uplift. This theory is a useful basis for interpretation of shore-lines in recently glaciated areas, but it should be remembered that even in these areas other possible factors, such as tectonic movements and downwarping of marginal areas, may be effective.

Outside these areas, both eustatic changes and tectonic movements may combine or act singly to produce shore-lines. The diverse causes of shore-line displacement and changes of relative land/sea-level are best clarified by examining later in this chapter the evidence from three areas, in each of which a different combination of factors resulted in shore-line displacement. These are the Baltic, where eustatic and isostatic factors combine, the Netherlands, where tectonic sinking is important, and the Mediterranean, where eustatic effects may be predominant.

*Contemporary and recent changes in relative land/sea-level*

Such changes have been demonstrated by studies of tide-gauge records in Scandinavia, the British Isles and the North Sea area (fig. 8.2), and North America (fig. 8.3). The records show that updoming is still continuing in areas subject to heavy glaciation during the Pleistocene. The maximum rate of uplift observed is in the

*Fig. 8.2* Contemporary uplift and downwarping in north-west Europe. The isobases represent rate of change (+ or −) in mm/year, determined from tide-gauge records. Dashed isobases are less certain, and the dotted isobases are based on interpolation (after Fromm 1953 and Valentin 1954).

*Fig. 8.3* Contemporary uplift in eastern north America. The isobases represent rate of uplift in mm/year, determined from tide-gauge records (after Gutenberg 1941).

northern part of the Gulf of Bothnia, nearly 1 cm a year, and in each area the place of maximum uplift corresponds well with the centres of ice dispersal.

It has been estimated that the uplift in Scandinavia will not be complete for many thousands of years and this implies that there is a very considerable time lag between the end of isostatic recovery and the final disappearance of the Scandinavian ice cap about 6000 years ago.

*Fig. 8.4a* Elements of the shore zones on a well-developed coastline (after Johnson 1919).

*Fig. 8.4b* Section at Porthleven, Cornwall, showing re-excavation of 'fossil' wave-cut notch containing cemented beach material and exhumation of 'fossil' cliff by the sea. The present notch re-occupies the excavated 'fossil' notch, and the old wave-cut platform forms the present one (plate 13a).

*Fig. 8.4c* Schematic section through western part of the Netherlands, showing sediments formed during the Flandrian time of rising sea-level behind beach barriers (van Straaten 1961).

1. Sands of young coastal dunes (after twelfth century).
2. Tidal channel, flat and salt marsh deposits (Sub-Atlantic).
3. Spit barrier deposits (Sub-Boreal), beach sands, grading downwards into finer sands with mud layers, upwards into dune sands.
4. Relatively coarse grained sands of North Sea floor.
5. River deposits, partly contemporaneous with peat.
6. Clay of salt and brackish marshes and swamps (Atlantic and early Sub-Boreal).

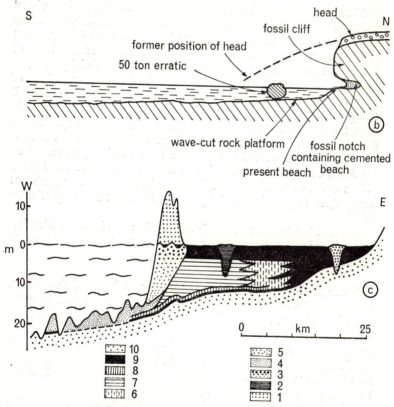

7. Sediments of tidal flat environment, channels, flats and marshes (Atlantic and early Sub-Boreal).
8. Lagoon clays (Atlantic).
9. Peat (late Boreal, Atlantic, Sub-Boreal and Sub-Atlantic). Much of this peat has been dug away by man. The diagram gives roughly the original situation.
10. Eolian and fluvial sands (Pleistocene and Pre-Boreal).

Outside the zero isobase for the present uplift, as seen in fig. 8.2, downwarping has been observed in the southern Scandinavian region and in the British Isles and North Sea region. It is not possible to say how much this is associated with independent tectonic changes and how much with any isostatic compensation following updoming further north.

### Evidence for changes of relative land/sea-level in the past

*Evidence for higher sea-levels than at present* (plate 13). Both erosional and constructional forms give evidence of higher sea-levels. Features associated with shore-lines are shown in fig. 8.4. Sea-cliffs, wave-cut platforms or marine terraces, wave-cut notches at the base of sea-cliffs, sea-cave systems and lines showing past activity of rock-boring molluscs have all been used to indicate past positions of sea-level. Off-shore deposits, off-shore bars, spits, beach gravels, all can give evidence of former marine transgression over the land. So does the alternation between estuarine and/or marine deposits and freshwater deposits. The contact between freshwater and brackish-water or marine deposits is called a transgression (freshwater to brackish) or regression (brackish to freshwater) contact, and these points of contact are important in determining how former sea-levels changed, as they register salinity changes of the water at particular heights.

Aggradation terraces of the lower reaches of rivers are also important for determining former sea-levels, as the terrace profile tends to flatten out when near sea-level (fig. 8.5).

*Evidence for lower sea-levels than at present.* Submerged shore-lines, submerged deltas and the extension of valley systems well into the sea, give evidence of former lower sea-levels. As an example of the last, the Elbe valley is recognisable in charts to a distance of 500 km from the shore, and to a depth of $-80$ m suggesting a former relative sea-level of at least that depth. The lowered sea-level would also be likely to change the regimen of the rivers concerned, which would start downcutting in their lower reaches, the downcutting working back as a nick-point in the long profile of the river (fig. 8.5). Many such nick-points have been identified in the Thames profile.[27]

Sediments also give clear evidence of former low sea-level in the occurrence below present mean sea-level of brackish or freshwater sediments intercalated in marine or estuarine series of deposits (fig. 8.4c).

*Fig. 8.5* Long profiles of rivers with down-cutting and aggradation phases associated with changing sea-levels. Fine dots, alluvium of temperate stages; large dots, sands and gravels of cold stages.

a. Preglacial valley, river rejuvenated by low sea-level of glacial times Nick-point marks the head of rejuvenation.
b. Aggradation as a result of a rising interglacial sea-level.
c. A further glacial low sea-level results in down-cutting in the lower parts of the valley and aggradation of outwash and weathering debris in the upper part.
d. Further aggradation during a second interglacial stage of higher sea-level.

### The interpretation of evidence concerning former sea-levels

It is thought that a world-wide chronology of the Pleistocene can be based on eustatic changes of sea-level, as indicated by former shore-lines. Such a chronology may indeed be possible, but there are two major groups of difficulties affecting its attainment. One is the difficulty of determining the eustatic component of any changes which have resulted in shore-line displacement, and adjusting for local isostatic and tectonic effects. The older the displaced shore-line, the more difficult it is to isolate the effective factors. It must be known whether the area under study is a stable area, or one subject to isostatic recovery or to tectonic activity. If a shore-line is level over a long distance, it is probably in an area of relative stability. But there are few areas where such stability can be well demonstrated.

144    PLEISTOCENE GEOLOGY AND BIOLOGY

The other group of difficulties concerns the actual height relation of a geological feature to the sea-level at the time it was formed. It is not easy to relate the position of the notch, the height of the wave-cut platform, the break of slope at the back of a platform, to a particular sea-level, as the position will vary with tidal range, the nature of the rock, whether it is well bedded horizontally or not, and the exposure of the coast. The relation of raised beach heights to sea-level is also difficult, as witness the height of the present Chesil beach up to forty feet above sea-level. There is also the possibility of sheets of beach gravel being formed as the regression of the sea occurs. These beach gravels will then not represent high still-stands of sea-level. Neither has any absolute datum been used for determination of former sea-levels over wide areas. These uncertainties can be reduced by accurate measurements and by reports on the reliability and meaning of the particular features measured, but substantial sources of variability remain.

With transgression and regression contacts, the evidence for salinity change and its relation to height is more objective, but here again there are such sources of error as compaction of sediments[14] and the possibility of changes in salinity by coastal changes rather than by changes in sea-level.

Though these difficulties remain, much has been done to elucidate relative land/sea-level changes, as will be seen in the subsequent examples. It is in the sphere of a eustatic chronology that the difficulties are most apparent. The problem is to relate the high inter-glacial still-stands of sea-level with particular interglacials, and in doing this the cycle of change of sea-level related to climatic change must be remembered. There will be transgression, still-stand and regression in each cycle, and it is difficult and important to relate particular features to particular parts of the cycle.

### Dating of displaced shore-lines

*Height.* Height has been used extensively in correlating shore-lines, especially in areas thought to be so stable that eustatic changes of sea-level are closely related to the displacement of the shore-lines.

*Stratigraphy.* The relation of shore-line deposits to solifluction sheets (head), tills and interglacial deposits has been one of the most effective methods of dating shore-lines.[24]

*Contained fossils.* These include pollen grains, molluscs, vertebrates, and even artefacts, as for example, in the dating of the raised beach in Sussex containing Acheulian implements to the interglacial (Hoxnian) in which these artefacts are characteristic. Changes of pollen content at transgression and regression contacts between terrestrial and marine or estuarine sediments have proved useful in dating sea-level changes in the Flandrian.[9] Likewise land uplift in Scandinavia has been documented by pollen studies of peats associated with particular shore-line stages.

*Absolute dating.*[10, 19] Radiocarbon dating of organic materials found in close relation to transgression and regression contacts of organic sediments has been successfully used to determine past sea-levels (fig. 8.7). The geological context of any sample to be dated should be quite clear. Ideally there should be no evidence of unconformity between the two sides of the regression or transgression contact, and that the sediment dated is close in age to the time of the transgression or regression. Shells have also been used to determine ages of raised beaches, especially in the Arctic.

### The graphical expression of changes in relative land/sea-level

*Isobase maps* (fig. 8.10). In these maps, lines joining points of equal uplift at particular times show the process of deformation of the earth's crust. The points are based on shore-line displacement studies. In the construction of such a map, the dating of the shore-lines is obviously of prime importance.

*Shore-line diagrams* (fig. 8.6).[3] These diagrams show the height of distinct shore-lines (y-axis) at different distances (x-axis) from the margin or centre of the area of uplift (distance diagram) (fig. 8.6a). Or they may be drawn so that a well-developed and well-dated shore-line is used as a reference level, drawn in as a straight tilted line, and other shore-lines then inserted in relation to the reference level (relation diagram). Fig. 8.6a is a diagram of the former type from the British Isles. Fig. 8.6b is an example of the latter type,[5] of two raised beaches in Spitsbergen, identified as belonging to particular times by the presence of pumice which had drifted on to them when they were formed. The reference level used is the straight tilt of the lower of the two pumice horizons. Fig. 8.9 shows a more complicated relation diagram from Finland.

### Examples of studies of past sea-level changes

*The Netherlands.* Relative land/sea-level changes in the Netherlands during the Flandrian have been studied by Jelgersma[12] in particular detail by means of radiocarbon dating of horizons significant for tracing the relative rise of sea-level at this time. Three factors are important in the Netherlands in determining the rate of Flandrian sea-level rise. Eustatic change of sea-level, tectonic downwarping during the subsidence of the North Sea basin, and the compaction of the soft Flandrian sediments, which cover a large part of the west of the country. It is difficult to separate the first two factors and to

*Fig. 8.6a* A shore-line diagram and late Pleistocene ice limits in the north of Ireland and south-west Scotland. The letters A, B, C ... refer to sites surveyed by Stephens and Synge, and the numbers to sites surveyed by Donner. All sites have been projected to the common baseline and the shoreline diagram constructed. The dots represent wave-cut notches in drift, the thick horizontal bars are strong terrace levels, and ml signifies the marine limit (Stephens and Synge, 1966).

decide what part of the rise in sea-level is caused by tectonic subsidence known to occur in the Netherlands in the pre-Flandrian,
and what part by eustatic rise. Only the net effect of these two can be
measured, and this has been done by making radiocarbon datings of
fen peat layers lying immediately on top of the older sands whose
surface dips seawards. The formation of this fen peat results from
a rise of water-level in the sand following rise in sea-level. Peat

*Fig. 8.6b* Shore-line relation diagram of pumice levels in the northern
part of Hinlopenstretet, Nordaustlandet, Spitsbergen. The position of
the sites is shown on the map (Donner and West 1956).

L

samples from local depressions in the basal sands or ombrogenous peats whose formation is not related to ground water are avoided. In this way the results of compaction of the soft Flandrian sediments are avoided, as the basal sand is hardly affected by compaction.

Fig. 8.7 shows the time/depth relations as determined by datings of the lowermost peats, and it covers the period 9300 years B.P. to

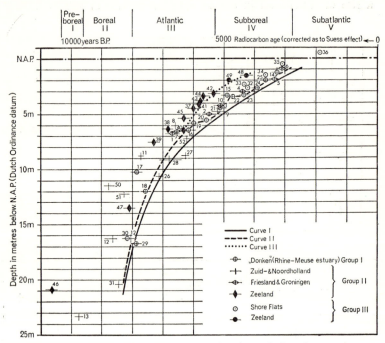

Fig. 8.7 Time-depth graph with curves showing relative changes in sea-level in the Netherlands (Jelgersma 1961). Each point represents a peat at depth, radiocarbon dated. The peats dated are divided into three groups. Group I, peat-beds in the Rhine-Meuse estuary; Group II, peats on Pleistocene aeolian sands in Zeeland, Holland, Friesland and Groningen; Group III, peats on sandy marine facies. The horizontal bar through the points gives the size of the standard deviation in age. For explanation of curves, see text.

2500 years B.P. The first curve is based on the assumption that peat growth may have started at different heights above high tide level and is drawn through the lowermost points of any given age. The second curve connects datings from the Rhine-Meuse estuary as it is believed the peats concerned were deposited close to sea-level. The

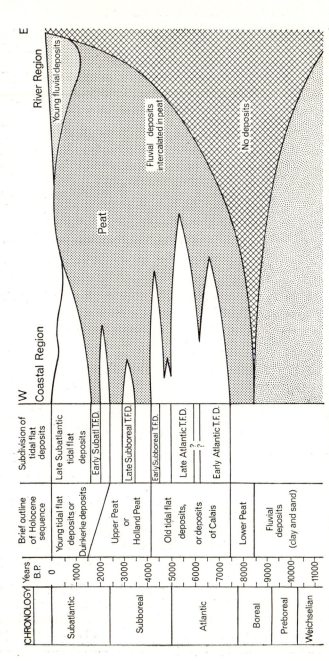

*Fig. 8.8* Schematic section through Late Pleistocene (Weichselian and Flandrian) deposits of the western part of the Netherlands. Horizontal distances not to scale; vertical distances based on a time-scale (Jelgersma 1961).

third curve shows datings from the province of Zeeland, and is higher than the others, perhaps due to greater tidal range in this area or because tectonic subsidence has been less.

The geological section in fig. 8.8 shows the accumulation of sediments during the Flandrian in the Netherlands. The accumulation of sediments closely followed the sea-level rise, so that alternations of tidal flat and freshwater peats form the succession. It should again be stressed that the positive change in sea-level has a component of subsidence as well as eustatic rise. If subsidence is small, it appears from the time-depth curve that the eustatic rise continued till recently and that there have been no substantial eustatic fluctuations during the time represented, nor any rise much above present sea-level. However, as the Netherlands is an unstable area, the curve shown in fig. 8.7 should not be regarded as representative of a wider area, and certainly not a definitive curve for the Flandrian eustatic rise.

*Relative land/sea-level changes in the Baltic area.* This is the classic area for the study of displaced shore-lines of the Late Weichselian and Flandrian. These past shore-lines of the Baltic are widely distributed but usually discontinuous, so that it may be difficult to trace the same shore-line for any distance. The shore-lines are present as beaches fronting slopes of till or of rock washed free from drift, and as shore bars and terraces in front of glacial sand and gravel deposits such as eskers and deltas. As the tidal ranges in the Baltic are small the old sea-levels can be determined by the position of the beaches and wave-cut features to accuracies of less than one metre.

The shore-line displacement reflects the changes in the height and area of the Baltic as deglaciation proceeded, and as lake levels were affected by the isostatic uplift following deglaciation and by the Flandrian eustatic rise. The isostatic component is the most important and it has been estimated that the total uplift at the centre of uplift has been in the order of 500 m.

The data required to reconstruct the history of the Baltic are mapping of the shore-lines, the measurement of their heights, and their dating into the Flandrian pollen-zone system. The relation of the ice retreat to the Baltic stages is shown by determining whether a shore-line is terminated by the line marking the ice margin at any particular time.

The dating of the shore-lines and correlation of disjunct stretches of shore-line are the main difficulties in the reconstruction of isobase maps showing the warping of shore-lines formed at different times in the past, examples of which are shown in fig. 8.10. Such maps demonstrate a dome-like upwarping with a centre in the northern part

of the Gulf of Bothnia, similar in kind to the upwarping trend
demonstrated by the isobases of contemporary uplift (fig. 8.2). The
isobases may be somewhat closer near the centre of upwarping,
implying increased uplift nearer the centre and so crustal bending.
In a shore-line diagram of the shore-lines of the principal Baltic
stages (fig. 8.9) the vertical profiles of each shore-line show that
differences in the angles of slope occur, indicating that the rate of

*Fig. 8.9* Shore-line relation diagram giving the heights of the shore-lines
in central Finland of the Baltic Ice Lake (BI–BVI), the Yoldia Sea (YI–
YIV), the Echineis Sea (E) and the Ancylus Lake (A) in relation to the old
level of Lakes Saimaa and Päijänne (MS1 and MP1) and to lower shore-
lines of Lake Saimaa (MS3 and MS4). The arrows show the altitudes of the
successive overflow channels for Lake Päijänne (P1–P3) and Lake Saimaa
(S1–S5) (Donner 1965).

uplift has differed from time to time. Sauramo[20] has described
sudden changes in the slope of some shore-lines which he ascribed
to movement at a hinge. The demonstration of such a hinge-line
requires accurate dating of the shore-lines on either side of the
hinge-line, and this has not yet been provided in the critical areas.

We may now follow through the history of the Baltic, as described
by Sauramo.[21] The stages are here simplified. Most of them have
several episodes of shore-line displacement within them (see fig. 8.9).
The sequence of shore-lines within the older stages are based on the
form of the shore-lines and on the varved clay chronology, whereas
those of the younger stages are dated by shell beds, peat stratigraphy,
pollen analysis and archaeology. The isobase maps for the different
stages are shown in fig. 8.10.

ice lake

*Fig. 8.10* Isobase maps (m) of stages in the history of the Baltic. The maps also show the extent of the ice and dry land at each stage (Sauramo).

    a. Late-glacial Yoldia Sea.
    b. Baltic Ice Lake.
    c. Yoldia Sea (first stage).
    d. Ancylus Lake.
    e. Littorina Sea.

fresh water lake

a. *The late-glacial Yoldia Sea (or Karelian Ice Sea)*. This is a marine stage, during which the Baltic was connected with the White Sea in the east and the North Sea to the west.

b. *The Baltic Ice Lake*. Uplift in the areas where there had formerly been ocean connections resulted in the isolation of the Baltic Ice Lake, which drained westwards through central Sweden at Billingen, and northwards marginal to the eastern limit of the ice sheet at this time. The ice lake was contemporary with the ice-marginal moraines of the Salpausselkä in Finland and the middle Swedish moraines.

c. *The Yoldia Sea* (named after the marine mollusc *Yoldia arctica*). Retreat of the ice led to the rapid fall of the lake level as new outlets were exposed in central Sweden. Eustatic rise in sea-level brought marine conditions to the Baltic again.

d. *The Ancylus Lake* (named after the freshwater mollusc *Ancylus fluviatilis*). The period of submergence was brought to an end by the rapid rise of the land, and again the Baltic became a freshwater lake, with its first outlet through the Svea river in south Sweden. Progressive tilting of the land transferred the outlet south to the Danish Sound. During this time the Ancylus Lake waters transgressed far more in the south of the Baltic than in the north, where land uplift was greater than in the south.

e. *The Littorina Sea* (named after the winkle *Littorina*). The sea then transgressed the Danish Sound bringing marine conditions to the Baltic again. This is the fore-runner of the present Baltic, which is less saline than the Littorina Sea, perhaps because its greater shallowness, related to uplift since *Littorina* times, prevents penetration of undercurrents of saline water far into the Baltic.

The relation of these Baltic stages to the chronology of the Flandrian is shown in table 8.1.

*The Mediterranean shore-lines*. The shore-lines of the Mediterranean have provided a sequence of past sea-levels which have been used as a basis for a world-wide chronology of eustatic changes of sea-level. The sequence was first made a 'general' Mediterranean one by Depéret[2] who named shore-lines as follows:

| | |
|---|---|
| Sicilian | 90–100 m |
| Milazzian | 55– 60 m |
| Tyrrhenian | 28– 30 m |
| Monastirian | 18– 20 m |

Later, a lower level of 6 to 8 m was named Monastirian II, and an even lower level of about 3 m has been described as Epi-Monastirian.[26]

*Table 8.1* Correlation of Baltic stages with ice retreat stages and pollen zones in Finland (Donner 1965b)

| Years A.D./B.C. | Stages of ice retreat | Pollen stratigraphy (southern Finland) | | Stages in the development of the Baltic Sea |
|---|---|---|---|---|
| 1000 | | | | Mya Sea |
| | | IX | Sub-Atlantic (spruce, pine) | |
| 0 | | | | Limnaea Sea |
| 1000 | | VIII | Sub-Boreal (birch, pine, spruce, elm, oak, linden) | *LVI* *LV* *LIV* |
| 2000 | | | | Littorina Sea |
| | | | | *LIII* |
| 3000 | Postglacial | Post-glacial | | *LII* |
| | | | | *LI* |
| 4000 | | VII | | |
| 5000 | | | Atlantic (birch, pine, elm, oak, linden) | Mastogloia Sea |
| | | VI | | |
| 6000 | | V | Boreal (pine) | *A*    Ancylus Lake |
| | | | | *E*    Echineis Sea |
| 7000 | Finiglacial | IV | Pre-Boreal (birch) | *YV* ↑ *YI*    Yoldia Sea |
| 8000 | Salpausselkä III Salpausselkä II Salpausselkä I | III | Younger Dryas (tundra) | *BVI* ↑ *BI*    Baltic Ice Lake |
| 9000 | | Late glacial | | |
| | Gothiglacial | II | Alleröd | Late-glacial Yoldia Sea |
| 10,000 | | | | |

Higher levels, up to 325 m, have been described in parts of the Mediterranean, e.g. in Algeria and Tunis[16] and in Cyrenaica,[17] and these are believed to be of late Tertiary or early Pleistocene age. Some of the altimetric names have also been used to denote particular marine faunas, and the equivalence between these faunas and the altimetric divisions is shown in table 8.2. The Tyrrhenian faunas are indicative of warmer conditions than now present and include species such as *Strombus bubonius* which are now found no further north than the coast of Senegal.

*Table 8.2* Shore-line and faunal stages in the Mediterranean and Black Sea

| Faunal stages | Altimetric stages (Depéret, Zeuner) | Libya shore-lines (figure 8.11a) | Black Sea shore-lines (figure 8.11b) |
|---|---|---|---|
| Calabrian | Calabrian | 140–200 m | |
| Sicilian | Sicilian 90–100 m | 70–90 m | 100 m |
| | Milazzian 55–60 m | | 60 m |
| Tyrrhenian | | 44–55 m | |
| | Tyrrhenian 28–30 m | 35–40 m | 40 m |
| | Main Monastirian 18–20 m | 15–25 m | 25 m |
| | Late Monastirian 6–8 m | 6 m | 13 m |
| | Epi-Monastirian 3 m | | 5 m |

The Sicilian fauna contains some Mediterranean species together with Atlantic species, such as *Cyprina islandica*, considered to indicate colder conditions.

The advantage of the Mediterranean as a type area for eustatic changes of sea-level is that tidal ranges are low and there are very extensive lengths of coast, often of limestone, suitable for shore-line studies. The difficulties are that it is hard to correlate the sea-level changes with particular events of the glacial and interglacial chronology (except perhaps in the instance of the 6 to 8 m beach discussed below), and that tectonic effects may have been important

Fragments of shoreline, whose continuity
has been established by visual means.
Correlations regarded as 'almost certain'.
Correlations regarded as 'very probable'.

*Fig. 8.11a* Raised shore-lines between Ras Aamer and Derna, Libya (McBurney and Hey 1955).

*Fig. 8.11b* Raised and deformed shore-lines of north-eastern coast of the Black Sea from the Taman Peninsula to Batum. Shore-lines (with heights in areas little deformed): 1, Chandian (100 m); 2, ancient Euxinian (60 m); 3, Uzunlar (40 m); 4, Karangat, upper (25 m); 5, Karangat, lower (13 m); 6, neo-Black Sea (5 m) (after Fedorov).

in determining shore-line levels as well as eustatic effects, particularly in areas such as Sicily and southern Italy.

The type of evidence of shore-line movement most acceptable is from shore-line diagrams. Few of these have been produced in the Mediterranean. Fig. 8.11 shows such a diagram for Cyrenaica[17] and also one for the north-east shore of the Black Sea.[7] They show some areas of warping, but with the lower shore-lines there is little warping, and the heights in the two areas show some agreement (table 8.2).

The main conclusion is that there is a well-documented series of shore-lines, five of which are widespread (Depéret's and the 6 to 8 m shore-line). These must represent important stages of sea-level still-stand, even if the exact levels of these still-stands are not clear. There is much doubt about the age of the levels in the terms of the glacial/interglacial sequence. The Milazzian is often said to be Günz/Mindel interglacial, the Tyrrhenian (altimetric) Mindel/Riss interglacial, and the Monastirian I and II Riss-Würm. As might be expected the most widespread shore-line is also one of the most recent; it is the 6 to 8 m (Monastirian II) shore-line. Shore-lines at this level have been observed in North Africa, South France, South Africa,[15] southern England and eastern North America (the Suffolk Scarp). In southern England it is associated with interglacial deposits of Ipswichian (Eemian) age.[24] But the dating of the other shore-lines is far from satisfactory.

# REFERENCES

STEPHENS, N. and SYNGE, F. M. 1966. 'Pleistocene Shorelines', in *Essays in Geomorphology*, ed. G. H. Dury. London: Heinemann.

1 DALY, R. A. 1938. *Architecture of the Earth*. New York: D. Appleton-Century.
2 DEPÉRET, C. 1918. 'Essai de coordination chronologique générale des temps Quaternaires', *C.R. Acad. Sc. Paris*, **167**, 418–22.
3 DONNER, J. J. 1965a. 'Shore-line diagrams in Finnish Quaternary research', *Baltica*, **2**, 11–20.
4 DONNER, J. J. 1965b. 'The Quaternary of Finland', in *The Quaternary*, vol. **1**, ed. K. Rankama. New York: Interscience.
5 DONNER, J. J. and WEST, R. G. 1956. 'The Quaternary geology of Brageneset, Nordaustlandet, Spitsbergen', *Norsk Polarinstitutt Skrifter*, No. 109.
6 FAIRBRIDGE, R. W. 1961. 'Eustatic changes in sea-level', *Phys. and Chem. of the Earth*, **4**, 99–185.
7 FEDEROV, P. V. 1960. 'Drevnie beregovie linii chernogo mora na no-beresche Kavkaza', *Izvest. Acad. Nauk. U.S.S.R.*, Ser. Geol., Pt. 2, 56–64.

8 FROMM, E. 1953. 'Map of glaciations and changes of level', in *Atlas over Sverige*. Stockholm: Generalstabens Litografiska Anstalts Förlag.

9 GODWIN, H. 1945. 'Coastal peat beds of the North Sea region, as indices of land- and sea-level changes', *New Phytologist*, **44**, 29–69.

10 GODWIN, H. 1960. 'Radiocarbon dating and Quaternary history in Britain', *Proc. Roy. Soc. London*, B **153**, 287–320.

11 GUTENBERG, B. 1941. 'Changes in sea level, postglacial uplift, and mobility of the earth's interior', *Bull. Geol. Soc. America*, **52**, 721–72.

12 JELGERSMA, S. 1961. 'Holocene sea level changes in the Netherlands', *Med. Geol. Stichting*, Serie C-VI, No. 7.

13 JOHNSON, D. W. 1919. 'Shore processes and shoreline development', New York: Wiley.

14 KAYE, C. A. and BARGHOORN, E. S. 1964. 'Late Quaternary sea-level change and crustal rise at Boston, Massachusetts, with notes on the autocompaction of peat', *Bull. Geol. Soc. America*, **75**, 63–80.

15 KRIGE, A. V. 1927. 'An examination of the Tertiary and Quaternary changes of sea-level in South Africa, with special stress on the evidence in favour of a recent world-wide sinking of ocean level', *Ann. Univ. Stellenbosch*, **5**, 1–81.

16 LAMOTHE, DE L. 1911. 'Les anciennes lignes de rivage du Sahel d'Alger et d'une partie de la côte algérienne', *Mem. Soc. Géol. France*, 4th ser., **5**, 559–71.

17 MCBURNEY, C. B. M. and HEY, R. W. 1955. *Prehistory and Pleistocene geology in Cyrenaican Libya*. Cambridge University Press.

18 NISKANEN, E. 1939. 'On the upheaval of land in Fennoscandia', *Ann. Acad. Sc. Fennicae*, Ser. A, **53**, No. 10.

19 OLSSON, I. and BLAKE, W. 1961. 'Problems of radiocarbon dating of raised beaches based on experience in Spitsbergen', *Norsk Geografisk Tidsskrift*, **18**, 1–18.

20 SAURAMO, M. 1955. 'Land uplift with hinge-lines in Fennoscandia', *Ann. Acad. Sc. Fennicae*, Ser. A III, No. 44.

21 SAURAMO, M. 1958. 'Die geschichte der Ostsee', *Ann. Acad. Sc. Fennicae*, Ser. A III, No. 51.

22 VALENTIN, H. 1954. 'Gegenwärtige Niveauänderungen im Nordseeraum', *Petermann's Geographische Mitteilungen*, **98**, Jahrgang (1954), 103–8.

23 VAN STRAATEN, L. M. J. U. 1961. 'Sedimentation in tidal flat areas', *J. Alberta Soc. Petroleum Geologists*, **9**, 203–26.

24 WEST, R. G. and SPARKS, B. W. 1960. 'Coastal interglacial deposits of the English Channel', *Phil. Trans. R. Soc. London*, B, **243**, 95–133.

25 WRIGHT, W. B. 1937. *The Quaternary Ice Age*, 2nd edn. London: Macmillan.

26 ZEUNER, F. E. 1955. 'The three Monastirian sea-levels', *Actes du IV Congrès International du Quaternaire (1953)*, **4**, 1–7.

27 ZEUNER, F. E. 1959. *The Pleistocene period*, 2nd edn. London: Hutchinson.

# CHAPTER 9

# CHRONOLOGY AND DATING

C HRONOLOGY concerns the dating of events in geological time and aims at establishing a series of geological events on a scale of absolute time. The dating of these events varies in accuracy from a few tens of years to a few thousands or more, according to the methods used, so that the building-up of a chronological series is a difficult matter. In the determination of the passage of time, measurements of geochemical changes associated with the passage of time are of prime importance. They have largely replaced older methods involving estimates of the passage of time based on the rates of geological processes, such as deposition, weathering and erosion.

The dating of events to years has been called absolute or chronometric dating, in contrast to so-called relative dating, which places one event in time relative to another, but with no reference to absolute time.

Chronology provides a time-scale of events of known position in a stratigraphical succession, so that chronology and stratigraphy combine to give a history of geological events. The chronology of the Pleistocene is far from being known in any detail, except in the most recent parts, but nevertheless more is known than that of earlier geological times. We shall be concerned with relative dating and some methods available for widespread correlation of dates, estimates of the passage of time based on geological processes, and measurements based on natural rhythmic processes and on geochemical change. Finally an outline chronology for the Pleistocene is constructed.

## DETERMINATIONS OF RELATIVE AGE

These determinations are mostly based on stratigraphical relations. Oakley (1964) has devised a system for making the basis of such determinations clear. He has distinguished four categories of relative age determination, especially in connection with the dating of fossil man: R1, when the object or event is related to the deposit containing it; R2, when the containing deposit is referred to the local geological succession, and R3 when the latter is correlated to a wider scheme of stratigraphy; and R4, when the relative age determination is based on form or morphology, e.g. of a bone. The category R1 has been divided into a number of classes intended to indicate whether the fossil is contemporaneous with the containing deposit, or is approximately contemporaneous, or is intrusive and therefore younger than the deposit. This system has the merit of indicating briefly the circumstances of a fossil find and the nature of its relative age determination.

The fluorine method[22] is useful for the relative dating of animal skeletal remains found in sand and gravel. Bones and teeth contain a proportion of hydroxy-apatite (calcium phosphate), which traps fluorine in groundwater and forms stable fluorapatite, the quantity of which can be measured by X-ray diffraction methods. The fluorine to phosphate ratio in bones and teeth is in part a measure of the time the fossils have been able to trap fluorine, so that bones in the same deposit which have suffered the same groundwater conditions should show similarities in fluorine content. Thus a mixture of bones in the same deposit but of different age may be revealed by measurement of the fluorine-phosphate ratio. The fluorine content of bone and antler is greater than that of teeth of the same age found in the same deposit, so measurements are best made on the same type of skeletal material.

Other methods, such as nitrogen and uranium analyses[28, 34] have also been used to determine relative ages of bones and teeth, e.g. in the study of the Piltdown fossils which resulted in the exposure of the hoax.[34]

### DATING BY FAUNA AND FLORA

Changes in the composition of faunas and floras have been used as a means of relative dating in the Pleistocene as with the earlier geological epochs. But the effects of the rapid climatic changes on fauna and flora tend to mask the evolutionary changes important for the stratigraphy of older deposits, and the shortness of Pleistocene time, as well as the greater detail of chronology required, tend to make the criteria used for the older rocks inapplicable. However, evolutionary changes have been used as a basis for chronology in Foraminifera studies of deep-sea sediments.[6a]

Because of the widespread occurrence of pollen in Pleistocene sediments, pollen analysis has become an important method of relative dating. The development of pollen analysis of Flandrian peats and other sediments in north-west Europe has led to the subdivision of Flandrian time into a number of pollen-analytical zones, each characterised by a particular assemblage of forest trees (table 12.10). This succession has been related to the climatic succession of Blytt-Sernander in Scandinavia and has become a basis for relative dating on the assumption that the pollen zones are to some extent synchronous. This method of relative dating has been much used in north-west Europe, in relation to vegetational history, climatic episodes and archaeology. But the basis for subdivision of Flandrian time has now passed to radiocarbon dating, though in many instances pollen analysis is still a useful method of relative dating within restricted areas. With deposits beyond the range of radiocarbon dating, for example interglacial or interstadial deposits, pollen analysis is still of prime importance in revealing the vegetational histories characteristic of each interglacial, and in this field it remains an important method of relative dating.

## TEPHROCHRONOLOGY[36]

This is a method of establishing a chronology based on ash falls. A volcanic eruption produces a widespread deposition of ash, and if such a layer becomes preserved in a sedimentary sequence (continental or marine), its wide occurrence will permit correlations. Thus sequences of ash layers in Iceland,[33] Patagonia[1] and elsewhere have been extensively used as marker horizons. Some ash falls have been dated, such as the Laacher See ash of the Eifel, found in Allerød (zone II, Late Weichselian) sediments in south-west Germany, or the Mazama ash from Crater Lake in Oregon, dated to about 6600 years ago, which covered much of north-western United States and adjacent Canada. An important older ash fall is the Pearlette ash of late Kansan age in the United States which spread over large parts of the Great Plains.

## PALAEOMAGNETISM CHRONOLOGY[5]

The earth's magnetic field changes in time, in direction over short intervals of time, and in becoming reversed over much longer periods. Certain rocks, including igneous rocks and some sedimentary rocks, become magnetised by the earth's field at the time they are formed, so that by measuring the direction of their magnetism, the earth's field may be determined at the time of rock formation. If volcanic rocks are used to determine palaeomagnetic fields, samples of the same origin can be used for potassium-argon dating. Thus a chronology can be built up showing polarity epochs of normal and reversed magnetism dated by the potassium-argon method. Magnetic directions between reversed and normal are rare, so it is thought that the transition times are short compared to the length of the polarity epochs.

There are several possible sources of error in the method, including self-reversal during initial magnetisation, slow magnetisation after initial magnetisation, and magnetisation changes imprinted during chemical alteration, such as haematite formation during weathering.

*Fig. 9.1* Correlations between the western United States, southern Europe, and Africa, based on palaeomagnetic and radiometric data.

Closed circles, normal polarity; open circles, reversed polarity; large circles, radiometric dates; small circles, no radiometric dates; G, glacial deposits; F, fossils. Cross-hatched areas indicate range of uncertainty in mammalian stage boundaries (after Cox, Doell and Dalrymple 1965).

However, enough determinations of polarity and age have been made on volcanic rocks to suggest that the combination of methods may be of value for Pleistocene chronology and correlation. The polarity epochs demonstrated, their duration, and correlations based on measurements from different continents are shown in fig. 9.1.

**Plate 1.** Oblique aerial photograph (20,000 ft.) of glaciers in north-east Baffin Island (69° 25′ N, 68° 52′ W).

There are small ice caps in the middle distance, left and right, with a piedmont glacier in the centre middle distance draining the ice cap to the left, and some valley glaciers. End moraines girdle the termini of the glaciers and are pierced by melt-water streams. Medial moraines are seen on the glacier in the right foreground. The melt-water drainage is north, then east in the middle distance. There is a small corrie glacier in the centre near distance. Note the different degrees of end-moraine development at the different glacier termini. *Copyright, Mines and Technical Surveys, Canadian Government. Photo T 219 R (101), July 1948.*

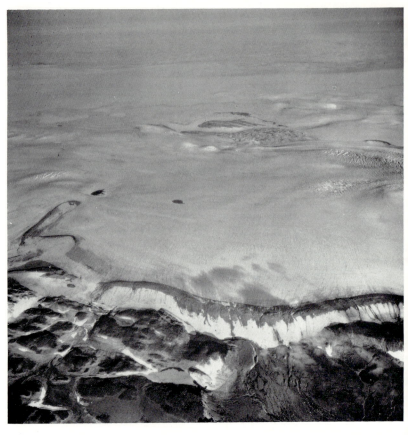

**Plate 2.** Oblique air photo of the margin of the Vestfonna ice sheet in Nordaustlandet, Spitsbergen, near the North Franklin Glacier. The end-moraine is well developed here, and is associated with shear structures in the ice, shown as slight lines parallel to and close to the edge. A braided stream system is seen in the foreground, and the surface drainage channels of the ice sheet can also be seen. The topography of the inland ice can be clearly seen in the middle and far distance. *Copyright, Norsk Polarinstitutt, Oslo. Photo Le 77a, 691.*

**Plate 3.** Finnish varves and their connection (from Sauramo 1929).
a. Three samples of the varved Late-Glacial clay in the valley of the Kalajoki River in Ostrobothnia, correlated with each other. Sample I from a locality lying 6 kilometres, and sample II 2 kilometres northwest, and sample III 8 kilometres southeast of the church of Haapajärvi.
b. Diagram of the connected clay samples named above showing the variations of the thickness of the varves. The bottom of the sections to the right. The dotted line bounds that part of the samples shown above in a.

**Plate 4.**
**a.** Thin section of a diatactic varve from Leppäkoski, Finland, ×12 (from Sauramo 1923).
**b.** Thin section of a symmict varve from Mattila, Finland, ×12 (from Sauramo 1923).
**c.** Thin section of early glacial (Gippingian) varved clay at Marks Tey (Essex). ×31.
The lamination is caused by strongly graded bedding of inorganic sediment. The lower part of each lamina contains abundant angular quartz grains, and the upper part clay minerals. *Photo by C. Turner.*
**d.** Thin section of laminations in interglacial lacustrine clay-mud of Hoxnian age (zone II). ×8. The light layers are very rich in diatoms (principally *Stephanodiscus astraea*) packed in a calcareous matric. This layer grades upwards into a darker more organic sediment. The pairing may be annual, the light layer resulting from a spring flush of the diatom *Stephanodiscus. Photo by C. Turner.*

**Plate 5.**

a. Fresh morainic landforms and kettle holes, part of the Southern Irish end-moraine (Weichselian maximum), near Blackwater, Co. Wexford, Eire.

b. Drumlins submerged by the Flandrian rise in sea level. Clew Bay, Co. Mayo, Eire.

*Both photographs by J. K. St. Joseph. Cambridge University Collection.*

a

b

**Plate 6.**
**a.** Esker and kames, near Clonmacnoise, Co. Offaly, Eire.
**b.** U-shaped valley and corries. Glen Dee, Aberdeen, looking north to the Pool of Dee. *Both photographs by J. K. St. Joseph. Cambridge University Collection.*

a

**Plate 7.**
**a.** 4″ diameter core through re-worked and brecciated lake deposits at Hoxne, Suffolk, × ½. The mottled sediments are largely clay-mud fragments reworked from marginal deposits and removed to the centre of the basin by solifluction; they also contain pebbles of chalk from the surrounding till on which the lake deposits lie. Pale bedded lacustrine silts were deposited at periods of higher water level.
**b.** Slump structures in laminated interglacial lacustrine clay-mud of Hoxnian age at Marks Tey, Essex. × ½. *Photo by C. Turner.*

b

**Plate 8.**

**a** Section in a peatdigging at Westhay (Godwin's Piece), Somerset Moors (photo by H. Godwin). Changes in peat composition indicate two horizons of flooding (layers 2 and 5) within a sequence of raised bog peats. Depth of section 1 metre. Section as follows:

1. Highly humified *Sphagnum-Calluna* peat.
2. Aquatic *Sphagnum* peat, with some *Eriophorum vaginatum* (precursor peat). This represents a flooding horizon in the peat sequence and its formation precedes the renewed growth of fresher *Sphagnum* peat.
3. Fresh *Sphagnum* peat. Renewed growth of the bog surface ('regeneration-complex' peat).
4. Humified *Sphagnum-Calluna* peat, with *Eriophorum vaginatum*.
5. Laminated peat with aquatic *Sphagna* and *Scheuchzeria* rhizomes, the latter prominent in the peat face. A second flooding horizon.
6. Mouldered humified *Sphagnum* peat.

The peat blocks cut from the face (from layer 3) show the banding characteristic of 'regeneration-complex' peat, resulting from alternate layers of darker more humified *Sphagnum-Calluna* peat with much fresher *Sphagnum* peat. These variations in peat type are associated with the pool and hummock complex of regenerating bog surfaces.

**b.** Interglacial raised beach gravel at Selsey, Sussex. This beach gravel is of the same age (Ipswichian) as that under the head at Brighton (Plate 13b). It is overlain by brickearth of aeolian origin, probably formed during the Weichselian.

a

b

c

d

1 m m

**Plate 9.** Organic sediments.
**a.** Fine detritus gyttja.
**b.** Coarse detritus gyttja.
**c.** Parvocaricetum peat. The radicells (cells with thickened or protruding walls) characteristic of Cyperaceae roots are seen near the base of the photo.
**d.** *Sphagnum* peat. The peat is unhumified and shows the characteristic structure of the leaves of *Sphagnum*.

a

b

**Plate 10.**
**a.** Non-sorted networks and stripes manifested as vegetation patterns. Brettenham Heath, Thetford, Norfolk. The networks occur on level ground, the stripes on slopes. Age Weichselian.
**b.** Network of tundra polygon type on surface of a Weichselian terrace, near Colne, Hunts.

*Both photographs by J. K. St. Joseph. Cambridge University Collection.*

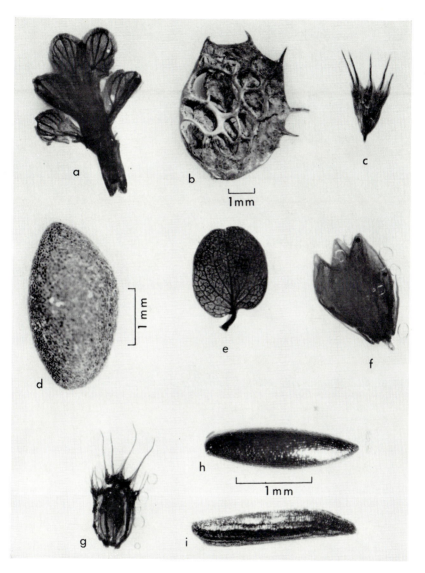

**Plate 11.** Macroscopic plant remains.
**a.** *Saxifraga oppositifolia*, leafy shoot.
**b.** *Onobrychis vicifolia*, pod.
**c.** *Armeria maritima*, calyx.
**d.** *Naias marina*, fruit.
**e.** *Salix polaris*, leaf.
**f.** *Helianthemum canum*, capsule.
**g.** *Scabiosa columbaria*, fruit.
**h.** *Naias flexilis*, fruit.
**i.** *Naias minor*, fruit.
**a, b, c, e, f, g,** from Weichselian deposits at Earith, Hunts.
   (*Photos by F. G. Bell*). *All to same scale.*
**d, h. i,** from Ipswichian deposits at Bobbitshole, Ipswich.

a

b

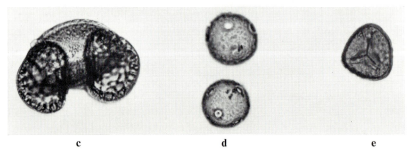

c                                    d                                    e

**Plate 12. Plant remains.**
**a.** Slide of reference material, fruits and nuts of *Carex* spp. Each column contains examples of a single species, identified by a number (London Catalogue number).
**b.** A pollen preparation from a late Flandrian peat in Scotland. × 260. 1, 3-pored grain of *Corylus*; 2, 3-pored (septate pores) grain of *Betula*; 3, 3-furrowed grains of *Quercus*; 4, *Filicales* spores.
**c.** Pollen grain of *Pinus sylvestris*. × 480. The central body and two wings is characteristic of many species of conifers.
**d.** Pollen grains of *Plantago lanceolata*. × 480. The grains have a verrucate surface and bordered pores scattered on the surface (periporate). This pollen grain is frequently associated with land-clearance phases of the late Flandrian.
**e.** Spore of *Sphagnum recurvum*, with the trilete scar often found in lower plants. × 400.

a

b

**Plate 13.**
**a.**   Ancient rock-platform at Porthleven, Cornwall. The present sea-level closely approximates to that of the time when the platform was cut, and the sea is now re-excavating the notch at the base of the cliff, partly filled with ancient beach material. A large erratic of gneiss is in the right middle distance, possibly dropped by drifting ice. The age of the platform is probably pre-Hoxnian.
**b.**   Black Rock, Brighton. A sea cliff of chalk formed during the Ipswichian interglacial is in the centre of the photo. Solifluction during the Weichselian has led to the formation of the bedded solifluction deposits (head) now resting on the face of the cliff and on the interglacial beach, present at the base of the section on the left.

a

b

**Plate 14.**
**a.** Terrace sands and gravels of Weichselian age at Earith, Hunts. The cast of a large ice-wedge is seen in the centre. The surface expression of similar casts on the same terrace in a nearby locality is seen in Plate 10b.
**b.** Coarse gravels and sand of the crevasse filling at Blakeney, Norfolk. The gravels are largely unsorted and abrupt changes of lithology occur. A period of frost-heaving has resulted in the upright arrangement of stones near the top on the left hand side of the photo.

**Plate 15.**
**a.** Cliffs at West Runton, Norfolk. Peat of the Cromerian temperate stage outcrops at the base of the cliff, itself composed of glacial deposits of the earliest glaciation of East Anglia.
**b.** Cliff section at Beeston, Norfolk. Glacial deposits, mainly till, contorted by ice-push and containing lenses of ice-contact stratified drift, mainly sand.

**Plate 16.** Fossil non-marine molluscs and insects.

**a.** *Columella columella* (Benz). ×15. Gippingian, from tjaele gravel at Thriplow, Cambs. Photo by B. W. Sparks (*Geol. Mag.*, **94** (1957), Plate VII).

**b.** *Belgrandia marginata* (Michaud). ×24. Ipswichian, from organic deposits at Bobbitshole, Ipswich. Photo by B. W. Sparks (*Phil. Trans. R. Soc.*, B, **241** (1957), Plate 3).

**c.** *Potamida littoralis* (Cuvier). ×1. Ipswichian, from terrace gravels at Barnwell, Cambs. Photo by B. W. Sparks.

**d.** *Stenus brunnipes* Steph. (Staphylinidae). ×110. Aedeagus, Hoxnian, from interglacial deposits at Nechells, Birmingham. Photo by Professor F. W. Shotton and P. J. Osborne (*Phil. Trans. R. Soc.*, B, **248** (1965), Plate 30).

**e.** *Hippodamia arctica* Schneid. (Coccinellidae). ×16. Left elytron showing characteristic pattern. Weichselian (Upton Warren Interstadial Complex), from terrace deposits of the Tame Valley, Warwicks. A non-British northern species of Fennoscandia. Photo by G. R. Coope and C. H. S. Sands (*Proc. R. Soc.*, B, **165**, Plate 50).

**f.** *Chiloxanthus stellatus* Curtis. (Saldidae). ×17. Hemielytron, showing characteristically patterned wing. Weichselian (Upton Warren Interstadial Complex), from terrace deposits of the Tame Valley, Warwicks. A non-British species of bug, with a northern circumpolar distribution. Photo by G. R. Coope and C. H. S. Sands (*Proc. R. Soc.* B, **165,** Plate 50).

## GEOLOGICAL PROCESSES INVOLVING PASSAGE OF TIME

Estimates of time based on these processes had been made in several areas before the advent of the more rigorous methods of dating. We may take some examples to illustrate the methods involved.

Penck[25] made estimations of the duration of interglacial stages in the Alps. Comparing the intensity of the weathering of the Decken-schotter of Mindel age around München with that of the Riss gravels, he concluded that the interglacial between the two was four times as long as during the Riss-Würm interglacial. On a similar basis, he estimated that the latter was three times as long as the post-Würm interval. From the observation that the two Deckenschotters (Günz and Mindel) bear the same relation to one another as the Riss gravels do to the Würm gravels, the duration of the Günz-Mindel inter-glacial was thought to be similar to that of the Riss-Würm inter-glacial. The relative lengths of the interglacials thus computed are shown in table 9.1.

*Table 9.1* Penck's estimates of interglacial time in the Alps

|                  | Günz-Mindel | Mindel-Riss | Riss-Würm | post-Würm |
|------------------|-------------|-------------|-----------|-----------|
| Relative duration | 3           | 12          | 3         | 1         |
| Duration in years | 60,000      | 240,000     | 60,000    | 20,000    |

Estimations of the length of the post-Würm interval, based in part on the growth of a delta into Lake Lucerne after the retreat of the Bühl-stadium towards the end of the Würm glacial stage, gave a time span of 20,000 years for this interval, thus giving the duration figures in table 9.1 for the interglacials.

Estimates of the durations necessary for interglacial weathering of tills were made by Kay[19] in Iowa. He assumed that the time available for leaching of the Wisconsin glacial deposits was some 25,000 years and estimated that the average depth of leaching was 2·5 feet in this time. The depths of leaching he found on older glacial gravels were 12 feet on Illinoian deposits, 30 feet on Kansan deposits and 20 feet on Nebraskan deposits. Assuming that the depth of leaching is pro-portional to time, he suggested that the lengths of the post-Illinoian (Sangamon) interglacial was 120,000 years, of the post-Kansan (Yarmouth) interglacial 300,000 years, and of the post-Nebraskan (Aftonian) interglacial 200,000 years.

Other estimates have been based on the rates of recession of waterfalls, and on accumulation of peat, travertine and ocean sedi-ments. Prestwich's[27] estimate in 1888 of 15 to 25,000 years for the duration of the Glacial Epoch and 8 to 10,000 years for the length of

M

post-glacial time, was based on the dissection of the landscape in north-west Europe. The latter is very near what we now believe to be the truth, but the former, though near to the present estimates of the duration of the most recent extension of the ice sheets in northern Europe and North America, is very much less than the minimum now thought possible for the length of the glacial period. Prestwich's estimates were based on his own observations and on his belief that estimates of the same periods by others at that time were far too great.

In all these estimations based on deposition, weathering and erosion, it should be remembered that time is merely one factor of many that affect rates of the processes concerned. With regard to weathering, factors of climate, soil texture and drainage will affect rates of leaching, and in the question of sediment deposition, the stream gradients, load and surrounding vegetation will all affect the rate of deposition. For these reasons such estimates of time are very liable to error, and in fact, by comparison with more recent methods, have in most instances been proved unreliable. Nevertheless, they were made at a time when no other methods were available, and they at least correctly gave a rough order of magnitude to Pleistocene time.

### ABSOLUTE OR CHRONOMETRIC DATING

The measurement of the passage of time is most reliably obtained by counting a sequence which results from the annual recurrence of the natural rhythmic processes of varve deposition and tree-ring formation, or by the measurement of geochemical changes as a result of radioactivity. We first consider the use of natural rhythmic processes.

### Dendrochronology[9, 14, 15]

Seasonal changes in the wood growth of trees produce annual rings. In spring wood cell-elements with large lumens are produced, while in the summer and autumn the cells become smaller. Thus a year's growth starts with larger cells and ends with smaller cells and both types comprise an annual ring (fig. 9.2).

Dendrochronology is the study of tree-rings for the purposes of dating. The time range covered can extend back some three or four thousand years in areas where trees of such ages survive, but the method has been most widely used as a means of dating prehistoric settlements with buildings constructed partly of wood in the south-west of North America in the last millennium.

Within a particular climatic province dendrochronology is a very accurate method of dating. The determination of the age of trees in forest stands gives means of dating the minimum age of the soil on which they are growing, for example the minimum age of alluvial deposits, glacial moraines or landslide deposits. At an upper forest or tree limit in a montane area, dating of the marginal trees may give an indication of the date of environmental changes which have allowed a rise or fall of the limit. In these instances the age determination results from the counting the number of tree-rings.

Environmental factors control the degree of growth of an annual ring. Thus changes in the size of the annual rings are an indication

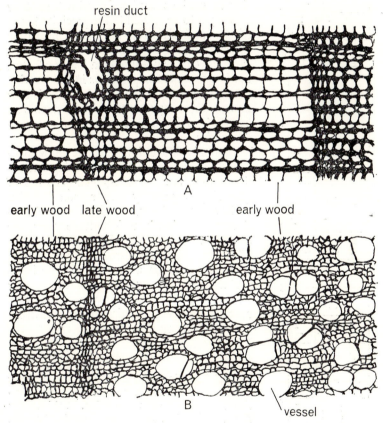

*Fig. 9.2* Transverse sections (×35) through A, a conifer, *Pinus strobus*, and B, an angiosperm, *Salix nigra*, showing the cell arrangement in annual rings (after Esau).

of past environmental changes and their dates. The growth of a ring is related to the food manufactured by the tree, and so is controlled by the climatic factors which limit photosynthesis and thus food reserves. It is therefore necessary to know the relation between ring width of a particular tree species and environmental factors before embarking on an investigation of past climates involving dendrochronology. In semi-arid climates, droughts limit growth, and the width of tree-ring in conifers used for dendrochronology is thought to be related to the precipitation in the late-summer to spring period preceding the start of the annual growth. In northern climates water is not usually a limiting factor, but low summer temperatures in the growing season reduce the ring width. As far as is now known there appear to be no significant correlations between solar cycles and tree-ring series.

The main difficulties attendant on building up a chronology of past climates using dendrochronology are the occasional presence of false rings, caused by early season droughts or low temperatures, the absence or discontinuity of a ring in unfavourable years, the changes in ring width which are a function of the age of a tree (growth function) and which have to be allowed for in the interpretation, and finally the fact that there may be a serial correlation between widths of successive rings independent of other environmental effects on ring width.

*Fig. 9.3* Tree-ring plots from two trees of *Pinus ponderosa* at the forest border in northern Arizona, showing good cross-dating. T, thick ring; DBL, double ring. The longer the vertical lines the narrower is the growth layer, as judged by eye. Rings of normal thickness are not shown, but are counted (Glock 1950).

The trees which have been mostly used in dendrochronology are conifers, especially species of pine and spruce in the north and species of pine (*Pinus aristata, Pinus flexilis*) in semi-arid regions in North America. *Sequoia* was extensively used in early studies, but the rings have a high degree of serial correlation.

Methods of obtaining samples for tree-ring analysis have been described by Glock.[14] Either blocks of wood reaching to the centre near the base of a tree or samples taken with a tree auger are used. There are three stages in building up a chronology. First the selection of different sites where the tree-ring sequences or series of particular species appear sensitive to climatic change (sensitive series) and also where they show little variation apart from growth function (complacent series). Then a process of cross-dating is carried out to overcome the difficulties of false and absent rings; a large number of trees of a number of species from different sites are sampled and their tree-ring series worked out with a low-power binocular microscope. In particular, samples are taken from slow-growing trees at stress sites, as these are important for climatic indications, and from quicker growing trees on favourable sites where all rings should be present. Drought years with thin rings are the best indicators for correlation (fig. 9.3). Finally, the tree-ring series from different species and different sites are built up into an overall chronology showing periods of drought or low summer temperature back over as long a time as that covered by the oldest trees. Chronologies may

*Table 9.2* Tree-ring averages in the sixteenth century A.D. expressed as a percentage of the mean for the period 1851–1950 (Fritts 1965)

A Temperature-sensitive chronologies at the northern tree limit (June–July mean)

|  | 1501–1550 | 1551–1600 | Mean | |
|---|---|---|---|---|
| Alaska (*Picea* spp.) | 111 | 105 | 108 | ($\leqslant$ + 0·8°C.) |
| Mackenzie Valley (*Picea* spp.) | 93 | 88 | 90 | ($\leqslant$ − 1·0°C.) |
| Northern Fennoscandia (*Pinus sylvestris*) | 103 | 107 | 105 | ($\leqslant$ + 0·5°C.) |

B Precipitation, drought-sensitive chronologies at the lower forest limit in the United States (a, winter-spring total; b, annual total)

|  | 1501–1550 | 1551–1600 | Mean |
|---|---|---|---|
| Montana (*Pinus flexilis* v. reflexa) | 94 | 86 | 90 |
| a California (*Pinus aristata*) | 97 | 95 | 96 |
| b Arizona, Flagstaff area (*Pinus ponderosa*) | 83 | 97 | 90 |

also be erected on samples from prehistoric dwellings and such a 'floating' chronology may be tied to an absolute chronology if it overlaps a series based on living trees in the same region.

As regards the distance within which correlations can effectively be made, in western North America, within a particular climatic province, significant correlations can generally be made between chronologies 500 km apart, and some significant correlations have appeared at distances of up to 1750 km. Thus the method can be used to date climatic changes over wide areas, and differences in climatic change in the different areas may reveal changes in past weather patterns. Table 9.2 shows changes during the sixteenth century A.D. in mean June–July temperature in three areas in northern latitudes and changes in precipitation (winter-spring and annual) in the western United States.

*Varves and other laminated sediments*

Laminated sediments or rhythmites, showing regular and repeated alternations of two sediment types, are commonly found in the Pleistocene. The sediments may be principally inorganic in origin, as in varved clays, or the alternation may be caused by organic-rich and organic-poor layers. The word varve was originally applied by de Geer[11] to describe 'periodically laminated sediments in which the deposition for every single year can be discriminated'. The sediments concerned were the late- and post-glacial varved clays of Sweden. The origin of these clays has already been described (Chap. 3) and the annual repetition of the pairs of sediment types, coarse and fine, is well established. Other rhythmites with an apparent annual origin are those described by Welten[35] from the Faulenseemoos in Switzerland. They show alternate light layers, the summer layer, rich in diatoms and calcium carbonate, and dark layers with fewer diatoms and rich in organic matter, the winter layer. The time represented by a column of these Flandrian sediments, taking the pairs as annual, agrees with estimates of Flandrian time from other sources. Laminated marine sediments with banding caused by alternate diatom-rich and clay-rich sediments have been described from the Gulf of California by Calvert,[4] and these are preserved as well-laminated sediments by the relative absence of burrowing organisms in an oxygen-poor environment. Freshwater laminated diatomites of the Luneburg Heath in north Germany have been described by Selle[31] and estimates of time represented have been made. It is obvious that the annual (or other periodic) origin of the sediment pairs must be established before a chronology can be attempted, and it is often difficult to prove that the pairs represent a particular span of time. Even in the instance of the classic varved clays, minor laminations within a single pair may confuse correlations and so render a chronology doubtful. Such minor laminations may arise from redeposition of sediments after storms.

As varved clays have been extensively used as a basis for a chronology, especially in Scandinavia, it is necessary to consider the methods and difficulties of this type of dating. Each sediment pair (varve) results from a year's deposition, coarse in the spring melt period, to finer in later summer and winter as the clays settle out. An exposure of varved clays shows a number of such pairs. Successive pairs will vary in thickness, depending on the amount of material fed into the extra-glacial lake in which the sediments were formed. De Geer, the pioneer of varve chronology, assumed that the climatic variation over a wide area was similar and caused the thicknesses of sediments deposited in any year to vary in a similar way. Thus changes in thickness in successive varves could be used to correlate varve successions from one section to the next (plate 3). Each section shows a set of varves covering a short time, the northern areal limit of each varve being the ice limit at the time of deposition of that varve. Each varve will overlap its predecessor northwards as the ice retreats. By taking a north–south transect at right angles to the direction of ice retreat in Sweden, counting the varves in sections as close as possible, then correlating them by thickness variation de Geer[13] was able to erect a chronology of the retreat of the ice sheet for the last 17,000 years, covering several hundred kilometres of retreat of the ice front of the Weichselian (last) Glaciation. The later part of the chronology agrees with that obtained by radiocarbon dating, but the earlier part has been disputed because of the possibility of extra laminations (not of annual origin) (e.g. 'storm-laminations') being interpreted as varves.

Sauramo[30] did not believe that de Geer's method of correlation based on thickness of individual varves was adequate because of local environmental effects on varve thickness. In producing a varve chronology for Finland he relied mainly on the correlation of varve series, each series showing particular characters of the varves in colour, in coarseness of grain, and in the arrangement of the coarse layers. He thus relied on the physical characters of the varves for his principal correlations. The datings he arrived at for Finland are supported by radiocarbon chronology.

Some attempts have been made to relate varve sequences in the Old and New Worlds, so-called tele-connections[12] as opposed to close connections. It has yet to be proved that such correlations are valid.

*Geochemical methods of dating*[2]

A number of methods of dating are based on the measurement of amounts of elements which in the process of time are either formed by or are subject to radioactive decay. The rate of decay being known, the time-interval may be determined between the present and the time when the particular parent element was fixed and its decay began.

Table 9.3 summarises the isotopes concerned in these dating methods and the applications of each method. Radiocarbon and potassium-argon dating are the most important of these methods at present and will be described first. Other methods are in the course of development although some (e.g. the $Pa^{231}/Th^{230}$ method) have been used considerably, and in the future they will assume greater importance.

*Table 9.3* Pleistocene geochemical dating methods
(after Broecker 1965)

| Isotope | Half-life $10^3$ years | Method | Range $10^3$ yrs | Materials | Ocean temp. | Sea level | Glacier extent | Arid lakes | Pollen sequence |
|---|---|---|---|---|---|---|---|---|---|
| $C^{14}$ | 5·7 | Decay | 0–35 | Organic, $CaCO_3$ | + | + | + | + | + |
|  |  |  | 35–70* | Organic |  |  |  |  |  |
| $Pa^{231}$ | 32 | Decay $Th^{230}$ normal | 5–120 5–120 | Red clay or *Globigerina* ooze | + | 0 | 0 | 0 | 0 |
| $Th^{230}$ | 75 | Decay | 5–400 | Red clay or *Globigerina* ooze | + | 0 | 0 | 0 | 0 |
| $U^{234}$ | 250 | Growth Decay | 0–200 50–1000 | $CaCO_3$ (biogenic) Coral | 0 0 | + + | 0 0 | + 0 | + 0 |
| $He^4$ | — | Growth | No limit | Molluscs, coral | 0 | + | 0 | + | 0 |
| $Ar^{40}(K/A)$ | — | Growth | No limit | Volcanic | + | + | + | + | + |

\* With low-background detectors and pre-enrichment of $C^{14}$

*Radiocarbon dating.*[21] This method is based on measuring the radio-carbon ($C^{14}$) activity of biogenic material such as wood, peat and shells. Radiocarbon is produced in the upper atmosphere by the interaction between nitrogen and cosmic ray neutrons (fig. 9.4). The radiocarbon is oxidised to carbon dioxide and mixes with the atmospheric carbon dioxide. It is then taken up by plants and animals and also becomes dissolved in sea and freshwater. Here it will be taken up by living organisms and exchange reactions will also occur between dissolved carbon dioxide, carbonates and bicarbonates to

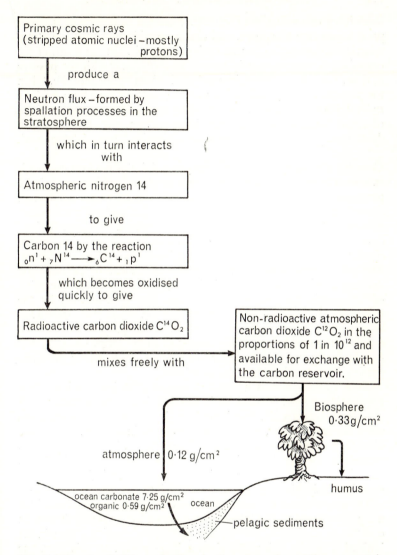

Fig. 9.4 Sketch of $C^{14}$ production in the atmosphere. The amount is shown of carbon ($C^{12}$ and $C^{14}$) in different parts of the exchange reservoir, expressed as grams of carbon in exchange equilibrium with the atmospheric carbon dioxide for each square centimetre of the earth's surface. The main reservoir is in the ocean carbonate.

form inorganic sediments (fig. 9.4). Thus the radiocarbon is incorporated into the biosphere, and reaches equilibrium with the atmospheric, freshwater and ocean carbon reservoir. On the death of the organism the radiocarbon is trapped and will decay with the passage of time. The rate of decay, immutable, is given by the half-life, taken for purposes of age calculation as 5568 years. In that time half the radioactivity will be lost. Therefore by measuring the radioactivity of fossil biogenic material containing carbon, the date at which death took place and equilibrium not maintained, can be determined.

*Counting the radioactivity.* The specific activity of modern carbon is extremely low, about 13·8 disintegrations of radiocarbon per minute per gram of carbon. It would be impossible to measure such a small amount in any detecting instrument in the presence of much larger amounts of cosmic ray mesons and soft gamma radiation derived from the surroundings. The effects of this unwanted radiation may be eliminated to a large extent by appropriate shielding of the detector. The soft gamma radiation is severely attenuated by housing the detector in a massive metal shield made of lead or iron. The effect of the cosmic ray mesons may be cancelled electronically by the principle of anticoincidence. The radiocarbon detector is surrounded by a ring of geiger counters such that with the appropriate electronics a pulse produced by a cosmic ray meson in the geiger counters will automatically prevent the record of a pulse produced by the same particle in the radiocarbon detector itself.

Since radiocarbon is a weak $\beta$ emitter (154 kev) and has low penetrating power, it must be introduced inside the detector itself in order to be detected. This is achieved in a detector known as a gas proportional counter, where the carbon is introduced as carbon dioxide, methane or acetylene gas. The emission of a radiocarbon $\beta$ particle causes an ionisation of the gas which is amplified and recorded electronically. The gas is kept at pressure within the counter since it is desirable to get as much carbon into the counter as possible.

The proportional counter is so named because the pulses obtained are proportional to the initial energy expended by the radiation (in contrast to a geiger counter where any discharge which results in the ionisation of the filling gas gives a large pulse). In this way, the particular pulses caused by decay of radiocarbon can be isolated from pulses caused by other radioactive materials, such as radon, which give much higher pulses from the $\alpha$ radiation.

Another counting technique involves measurement of scintillation in organic liquid made from the sample.

The size of the counter is governed by the size of samples available.

Thus for small samples, a small counter at high pressure (2 to 3 atm) and with low background (say 2 to 6 counts per minute) gives the best accuracy. A larger counter, holding more carbon, with a similar background will give higher accuracy. In other words, the 'signal to noise' ratio for a large counter is greater than with a small one.

The age is calculated as follows:

$$\frac{T}{\log_e 2} \times \log_e \frac{(S - b)}{(S_0 - b)}$$

where $T$ = half life,
$S$ count of fossil sample,
$b$ background count, and
$S_0$ contemporary count.

*Assumptions made in radiocarbon assay.* Several assumptions have to be made in using the method for dating. In general, these assumptions appear to be valid as shown by dating of samples of known age. The assumptions are:

1. That the specific radioactivity of living organic material has not varied in the past; i.e. that the concentration of radiocarbon in the atmosphere has remained constant and that any isotopic fractionation by organisms taking it up has remained the same (in living wood $C^{12} : C^{13} : C^{14} = 98\cdot9 : 1\cdot1 : 1\cdot07 \times 10^{-10}$). The constancy of the activity in the atmosphere will depend on the constancy of production of radiocarbon, on the loss of radiocarbon by sedimentation and on the isotopic equilibrium between different parts of the reservoir (fig. 9.4). Small variations in the order of one to two per cent in the atmospheric activity have been found by dating tree-rings over the past 1000 years,[37] which lead to dating errors of $\pm$ 100 years, and excesses of $C^{14}$ of as high as eight per cent (corresponding to an error of about 620 years) have been recorded from woods of known age up to 5000 years B.C. Some caution is therefore necessary at present in the equation of radiocarbon years to absolute sidereal years.[6]

2. That the atmospheric source of radiocarbon is geographically constant in its specific activity, so that dates from different continents, say, are comparable.

3. That the half-life has been accurately determined. The half-life has been measured several times and its mean value is taken as 5730 $\pm$ 30 years. Nevertheless, the Libby standard of 5568 years is used to achieve continuity of definitive publication in the journal *Radiocarbon*.[18]

4. That there has been no exchange of radiocarbon since the death of the organism which incorporated it. Here there are possibilities for exchange and contamination, and these are considered next.

*Sources of error.* Sources of possible error are many, ranging from isotopic fractionation in the plant or shell during measurement, to contamination in sample-taking and storage.

1. Isotopic fractionation during processing occurs; very small amounts of radiocarbon are lost and this may become significant in

*Fig. 9.5* Initial $C^{14}$ activity of each of 25 samples (measured in three radiocarbon laboratories) taken at 50-year intervals from *Sequoia gigantea*, represented as a percentage variation from the activity of the wood from the 1859 tree-ring. The dotted curve is a visual aid only (Willis, Tauber and Münnich 1960).

samples older than a few thousand years. If the proportion in the samples of $C^{12}$ to $C^{13}$ is known (measured by mass spectrometry) a correction for this loss can be made.

There is evidence that isotopic fractionation in plants leads to enrichment of $C^{12}$ during photosynthesis, while in the surface waters of oceans the activity is lower than average because of mixing between the surface radiocarbon atoms and those of greater age in the deeper oceans.[24] Thus in the Atlantic, surface water has an apparent age of about 450 years.

2. Intrusion of younger carbon into samples. Carbon contained in humic acids or in recent roots may give much greater radioactivity and therefore reduce the apparent age of samples. This is particularly

important in dating old samples near the limit of radiocarbon dating, where even the introduction of very small amounts of radiocarbon will give an apparent age to a sample too old to have any measurable activity of its own. With humus, the humus fraction may be separated and dated separately to test its age. Where recent roots are found in near-surface samples, it may be necessary to abstract all fossil leaves, twigs, seeds, etc., from a sample and date these. It is some-times very difficult to separate recent intrusive plant organs from

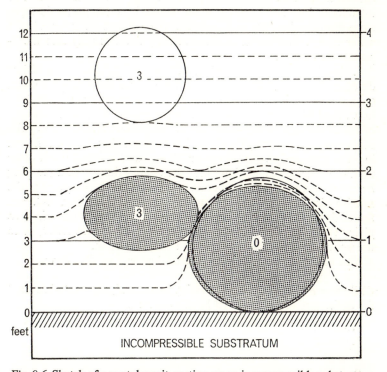

*Fig. 9.6* Sketch of a peat deposit, resting on an incompressible substratum, showing compaction effects in relation to two logs of different ages in the peat (after Kaye and Barghoorn 1964). The figures on the right and the solid lines indicate lines of sediment deposited at the same time (deposi-tional isochrons) before compaction. The empty circles show the positions of two logs at time of deposition, the figure in each referring to the time of deposition in relation to the isochrons.

The dashed lines, numbered on the left, are depositional isochrons after compaction of the peat to one-third of its thickness. The stippled logs show their position after compaction.

organic sediments. Exchange of carbonate with that in percolating waters may lead to greater radioactivity of the outer rinds of shells; and here it is necessary to wash the shells in dilute hydrochloric acid to remove the outer layers. There may also be contamination by radiocarbon via washing samples during their preparation, as has been shown by dates obtained from Tertiary shells.[24] Introduction of recent radiocarbon may also occur during storage of samples.

3. Intrusion of old carbon. Here there is the possibility of older carbon introduced in the form of fragmentary coal in sediments, or introduced into submerged aquatic plants by photosynthesis when the water contains dissolved carbonate from surrounding rocks (hard water error). Freshwater and land-living molluscs may also incorporate old carbon.

4. Stratigraphical sources of error. The relation between the object dated and the geological context of the sample must be quite clear, so that the date is meaningful in geological terms. For example, logs in a raised beach may not be contemporaneous with the formation of the beach, and so will not date it. An artefact may not be of the same age as the dated organic sediment containing it. The charcoal in an archaeological site may result from burning wood much older than the time of occupation. And the compaction of peat (varying from one-half to one-seventh of its original thickness) may lead to the relative displacement of peat and its contained wood (fig. 9.6).[20] In the dating of trees it is necessary either to use the outer rings as giving the nearest date to the time the tree died or was felled, or to use young trees or twigs covering a small time span.

This source of error can be greater than any of the above.

*Collection and treatment of samples.* In general, the materials used for dating are to be preferred in this order:

1. charcoal
2. wood
3. peat
4. bone
5. shell

Bone is not normally recommended because its carbon content is low, the structure porous and there are possibilities of alteration taking place. However, the collagen is thought to be stable, and, if extractable, can be very valuable for dating.

The samples for dating should be taken with extreme care, if possible out of range of penetration of recent roots and other types of contamination. The samples should be stored dry in sealed polythene bags. Pretreatment of organic materials[23] is necessary to remove carbonates (hot dilute hydrochloric acid) and humic acids (dilute sodium hydroxide), while with shell samples it is necessary to treat with dilute hydrochloric acid to remove surface layers which may have exchanged carbon with percolating waters. With peat and wood it may be necessary to separate the lignin and cellulose fraction in expectation that a contaminant will be eliminated or will follow either fraction, as will be seen from the separate dating of each fraction. In washing samples to extract organic material it is necessary to use boiled distilled water or dilute hydrochloric acid.[24]

The amount of material required for dating naturally varies with the carbon content of the sample. In general 3 to 5 gm of carbon is required, depending on the size of the counter. Thirty gm dry weight of sample is easily sufficient where carbon content is high, but where it may be low (e.g. partly inorganic sediments) much more (200 to 300 gm) may be necessary.

*Interpretation of dates.* In the calculation of the age of a sample, the half-life for calculation is now taken as 5568 years,[18] and the common standard for recent radioactivity of living material is taken as ninety-five per cent of the activity of oxalic acid provided by the US Bureau of Standards. The use of this standard avoids the danger of different laboratories using different standards for modern activity, some of which may suffer from increased radioactivity as a result of nuclear weapon tests and others from decreased activity as a result of infusion of dead carbon into the atmosphere by industrial processes using coal and other fuel. The ninety-five per cent activity of the standard oxalic acid is close to the activity of wood formed towards the end of the last century, prior to the fossil fuel dilution effect.

With marine shells there is a difficulty in obtaining a modern standard activity. Recent marine shells may give an apparent age of a few hundred years,[24] but this varies according to the particular ocean environment in the area, an effect already discussed.

A correction, normally small for wood and peat, has also to be made for isotope fractionation of radiocarbon during assay.

The date itself is stated in terms of measured probabilities because of the random nature of radioactive decay. A date is given as a time interval within which the true date will lie with a certain probability. The error given for each determination is calculated on the counting statistics and refers to one standard deviation, within which there is a sixty-eight per cent probability that the real date lies. The results of the assays are given as radiocarbon age B.P. (before the present), taken as 1950, or as a date A.D./B.C.

The limit of radiocarbon dating is up to about seven half-lives (30,000 to 40,000 years) unless a process of isotopic enrichment[17] has been carried out. Using the latter process, some dates up to 64,000 years have been obtained.

The main advantage of radiocarbon dating, as opposed to, for example, varve chronology, is that it is a method which is very widely applicable and results in long-distance correlations. It has been extensively used to date archaeological, vegetational and climatic events revealed in organic sediments, and changes in sea-level as revealed by sections showing transitions between fresh and sea water sediments. Its use is more limited where shells are concerned because of the possible errors already discussed. The method has also been used to determine the minimum age of soils by the assay of humic materials of B-horizons of podsols.[26]

*Potassium-argon dating.*[7] A long-lived and naturally occurring isotope of potassium, $K^{40}$, decays to argon, $A^{40}$. By measuring the ratio of $A^{40}$ produced to the remaining $K^{40}$, the time of origin of crystals or whole rocks containing potassium can be dated. The decay product is not a normal constituent of rocks, but assumptions have to be made concerning trapping of argon after the time of crystallisation, no loss of argon in time by diffusion, no changes of potassium content after crystallisation, and no reheating by later intrusions, resulting in the alteration of the K-A ratio. There is also the difficulty that a volcanic rock may contain older rock detritus which would increase the age significantly. These sources of error may lead to much greater percentage errors than with radiocarbon dating.

The method has been developed so that Pleistocene volcanic rocks and their crystal constituents can be dated, and it has great promise for the dating of Pleistocene events beyond the range of radiocarbon dating.

A number of dates have been obtained which have a bearing on the Plio/Pleistocene boundary. A date of 1·61 m.y. (million years) has come from a basalt in southern France of probable Lower Villafranchian (c. Lower Pleistocene) age; and a date of 1·75 m.y. has been given by probable Lower Villafranchian volcanic rocks in East Africa at Olduvai Gorge.[10] Dates of 1·5 to 3·5 m.y. have been obtained from volcanic rocks of Blancan age (supposedly near the Plio/Pleistocene boundary) in North America.[7] The lower boundary of the Pleistocene therefore appears to have an age within the bracket 1·5 to 3·5 m.y. The size of the bracket is probably related in part to the different bases for determining the Plio-Pleistocene boundary in different parts of the world.

Another series of measurements[8] on the Laacher (Eifel) volcano products found in the Rhine terraces has given an indication of the age of these terraces (table 9.5).

*Other geochemical methods.*[2, 38] The long-lived uranium isotopes, $U^{238}$ and $U^{235}$, decay through short-lived isotopes to lead. Some of these intermediate isotopes have half-lives suitable for Pleistocene dating. These are shown in table 9.4. There is also the measurement of accumulation of helium, produced by the decay of $U^{238}$.

These geochemical methods of dating based on the Uranium series are under active development at present, and they will certainly contribute much to Pleistocene chronology in the future. The bases and use of some of the uranium decay isotopes is briefly as follows:

1. *$Th^{230}$ deficiency.* In some biogenic substances (marine carbonates, peat) there is an initial deficiency of $Th^{230}$, but in time there is a growth towards equilibrium with uranium.

The $Th^{230}/U^{234}$ method has been used for dating marine mollusc shells. Assuming that the carbonate, shortly after death of the mollusc, contains uranium but no thorium, and that the carbonate system remains closed, then the ratio $Th^{230}/U^{234}$ is a function of age until equilibrium is reached at 0·5 m.y. Using this method, apparent ages of molluscs from the Mediterranean and Moroccan raised beaches show some consistency and agreement with independent evidence of age (table 9.5). The dates suggest two periods of high sea-level (non-glacial intervals) at 140,000 to 115,000 years B.P. and 75,000 to 90,000 years B.P. The latter dating agrees with other evidence for the age of the last warm period (Eemian) based on the $Pa^{231}/Th^{230}$ ratio in deep-sea sediments and on extrapolation from radiocarbon dates.

2. *$Th^{230}$ excess.* In ocean sediments $Th^{230}$ decays with time. Assuming the excess $Th^{230}$ of recent sediments has remained constant in time at any point on the ocean floor, the amount of decay with depth gives rate of accumulation of sediment. A similar method has been devised based on the decay of $Pa^{231}$.

3. *$Pa^{231}$–$Th^{230}$ method.* In recent ocean sediments, it is assumed that the ratio of $Pa^{231}$ and $Th^{230}$ is constant, as it is related to the $U^{238}$ and $U^{235}$ abundance in the oceans. As decay rates of the two isotopes are different, the change in ratio of the two with depth of sediment will give the rate of accumulation of sediment. This method has been successfully used in dating marine sediments used for isotopic temperature determinations (table 9.5) (fig. 10.9).

N

4. *Tritium method.* Tritium, $H^3$, formed by cosmic ray bombardment, has a half-life of about 12 years. On oxidation to water it enters into glacier ice, and its abundance in ice may be used to date ice within the last 50 to 100 years.

*Table 9.4* Decay series of uranium isotopes used in Pleistocene dating, showing half-lives of the various isotopes (after Broecker 1965). Principal isotopes underlined.

*Astronomical method.* On the supposition that terrestrial climatic changes are determined by variation in elements of the earth's orbit round the sun, and because these variations can be calculated for past ages, it should then be possible to calculate the frequency and nature of past climatic changes. The theory of the relation between terrestrial climate and insolation changes resulting from variation in orbit is associated with the name of Milankovitch, and the theory has been developed by Zeuner (1958) and Broecker.[3] It is to be expected that there is a relation between orbit and climate, and it will be of great interest to see whether the geological sequence and its chronology based on absolute methods of dating will lend practical support to Milankovitch's ideas.

## CHRONOLOGY OF THE PLEISTOCENE

Various methods have been used to date continental and marine Pleistocene events, and times of high sea-level thought to be inter-glacial. They are summarised in table 9.5. In this table events of known geological context or of periods when sea-level was near

| Time scale 10³ yrs (not linear) | C¹⁴ N-W Europe[16] | K/A Europe | K/A Africa | K/A N. America | Pa²³¹/Th²³⁰ related to O¹⁶/O¹⁸ episodes in Caribbean marine deposits (fig. 10.9)[20] | Th²³⁰/U²³⁴ (coral, shell, oolite near or above present sea level—i-g) Mediterranean, Morocco[31] | Th²³⁰/U²³⁴ elsewhere[a] |
|---|---|---|---|---|---|---|---|
| 10 | Flandrian ——10,250 B.P. | | | | | | |
| 20 | Weichselian | | | | | | |
| 30 | | | | | | | |
| 40 | | | | | | | |
| 50 | | | | | | | |
| 60 | Brørup i-s | | | | | | |
| 70 | | | | | colder (g) | | |
| 80 | Eemian i-g | | | | warmer (i-g) | Ouljian (5–8 m) sl | Bahamas sl |
| 90 | | | | | colder (g) | | |
| 100 | | | | | | | |
| 125 | | Holstein i-g | | | warmer (i-g) | Tyrrhenian? sl | Eniwetok, Florida Keys sl |
| 150 | | | | | colder (g) | | |
| 200 | | Mindel g (Rhine middle and old Middle Terrace) | | | | Anfatian sl (25–34 m) | |
| 250 | | | | | | | |
| 300 | | Cromer i-g | | | | | |
| 350 | | Günz g (Rhine High Terrace) | | | | | |
| 400 | | | | | | | |
| 450 | | | | | | | |
| 500 | | | | | | | |
| 550 | | | | | | | |
| 600 | | | | | | | |
| 1000 | | Villafranchian f (S. France) | | Irvingtonian f | | | |
| 2000 | | | Olduvai (Villafranchian f) | Blancan f | | | |
| 3000 | | | | | | | |

features dated: f fauna    i-s interstadial
g glacial    sl sea-level
i g interglacial

or above present sea-level are placed according to the particular dating method used. It is apparent from the table that the outline chronology back to about 120,000 years is fairly satisfactory, but beyond this correlations of marine and continental events are uncertain and datable events are few. If the Plio/Pleistocene boundary is below deposits with the Villafranchian type fauna, then the age of the boundary is probably between 2 to 3 m.y., as already discussed. It is evident that there is much yet to be found out about the geology and life of the lengthy Lower Pleistocene.

# REFERENCES

HAMILTON, E. I. 1965. *Applied Geochronology*. London: Academic Press.
OAKLEY, K. P. 1964. *Frameworks for dating fossil man*. London: Weidenfeld and Nicholson.
ZEUNER, F. E. 1958. *Dating the Past*. 4th edn. London: Methuen.

1 AUER, V. 1956. 'The Pleistocene of Fuego-Patagonia', *Ann. Acad. Sc. Fennicae*, Ser. A III (Geologica-Geographica), No. 45.

2 BROECKER, W. S. 1965. 'Isotope geochemistry and the Pleistocene climatic record', in *The Quaternary of the United States*, eds. H. E. Wright and D. G. Frey. Princeton University Press.

3 BROECKER, W. S. 1966. 'Absolute dating and the astronomical theory of glaciation', *Science*, **151**, 299–304.

4 CALVERT, S. E. 1964. 'Factors affecting distribution of laminated diatomaceous sediments in Gulf of California', in *Marine geology of the Gulf of California—a Symposium*. Memoir No. 3, Amer. Assoc. Petrol. Geologists. 311–30.

5 COX, A., DOELL, R. R. and DALRYMPLE, G. B. 1965. 'Quaternary palaeomagnetic stratigraphy', in *The Quaternary of the United States*, eds. H. E. Wright and D. G. Frey. Princeton University Press.

6 DAMON, P. E., LONG, A. and SIGALOVE, J. S. 1963. 'Arizona radiocarbon dates IV', *Radiocarbon*, **5**, 283–301.

6a ERICSON, D. B., EWING, M. and WOLLIN, G. 1964. 'The Pleistocene Epoch in deep-sea sediments', *Science*, **146**, 723–32.

7 EVERNDEN, J. F., SAVAGE, D. E., CURTIS, G. H. and JAMES, G. T. 1964. 'Potassium-argon dates and the Cenozoic mammalian chronology of North America', *Am. J. Science*, **262**, 145–98.

8 FRECHEN, J. and LIPPOLT, H. J. 1965. 'Kalium-Argon-daten zum alter des Laacher Vulkanismus, der Rheinterrassen und der Eiszeiten', *Eiszeitalter und Gegenwart*, **16**, 5–30.

9 FRITTS, H. C. 1965. 'Dendrochronology', in *The Quaternary of the United States*, eds. H. E. Wright and D. G. Frey. Princeton University Press.

10 FUNNELL, B. M. 1964. 'The Tertiary period', in *The Phanerozoic time-scale, Q. J. Geol. Soc. London*, **120s**, 180–91.

11 GEER, G. DE 1912. 'A geochronology of the last 12,000 years', *C.R. XI Int. Geol. Congress (Stockholm)*, **1**, 241–53.

12 GEER, G. DE 1934. 'Geology and Geochronology', *Geogr. Annaler*, **16**, 1–52.

13 GEER, G. DE 1940. 'Geochronologia Suecica Principles', *Kungl. Svenska Vetensk. Handl.*, Ser. 3, **18**, No. 6.

14 GLOCK, W. S. 1937. *Principles and methods of tree-ring analysis. Carnegie Inst. Publ. (Washington)*, No. 486.

15 GLOCK, W. S. 1950. 'Tree growth and rainfall', *Smithsonian Misc. Coll.*, **111**, No. 18.

16 HAMMEN, T. VAN DER, MAARLEVELD, G. C., VOGEL, J. C. and ZAGWIJN, W. H. 1967. 'Stratigraphy, climatic succession and radiocarbon dating of the last glacial in the Netherlands', *Geol. en Mijnbouw*, **46**, 79–95.

17 HARING, A., DE VRIES, A. E. and DE VRIES, H. 1958. 'Radiocarbon dating up to 70,000 years by isotopic enrichment', *Science*, **128**, 472–3.

18 JOHNSON, F. 1966. 'Half-life of radiocarbon', *Science*, **149**, 1326.

19 KAY, G. F. 1931. 'Classification and duration of the Pleistocene Period', *Bull. Geol. Soc. America*, **42**, 425–66.

20 KAYE, C. A. and BARGHOORN, E. S. 1964. 'Late Quaternary sea-level change and crustal rise at Boston, Massachusetts, with notes on the autocompaction of peat', *Bull. Geol. Soc. America*, **75**, 63–80.

21 LIBBY, W. F. 1965. *Radiocarbon Dating*. 2nd edn., with additional notes. Chicago: Phoenix Science Series.

22 OAKLEY, K. P. and HOSKINS, W. R. 1950. 'New evidence on the antiquity of Piltdown man', *Nature*, **165**, 379–82.

23 OLSON, E. A. and BROECKER, W. S. 1958. 'Sample contamination and reliability of radiocarbon dates', *New York Acad. Sci. Trans.*, Ser. II, **20**, 593–604.

24 OLSSON, I. U. and ERIKSSON, K. G. 1965. 'Remarks on the $C^{14}$ dating of shell material in sea sediments', *Progress in Oceanography*, **3**, 253–66.

25 PENCK, A. 1908. 'Das Alter des Menschengeschlechtes', *Zeit. für Ethnol.*, **40**, 390–407.

26 PERRIN, R. M. S., WILLIS, E. H. and HODGE, C. A. H. 1964. 'Dating of human podzols by residual radiocarbon activity', *Nature*, **202**, 165–6.

27 PRESTWICH, J. 1888. *Geology*. Vol. 2, Stratigraphical and physical. Oxford: Clarendon Press.

28 PYDDOKE, E., ed. 1963. *The scientist and archaeology*. London: Phoenix House.

29 ROSHOLT, J. N., EMILIANI, C., GEISS, J., KOCZY, F. F. and WANGERSKY, P. J. 1962. '$Pa^{231}/Th^{230}$ dating and $O^{18/16}$ temperature analysis of core A254-BR-C', *J. Geophys. Res.*, **67**, 2907–11.

30 SAURAMO, M. 1923. 'Studies on the Quaternary varve sediments in southern Finland', *Comm. géol. de Finlande Bull.*, No. 60.

31 SELLE, W. 1955. 'Die Vegetationsentwicklung des Interglazials vom Typ Ober-Ohe', *Abh. naturw. Verein. Bremen*, **34**, 33–46.

32 STEARNS, C. E. and THURBER, D. L. 1965. 'Th$^{230}$–U$^{234}$ dates of late Pleistocene marine fossils from the Mediterranean and Moroccan littorals', *Quaternaria*, **7**, 29–42.

33 THORARINSSON, S. 1944. 'Tefrokronologiska studier på Island (with English summary)', *Geogr. Annaler*, **26**, 1–215.

34 WEINER, J. S. *et al.* 1955. 'Further contributions to the solution of the Piltdown problem', *Bull. Brit. Mus. (Nat. Hist.), Geology*, **2**, No. 6.

35 WELTEN, M. 1944. 'Pollenanalytische, stratigraphische und geochronologische Untersuchungen aus dem Faulenseemoos bei Spiez', *Veröff. Geobot. Inst. Rübel*, **21**.

36 WILCOX, R. E. 1965. 'Volcanic ash chronology', in *The Quaternary of the United States*, eds. H. E. Wright and D. G. Frey. Princeton University Press.

37 WILLIS, E. H., TAUBER, H. and MÜNNICH, K. O. 1960. 'Variations in the atmospheric radiocarbon concentration over the past 1300 years', *Radiocarbon*, **2**, 1–4.

38 WISEMAN, J. D. H. 'Deep sea cores as an aid to absolute dating in the Quaternary Period', *Report VI Int. Congr. on Quaternary (1961)*, **1**, 743–66.

# CHAPTER 10

# CLIMATIC CHANGE

THE importance of climatic change in the Pleistocene is made evident by its use as the basis for classification of the Pleistocene. There is a great contrast between the climatic fluctuations in the Pleistocene and the lesser changes known from Tertiary time, as shown in fig. 10.1.

The historical records of climatic change, of changes in such external factors as atmospheric circulation, and of changes in the distribution of plants and animals, give an inkling of the complex relations between climate, glacier advance or retreat and life; they allow theoretical models to be made of possible causes and of some effects of climatic change. Such models may in the future be a basis for relating environmental changes of recent prehistoric time to climatic change, and from these it may then be possible to extrapolate back to explain the older Pleistocene climatic fluctuations. A more detailed knowledge of the nature, magnitude and succession of climatic changes will be the necessary prerequisite for finding the causes of climatic change.

The important climatic factors are temperature and precipitation (solid and rain), not only their absolute amounts but, just as important, their seasonal distribution throughout the year. Correlated with these changes are changes in atmospheric circulation, storminess and windiness, which greatly affect the climate of such an oceanic area as Britain. There is also the possible variation from an oceanic climate with high rainfall and low variation in temperature to a continental climate with a more seasonal distribution of rain and greater seasonal differences of temperature.

As well as these regional climatic changes, we have also to consider climatic conditions which may be prevalent on a much more local scale. It is important to distinguish between those evidences of climate which give regional information and those which give microclimatic information. Day-length and angle of insolation, dependent on latitude, will also be important factors, such as where they may determine species presence, or the duration of freeze-thaw cycles.

There is also the question whether the presence of the ice sheets affected local or regional climates. Without doubt, they affected areas near the ice margins, and must have lowered mean temperatures by a few degrees. Whether they had a much wider effect on climate is not clear.

*Fig. 10.1* Diagram of fall of mean annual temperature in the Lower Rhine valley in Tertiary and Pleistocene times (after Teichmuller). Only the early fluctuations of the Pleistocene are shown. Fluctuations in Tertiary time may have occurred, but not about the low mean temperatures seen in the Pleistocene.

The existence of colder conditions in more southerly latitudes than they are now present brings the certainty that periglacial climatic conditions are not repeated in the present climatic systems. This makes for difficulty in reconstructing glacial climates. However, enough has been said of the complexities of climate and the interpretation of palaeo-climates, and we shall now examine briefly the principal lines of evidence which enable us to estimate the nature and magnitude of past climatic change. First to be considered are indices of past climatic change, then evidence of change in historic time.

### INDICES OF PAST CLIMATIC CHANGE

The evidence to be considered is biological, geological, geomorphological and geochemical.

#### Biological evidence

This type of evidence has already been discussed to some extent in Chapter 7.

*Faunal evidence from marine sediments.*[11, 12, 46] As the temperature of surface sea water is in equilibrium with the temperature of the air above, and the abundance and distribution of pelagic species is correlated with temperature, there is a record of temperature change in the sediments containing fossil planktonic species of Foraminifera. Both the species distribution and the abundance of Foraminifera reflect temperature change.

Fig. 10.2 shows climatic curves deduced from faunal studies of a Caribbean core. The curves are derived from changing percentages (curve b) of temperate-indicating Foraminifera (e.g. *Globorotalia menardii*) and cold-indicating Foraminifera (e.g. *Globigerina pachyderma*), and the abundance of *Globorotalia menardii* (curve c). Isotopic temperatures from the same core, discussed later, are shown in curve d. On the basis of the foraminiferal studies, a series of faunal zones allied to the climatic episodes have been proposed for the Atlantic and Caribbean cores and are shown in fig. 10.2, curve a.[11]

In the Atlantic high productivity is associated with temperate climates as indicated by the correspondence of productivity and species curves. In the Pacific high productivity appears to be associated with cold climates; when cold ocean currents from the south come further into the tropics, they bring an improved supply of nutrients to the surface waters.

Details of temperature and other environmental changes have also been deduced from studies of Foraminifera and molluscs of inshore deposits, particularly in southern Norway.[6, 15] In fact, the climatic optimum of the Flandrian was first postulated by Lloyd Praeger as a result of his investigations of the fauna of estuarine clays of northern Ireland.

*Other faunal evidence.* Some wide-ranging animals with distribution governed by vegetation give regional evidence of climate, for example, the relation of horse and steppe. Each of the vegetation regions shown in fig. 10.3 will have its own characteristic fauna. Narrow-ranging organisms, for example, terrestrial molluscs, give

*Fig. 10.2* Palaeotemperature curves derived from ocean cores (after Ericson, Ewing, Wollin and Heezen 1961).

a. Generalised climatic curve with average thickness of sediments in the deep Atlantic and Caribbean, showing foraminiferal zones.

b. Climatic curve from Caribbean core A 179–4, based on relative numbers of warm- and cold-water planktonic Foraminifera. C, relatively cold climate; W, relatively warm climate.

c. Climatic curve from the same core, based on ratios of numbers of *Globorotalia menardii* to weight of material coarser than 74 $\mu$ in each sample, with Pleistocene chronology interpreted by Ericson *et al.* (1961).

d. Climatic curve from the same core based on isotopic temperatures obtained by Emiliani (1955) from the tests of *Globigerinoides sacculifera*, with Pleistocene chronology interpreted by Emiliani. Radiocarbon dates from the core are shown at the top left of the column.

indications of local climatic conditions, and assemblages may show a regional property of the climate, for example, the indication of warm summer temperatures by the presence of *Corbicula fluminalis* and *Belgrandia marginata*, both species now found in the Mediterranean region. There is here the usual difficulty of determining what are the climatic factors which really control the distribution of the species (living or extinct) found fossil. For example the climatic regime under which the extinct Siberian mammoth lived is unknown, though from its association with living cold-indicating mammals, its presence is usually thought to indicate a cold climate.

*Fig. 10.3* Pleistocene biotopes in Europe (Zeuner 1959).

*Evidence from fossil plants.* As we have seen in Chapter 7, pollen assemblages give evidence of regional vegetation types, which, by analogy with the distribution of present-day vegetation types, indicate regional climatic type (fig. 10.3). Thus assemblages indicate a temperate forest climate, oceanic or continental according to the genera represented, or an open vegetation climatic type, such as tundra or steppe, each with its own characteristic climate. Occasionally single genera may give such climatic indications; for example the abundance of *Ilex*, a tree of oceanic distribution type, far east of its present limits in Middle Europe in the Hoxnian interglacial, suggests that the climate of this interglacial was more oceanic than that at present. The climatic optimum of the Flandrian was early demonstrated by the fossil occurrence of thermophilous plant species north of their present range (fig. 10.4).

Macroscopic plant fossils of local derivation are of particular use as indicating local habitat conditions. Individual species may indicate particular climatic conditions, depending on whether enough is known of the present-day distribution of the species and the climatic conditions governing its distribution. Aquatic plants in particular have been considered good indicators of regional climate, because

*Fig. 10.4* Fossil Flandrian occurrences of *Corylus avellana* and *Trapa natans* in western Scandinavia (after Andersson 1910).

of the more uniform environment they live in.[22, 44] Seasonal temperatures have been estimated from studies of climatic conditions thought to be important in determining present distributions. The pollen frequencies of *Viscum*, *Hedera* and *Ilex* in Denmark have been used to determine climates in the Flandrian of Denmark,[20] on

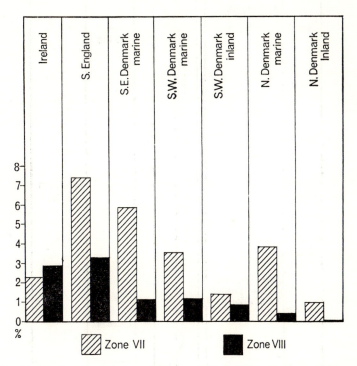

*Fig. 10.5* Pollen frequencies of *Hedera helix* in Atlantic (zone VII) and Sub-Boreal (zone VIII) times in north-west Europe (Iversen 1960). The basis for calculation of the frequency is total tree pollen excluding *Corylus*. The Atlantic frequencies are greatest to the west and in the east where coastal influence is present (in marine deposits). The fall across the Atlantic–Sub-Boreal boundary is greatest in the east, least in the oceanic west.

the basis that their flowering and optimum growth in the recent past can be related to particular conditions of summer and winter temperature. For example, *Hedera*, whose northern and eastern limits for normal growth in northern Europe are set by mean temperatures for the coldest month being warmer than −1·5°C, or

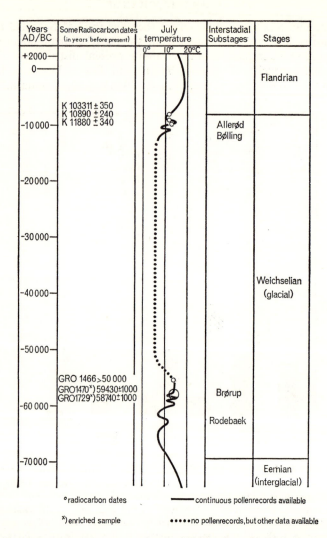

| Years AD/BC | Some Radiocarbon dates (in years before present) | July temperature | Interstadial Substages | Stages |
|---|---|---|---|---|
| +2000—<br>0— | | 0°  10°  20°C | | Flandrian |
| -10 000— | K 103311 ± 350<br>K 10890 ± 240<br>K 11880 ± 340 | | Allerød<br>Bølling | |
| -20 000— | | | | |
| -30 000— | | | | |
| -40 000— | | | | Weichselian (glacial) |
| -50 000— | | | | |
| -60 000— | GRO 1466 > 50 000<br>GRO1470ˣ) 59430±1000<br>GRO1729ˣ)58740±1000 | | Brørup<br><br>Rodebaek | |
| -70 000— | | | | Eemian (interglacial) |

° radiocarbon dates      —— continuous pollenrecords available

ˣ) enriched sample      ••••• no pollenrecords, but other data available

*Fig. 10.6* July temperature curve for the Weichselian glacial in Denmark, based on fossil floras and on the present-day distribution in north and central Europe of higher plant species found fossil (Andersen, de Vries and Zagwijn 1960). The estimated temperatures should be considered minimum and maximum for warm and cold intervals respectively.

*Viscum*, which thrives where mean temperatures of the warmest month are higher than 16° to 18°C. The fall in *Hedera* pollen frequencies at the change from Atlantic to Sub-Boreal times in the more continental parts of northern Europe, as shown in fig. 10.5, is interpreted to indicate a fall in mean winter temperatures at this time in the more continental areas, contrasted with the smaller fall (or rise in Ireland) in the more oceanic west. The work by Iversen[21] and Andersen[1] (fig. 10.6) on the Danish floras of Late Weichselian and Weichselian times respectively are also good examples of climatic determination using fossil floras.

Table 10.1 (p. 194) shows estimations of part conditions of climate based on both plant assemblages and on individual species.

*The Blytt-Sernander scheme of post-glacial climatic change in Scandinavia.* The Norwegian botanist Axel Blytt[4] described arctic, sub-arctic, boreal, atlantic, sub-boreal, sub-atlantic elements in the Norwegian flora. He supposed that these elements immigrated into Norway in this order during alternating dry and wet periods. He sought to demonstrate this by a study of tree layers in peat deposits, the drier (continental) periods (boreal, sub-boreal) being marked by tree stump horizons, the wetter (oceanic) periods (atlantic, sub-atlantic) by active peat growth. R. Sernander[40] considered that Blytt's scheme could be applied with some modifications to Swedish peat deposits, and it was his work which led to the wider use of the terms Boreal, Atlantic, Sub-Boreal, Sub-Atlantic to denote climatic phases of the Flandrian. He related these phases to the stages of the Baltic and thus gave them a stricter chronological meaning. And at a later date, they were related to the Scandinavian pollen zonation.

On the other hand, these ideas, formulated by the Uppsala school, were hotly contested by others, especially G. Andersson,[3] who thought there was no good evidence for these divisions, but rather a single climatic optimum, then deterioration.

However, the Blytt-Sernander periods are often used at present as names of divisions of Flandrian time, but their reality in climatic terms is still a matter for discussion.

## Geological evidence

*Sediments.* Glacial deposits, both on land and in water, though the most obvious products of glaciation, give little evidence of the detail of climatic change. The spread of glaciers in the Alps and Scandinavia appears to be related to lower temperatures as indicated by the

Table 10.1 Some estimates of Pleistocene temperature change

| Type of evidence | Area | Age | Parameter | Temperature difference from present value in area concerned | Reference |
|---|---|---|---|---|---|
| Plants | Denmark | Flandrian, Atlantic, Sub-boreal | July mean | +2°C | Iversen 1944 |
| | Scandinavia | Late Weichselian zone III | July mean | −6°C | Iversen 1954 |
| | S. Germany | Late Weichselian zone III | July mean | −5·6 to −7°C | Firbas 1949–52 |
| | Scandinavia | Late Weichselian zone II (Allerød) | July mean | −2°C to −3°C | Iversen 1954 |
| | England (Fladbury) | Middle Weichselian | July mean | −5½°C | Shotton 1960 |
| | England (Chelford) | Early Weichselian Chelford interstadial | July mean | −2°C to −3°C | Shotton 1960 |
| | Denmark | Eemian, zone f | July mean | +2°C | Jessen and Milthers 1928 |
| | S. Poland | Günz glacial (Mizerna II/III) | annual mean | −4°C to −5°C | Szafer 1954 |
| Animal (*Emys orbicularis*) | Denmark | Flandrian, Atlantic, Sub-boreal | July mean | +2°C to +3°C | Degerbøl and Krog 1951 |
| Periglacial (patterned ground) | E. England | Weichselian | annual mean | > −12½°C | Shotton 1960 |
| Geochemical | Atlantic | Pleistocene | oscillation amplitude about 6°C | | Emiliani 1955 |

fact that former estimated snow-lines are lower but parallel to present snow-lines, but in other areas, for example, the Arctic, glacial advances appear to have been produced by precipitation changes. The formation and spread of glaciers and ice sheets are merely one result of climatic change. The size or duration of the change is not to be found by studying glacial deposits. Great thicknesses of till can be deposited in a short time, or none at all in a long time, such are the variables governing erosion and deposition. However, the areal extent of drift sheets does give some evidence of climate, because drift limits tend to be parallel to present summer isotherms, corresponding to the relation between existing firn limits and summer temperatures, so suggesting summer atmospheric circulation similar to that of the present. The presence of organic rather than inorganic sediments may argue for amelioration of climate, but often local environmental factors determine which will be formed, for example, the provision of inorganic sediments by solifluction, or the organic fill of abandoned meanders in outwash plains. The presence of loess sheets and other aeolian deposits, again gives only general conditions of climate. At present loess accumulates under steppe climates, but is rare in wet climates, and thus loess is usually associated with dry continental climates, where silts are available for redistribution by wind. During the glacial stages the sources of silt (e.g. from outwash) were more widespread, and the presence of arctic species in loess faunas shows the loess climate of the past was not necessarily similar to that of today. The directions of prevalent winds have been estimated[31] from dune orientation and the wind circulation from dune structures.[35] Such evidence is important in determining regional circulation changes associated with glaciation.

*Periglacial phenomena.* The climatic significance of various periglacial features has already been mentioned in Chapter 5. Structures resulting from freeze-thaw effects give evidence of alternation of temperatures across freezing-point—thus implying low winter temperatures, but not necessarily permanently frozen ground, of which the best indication appears to be deep and well-marked casts of ice-wedges, which only form where a negative mean temperature (below about −6°C) is maintained. For example, the relation between isotherms and ice-wedge formation in Alaska has already been mentioned (fig. 5.10). Solifluction is not necessarily a sign of permanently frozen ground; with permeable sediments subsurface frozen ground is required (say in the spring) to hold up the water in the thawed layer so that downslope creep of this layer develops. In Britain, solifluction is more prevalent than loess deposition, which is more or

o

less confined to the south and east. This is presumably related to oceanic influence on the climate.

An estimate of seasonal temperature in the last glaciation for the foothills of the eastern Alps has been made based on the relation between permafrost and tree growth.[34] In the west there is evidence for tundra and permafrost, to the east in Hungary for tree growth and permafrost. The northward limit of trees is said to be around the 10°C July isotherm, and the maximum annual mean temperature for permafrost around −2°C. Then, where the tree limit meets the permafrost limit in the area studied, the July temperatures would be about 10°C and the annual mean −2°C. Estimations of monthly temperatures based on these figures are:

*Table 10.2* Estimations of mean monthly temperatures based on tree limit and permafrost distribution

| J | F | M | A | M | J | J | A | S | O | N | D |
|---|---|---|---|---|---|---|---|---|---|---|---|
| −14 | −12 | −8 | −2 | 4 | 8 | 10 | 8 | 4 | −2 | −8 | −12° C |

To the west, decreased summer temperatures resulted in less summer thaw and prevented tree growth, and the converse to the east.

*Geomorphological evidence.* Terraces demonstrating higher lake levels than at present may be evidence of former higher precipitation but they may also indicate lower temperatures, resulting in reduced evaporation. Such a relation as the latter is apparent from the Great Salt Lake in Utah, where a drop of level was accompanied by an increased temperature in the period 1875–1937. In assessing the meaning of changed lake levels it is obviously important to know whether other factors—changed outlets, damming by lava flows or earth movements—have been important on determining lake level.

The significance of marine terraces as indicators of interglacial climates has already been discussed (Chapter 8). Conversely, deep channels in present river systems and on the continental shelf are related to glacial stages by reason of the expected eustatic lowering during these stages.

Cirques are important in determining former local (orographic) snow-lines, because they form near or at the firn limit (Chapter 3). Thus the altitude of a group of cirque floors should indicate the snow-line at the time they were forming. So the altitude difference between this and the present snow-line, will indicate the lowering of the snow-line during cirque formation. If we disallow changes in snowfall and apply the lapse rate (0·6°C for 100 m), a rough figure can be obtained for mean summer temperature change. The mean difference for the world as a whole has been calculated[5] at 760 m, giving a figure about 4·5°C temperature difference between glacial maxima and the present. This figure will be less if snowfall increased.

*Soils.* Chemical and physical weathering processes produce soil on the parent rock. The course of development of the soil depends on the parent rock type, on the climate, on vegetation growing on the soil, and on the time that has been available for soil development. The great zonal soil groups (e.g. podsol, brown earth, chernozem) are related to climate and vegetation. So the identification of a fossil soil to a particular zonal type may give information regarding the climate and vegetation of the time during which it formed. The main zonal soils and the climates relating to them are as follows:

1. Podsol. Developed under humid conditions with free drainage, with a grey bleached zone in the A* horizon caused by leaching, with an accumulation of sesquioxides in the B horizon, carried down with the humic acids. The vegetation is usually heath or coniferous forest.

2. Brown-earths. These form under warmer or drier conditions than podsols, so that instead of a predominant leaching, the A horizon is well aerated and organic matter quickly oxidised. Less acid humus is produced, and sesquioxides are not leached much from the A horizon. There is loss of bases by leaching. A distinct B horizon is not usually present, and the colour of the soil is caused by the presence of oxidised and hydrated iron. The vegetation typically associated with brown-earths is temperate deciduous forest.

    The grey-brown podsolic soils are intermediate between podsols and brown-earths; they have a lower base-status than brown-earths and some podsolisation has occurred as a result of movement of sesquioxides.

3. Chernozems (black-earths). These form under conditions of continental climate with warm dry summers, with rain mainly in the spring and autumn. The main characteristic is the deep humus-rich A horizon, enriched with calcium carbonate near the base, and the absence of a B horizon. There is not sufficient rainfall for complete leaching of the bases, and the upward capillary movement of water in the summer leaves the carbonate in the basal layer of the A horizon where it concentrates to form concretions. The

* The following simplified horizon nomenclature is used:
A horizon: humus horizon, active biologically.
B horizon: enriched in iron and clay (not always present).
C horizon: parent rock.

natural vegetation associated with the soil is short-grass prairie or steppe.

4. Chestnut soils. These occur under conditions of increased summer temperatures and decreased precipitation. The A horizon contains less humus, and calcium carbonate is well distributed throughout the profile. The vegetation is steppe.

5. 'Mediterranean' soils. Under conditions of warm dry summers and milder wet winters, the processes forming brown-earths proceed but there is a greater drying in the summer. This leads to strong oxidation, and there is less degree of hydration of the free ferric oxide, which results in red coloration of the soil.

6. Desert soils. These are often rich in alkalis or calcium carbonate, which may form encrustations or nodules (caliche) near or at the surface. Thus accumulation results from an upward movement associated with evaporation.

Such soil types as these merely show the tendency of soil development under particular climatic conditions. There are very many more types recognised, and for diagnoses and descriptions of European soil types reference should be made to Kubiena's *Soils of Europe*.[25]

The problems of interpreting fossil soils are several. The first is in the recognition of a fossil soil. An iron rich or ferrocrete or a calcrete layer, may be the result of post-depositional changes related to former or present water levels or to impermeable layers holding up drainage. A horizon rich in organic matter may be a result of primary sedimentation.

A well-developed fossil soil may be classifiable into its major type showing the general climatic regime under which it was formed. More often the profile is truncated, or the soil horizons disturbed, so that identification is made difficult. The fossil soil may be the end-product of a time of changing climate, or it may have developed during a time of no climatic change. There may be also local topographic factors influencing soil formation which are not evident in a section of sediments.

Three examples of the interpretation of fossil soils will be mentioned.

1. Fossil soils associated with loess in Europe. Much work has been done on these soils and their relation to climatic change and to chronology of the glacial and interglacial stages. The climatic interpretation of the soils has been improved by studies of thin sections of soils and by studies of the associated mollusc faunas. Fig. 10.7 shows soil types associated with loess in three soil provinces, arctic, Baltic (more oceanic) and Pannonian (more

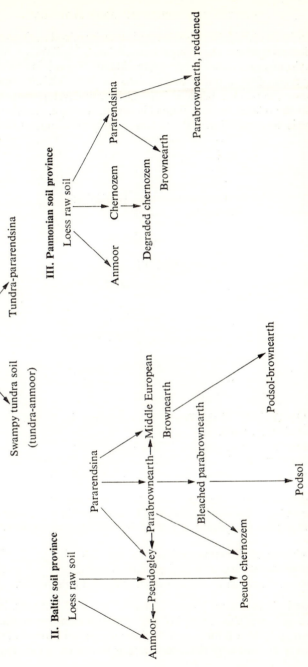

*Fig. 10.7* Developmental relations of recent and fossil loess soils in the Arctic, Baltic and Pannonian soil provinces (Kubiena 1956).

continental). Fig. 10.8 shows a typical series of soil horizons within a loess sequence. The interpretation of such fossil soils as these in environmental terms is extremely difficult,[24] and it is much aided by finds of fossil molluscs associated with the soils.[30] Table 10.3 shows the relation between interglacial soil development on loess and the related mollusc faunas in central Europe. Another problem is the correlation of the soil horizons from one area to another.

*Fig. 10.8* Division of the Würm loess sequence in Hessen, Germany (Schönhals *et al.* 1964).

    a. Riss/Würm interglacial soil (Homburger soil);
    b. humus zones of the Early Würm (Mosbacher Humuszonen);
c, d. two soils in the loess of the Middle Würm (Gräselberger and Hahn-stätter soils);
    e. soil horizons in the Late Würm loess, more weakly developed than c and d (Erbenheimer soils). At f there is a tuff layer (Kärlicher tuff) important for synchronisation of the different loess sections.

A change of climatic province will lead to a change of soil type, and perhaps, if a continental extreme is reached the lack of appearance of a soil, as loess deposition remained continuous.

2. Gumbotil in central United States.[37] Gumbotil is a grey, leached and reduced clay overlying and grading down into till. It is thought to be a B horizon of an interglacial soil formed in upland poorly drained clay-rich areas, and is found on all of the three

*Table 10.3* Correlation between development of terrestrial deposits and molluscan fauna in Pleistocene warm periods in Central Europe (Lozek, 1965)

| Sedimentation, soil formation | | Molluscan fauna |
|---|---|---|
| Renewed sedimentation, at the beginning very slow, with concomitant formation of soils of the chernozem series in dry regions (beginning of the new cold phase) | early glacial | Disappearance of woodland species, arrival of steppe assemblages with *Chondrula tridens, Helicopsis striata, Pupilla muscorum*, persistence of *Bradybaena fruticum, Arianta* |
| Intensive soil-forming processes—climax stages of brown-earths—parabraunerde, braunerde, terra fusca, pseudochernozem, pseudogley. Cessation of the formation of calcareous tufas | climatic optimum | Fully developed woodland assemblages with slowly receding southern species, abundant in the preceding periods: *Helicodonta obvoluta, Helix pomatia, Cepaea, Clausiliidae, Zonitidae* |
| Sedimentation and denudation cease. Soils attain the climax stage due to intensive soil processes. A strong removal of lime into subsoil and weathering | climatic optimum | Fauna of climatic optimum. Maximum distribution of rich moisture-requiring assemblages—*Banatica* or *Ruderatus* fauna fully developed, disappearance of steppe species |
| Moderate hillwash, weathering and consolidation of the ground surface more intense; soils still in initial stages (frequently calcareous up to the surface), soil sediments weakly humic | climatic optimum | Towards the close of the interval fully developed forest faunas with a great proportion of warmth- and moisture-requiring species appear, wide distribution of molluscs on the soils, still calcareous up to the surface, enclaves of steppe assemblages pushed back by forest |
| Hillwash still relatively intense, start of weathering and formation of soils; on the slopes coarser waste appears; start of formation of calcareous tufas | | Arrival of warmth-loving fauna, thermophilous steppe elements penetrate to steppes (e.g. *Abida, Cepaea vindobonensis* locally also high up into the mountains), at first prevalence of tolerant species (see below), the share of less tolerant ones gradually increasing—*Cochlodina laminata, Aegopinella minor, pura, Clausilia cruciata, Discus ruderatus, Gastrocopta theeli* |
| Intense hillwash and moderate solifluction; in cold phases yellow-brown loams with a slightly increased humus content; angular small-size rock waste. Cessation of loess sedimentation | late glacial | Tolerant, more or less moisture-requiring assemblages, faunas with *Arianta arbustorum, Vitrea crystallina, Perpolita radiatula, Perforatella bidentata*; in warm localities *Chondrula tridens, Helicopsis striata*, arrival of *Cochlicopa lubricella* and *Truncatellina cylindrica*, disappearance of *Columella columella* and *Vallonia tenuilabris* |
| Loess sedimentation | glacial | Loess faunas: *Columella columella, Vallonia tenuilabris, Pupilla loessica, Vertigo parcedentata*; only tolerant species of open environments |

older till sheets in the United States (Nebraskan, Kansan and Illinoian). The presence of gumbotil has been taken to be one of the main criteria in separating the times of till-sheet formation from one another by interglacial stages. More exact climatic conditions under which the gumbotils formed are not known. Partly the difficulty is one of nomenclature. Various soil types and also possibly sediments which have accumulated in depressions—the so-called accretion gleys—have been included in the term gumbotil, and this has led to discussion on the meaning and significance of gumbotil.

3. Recurrence surfaces in ombrogenous peats.[17, 18, 38] Some sections through ombrogenous (see p. 51) peats show bands of dark highly humified peat overlain by lighter fresh peat (plate 8). The humification and oxidation is caused by a slowing down or cessation of peat growth caused by drying out of the surface, that is, it is incipient soil formation. Both the local hydrology of the peat bog and regional climatic changes may be responsible for the formation of such recurrence surfaces. Whether these are synchronous or not in the same or different areas of peat accumulation is important. If they are, regional climatic tendencies to drying out are suggested. If not, the hydrological balance may be locally affected only, perhaps by an increased curvature of the bog surface or by a changing relation to the surrounding water table.

The most obvious recurrence surface in north European bogs is Weber's '*Grenzhorizont*', believed to have been caused by the bog surfaces drying out in Sub-Boreal time, followed by rapid peat accumulation in Sub-Atlantic time. Many other recurrence surfaces of different age are known, but their correlation over large areas remains in some doubt. Even within one bog it is known that surfaces in different parts of the bog were not necessarily formed in the same periods,[38] suggesting local factors at work controlling the rate of growth.

### Isotopic determination of temperature[8]

The relative abundance of oxygen isotopes $O^{16}$ and $O^{18}$ in biogenic carbonates (tests of Foraminifera, mollusc shells) secreted by animals living in water is related to the abundance of these isotopes in the water at the time the carbonate was formed. The ratio in water will depend on the temperature amongst other factors. Therefore by measuring the $O^{18/16}$ ratios in calcium carbonate skeletons, say tests of Foraminifera found at successive levels in deep-sea cores, it is thought possible to deduce past temperature changes which took place while the sediment was forming. The ratio of the isotopes in the carbonate is measured by a mass-spectrometer. The ratio changes are very small ($O^{18}$ enrichment in respect to $O^{16}$ increases 0·02 per cent per 1 °C temperature fall) and the instrument used has to be very sensitive.

Ocean carbonates are the subject of measurement because of the possible variations in $O^{18/16}$ ratio in shallow marine and inland waters. By measuring the ratios in tests of pelagic Foraminifera, surface water isotopic temperatures are obtained, while the ratios in benthonic Foraminifera show isotopic temperatures for bottom waters. The isotopic temperatures have to be converted to true temperature, and to do this the isotopic ratio of the ocean at the time of carbonate formation should be known. The ratio is liable to be altered by other factors than temperature, e.g. enrichment of $O^{18}$ in the oceans during glacial times as a result of deficiency of $O^{18}$ in glacial ice. Variations of $O^{18/16}$ surface ocean water also results from evaporation ($H_2O^{16}$ evaporates more quickly than $H_2O^{18}$) thus giving variation between the ratio in tropical and arctic waters. The importance of these factors remains to be evaluated in detail. The $O^{18}$ enrichment factor in particular may be more effective than hitherto assumed.

Fig. 10.9 shows the isotopic temperature curves from ocean cores from the Caribbean. If corrections for various factors affecting the isotopic ratio are made, the maxima are lowered by about 1·3°C and the minima raised by about 1·7°C. The results show fluctuations of surface water (true) temperature, based on measurements of tests of pelagic Foraminifera of about 6°C. Measurements on the calcareous tests of benthonic Foraminifera show a depression of about 2°C for bottom water in the eastern equatorial Atlantic during glacial stages, but little change from the present in the equatorial Pacific. This may be related to the large area of ice in the North Atlantic during the glaciations. The curves for surface water in the Pacific show little variation, in contrast to that in the Caribbean and Atlantic and this lack of variation may have its origin in local oceanographic conditions in the Pacific.

The curves obtained are important in showing that surface ocean waters fluctuated in temperature, but perhaps rather less than the estimated temperature change of the continental lowlands of present temperate regions, and that the successive fluctuations were of a similar order of magnitude. There are, however, several difficulties inherent in the use of the curves as absolute indicators of change in temperature with time. First there may be difficulties in applying the method, resulting from changes in the isotope ratio because of exchange or because some organisms (e.g. coral) appear to show

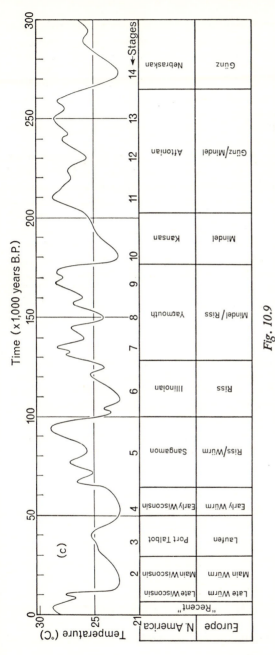

*Fig. 10.9*

a. Isotopic temperature curve from the Caribbean core A 240–M1, with absolute dates obtained by the $Pa^{231}/Th^{230}$ method (Rosholt *et al.* 1961).

b. Isotopic temperature curves from Caribbean core A 179–4, from tests of *Globigerinoides rubra* (a), *Globigerinoides sacculifera* (b), *Globigerina dubia* (c), and *Globorotalia menardii* (d) (Emiliani 1955). There is good agreement between the curves from the four species.

c. General temperature curve and time scale (beyond 150,000 years obtained by extrapolation), with Emiliani's correlations to the continental Pleistocene (Emiliani 1961).

carbonate deposition unrelated to the environmental ratio. The curves do not show some details of temperature change which are known from studies of continental deposits. For example, an abrupt change in surface water temperature at 10,800 years ago is deduced, but no details of fluctuation around this point, as shown by the Late Weichselian zones I, II and III, are indicated. On the other hand there is a considerable degree of agreement between major climatic trends of the Weichselian in north-west Europe and the isotopic evidence from Atlantic cores.[19]

Another difficulty results from the possibility that the record from some cores may be incomplete; parts may have been lost by slumping, etc., and so an unknown number of cycles of climatic change may be missing. Then there is the difficulty of correlating the temperature minima and maxima with the continental glacial and interglacial sequence. Lastly there is the difficulty that curves based on isotope ratio and species assemblage changes do not always tally, as shown in fig. 10.2, and this leads to various versions of correlation with the continental sequence, also shown in fig. 10.2. However there does appear to be agreement between the two back to some 60 or 70,000 years, that is to the end of the last (Eemian) interglacial.

*Precipitation changes*

Evidence for precipitation changes is more slender. On the one hand there are the supposed pluvial periods when lakes in the middle and equatorial latitudes stood higher than present, and these periods are usually correlated with glacial stages. There is the suggestion that the ice sheets forced southwards the depression tracks bringing rain. On the other hand, there are observations on snow-line changes, for example, in the Alps, which demonstrate that snow-line depression was not accentuated in the direction of normal rain-bearing winds. Such would be expected if there was much increase in precipitation. In fact, there is some evidence for decreased precipitation as a whole during glacial stages. For example, it has been estimated[32, 33] that in the last glacial stage, the precipitation over the highlands in Britain only reached eighty per cent of today's value. This figure was suggested by the absence of cirques in southern Britain, which would have been caused by a lower firn limit related to greater precipitation, whereas much higher firn limits related to much decreased precipitation would not have produced the known ice sheets.

The lower precipitation suggested does not conflict with great expansion of ice. Lower temperatures mean less ablation, very significant for ice accumulation. Thus the various evidences regarding precipitation indicate that world-wide change in temperature resulted in a changed precipitation pattern.

It is very probable that a pattern of precipitation changes accompanied each ice advance. Perhaps regional precipitation increased during the early parts of the ice advances as belts of cyclonic activity moved south, and later during the glacial, at the time of maximum cold, the colder seas resulted in less moisture being available and less precipitation in the belts of cyclonic activity.

### Conclusions—past climatic change

Of all the factors involved in climatic change in the Pleistocene, it is clear that temperature changes are best documented. The magnitude of these according to various types of evidence is indicated in table 10.1. Estimates of the amount of fluctuation of temperature between the temperate and cold stages vary between 3°C and 15°C, but 5° to 8°C fluctuation of mean annual temperature is a value generally considered to be near the mark. As we have seen, there are considerable difficulties in deducing seasonal changes of temperature and precipitation values. Combination of various types of evidence often proves rewarding, and an example of such an approach is shown in fig. 10.10, giving conclusions about the Late Weichselian climate of the British Isles.[32, 33]

*Fig. 10.10* Suggested isotherms for the Allerød interstadial (zone II) and the succeeding climatic recession of zone III, during the Late Weichselian of the British Isles (Manley 1951).

## RECENT CLIMATIC CHANGE[29, 32]

We may gain some insight into climatic change by studies of recent changes and associated effects in Britain.

In brief the major changes which are believed to have occurred over the period of the last 7000 years are as follows.

*Table 10.4* Recent climatic change in Britain

| | |
|---|---|
| 5000–3000 B.C. | Flandrian climatic optimum. Annual mean temperatures about 2°C above present. |
| 500 B.C. | climatic deterioration of the Sub-Boreal. |
| 1000–1300 A.D. | lesser climatic optimum. |
| 1300 A.D. | climatic deterioration set in. |
| 1550–1850 A.D. | 'little ice age'. |
| 1850–1940 A.D. | warmth increase. |
| 1950 A.D. to present | warmth decrease. |

The detailed instrumental records over the last hundred years or so are of particular interest. There has been a general warming, arctic sea ice has thinned and decreased in area, deglaciation has been prevalent, and plants and animals have changed their ranges in response to the amelioration.[13, 29] Fig. 10.11 gives details of temperature, precipitation and westerly wind incidence in this period in the British Isles. Higher temperatures were characteristic of three or four decades around 1930, and terminated a long period of temperature rise. Annual rainfall increased in Europe, including Britain, and in much of western Asia and the western parts of other continents, and there was also a general increase of snow and rain at higher latitudes. There was also an increase in the incidence of westerly winds, involving an increase in strength of the world's main wind-streams. This period also appears to have been a time of minimum precipitation in the eastern parts of temperate continents and intensification of desert conditions in arid regions. A weaker circulation has predominated in more recent years, especially since 1958; westerlies have decreased and so have temperatures and rainfall.

The atmospheric circulation is an important part of these changes, both in intensification, making the polar regions warmer by the penetration of warm westerly wind-streams to the north, and by encouraging warm ocean currents northwards as well. As a result storminess in middle latitudes decreases and the climate generally ameliorates. Conversely, weakening of the circulation and an increase of northerly and easterly winds at the expense of westerlies, as observed since 1940, is related to climatic deterioration, as shown by the increase of sea ice during the last decade in the Arctic and in the

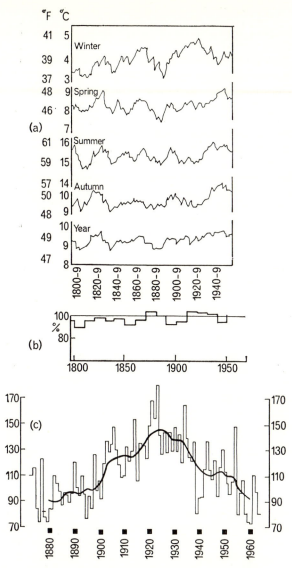

*Fig. 10.11* Recent climatic changes in Britain.
a. Average temperatures in Central England (°C), shown by 10-year running means for each season and for the year (after Manley).
b. Rainfall in England and Wales, plotted as decade averages which are
shown as percentages of the average 1900–1939 (932 mm) (Lamb 1965).
c. Number of days classified as westerly type for each year since 1873
in the British Isles (Lamb 1965).

north Atlantic. A general correlation can be seen here of temperature, rainfall and circulation.

The question is whether there is a relation between an external factor such as intensity of solar radiation and the atmospheric circulation. There have been suggestions of the relation of sunspot activity and ultraviolet intensity to circulation changes, but it remains to be demonstrated exactly what is the relation between circulation itself, dependent on the unequal heating of the equatorial and polar areas, and external factors which might produce changes in the thermal gradient. Other factors will also affect the thermal gradient, e.g. the high albedo of snow and ice will give significance to the area covered by seasonal or perennial snow and ice; and also changes in moisture content of atmosphere and cloudiness, themselves dependent on the general atmospheric circulation.

## CAUSES OF CLIMATIC CHANGE

A large number of hypotheses have been put forward to account for the multiple glaciation characteristic of the Pleistocene. Any explanation should say why at the end of the Tertiary, during which there was a gradual decrease in temperature, world-wide temperatures were depressed sufficiently to ensure formation and expansion of glaciers in mountainous areas where precipitation was high enough. And it should also account for the fluctuations in temperature after this time, fluctuations of the magnitude of 5 to 8°C. Any theory of causation of ice ages should also be applicable to the pre-Pleistocene glaciations, such as those of the Permo-Carboniferous and Eo-Cambrian.

We can first briefly mention the factors which have been regarded as possible agents of climatic change. These are terrestrial and extra-terrestrial. The terrestrial factors suggested include changes in configuration of land and sea, the increased building of highlands in the late-Tertiary on which glaciers could develop, and the effect of changes of carbon dioxide concentration in the atmosphere (increase leads to inhibition of outgoing radiation from the earth to space, and more absorption of the incoming solar radiation on its passage through the atmosphere, resulting in raised temperatures at the earth's surface), and increased cloudiness (leading to depression of temperatures by loss of radiation by reflection). Extra-terrestrial factors involve variations of the solar radiation 'constant' in time (as yet unproven) and the possibility of variation in solar radiation received by the earth because of interception by inter-stellar matter. A third class of factors involve changing the radiation received on various parts of the earth because of variation in the elements of the earth's orbit round the Sun.

To illustrate hypotheses put forward we may take three examples. One dependent on change in solar radiation, one dependent on terrestrial changes, and one combining the two.

| Radiation | World temp | Precipitation | Glaciated regions | | Whole earth |
|---|---|---|---|---|---|
| CAL/CM²Min | °C | CM/Year | Ice-cap | Climate | Precipitation |
| $S_D$ Increasing | $T_D$ Increasing | $P_D$ Increasing | E, D | Warm-wet Interglatial | Very wet, D, Pluvial |
| $S_C$ | $T_C$ | $P_C$ | C | Glacial | Wet, C |
| $S_B=1.95$ Decreasing | $T_B=14°C$ Decreasing | $P_B=74$ Decreasing | B, A  80 70 60 50°N  Latitude | Present day / Cold-dry Interglacial | Dry, B / Very dry, Interpluvial |
| a | b | c | d | e | f |

*Fig. 10.12* Relation between solar radiation and climatic change according to Simpson's hypothesis (Simpson 1957). Point B gives conditions at present day in terms of solar 'constant' (S), mean temperature (T) and annual precipitation (P) of the earth.

## Simpson's hypothesis[42, 43]

This is interesting as an attempt to demonstrate that an increase in solar radiation results in multiple glaciation. The course of events is shown in fig. 10.12. From point A to point C solar radiation increases, temperature rises, circulation between the Equator and the Poles increases as a result and results in increased cloudiness and precipitation. This increased precipitation lowers the snow-line and glaciation ensues. From point C to point D there is a continued rise in radiation, the temperature increases further, snow-lines rise and glaciation ends. The process reverses during a decrease of radiation. Thus Simpson obtains (fig. 10.12), during an oscillation of the solar 'constant', a glaciation preceded by a cool dry interglacial and

P

followed by a warm wet interglacial. In the extra-glacial area these fluctuations would be represented by an arid interpluvial period and a pluvial period.

There is in fact no evidence from interglacial climates to support the two types of interglacial resulting from this scheme. But the ideas are valuable in demonstrating possible links between radiation changes and climatic events in the Pleistocene.

### Ewing and Donn's hypothesis[14]

This tries to explain recurrent glaciation as a result of terrestrial changes, on the premise that an ice-free Arctic ocean favours the formation of glaciers on the surrounding land masses. During a warm (interglacial) period the Arctic is ice free as a result of a flow of warm water north from the Atlantic. This may have been the cause of increased precipitation, and thus glacier growth, in the surrounding areas, with a resultant lowering of world sea-level. This causes the shallowing of the sea or the emergence of a land bridge between Iceland and the Faroes, preventing a northerly penetration of warm waters. The Arctic Ocean freezes over, precipitation to the surrounding glaciers and ice sheets is reduced and they wane. Sea-level is restored, the Arctic Ocean ice melts and the cycle starts again.

The cycles began, according to this hypothesis, when the North Pole reached a position favourable to the process, at the beginning of Pleistocene time.

There are several objections to this hypothesis. For example, there is little evidence for much polar wandering in the late Tertiary, and if the source of precipitation was the Arctic Ocean, there surely would have been more glaciation north of the mountains of Alaska and Anadyr than is now recognised.

### Solar-topographic hypothesis of R. F. Flint

This relies on the observed relation between late-Tertiary mountain-building and the advent of Pleistocene ice sheets and glaciers to bring about the first cold period of the Pleistocene, and on fluctuations in solar radiation to produce temperature fluctuations thereafter. Regarding the latter, there has been suggested[45] a relation between solar fluctuation and glacial fluctuation, the glaciers shrinking in high sunspot number periods and expanding in low sunspot number periods. Even if this is so the mechanism linking changes in solar energy output (in kind or quantity) and the changes demonstrated by Pleistocene geology and biology are unknown.

At the moment the solar-topographic hypothesis seems the most reasonable general explanation for recurrent glaciation in the Pleistocene. But whether variation in the received radiation depends on variation in solar 'constant' or on changes in the elements of the earth's orbit, or both, it is not possible to say. If there was a correlation between a Milankovitch-type curve and the geological evidence for climatic change, then the point might be decided.

If the major climatic changes are caused in the way suggested by the solar-topographic hypothesis, it may still be possible that minor fluctuations, such as those occurring within glaciations, are caused by other factors, such as changes in distribution of land and sea or ice surges.

As stated at the beginning of the chapter, we need more evidence of the nature, magnitude and succession of climatic change before we can find the cause or causes, and the link between cause and effect, in this matter.

## REFERENCES

BOWEN, R. 1966. *Palaeotemperature analysis*. Amsterdam: Elsevier.

MITCHELL, J. M. 1965. 'Theoretical palaeoclimatology', in *The Quaternary of the United States*, eds. H. E. Wright and D. G. Frey. pp. 881–901. Princeton University Press.

NAIRN, A. E. M. (ed.). 1961. *Descriptive palaeoclimatology*. London: Interscience.

SCHWARZBACH, M. 1963. *Climates of the Past*. London: van Nostrand.

WRIGHT, H. E. 1961. Late Pleistocene climates of Europe: a review. *Bull. Geol. Soc. Amer.*, **72**, 933–84.

1 ANDERSEN, S. T. 1961. 'Vegetation and its Environment in Denmark in the Early Weichselian Glacial', *Danm. Geol. Unders.*, II Raekke, No. 75.

2 ANDERSEN, S. T., DE VRIES, H. L. and ZAGWIJN, W. H. 1960. 'Climatic change and radiocarbon dating in the Weichselian glacial of Denmark and the Netherlands', *Geol. en Mijn.*, **39**, 38–42.

3 ANDERSSON, G. 1910. 'Swedish climate in the Late-Quaternary Period', in *Die Veränderungen des Klimas seit dem maximum der letzten Eiszeit*, pp. 247–94. XI Int. Geol. Congress. Stockholm. Stockholm: Generalstabens Litografiska Anstalt.

4 BLYTT, A. 1876. *Essay on the immigration of the Norwegian flora during alternating rainy and dry periods*. Christiania: Cammermeyer.

5 BROOKS, C. E. P. 1951. 'Geological and historical aspects of climatic change', in *Compendium of Meteorology*, ed. Malone, T. F. pp. 1004–23. Boston: American Meteorological Soc.

6 BRØGGER, W. C. 1900–01. 'Om de senglaciale og postglaciale nivå-forandringer i Kristianfeltet (Molluskenfaunan)', *Norges Geol. Unders.*, No. 31.

7 DEGERBØL, M. and KROG, H. 1951. 'Den europaeiske Sumpskildpadde (*Emys orbicularis L.*) i Danmark (with English summary)', *Danm. Geol. Unders.*, II Raekke, No. 78.

8 EMILIANI, C. 1955. 'Pleistocene temperatures', *J. Geol.*, **63**, 538–78.

9 EMILIANI, C. 1961. 'Cenozoic climatic changes', in *Solar variations, climatic change, and related geophysical problems*, ed. R. W. Fairbridge. *Ann. N.Y. Acad. Sci.*, **95**, 1–740.

10 EMILIANI, C. 1964. 'Palaeotemperature analysis of the Caribbean cores A 254-BR-C and CP-28', *Bull. Geol. Soc. Amer.*, **75**, 129–44.

11 ERICSON, D. B., EWING, P. M. and WOLLIN, G. 1964. 'The Pleistocene epoch in deep-sea sediments', *Science*, **146**, 723–32.

12 ERICSON, D. B., EWING, M., WOLLIN, G. and HEEZEN, B. C. 1961. 'Atlantic deep-sea sediment cores', *Bull. Geol. Soc. Amer.*, **72**, 193–286.

13 ERKAMO, V. 1956. 'Untersuchungen über die pflanzenbiologischen und einige andere folgeerscheinungen der neuzeitlichen klima-schwankung in Finnland', *Ann. Bot. Soc. 'Vanamo'*, **28**, No. 3.

14 EWING, M. and DONN, W. L. 1958. 'A theory of ice ages', *Science*, **127**, 1159–62.

15 FEYLING-HANSSEN, R. W. 1964. 'Foraminifera in Late Quaternary deposits from the Oslofjord area', *Norges Geol. Unders.*, No. 225.

16 FIRBAS, F. 1949–52. *Waldgeschichte Mitteleuropas*. Jena: G. Fischer.

17 GODWIN, H. 1954. 'Recurrence-surfaces', *Danm. Geol. Unders.*, II Raekke, No. 80, 22–30.

18 GRANLUND, E. 1932. 'De svenska högsmossarnas geologi', *Sver. Geol. Unders.*, Ser. C., No. 373.

19 HAMMEN, T. VAN DER, MAARLEVELD, G. C., VOGEL, J. C. and ZAGWIJN, W. H. 1967. 'Stratigraphy, climatic succession and radio-carbon dating of the last glacial in the Netherlands', *Geol. en Mijnbouw*, **46**, 79–95.

20 IVERSEN, J. 1944. '*Viscum, Hedera* and *Ilex* as climate indicators', *Geol. Fören. Förh.*, **66**, 463–83.

21 IVERSEN, J. 1954. 'The Late-Glacial Flora of Denmark and its Relation to Climate and Soil', *Danm. Geol. Unders.*, II Raekke, No. 80, 87–119.

22 IVERSEN, J. 1960. 'Problems of the Early Post-glacial forest development in Denmark', *Danm. Geol. Unders.*, IV Raekke, **4**, No. 3.

23 JESSEN, K. and MILTHERS, V. 1928. 'Stratigraphical and palaeonto-logical studies of interglacial freshwater deposits in Jutland and north-west Germany', *Danm. Geol. Unders.*, II Raekke, No. 48.

24 KLIMA, B., KUKLA, J., LOZEK, V. and DE VRIES, H. 1962. 'Stratigraphie des Pleistozäns und alter des Paläeolithischen rastplatzes in der Ziegelei von Dolni Vestonice (unter-Wisternitz)', *Anthropozoicum*, **11**, 93–145.

25 KUBIENA, W. L. 1953. *The soils of Europe*. London: Murby.

26 KUBIENA, W. L. 1956. 'Zur Micromorphologie, Systematik und Entwicklung der rezenten und fossilen Lössböden', *Eiszeitalter u. Gegenwart*, **7**, 102–12.

27 LAMB, H. 1961. 'Fundamentals of climate', in *Descriptive Palaeoclimatology*, ed. A. E. M. Nairn, pp. 8–44. London: Interscience.

28 LAMB, H. 1964. 'Climatic changes and variations in the atmospheric and ocean circulations', *Geol. Rundschau*, **54**, 486–504.

29 LAMB, H. 1965. 'Britain's changing climate', in *The biological significance of climatic changes in Britain*, ed. C. G. Johnson, pp. 3–34. London, Institute of Biology: Academic Press.

30 LOZEK, V. 1965. 'The relationship between the development of soils and faunas in the warm Quaternary phases', *Sbornik geologickych Ved*, Antropozoicum, řada A, sv. 3, 7–33.

31 MAARLEVELD, G. C. 1960. 'Wind directions and cover sands in the Netherlands', *Biul. Peryglacjalny*, **8**, 49–58.

32 MANLEY, G. 1951. 'The range of variation of the British climate', *Geogr. J.*, **117**, 43–68.

33 MANLEY, G. 1959. 'The Late-glacial climate of north-west England', *Liverpool and Manchester Geological Journal*, **2**, 188–215.

34 POSER, H. 1948. 'Boden- und Klimaverhältnisse in Mittel und Westeuropa während der Würmeiszeit', *Erdkunde*, **2**, 53–68.

35 POSER, H. 1954. 'Zur rekonstruktion der Spätglazialen Luftdruckverhältnisse in Mittel- und Westeuropa auf Grund der vorzeitlichen Dünen', *Erdkunde*, **4**, 81–8.

36 ROSHOLT, J. N., EMILIANI, C., GEISS, J., KOCZY, F. F. and WANGERSKY, P. J. 1961. 'Absolute dating of deep-sea cores by the $Pa^{231}/Th^{230}$ method', *J. Geol.*, **69**, 162–85.

37 RUHE, R. V. 1965. 'Quaternary palaeopedology', in *The Quaternary of the United States*, eds. Wright, H. E. and Frey, D. G. pp. 755–64. Princeton University Press.

38 SCHNEEKLOTH, H. 1965. 'Die rekurrenzfläche in Grossen Moor bei Gifhorn —eine zeitgleiche Bildung', *Geol. Jb.*, **83**, 477–96.

39 SCHÖNHALS, E., ROHDENBURG, H. and SEMMEL, A. 1964. 'Ergebnisse neuer Untersuchungen zur Würmlöss-Gliederung in Hessen', *Eiszeitalter u. Gegenwart*, **15**, 199–206.

40 SERNANDER, R. 1908. 'On the evidence of Postglacial changes of climate furnished by the peat-mosses of Northern Europe', *Geol. Fören. Förh.*, **30**, 465–78.

41 SHOTTON, F. W. 1962. 'The physical background of Britain in the Pleistocene', *Adv. Sci.*, **19**, 1–14.

42 SIMPSON, G. C. 1957. 'Further studies in World Climate', *Quart. J. R. Meteor. Soc.*, **83**, 459–85.

43 SIMPSON, G. C. 1959. 'World temperatures during the Pleistocene', *Quart. J. R. Meteor. Soc.*, **85**, 332–49.

44 SZAFER, W. 1954. 'Pliocene flora from the vicinity of Czorsztyn, (West Carpathians) and its relationship to the Pleistocene', *Instytut Geologiczny*, Prace Tom XI. Warsaw.

45 WILLETT, H. C. 1951. 'Extrapolation of sunspot-climate relationships', *J. Meteorology*, **8**, 1–6.
46 WISEMAN, J. D. H. and OVEY, C. D. 1950. 'Recent investigations of the deep sea floor', *Proc. Geol. Assoc. London*, **61**, 28–84.
47 ZEUNER, F. E. 1959. *The Pleistocene period*. 2nd ed. London: Hutchinson.

# CHAPTER 11

# PLEISTOCENE SUCCESSIONS AND THEIR SUBDIVISION

*Development of the detail of Pleistocene successions in Europe*

D URING the middle of the nineteenth century the acceptance of the glacial theory for the origin of the Pleistocene drifts in northern Europe led to the recognition of the Pleistocene Ice Age. Soon after came the idea of polyglacialism, involving a number of distinct ice advances over the area. Trimmer in 1858 described two tills on the coast of East Anglia and Geikie in 1877 recognised four glaciations in the East Anglian drift sequence. Later, in 1895, Geikie[4] (table 11.1) put forward a sequence of glacials and interglacials in northern Europe. Geikie's system was not, however, widely adopted as a basis for the subdivision of the Pleistocene; the evidence at that time hardly merited a comprehensive scheme. It was not until the classic work of Penck and Brückner[11] in the Alps that a general scheme, involving fourfold glaciation, became widely accepted in Europe (table 11.1).

In Europe Penck and Brückner's scheme remained authoritative for many years. It was used, and still is, in many areas beyond the Alps: for example, the names of the Alpine glacial stages are widely used by archaeologists in many parts of Europe. In some ways it is unfortunate that Penck and Brückner's scheme became so widely used. Unlike the clearer sequence of glacials and interglacials in northern Europe, the original work on the fourfold glaciation of the Alps was done in a much more difficult area—certain valleys of the northern foreland of the Alps (figs. 11.1 and 11.2). The sequence was mainly based on relative levels of outwash bodies with interglacial periods deduced from weathering, soil profiles, and the extent of downcutting between the deposition of the successive outwash bodies.

The succession of ice advances of the Scandinavian ice sheet became formalised in the 1920's (table 11.1). The drift borders of these different glacial stages are shown in fig. 11.4. There was a considerable distance between the Alpine and Scandinavian ice sheets at the

*Fig. 11.1* Southern Germany, showing the approximate margin of the Würm glaciation (dashed line) and the foreland with older drifts to the north, drained by the Danube. Rivers in the foreland area give their names to the Alpine stages.

*Fig. 11.2* Long profile of the gravel terraces of the river Iller (see fig. 11.1) and their relation to moraines (Wright 1937).

# *Table 11.1* Classification of the Pleistocene

Names on the left of each column are cold or glacial stages, and those on the right, temperate stages. Above the double line are the classical glacial and interglacial stages of the Pleistocene; below it is the 'preglacial' part of the Pleistocene. Present conventional correlations are shown by lines connecting stage names.

| N. America [2] | N. Europe [4] | Alps [15] | N.W. Europe [15] | European U.S.S.R. [7] |
|---|---|---|---|---|
| Wisconsin | Mecklenburgian | Würm | Weichselian | Waldai |
| Sangamon | Neudeckian | R/W | Eemian | Mikulino, Mgi |
| Illinoian | Polandian | Riss | Warthe | Moscow |
| Yarmouth | Helvetian | M/R | ? | Odintzovo |
| Kansan | Saxonian | Mindel | Saale | Dnieper |
| Aftonian | Norfolkian | G/M | Holstein | Lichwin |
| Nebraskan | Scanian | Günz | Elster | Oka |
| | | | Cromerian | Belovezhsky |
| | | Donau | Menapian | (Apsheron and |
| | | | Waalian | Akchagyl |
| | | Biber | Eburonian | formations) |
| | | | Tiglian | |
| | | | Praetiglian | |

time of maximum glaciation, as seen on the map of Europe showing the distribution of Pleistocene ice (fig. 11.3), and the exact correlation of the Alpine and Scandinavian glacial advances is still a matter of some doubt.

The advances in the subdivision of the European Pleistocene really stem from the work of Jessen and Milthers[5] in 1928 on freshwater

*Fig. 11.3* Ice limits in Europe at time of maximum glaciation. The Scandinavian ice is shown confluent with British and Irish ice to the west and with the Urals and Novaya Zemlya ice to the north-east. Minor glaciated areas are also outlined or spotted (after Flint 1957).

interglacial deposits. They showed that each of two interglacial periods they identified had a characteristic vegetational sequence revealed by pollen analysis. Thus for the first time was it possible to introduce definite correlations of interglacials, and hence glacials, over wide areas of northern Europe.

Moreover, as a result of Jessen and Milthers's work, it has become

*Fig. 11.4* Limits of the ice of the Scandinavian and neighbouring ice caps during the main glacial stages. E, Elster/Oka; S, Saale/Dnieper; Wa, Warthe/Moscow; W, Weichsel/Moscow; W, Weichsel/Waldai maximum; w, retreat stages of the Weichselian ice; w1, Pomeranian; w2, Frankfurt/Poznan; w3, Riga; w4, Salpausselka (after Woldstedt 1958).

*Table 11.2* Climatic development of interglacials and interstadials
(Jessen and Milthers, 1928)

| *Glacial or periglacial deposits* | |
|---|---|
| *Interstadial climatic development* | *Interglacial climatic development* |
| arctic | arctic |
| sub-arctic | sub-arctic |
| boreal, with summer temperature essentially lower than in the Flandrian climatic optimum of the area in question | boreal |
| | temperate, with summer temperature at least as high as during the Flandrian climatic optimum of the area in question |
| sub-arctic | boreal |
| arctic | sub-arctic |
| | arctic |
| glacial deposits | |

customary to use interglacial and interstadial as terms to define particular types of non-glacial climatic conditions in temperate northwest Europe, as indicated by vegetational changes (table 11.2); interglacial to describe a temperate period with a climatic optimum at least as warm as the Flandrian climatic optimum in the region concerned, and interstadial to describe a period which was either too short or too cold to permit the development of temperate deciduous forest of the interglacial type in the region concerned. This use of the terms is preferable to their use as general indicators of non-glacial conditions (fig. 11.5), e.g. the use of the word interglacial in the purely stratigraphical sense of denoting any deposit between two tills, or its use as indicating a period of erosion between two tills, or its use on the evidence of high sea-levels.

The rapid development of pollen studies in the last twenty years has made wide correlations possible over the greater part of northern Europe. It is interesting to note, however, that few organic interglacial deposits occur in the Alps of certain date relative to the Alpine glacial stages, so correlation of glacial and interglacial stages in this area is not always clear.

The development of local Pleistocene successions which avoid the strait-jacket of the Alpine nomenclature has also resulted in advances in our knowledge of local stratigraphic sequences.

Two further advances in technique have also improved our knowledge of Pleistocene successions and hold out more promise for the future. These are dating by means of radioactive isotopes, both radiocarbon and potassium/argon dating, and palaeotemperature determinations. As we have seen in Chapter 9 potassium/argon dating has given a figure for the length of time occupied by the Pleistocene succession, and radiocarbon dating has given much detail to the Weichselian (last) glaciation and Flandrian sequences. Palaeotemperature determinations from ocean basin sediments promise to

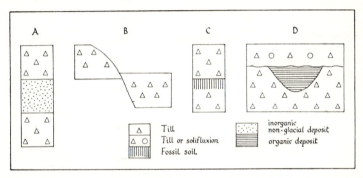

*Fig. 11.5* Four situations in which the term interglacial (or interstadial) has been used (West 1963).

a. Mid-glacial sands; no evidence of climate, only of ice recession. A 'stratigraphical' interglacial.

b. One till sheet separated from another by a period of dissection of the landscape. The erosional interval has been called interglacial.

c. Development of a soil on an older till, later sealed by deposition of a younger till. The soil type may give information on the climate of the non-glacial weathering phase. Such buried soils have been little used in British Pleistocene stratigraphy.

d. Deposition of organic deposits in a hollow in an older till during a non-glacial interval. Study of the fossils in the organic deposit gives much information on the flora, fauna and climate of the interval and can characterise it as interglacial or interstadial.

give a general scheme of climatic change during the Pleistocene which may eventually become the basis for a world-wide correlation of the Pleistocene succession.

At present, it may be said that the correlation of cold and temperate stages across Europe is far from satisfactory. The conventional correlations are shown in table 11.1. In particular the correlation of pre-Eemian interglacials across northern Europe is not clear, because of the problematical nature of the interval between the Saale/Warthe and Dnieper/Moscow[7] glacial advances. Secondly, the correlation of the Lower Pleistocene, i.e. what would be considered fifty years ago as 'pre glacial' or Pliocene, is uncertain because of the paucity of the evidence.

*Table 11.3* Subdivision of the Cainozoic in north-west Europe

| Geological time units | Era | Period | Epoch | Age |
|---|---|---|---|---|
| Stratigraphical units | | System | Series | Stage |
| **a.** *Present usage* | | | | |
| | | Quaternary | Holocene or Recent | Flandrian |
| | | | Pleistocene | Weichselian ↑ Pretiglian |
| | Cainozoic | Tertiary | Pliocene Miocene Oligocene Eocene Palaeocene | Reuverian |
| | Mesozoic | | | |
| **b.** *Suggested usage* | | | Pleistocene | Flandrian ↑ Pretiglian |
| | Cainozoic | (first period of Cainozoic) | Pliocene Miocene Oligocene Eocene Palaeocene | Reuverian |
| | Mesozoic | | | |

## Pliocene, Quaternary, Pleistocene, Holocene

According to present usage, the Pliocene is the final series of the Tertiary system, with the Pleistocene and Holocene series constituting the Quaternary system. The Tertiary and Quaternary together constitute the Cainozoic Era (table 11.3). However, the boundary between the Tertiary and Quaternary systems is not marked by such significant changes as characterise the older system boundaries, and it may therefore be better to consider the Tertiary and Quaternary as constituting together the first system of the Cainozoic era, as advocated by R. F. Flint.[2] The boundary between the Pleistocene and Holocene is no different in character to the boundaries between the preceding glacials and interglacials, and the Holocene would therefore be better considered as the most recent stage of the Pleistocene, rather than a separate series. The name Holocene should then be discarded and replaced by a stage name (Flandrian), and the name Pleistocene would revert to its first meaning, in which sense it is used in this book. These changes from present usage are shown in table 11.3.

Originally the name Pleistocene was coined by Lyell[8] in 1839 to include rocks with a molluscan fauna containing more than seventy per cent of living species; this included the post-Pliocene strata. But the term soon came to be synonymous with the Ice Age, thus implying that the Pleistocene was characterised by glacial climates. The boundary between the Pliocene and Pleistocene was formalised by a

*Table 11.4* Plio/Pleistocene boundary in Europe

(c, continental succession; m, marine succession)

|  | Italy (type area) | Netherlands (c) | East Anglia (m) |
|---|---|---|---|
| Pleistocene | Villafranchian (c) Calabrian (m) | Pretiglian | Red Crag |
| Pliocene | Astian (m) | Reuverian | Coralline Crag |

committee of the 18th International Geological Congress meeting in London in 1948.[6, 10]

They defined the boundary in a type area of marine sedimentation in Italy, as being at the base of the Calabrian stage or its supposed continental equivalent, the Villafranchian (table 11.4). The boundary is the horizon in the Italian Neogene succession where there is good palaeontological evidence for climatic deterioration, that is the appearance of cold-indicating Foraminifera and molluscs. This climatic deterioration has been used to mark the base of the Pleistocene else-where, as in the Netherlands, where there is a marked change of climate between the Reuverian stage of the Pliocene and the Pretiglian stage of the Pleistocene, as evidenced by great vegetational changes. The boundary also coincides in Europe with the spread of the genera *Elephas*, *Bos* and *Equus*, a spread previously considered to mark the base of the Pleistocene.

However, the criteria for the placing of the boundary even in the type area are disputed, and there is at present no possibility of good correlation of the type boundary with other horizons in other regions and in other environments of deposition.[3, 12]

### Subdivision of the Pleistocene

We now have to consider the methods by which subdivisions of the Pleistocene succession can be made. There are certain differences between the bases for subdivision in the Pleistocene and in older rocks. The time covered by the Pleistocene is, geologically speaking, relatively short, so that evolutionary changes found in older parts of the geological time scale are not so evident. But although short, the record of the rocks is known in great detail, so that we have preserved over the earth's surface synchronous deposits of many different environments, again a difference from the more incomplete record of the older rocks. This variety of environments of deposition is accompanied by a variety of geomorphological processes also recorded in the earth's landforms, the study of which also gives many clues to the succession of Pleistocene events.

The purpose of subdivision is twofold. First it is to split the succession into manageable units, and second it is to bring together by correlation the sequence of events and the units of the succession found in the many environments of Pleistocene time. The main difficulty of splitting the succession into units is that geological and climatic processes show continual gradual change, with few very abrupt changes. We have to decide on criteria which are at once objective and clearly expressed in the geological record, and these criteria will differ in different environments of sedimentation and landscape formation.

The ideal situation would be to find absolute age markers at all horizons in all environments, so that we could have a calendar of events divided say into 1000 year segments, giving complete correlations of sediments, processes and events over the earth's surface. The actual situation is that we have indications of absolute age (radiocarbon age) common in certain environments up to say 10,000 years ago and less common up to 60,000 years ago, and a few isotope-based dates in the middle and early part of the Pleistocene. Otherwise we have to rely for our subdivisions on the geological and geomorphological evidence for age and succession so that a series of manageable and objective units are obtained.

There are various methods of subdividing the stratigraphic succession and the time it represents.[1, 9]

The following types of subdivision may be mentioned:

*Units based on lithostratigraphy.* These units are subdivisions of the rock succession distinguished by their lithological characteristics.

*Units based on biostratigraphy.* These are subdivisions of the rock succession characterised by a particular content of fossils, e.g. pollen zones, mammalian faunal zones, foraminiferal zones in deep sea sediments. There are various types of zone: assemblage zone, characterised by a particular assemblage of species (e.g. a pollen zone); peak or acme zone, characterised by the exceptional abundance of a particular taxon.

*Units based on climatic change.* These are subdivisions of the succession representing inferred climatic episodes, e.g. glaciation, interglacial.

*Units of the rock succession,* thought to be of regional significance, which are related to type sections or areas, and characterised by a particular sequence of geological events. Both lithological and biostratigraphical evidence can contribute towards the definition of these units. For example, biostratigraphy leading to the definition of stages in the Pleistocene.

*Units based partly or wholly on geomorphology.* These are subdivisions of the Pleistocene resulting not wholly from the rock succession but from a consideration of the relation of constructional or erosional features to one another, e.g. a series of river terraces, or a series of marine levels reflecting eustatic changes of sea-level.

There are also the means of subdividing the rock succession provided by dating methods, already discussed in Chapter 9.

Table 11.5 gives the names of various categories used in subdividing the rock or fossil succession.

Because the Pleistocene is characterised by climatic change, and because it is probable that climatic fluctuation in the earth's atmosphere has governed the sequence of geological processes and events in different environments, it is usually thought that climatic change,

Q

*Table 11.5* Stratigraphical nomenclature

| | Basis for subdivision | | |
|---|---|---|---|
| | *Lithostratigraphical* | *Biostratigraphical* | *Standard stratigraphical* |
| subdivisions | group | zone | system |
| | formation | subzone | series |
| | member | zonule | stage |
| | bed | | substage |

as indicated by lithology, fossils and geomorphology, is a suitable basis for subdivision of the Pleistocene. Hence the climatic episode units (glaciation, interglacial, pluvial, interpluvial) mentioned above. But the climatic episodes are, except where extensive palaeotemperature records are found, based on interpretation of lithological, biostratigraphical and other lines of evidence, so that they are synthetic.

When the geological record of the Pleistocene is complete it will be seen how the succession of lithostratigraphical, biostratigraphical and other subdivisions mentioned above are related one to another. All types of subdivision are useful in that they will indicate a different facet of the sequence of events. Meanwhile, we must attempt to build up sequences in different areas which have a local validity and the most useful method of subdivision to fulfil the purposes of subdivision will vary from place to place, depending on the criteria available.

*Examples of subdivision*

We can now exemplify these principles by reference to particular areas and to particular environments of deposition.

*The Pleistocene sequence in north-west Europe.* The glacial/interglacial sequence in north-west Europe (table 11.1) was primarily based on the rock succession, tills and other glacial deposits alternating with non-glacial sediments such as peat. Thus the units of the subdivision were of a lithostratigraphical type.

The increased use of palaeobotanical data, especially that derived from pollen analysis, has given much detail of biostratigraphy, and a satisfactory series of units based on biostratigraphy has been used in the Netherlands (fig. 11.6) and the British Isles (table 11.6).

Fig. 11.6 Subdivisions of the Lower Pleistocene and Upper Pliocene in the Netherlands (Zagwijn 1960). The stages are based on biostratigraphical evidence (pollen diagrams).

*Table 11.6* Stages of the British Pleistocene

| | | | Stage | Climate | | |
|---|---|---|---|---|---|---|
| (Quaternary) | (Holocene) | | Flandrian | t | | |
| | Pleistocene | Upper | Weichselian | c | g | p |
| | | | Ipswichian | t | | |
| | | | Gippingian | c | g | p |
| | | Middle | Hoxnian | t | | |
| | | | Lowestoftian | c | g | p |
| | | | Cromerian | t | | |
| | | | Beestonian | c | | p |
| | | | Pastonian | t | | |
| | | Lower | Baventian | c | | p |
| | | | Antian | t | | |
| | | | Thurnian | c | | |
| | | | Ludhamian | t | | |

c, cold                           g, glacial deposits known
p, permafrost known               t, temperate

Briefly, the stages resulting from biostratigraphical evidence are alternating cold (sometimes glacial) and temperate stages, as indicated by biostratigraphy, the boundary between them being placed where the vegetation changes from an open sub-arctic park landscape to a wooded landscape with temperate trees, and vice-versa. These changes are recognised in pollen diagrams by changes in the tree/non-tree pollen ratio and the frequency of pollen of thermophilous trees.

This method of subdivision leads to the formulation of stages, climatically distinct. Whether these stages be termed time-stratigraphical or biostratigraphical or climatic is not so important. What is significant is that the stages and their boundaries can be determined objectively and have a practical use for formulating the local Pleistocene succession.

Similar biostratigraphical criteria can be used to define and limit interstadial intervals in the glacial stages. Such oscillations will be accompanied by the reappearance of forest, of a boreal type, not of the temperate type indicative of interglacials (table 11.2).

Clearly such a scheme of subdivision is only of local application. If we move away much in latitude, say, further north, the same pollen changes will not be synchronous as those further south. If we move in longitude to a more continental climate, the changes in tree/non-tree pollen ratio may reflect the change to a temperate steppe vegetation. Each region must clearly use its own criteria for boundaries, having regard to the overall climatic changes, presumably synchronous, which determine the regional fluctuations.

It is thus possible with the aid of pollen analysis to devise a system of objective units for our region, based on biostratigraphy. The major units in the Pleistocene will be stages and substages. The stages will be cold or temperate, glacial and interglacial respectively if glacial deposits are present. The substages will then be the subdivisions of the stages, e.g. the stadia and interstaidals of the glaciations or the major pollen zones of the cold or temperate stages.

There is also the question of the naming of stages and substages. This should be done on the type site system so that the fundamental evidence for the subdivisions is clear. Each cold, temperate and interstadial phase should have its own type site where the stratigraphical evidence is clear. There will then be the least confusion resulting from nomenclatorial difficulties. It will produce a number of new names, based on local sequences, but eventually when certain correlations emerge, regional names can replace more local ones.

There remains the question of the division of the Pleistocene into Upper, Middle and Lower. The placings of the divisions in table 11.6 are those used in north-west Europe. The Lower/Middle boundary is placed at the beginning of the first temperate period (the Pastonian) showing an absence of the so-called Tertiary relic plants, e.g. *Tsuga, Pterocarya*. The Middle/Upper boundary is placed at the end of the Hoxnian (temperate) stage.

*The Pleistocene sequence in the north American plain.* The lithostratigraphical basis of glacial and non-glacial deposits is used as a basis for division into stages (table 11.1). However, not much detail is known of the sequences within non-glacial stages and the upper and lower boundaries of the stages are not precisely fixed. Ancient soil horizons provide key evidence for non-glacial conditions between ice advances and so-called soil-stratigraphical units form an important component of the classification of the Pleistocene succession.

*Loess sequences in central Europe.* Loess sequences play an important part in determining the Pleistocene succession in periglacial areas. They are sensitive to climatic change, loess forming during periods of more rigorous climate and soils forming on cessation of loess formation in more temperate climates. The classification of such sequences is based on the sediments, including soils and on bio-stratigraphical evidence from non-marine molluscs. Both are used to formulate climatic episodes. The sequence of climatic episodes, together with radiocarbon and archaeological evidence is the basis for correlation with the glacial/interglacial sequence to the north. The respective climatic (and therefore sedimentary) provinces are very different and direct geological correlations on the basis of super-position are not possible.

*Stratigraphy of cave deposits and of periglacial sequences.* These are basically lithostratigraphical, as the successions concern the sequence of stalagmite, cave breccias and soils in the case of cave deposits, and sequences of solifluction, aeolian deposits, involutions, perma-frost structures and soils in the case of periglacial sequences. Climatic episodes are inferred from the sequences, and it is these which form the basis for correlations. Local factors of slope, hydrology, aspect and so on may affect the sequences, so that climatic interpretation may be difficult. The definition of lithostratigraphical units will not be so difficult, and the definition of major climatic stages should be clear. Substages may be far more difficult to define.

*Stratigraphy of limnic sediments.* Biostratigraphical evidence from pollen analyses will provide evidence for the definition of assemblage zones. The regional significance of such zones will appear after the detailed regional studies which allow local variants to be isolated from the regional succession. Lithostratigraphical successions are separate, but their evidence of climatic change, together with that from biostratigraphy, should be used to formulate climatic episode units.

*Sea-level sequences and terrace sequences.* Because of the incomplete record of geological events given by these sequences, they will not form a series of units filling Pleistocene time, as may sequences of a lithostratigraphical type. Major episodes of sea-level standstill or of terrace aggradation or of marine or fluvial erosion will be recorded. Whether these episodes will have a climatic significance will depend on the lithology of the sediments and on the faunas and floras associ-ated with them or on the theory that high and low sea-levels have climatic significance.

The correlation of these episodes with those of the general climatic sequence known from lithostratigraphical and biostratigraphical evidence may be very difficult, so that these geomorphologically-based episodes often form an independent sequence of events, whose exact relation with the sequence provided by other evidence is not clear.

*Faunal zones.* These are based on successions of faunas, each zone having a characteristic fauna. The zones so defined may cover several climatic stages, and so form an independent view-point of the Pleistocene succession.

*Measured ages or climatic characters.* A basic succession of radio-carbon years, with units of 100s or 1000s of years forms a distinct type of classification of Pleistocene time, and will be an important scale for the time covered by this method of dating. Subdivisions based on temperature changes, such as the fluctuations seen in cores of ocean sediments (fig. 10.2) may also be used to define climatic subdivisions, but the evidence for the relation of these subdivisions to continental climatic subdivisions is not so far advanced as to allow correlations beyond the last interglacial.

## REFERENCES

1 CODE OF STRATIGRAPHIC NOMENCLATURE (1961). *Bull. Amer. Assoc. Petrol. Geologists*, **45**, 645–65.

2 FLINT, R. F. 1957. *Glacial and Pleistocene geology*. New York: Wiley.

3 FLINT, R. F. 1965. 'The Pliocene-Pleistocene boundary', Spec. Papers Geol. Soc. America, No. 84, *International Studies on the Quaternary*, 497–533.

4 GEIKIE, J. 1895. 'The classification of European glacial deposits', *J. Geol.*, **3**, 241–70.

5 JESSEN, K. and MILTHERS, V. 1928. 'Stratigraphical and palaeontological studies of interglacial freshwater deposits in Jutland and north-west Germany', *Danm. Geol. Unders.*, II Raekke, No. 48.

6 KING, W. B. R. and OAKLEY, K. P. 1949. 'Definition of the Pliocene/Pleistocene boundary', *Nature*, **163**, 186–7.

7 KRASNOV, I. I. 1965. 'Regional unified and correlative stratigraphic scheme for the Quaternary of European U.S.S.R.', Spec. Papers Geol. Soc. America, No. 84, *International Studies of the Quaternary*, 247–71.

8 LYELL, C. 1839. 'On the relative ages of the Tertiary deposits commonly called "Crag" in the counties of Norfolk and Suffolk', *Mag. Nat. Hist.*, **3**, (N.S.), 313–30.

9 MILLER, T. G. 1965. 'Time in stratigraphy', *Palaeontology*, **8**, 111–31.

10 OAKLEY, K. P. 1949. International Geological Congress XVIIIth

Session, Great Britain, 1948. Proceedings of Sectional Meetings. Section H. 'Plio-Pleistocene boundary', *Geol. Mag.*, **86,** 18–21.

11 PENCK, A. and BRÜCKNER, E. 1909. *Die Alpen im Eiszeitalter*. Leipzig: Tauchnitz.

12 RUGGIERI, G. 1965. 'A contribution to the stratigraphy of the marine lower Quaternary sequence in Italy', Spec. Papers Geol. Soc. America, No. 84, *International Studies on the Quaternary*, 142–52.

13 WEST, R. G. 1963. 'Problems of the British Quaternary', *Proc. Geol. Assoc. London*, **74,** 147–86.

14 WRIGHT, W. B. 1937. *The Quaternary Ice Age*. 2nd ed. London: Macmillan.

15 WOLDSTEDT, P. 1958. *Das Eiszeitalter*. Bd II. Stuttgart: Enke.

16 ZAGWIJN, W. H. 1960. 'Aspects of the Pliocene and early Pleistocene vegetation in the Netherlands', *Meded. Geol. Stichting*, Serie C. III 1, no. 5.

# CHAPTER 12

# THE PLEISTOCENE OF THE
# BRITISH ISLES

THIS chapter gives a general introduction to the Pleistocene stratigraphy of the British Isles. There is a large literature on the subject; no single up-to-date book covers the field, but Wright's classic textbook on the Quaternary Ice Age[97] gives an extensive description of the Pleistocene history of the British Isles, and a shorter, more recent account has been given by the author.[85] A useful list of names which have been used in British Pleistocene stratigraphy has been published in the International Stratigraphical Lexicon series.[38] The bibliography to this chapter is not intended to be completely comprehensive, but to give access to the recent literature on the subject concerned.

Multiple glaciation of the British Isles resulted in the formation of the great drift sheets which cover much of the lowland area (fig. 12.1) except for southern Britain and small parts of southern Ireland. From the main centres of glaciation, ice spread in the directions shown in fig. 12.2. In the periglacial areas extensive spreads of solifluction deposits were formed, and, to the south and east, loess. During permafrost times ice-wedge polygon networks were formed. Terrace sands and gravels were deposited in the drainage-ways leading from the ice fronts, and deep channels were cut in valleys as a result of low sea-levels. During the warmer temperate stages between the glaciations, rivers deposited alluvium under conditions of rising sea-level, and forest reoccupied the land. Apart from the formation of terrace deposits, the temperate stages were probably rather quiet times in terms of landscape evolution, in contrast to the erosional and depositional processes accompanying glaciation, lowered sea-levels, periglacial climates, and incomplete vegetation cover.

The Pleistocene also covers a time of mainly marine deposition in basins round the edge of the North Sea in south-east Britain. The changing climate is recorded in these deposits not by glacial and interglacial deposits, but by faunal and vegetational changes. The deposits are often called 'preglacial', as they are found below the first true till, but their Pleistocene age is attested by their fauna and flora.

## A BRIEF HISTORY OF INVESTIGATION[42]

The diluvial theory of the origin of the drift was championed by Buckland in his Reliquae Diluvianae of 1823. He was later converted to the glacial theory by Agassiz and this theory was, later in the

*Fig. 12.1* Pleistocene drifts in the British Isles (after *Atlas of Britain* (Clarendon Press) and Geikie's Geological Map of Ireland (Bartholomew)).

century, accepted by most other geologists. Edward Forbes in 1846 gave detailed consideration to the effect of the northern drift ice on the distribution of plants and animals. About this time was started a long series of stratigraphical studies of the drift by officers of the Geological Survey and others. Joshua Trimmer recognised two tills in the cliff sections on the East Anglian coast, and James Geikie furthered the principle of polyglacialism by his recognition of four

*Fig. 12.2* The main Pleistocene ice streams of the British Isles, and the divisions used in the description of regional stratigraphy.

glaciations. By the end of the nineteenth century, much of our present knowledge of the drift sequence was obtained.

The origin of man in relation to the glacial period became an important point of discussion from the late eighteen-fifties onwards. There was dispute on the age of man—post-glacial or interglacial, and there was great interest in the relation of palaeolithic implements to the drift sequence. The archaeological side of the matter became rather confused towards the end of the century, with the fashion for pushing back the finding of artefacts to the older drift deposits; for example, the Kent eoliths described by Benjamin Harrison and his postulation of 'Plateau Man'.

The main difficulties of the interpretation of Pleistocene stratigraphy in the first half of this century were the lack of any reliable means of effecting correlations between distant drift sequences, and too facile correlation with the Alpine sequence. Often, at least in the south and east of Britain, correlations were based on artefacts, and a relative chronology based on them was widely mentioned.[8]

Detailed pollen-analytical studies of the Flandrian started to be made in the nineteen-thirties and by the end of that decade, the main outlines of climatic and vegetational history of this stage were known. The introduction of radiocarbon dating in the early nineteen-fifties put this climatic and vegetational history on a firm chronological basis. In the middle nineteen-fifties the main characters of the successive interglacials became clearer, largely as a result of pollen-analytical studies, and a firm basis for the correlation of till sheets was found. This also provided a scale of time to which palaeolithic cultures could be related.

A basis for a classification of the British Pleistocene was put forward in 1963,[84] and it is this classification which will be used in our description of the Pleistocene of the British Isles. Of course, this is only a provisional classification, and new evidence will lead to complication, but its use eases the task of giving order to a multitude of facts.

### CLASSIFICATION AND LOWER LIMIT OF THE PLEISTOCENE

As seen in figs. 11.3 and 12.2, the glaciation of the British Isles proceeded independently from that of continental north-west Europe, and we therefore require a separate classification of our deposits, not one based on continental stratigraphy. Believing that the major climatic changes in the whole of north-west Europe were more or less synchronous, even if differing in expression according to latitude and longitude, it follows that there should be eventually a close correlation between the sequence in the British Isles and that on the continent. But such correlation is not yet clear, again a reason for a separate classification.

Although the Pleistocene is associated strongly with glaciation and glacial deposits, a large part of the early Pleistocene in the British Isles shows no direct traces of glaciation. This 'preglacial' Pleistocene consists of marine, estuarine and, rarely, freshwater deposits, and it includes all the Crag deposits in East Anglia later than the Coralline Crag (table 12.1). The criteria used to determine this position of the Pliocene-Pleistocene boundary[5] are the presence of a stratigraphical break between the Red and Coralline Crags, a marked increase in the proportion of northern forms of marine molluscs and the first occurrence of Lower Pleistocene molluscs of northern aspect (both indicative of a cooling in climate), and, finally, the first arrival, in the Red Crag, of elephant and horse. As described in the previous chapter, the 'type' section for the Pliocene-Pleistocene boundary in Europe is in southern Italy where the fauna of a sequence of marine deposits shows a deterioration of climate and this is taken as indicating the Pliocene-Pleistocene boundary. The Coralline—Red Crag cooling gives similar evidence for the boundary in East Anglia.

This position of the Pliocene-Pleistocene boundary has come to be accepted in the last twenty years. At the time of the detailed studies of the British Early Pleistocene, from 40 to 100 years ago, the Pleistocene was synonymous with the glacial period, so that all our pre-glacial Pleistocene was included in the Pliocene.[52]

The division of the British Pleistocene succession into stages, on the basis of principles already discussed in Chapter 11, is shown in table 11.6. Flandrian is used as a stage name in place of Holocene, following the usage of naming temperate stages after their characteristic marine transgression. The divisions into Lower (Early), Middle and Upper (Late) Pleistocene are based on current usage in north-west Europe.

The sequence of Pleistocene stages is based on the East Anglian biostratigraphical and lithological evidence. In the Midlands too there is considerable biostratigraphical evidence, forming a reasonably secure basis for correlations with the East Anglian sequence of stages. Of Ireland, the same can be said. When we extend our survey to other areas, however, there is a paucity of biostratigraphical evidence, and this leaves the lithological and geomorphological evidence as the mainstay for correlation of the succession. In Wales, north and north-east England, and Scotland, till sequences are known, but few biogenic temperate deposits are known apart from those of the Flandrian. The correlation of the till sheets is problematical, especially the question of how many are of Weichselian age, for if that were known, then tills of the earlier glacial stages might be tentatively identified and correlated.

The identification of the limits of the Weichselian glacial advances, and the number of them are therefore of great importance. But there has been and still is much discussion over both these points.[47] Interstadial biogenic deposits are few and even fewer have been dated by radiocarbon assay. Fig. 12.3 shows limits of the Weichselian ice (depositing the so-called Newer Drift) which have been suggested by various authors. An important contribution towards Weichselian

*Fig. 12.3* Limits of the main glacial advances and of Weichselian retreat stages in Britain.

stratigraphy will be made from studies of the periglacial successions, but this has hardly been started.

Fig. 12.3 also shows the limit thought to have been reached by the older glacial advances. Again there is much discussion of the limits of these older glaciations and their correlation across the country.

In the following brief account of the Pleistocene succession in the various regions of the British Isles, we will start with the classic area of East Anglia, where the Pleistocene sequence is most complete, and where there is an abundance of biostratigraphical evidence concerning Lower, Middle and Upper Pleistocene deposits. In the other glaciated areas we will be mainly dealing with the Middle and Upper Pleistocene, and, as already mentioned, correlation with East Anglia may or may not be possible. Finally, it will be necessary to consider again general topics affecting the whole region, such as periglacial phenomena, changes of relative land/sea-level, dating, and the Late Weichselian and Flandrian.

## EAST ANGLIA

### The 'preglacial' succession

The west–east section in fig. 12.4 shows the general disposition of the 'preglacial' and 'glacial' parts of the Pleistocene succession in East Anglia. We first have to consider the Lower Pleistocene Crag deposits formed in a shallow basin of deposition in the east of the area. The contours of this basin and the Crag in it are shown in fig. 12.5.

*Fig. 12.4* Diagrammatic E–W composite section through the Pleistocene of East Anglia. 1, Ludhamian Crag; 2, Thurnian Crag; 3, Antian Crag; 4, Baventian sand and silt; 5, Pastonian estuarine silts; 6, Beestonian sands and gravels; 7, Cromerian freshwater muds; 8, Cromerian estuarine silts and gravels; 9, Early Lowestoftian sands and silts; 10, Cromer till; 11, Corton sands; 12, Lowestoft till; 13, Hoxnian clay-muds; 14, Gippingian gravels; 15, Ipswichian muds; 16, Weichselian terrace sands and gravels; 17, Flandrian alluvium of Fenlands, 17a Lower peat, 17b Fen clay (estuarine), 17c Upper peat, 17d Romano-British silt.

*Fig. 12.5* Contours of the base of the Crag (the grid refers to the New Series 1″ geological maps). By permission of the Institute of Geological Sciences; from internal report *The hydrology of the Pleistocene deposits of East Anglia* by J. H. Price and J. Tuson, and figure 7, Wartime Pamphlet 20, Pt X, *Water supply from underground sources of Cambridge–Ipswich district*, by A. W. Woodland.

The classic view of the Crag succession filling the basin was enunciated by Harmer[29] (table 12.1). This succession is largely founded on faunal rather than stratigraphical evidence, and this faunal evidence is viewed in the light of two assumptions, namely, that the proportion of northern marine molluscs increased throughout the Lower Pleistocene and the proportion of 'extinct' molluscs decreased during the same period. Both these assumptions may be questioned; the first in view of the fact that several Lower Pleistocene climatic fluctuations are known to have occurred, the second in view of the possibility that 'extinct' species may have returned with a change in climate.

The stages of the Lower Pleistocene shown in table 11.6 are based on pollen-analytical studies of a deep borehole in the Crag at Ludham,[82] and are supported by climatic evidence given by foraminiferal studies at the same locality.[23] Similar evidence from other boreholes supports this succession of stages. Fig. 12.6 shows a north–south section through the Crag basin. The relation between the

*Table 12.1* The Pleistocene Crag Succession of Harmer (1902)

| Harmer's stages | Lithological and Palaeontological Horizons |
| --- | --- |
| CROMERIAN | Cromer and Kessingland Forest Bed, zone of *Elephas meridionalis* |
| ICENIAN | Weybourne and Belaugh Crag, zone of *Macoma balthica* Chillesford Beds, zone of *Leda oblongoides* Norwich Crag: Upper division, zone of *Astarte borealis* Lower division, zone of *Mactra subtruncata* (in other Crag classifications by Harmer the Norwich Crag remained undivided in one zone of *Astarte borealis*) |
| BUTLEYAN | Butley and Bawdsey Crag, zone of *Cardium groenlandicum* |
| NEWBOURNIAN | Newbourne and Sutton Crag, zone of *Mactra constricta* |
| WALTONIAN | Essex Crag: Oakley horizon, zone of *Mactra obtruncata* Walton horizon, zone of *Neptunea contraria* |
| PLIOCENE | Coralline Crag |

R

*Fig. 12.6* Crag distribution in East Anglia (after Harmer) (the map includes areas where Crag is concealed by drift), and north–south section through the Crag basin in East Anglia. Letters on the left of the stratigraphical columns show Harmer's naming of the deposits: R(B), Butleyan Red Crag; N, Norwich Crag; C, Chillesford Clay and Sand; W, Weybourne Crag. Letters on the right of the stratigraphical columns show stages and correlations based on analyses of pollen and Foraminifera: L, Ludhamian; T, Thurnian; A, Antian; B, Baventian; P, Pastonian; Be, Beestonian; Cr, Cromerian.

classic Crag divisions and the stages at present known are shown on the figure. The critical areas are where the Crag succession meets the Cromer Forest Bed Series[89] at the north margin of the basin and where it meets the Red Crag to the south. The former relation is shown in fig. 12.7, but the latter relation is not very clear, and the age of the Red Crag in relation to the Lower Pleistocene stages is not certain.

The variation in depth of the Pastonian marine and estuarine deposits (fig. 12.6), as well as the basal Crag contours (fig. 12.5)

*Fig. 12.7* Sketch section at West Runton, about 450 m long and 7 m depth. a, Weybourne Crag (Beestonian/Pastonian); b, estuarine silts (Pastonian) pierced by ice-wedge cast of Beestonian age; c, sands and gravels, and a freshwater silt with arctic plants (d) (Beestonian); e, marl (Late Beestonian); f, muds and peats (Cromerian); g, weathered horizon (Cromerian 'soil'); h, estuarine silts and sands (Cromerian transgression deposits), pierced by ice-wedge cast of Early Lowestoftian age; i, Cromer Till (Lowestoftian). Chalk at base.

suggest tectonic movement in East Anglia during or later than the Lower Pleistocene, with relative uplift in the Chillesford and Southwold area and downwarping in the Ludham area. However, much more study of the Crag series is required before these tectonic movements can be reconstructed in any detail.

The Pleistocene preglacial stages may be briefly described as follows:

*Ludhamian.* Shelly marine sands, 25 m thick at Ludham, with a temperate fauna and flora, the latter with a characteristic north American and eastern Asia genus *Tsuga*, the hemlock spruce.

*Thurnian.* Marine (or estuarine) silty clays, 7 m thick at Ludham, with a foraminiferal fauna and a flora both indicating cool conditions. Deposits related to this stage are known from Ludham and Southwold.

*Antian.* Shelly marine sands, 3 m thick at Ludham with a temperate foraminiferal and mollusc fauna, and temperate flora, are known from Ludham and Easton Bavents. The flora again includes *Tsuga*.

*Baventian.* Marine (or estuarine) silty clays, 8 m thick at Ludham, with a cool flora and fauna, are known at Ludham, Easton Bavents, South Cove, Aldeby, and on the Norfolk coast.

*Pastonian.* Marine (or estuarine) silts, a few metres thick, with a temperate flora, but without *Tsuga*, are known from the Norfolk coast and inland at Bungay; beach gravels probably of this stage are also known (Westleton Beds). Possibly the marine faunas of the Norwich Crag belong partly to this stage.

*Beestonian.* Arctic freshwater plant beds and evidence of permafrost are found in sands and gravels a few metres thick overlying the Pastonian silts in the Norfolk coast.

*Cromerian.* Temperate freshwater muds (plate 15a), and, upon them, estuarine and beach deposits of a marine transgression, overlie the Beestonian sands and gravels on the Norfolk coast. They are up to 5 m thick, and are overlain by arctic plant beds and sands with evidence of permafrost conditions, both of these belonging to the earliest glacial stage of East Anglia, the Lowestoftian.

Table 12.2 shows the relation between these 'preglacial' stages and the formations included in them. The changes of relative land/sea-level implied by this succession is discussed later.

*The glacial/interglacial succession*[83]

Deposits of three glacial and three non-glacial temperate stages are known in East Anglia, with the relations as shown in table 12.2 and fig. 12.4. The locations of important sites are shown in fig. 12.8. The till sequence is best known in Suffolk, and is more confused in north-east Norfolk where the contorted glacial deposits (plate 15b) seen in the coast section remain to be studied in detail. The correlation of the till sequence about to be described with that of the three tills (Hanningfield, Springfield and Malden Tills) described in Essex[13] is also not yet clear. These stages are briefly as follows:

*Lowestoftian.*[2, 86] The North Sea Drift, including the Cromer Till, a blue-grey silty till and the Norwich Brickearth, a red silty till,

## Table 12.2 Pleistocene succession in East Anglia

| | |
|---|---|
| Flandrian | lake deposits, peat, alluvium, estuarine clays, blown sands |
| Weichselian Late | lake deposits of zones I, II and III |
|     Middle and Early | Intermediate and Low Terraces of the Cam<br>Fenland river gravels<br>March gravels<br>Hunstanton Till |
| Ipswichian | Interglacial deposits at Cambridge, Bobbitshole, Stutton, Wretton. High Terrace of the Cam |
| Gippingian | Tjaele gravels<br>Gipping Till, Cannonshot gravels of north Norfolk, kames and outwash plains |
| Hoxnian | Interglacial deposits at Hoxne, Marks Tey, Clacton (freshwater and marine), Nar Valley (freshwater and marine) |
| Lowestoftian | Lowestoft Till<br>Corton Beds (glaciomarine?)<br>Cromer Till, Norwich Brickearth<br>Upper Arctic Freshwater Bed of Cromer Forest Bed Series |
| Cromerian | estuarine silts<br>freshwater peat } of Cromer Forest Bed Series |
| Beestonian | sands and gravels<br>Lower Arctic Freshwater Bed } of Cromer Forest Bed Series |
| Pastonian | estuarine silts, freshwater peat of Cromer Forest Bed Series, Norwich Crag in part, Weybourne Crag in part, Westleton Beds |
| Baventian | Easton Bavents silt and sand, Weybourne Crag in part |
| Antian | shelly sand and gravel, Norwich Crag in part |
| Thurnian | shelly sand and silt (at depth) |
| Ludhamian | shelly sand and gravel (at depth) |

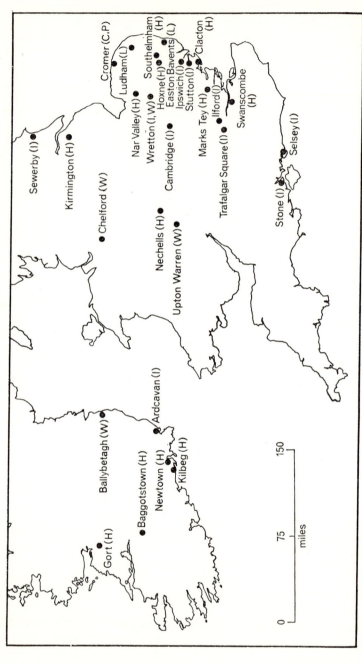

*Fig. 12.8* Important Pleistocene fossiliferous sites. L, Lower Pleistocene; P, Pastonian; C, Cromerian; H, Hoxnian; I, Ipswichian; W, Weichselian.

overlies the Cromerian on the Norfolk and Suffolk coasts. The ice advance, Cromer Advance (fig. 12.9), which deposited these tills came from the north-west. The exact relation between the two tills is uncertain, but since their stone orientation and stratigraphical positions are similar, they are ascribed to the same ice advance; the Norwich Brickearth is probably a weathered version of the Cromer Till. The Scandinavian erratics in the North Sea Drift have been taken to suggest an ice advance from the north over the North Sea, hence the

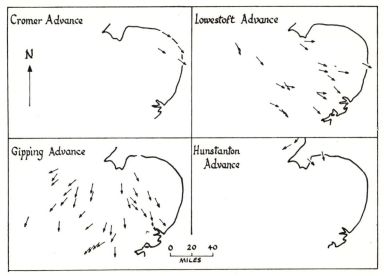

*Fig. 12.9* Directions of four ice advances in East Anglia and the east Midlands, based on stone orientation measurements (West 1963).

name. But possibly these erratics are derived from a secondary source in north-east England and have not travelled directly from Norway, and their presence does not controvert other evidence of a derivation in Norfolk from the north-west. The drifts of this early ice advance are overlain on the east coast by the Corton Beds, sands which contain a marine mollusc fauna. This fauna affords uncertain evidence of climatic conditions. Some consider it to be secondary, others contemporaneous, others both.[83] As there is no clear evidence of temperate climatic conditions, the sands probably represent an interval of deglaciation between two ice advances of the same major glaciation. It is possible that the lower part of the Corton Beds have an *in situ* marine fauna, deposited on the retreat of the North Sea Drift ice, while the upper part is related to the advance of the

Lowestoft ice. The level reached by the Corton Beds, 10 to 20 m O.D., suggests considerable ponding-up of water in this area (perhaps over the southern North Sea basin) during the lapse of time between the two ice advances. The ice advance which laid down the Lowestoft Till (Lowestoft Advance, fig. 12.9) moved east across Norfolk and Suffolk and deposited a blue-grey clay-rich till with Chalk and Jurassic erratics, the so-called Chalky-Jurassic Boulder Clay. To the north of Norfolk the till is far more chalky (Marly Drift).

A number of buried channels, the deepest lying at 106 m below O.D., are known beneath or in tills of Lowestoft age. They appear to be channels gouged subglacially during this ice advance.

*Hoxnian.*[80] Many lacustrine deposits up to 20 m thick, with a temperate fauna and flora and overlying the Lowestoft Till, are known in Norfolk, Suffolk and Essex. The type site for this temperate stage is at Hoxne, Suffolk, where an extensive series of lacustrine sediments covering a large part of this non-glacial time are preserved (fig. 12.10). Marine and estuarine sediments of the latter part of this stage are known at Clacton, Essex and in the Nar Valley, Norfolk.[66]

*Gippingian.*[2, 86] During this glacial stage (Gipping Advance, fig. 12.9), ice moved southwards over East Anglia, and deposited till of a paler and more chalky type than the Lowestoft Till. This Gipping Till is characterised by the presence of igneous erratics derived from the north of England. The area of extension of the Gipping Advance is problematical, and there are possibly interstadial deposits within this glacial stage, e.g. the lacustrine deposits at Mildenhall in Suffolk.[56] The morainic features found on the north coast of Norfolk near Holt, including outwash plains, kames and crevasse-fillings,[60] belong to a retreat episode of this glacial stage, as do tjaele gravels in the Cam Valley.[61]

*Ipswichian.*[81] A further series of temperate lacustrine or fluviatile deposits, up to 5 to 10 m thick, occur in the present-day valley systems, and are younger than the Gipping Till. They belong to the Ipswichian temperate stage, with the type site near Ipswich. Brackish deposits of this stage are known at Wretton, Norfolk.

*Weichselian.* The Ipswichian deposits are overlain by terrace or solifluction deposits of the Weichselian glacial stage, during which ice reached down to the north Norfolk coast and there deposited a red-brown till, the Hunstanton Till (Hunstanton Advance, fig. 12.9). This till is very similar to the upper (Hessle) till of the glacial sequence in east Lincolnshire and Holderness. It is associated with a few fresh landforms, such as the esker in Hunstanton Park. The March gravels of the Fenland, with a mainly marine fauna, may also be associated with marginal glacial action of the Weichselian.

*Flandrian.* Biogenic infillings of closed depressions (meres) and the freshwater and estuarine sequences of the Fenland basin[24] and Broadland[36] are of Flandrian age. In the last two there is a lower Flandrian freshwater peat, a middle Flandrian estuarine silt or clay, and an upper Flandrian freshwater peat, overlain by estuarine silts.

## Landform development

The landforms developed on the glacial deposits are generally subdued with few signs of end-moraine features. A few drainageways are known, such as the Little Ouse-Waveney Gap, of Gippingian or Weichselian age. As indicated in fig. 12.4, the Hoxnian temperate deposits are found in places isolated from the present valley systems, in strong contrast to the positions in valleys of the Ipswichian deposits. The landforms therefore took on their present aspect some time late in the Gippingian glacial stage. The terrace system of the Cam, the best known terrace system in East Anglia,[61] contains a high terrace, partly of Ipswichian deposits, and intermediate and low terraces of Weichselian age. Sections in the last two often show ice-wedge casts (plate 14a).

### THE MIDLANDS[74]

In the Midlands there is a substantial record of the Middle and Upper Pleistocene (table 12.3). Ice advances of the three glacial stages extended into the area, and their drainage was associated with terrace systems of the three main rivers, the Trent, Severn and Thames. The drifts of the two older glacial stages are found on the higher uplands, while the Weichselian glacial deposits are confined to the west Midlands lowlands. There is much dispute over the limits of the Weichselian ice, and the sediments originating from it, while the sequence of the older drifts appears better established. This older drift includes deposits of two glacial stages, which are correlated to the Lowestoftian and Gippingian glaciations of East Anglia. The link between the two areas is provided by temperate biogenic deposits at Nechells, Birmingham (fig. 12.10), and the till sheet of the Gipping ice advance, which, as the Eastern Drift or Midlands Chalky Boulder Clay, stretched into the heart of the Midlands.

Ice advanced into the Midlands from three main sources, each resulting drift type having its characteristic erratic suite. The Welsh drift contains Uriconian volcanic rocks, the eastern drift Mesozoic

Table 12.3 Pleistocene succession in the Midlands

| | | | | Avon Terraces | Ht. above alluvium, feet |
|---|---|---|---|---|---|
| Flandrian | | lake deposits, peat, alluvium | | | |
| Weichselian | Late | lake deposits of zones I, II and III | | | |
| | Middle and Early | Llay Readvance<br>Welsh Readvance<br>Main Irish Sea glaciation (Bar Hill-Wrexham moraine)<br>'Upton Warren interstadial complex'<br>Chelford Mud | Worcester Terrace<br>Main Terrace | Avon Terrace 1<br>Avon Terrace 2 | 10<br>30–40 |
| Ipswichian | | | Kidderminster Terrace | Avon Terrace 3<br>Avon Terrace 4 | 40–50<br>80–90 |
| Gippingian | | Moreton (Eastern) Drift, 2nd Welsh glaciation and Older Irish Sea glaciation | Bushley Green Terrace | Avon Terrace 5 | 140–150 |
| | | | Severn Terraces | Avon Terraces | Ht. above alluvium, feet |
| Hoxnian | | Nechells interglacial deposits | | | |
| Lowestoftian | | Bubbenhall Clay, 1st Welsh glaciation, Northern drift of Oxford region | | | |

rocks, and the northern or Irish Sea drift marine molluscs derived
from Irish Sea sediments and rocks from the Lake District and
Southern Uplands of Scotland. Judging from the present distribution
of these drift-types, during the two older glaciations the Welsh and
eastern ice streams were important, while in the youngest the Irish
Sea Ice was predominant.

*Fig. 12.10* Middle Pleistocene successions. a, at Hoxne, Suffolk (West
1956); b, north Birmingham (Kelly 1964).

The oldest glacial deposits[54] (First Welsh Glaciation) are thin Welsh drifts in the lower parts of the Severn river system, and northern drifts in the Coventry region, formed during ice advances from the west and the north. Of the same age may be the northern (plateau) drift of the Oxford region.[1] The succeeding temperate stage is recorded by peaty silts in Birmingham[32] which lie below gravels and tills correlated with the Gippingian glacial stage (fig. 12.10). Their stratigraphical position and vegetational history point to their

*Fig. 12.11* The Gipping Glaciation in the Midlands. Lake Harrison at its maximum stage is shaded. B, Birmingham; C, Coventry; G, Gloucester; L, Leicester; S, Stratford. 1, eastern ice margin at Lake Harrison maximum; 2, later stage of the eastern ice; 3, northern ice; 4, Severn Valley ice; 5, Moreton Moraine; 6, Lake Harrison overflows.

Hoxnian age. There is also an important erosional interval between the older glacial deposits and those correlated with the Gipping.

During this second glacial stage (Second Welsh Glaciation, Main Eastern Glaciation) three ice streams entered the Midlands as shown in fig. 12.11. The advance of the ice impounded a large proglacial lake in a 'proto-Trent' valley wending north-east;[54] this lake, named Lake Harrison, was at its maximum size 56 miles long and reached a height of 125 m O.D. The lake was eventually overridden by eastern ice, associated with a moraine at Moreton-in-the-Marsh. Overflows occurred from the lake into the upper Thames system,[3] and the link between the glacial sequence and the upper Thames terraces is given by the carriage of northern erratics (Bunter pebbles and flints), appearing in quantity in the Wolvercote Terrace of the Evenlode and Cherwell rivers. On the retreat of the eastern ice, additional stages of Lake Harrison developed, and on retreat of the western ice, the lake was drained into the Severn, and rapid erosion of the lake deposits ensued. The present Warwickshire Avon was thereby initiated.

The terrace systems of the Trent,[50, 68] Severn[92] and Avon began to form on the retreat of the ice. These terrace systems in outline divide into high terraces correlated with the glacial retreat, middle terraces with a warm fauna, probably Ipswichian in age, and low terraces of Weichselian age. Table 12.3 gives the succession of terraces in the Avon and Severn valleys.

The Midlands area is a critical one for Weichselian stratigraphy and the margin for this glacial stage is a subject of controversy. Meltwaters escaped east over the Pennine watershed and south through the Shropshire Hills, notably via the Ironbridge Gorge. Several proglacial lake systems, marginal drainage features and retreat stages of the Weichselian ice have been described from the Cheshire Plain.[46, 49] There is much discussion over the Weichselian stratigraphy of the region. Some suppose the existence of two tills separated by middle sands; from these middle sands at Chelford there is a radiocarbon date of 60,800 B.P. years of wood associated with a thin peat horizon.[57] This non-glacial interval, the Chelford interstadial, is an important feature of Weichselian stratigraphy in Britain. Others suppose a more complex sequence. For example, an early Main Irish Sea Advance extending far south, then the Ellesmere Readvance, then the Llay Readvance (fig. 12.3).[46] Yet others have supposed the Ellesmere moraine to be the margin of the Weichselian, and there is radiocarbon evidence to suggest an age bracket of 10,000–28,000 years B.P. for the time of its formation.[4] There is also the question of the relation of the Welsh ice to the main Irish Sea ice. The so-called Welsh Readvance may be of the same age or later than the Main Irish Sea Advance. Apart from these stratigraphical questions a number of climatic oscillations have been adduced from studies of floras and insect faunas in the west Midlands, and there are radiocarbon dates from many of these deposits. Fig. 12.12 shows a tentative synthesis of the course of Weichselian climatic change in north-west Europe and the position of various faunas or floras on the climatic curve.[15]

Local solifluction (tjaele) gravels and sands of the Severn and Avon

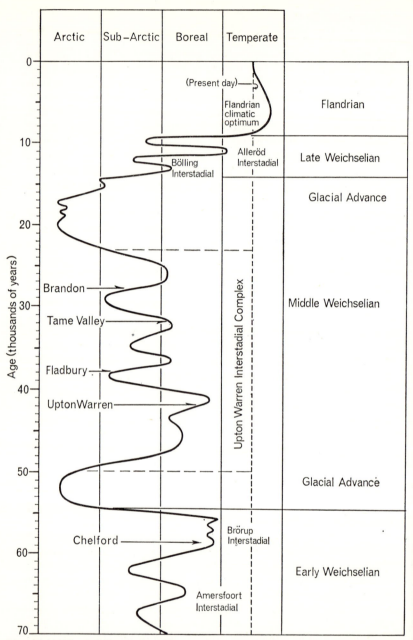

*Fig. 12.12* West Midlands fossiliferous sites, correlated to a curve of Weichselian climatic change in north-west Europe (after Coope and Sands 1966). The sites are named on the left of the curve, and correlations with the continental Weichselian are given on the right of the curve.

valleys are also associated with the Weichselian, as are fossil ice-wedge networks reported from the Low Terrace (No. 4) of the Avon.[55] Beyond the limit of the Weichselian ice, on the limestone of the Derbyshire dome, loess is admixed with weathering residues of the limestone.[48] This may be of Weichselian age, and its presence here, with the concealment of the weathered limestone surface contrasts with the bare limestone pavements of the northern Pennines, swept by the Weichselian ice.

### WALES

During the glacial stages Wales was overrun by ice from local ice sheets developing at various centres in the Cambrian Mountains and by ice from the Irish Sea ice sheet moving southwards and impinging on the Welsh coast. Local ice sheets developed in the north, in the mountains of Snowdonia, the Harlech Dome, Cader Idris, Arenig and Berwyn, and ice from these centres radiated west, north and east, to be confined by the Irish Sea ice at certain times. In central Wales ice moved east down the upper valleys of the Severn and Wye, and west from the Plynlimon range into Cardigan Bay. In southern Wales the principal ice centres were the Brecon Beacons and the Carmarthen Fans. Ice from these mountains filled the valleys of the Towy, Neath, Taff and Usk rivers and passed off into the Bristol Channel.

Little biostratigraphical evidence for the subdivision of the Welsh drifts has yet been obtained. Older and newer drifts have been separated on the basis of freshness of the landforms and weathering of the deposits. The most important evidence for subdividing the succession comes from cave deposits in South Wales (fig. 12.13), where a fossil soil and a cave earth with a temperate mammalian fauna separates two heads. The cave earth and fossil soil are considered to be Ipswichian in age and the two heads Gippingian and Weichselian. The sequence is shown in table 12.4.

The stratigraphy of the older drifts is not well known.[6] They are best exposed in the coastal sections of Cardigan Bay, where they have been seen to lie on a shore-platform at 3 to 4 m above H.W.M., and on associated raised beach deposits. But there has been much discussion on whether the deposits concerned are true tills or solifluction deposits. The erratics in the beach deposits suggest a glacial phase earlier than the time of beach formation. Over them is a sequence of older drift tills. All these are correlated with the Gippingian glacial stage.

The border of the Weichselian maximum is partly that of Irish Sea

*Table 12.4* Pleistocene succession in Wales

| | | |
|---|---|---|
| Flandrian | | lake deposits, peat, alluvium, estuarine clays |
| Weichselian | Late | III Corrie moraines, solifluction<br>II  muds of Allerød interstadial<br>I  Corrie moraines, solifluction |
| | Middle<br>and<br>Early | main Irish Sea glaciation, Cardiff-Llandaff moraine<br>cave heads |
| Ipswichian | | Llansantffraid soil, *Neritoides* Beach, cave earths |
| Gippingian | | Pencoed Mountain glaciation<br>Older Irish Sea glaciation (shelly till)<br>Newquay Mountain glaciation    Gower till and cave heads |
| Hoxnian | | *Patella* beach of Gower |
| Lowestoftian | | Aberarth drift, coastal erratics |
| Middle and Early<br>Pleistocene | | shore-platforms |

ice, partly of local Welsh ice. The Irish Sea ice mounted the northern slopes of Wales, moved south-west by the Lleyn Peninsula and south-east into the Cheshire Plain. An important stratigraphical point is that till was laid down in the Vale of Clwyd and sealed caves containing Palaeolithic ('Aurignacian') implements, suggesting this till was deposited in the later part of the Middle Weichselian. The Weichselian border in West and South Wales is controversial (fig. 12.3) and remains to be clearly demonstrated. In South Wales the Weichselian maximum is marked by end-moraines in the valleys. Large piedmont glaciers formed in Swansea Bay and in south-east Glamorgan.

Retreat phenomena of the Weichselian have been recorded in many parts of Wales, e.g. the fluvioglacial terraces of the Lleyn Peninsula and marginal glacial lakes and associated overflows of the south-west.[11] Late Weichselian glaciers in Wales left block-moraines, some of which have been dated to zone III.

Fig. 12.13 Coastal Pleistocene deposits in south-west Wales (Bowen 1966).
a, *Patella* beach; b, head; c, till; d, weathering horizon or interglacial soil;
e, cave earth; f, Minchin Hole sand; g, Minchin Hole cemented sand; h,
soliflucted till (part of upper head); i, silt horizon; j, ice-wedge casts; k,
involutions.

## LINCOLNSHIRE AND EAST YORKSHIRE

The margin of the Weichselian ice passes north–south through this
area east of the Yorkshire-Lincolnshire Wolds (fig. 12.3). The
southern part of the limit is again controversial, and the results of
the ice advance in pounding up the drainage of the Trent and
Fenland areas remain to be investigated in detail.[67, 68] The older
drifts include an upland chalky boulder clay of the Wolds, usually
correlated with the Gippingian. To the east of the Wolds, there is a
sequence of tills, as shown in table 12.5; the uppermost till of each
sequence is clearly Weichselian because of the fresh morainic features,
including many kettle-holes. In Holderness[9] the Drab and Purple
and Hessle Tills are separated from an older Basement Series of tills
by the Sewerby raised beach deposits, believed to be Ipswichian in
age. The tills above the beach deposits are thus Weichselian and
those below Gippingian or older.

In east Lincolnshire[68, 70] there is also difficulty about the division
of the till sequence into glacial stages. In the whole region there are

Table 12.5 Pleistocene succession of Lincs, East Yorkshire and Northern England

| | Lincolnshire | E. Yorkshire | Northern England |
|---|---|---|---|
| Flandrian | Lake deposits, peat, alluvium, estuarine deposits, raised beaches | | |
| Late | Lake deposits of zones I, II and III | | Zone III corrie moraines of Lake District. Allerod interstadial lake deposits |
| Weichselian — Middle and Early | Hessle Till (Burgh peat layer) Upper Purple Till Lower Purple Till | Hessle Till, Kelsey Hill shelly gravels Purple Till Drab Till Dimlington Moss Silts | Scottish Readvance Main Lake District Glaciation Early Scottish Glaciation |
| | | | Upper Till Middle Sands Lower Till |
| Ipswichian | | Sewerby beach deposits | |
| Gippingian | Chalky Till of Wolds, Basement Till of E. Lincs | Basement Till Series | Scandinavian drift |
| | | | E. Durham — Lake District |
| Hoxnian | Kirmington interglacial deposits (freshwater and estuarine) | Bridlington Crag | |

few biogenic temperate deposits. The most important is at Kirmington in the northern part of the Lincolnshire Wolds, where, between tills, there is a thin peat layer which is associated with estuarine and beach deposits.[7] These temperate deposits are probably Hoxnian in age and their place in the till sequence clearly requires renewed investigation.

Gravels rich in marine shells occur in several areas of Holderness and east Lincolnshire. These are often associated with morainic features, and they appear to be fluvioglacial gravels containing re-worked interglacial marine shells or ice-pushed interglacial gravels and silts.

## NORTHERN ENGLAND

Northern England was subject to glaciation by a local ice sheet forming in the mountains of the Lake District and by smaller ice sheets of the northern Pennines, and to glaciation by ice streams flowing from centres in the southern uplands of Scotland (fig. 12.14). The south-flowing Scottish ice was divided by the Lake District ice, the western stream being directed towards the Irish Sea, the eastern stream across the Pennines via the Tyne Gap and Stainmore.

Changes in the power and direction of these ice streams resulted in the deposition of till sequences,[59, 75] the identification of the different ice advances being facilitated by the many characteristic erratics of the drift, e.g. Norwegian erratics in the Scandinavian drift, Shap

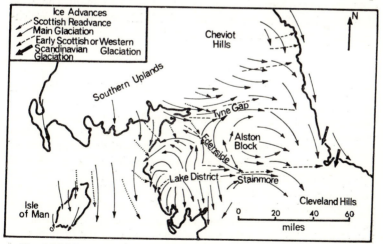

*Fig. 12.14* Ice streams in northern England (after Eastwood 1953).

granite in tills derived from the Lake District ice. The lack of biogenic temperate deposits within the till sequences make the correlation of ice advances with the known glacial stages difficult. In northern England, as in Holderness and east Lincolnshire the problem is really how many tills are Weichselian. The Weichselian margin in the Vale of York, at the York and Escrick moraines is a well-marked standstill phase, and a well-known system of ice-marginal features occurs in the Cleveland Hills of north York-shire.[28] But other moraine systems relating to ice retreat in the area are more difficult to interpret and their relation to the till sequence is difficult, as with the position of the Scottish Readvance within the Weichselian. There are, however, Late Weichselian zone III moraines in corries of the Lake District and Pennines. Table 12.5 shows the till sequence, with suggested correlations.

On the coast near Durham the oldest Pleistocene deposits are of particular interest. They include freshwater peats found in fissures in the Magnesian Limestone preceding the oldest till of the area, the Scandinavian Drift. The age of the freshwater deposits is problemati-cal. They have been described as Lower Pleistocene, but this corre-lation, based on fossil flora, requires re-investigation.

In the dales of the Pennines there are also several ice advances recognised.[51] Their correlation with ice advances further north is problematical.

In the Isle of Man there is also a good till sequence, with tills believed to be of Lowestoftian and Gippingian age, separated by sands thought to be marine, and a younger Weichselian till. The Bride Hills moraine of the northern part of the isle may mark a Weich-selian maximum or be a retreat stage.[93]

## SCOTLAND[58]

The ice streams developing during the Scottish glaciations are shown in fig. 12.2. In the Highlands ice flowed west and north-west over the Outer Hebrides and towards the east the flow was deflected by the presence of Scandinavian ice. In the south, the Highlands ice was deflected by the Southern Uplands ice, westward down the Firth of Clyde and Irish Sea, and eastwards along the Firth of Forth, where it was again deflected north and south by Scandinavian ice. The ice flowing east from the Southern Uplands was similarly deflected by the Scandinavian ice, while in the west of the Southern Uplands ice flowed partly into the Irish Sea, and partly south to the east of the Lake District ice, down the Vale of Eden and over the Pennines.

Apart from the mountainous areas, with all the normal signs of mountain glaciation, the glacial scenery is of two main types: the smooth and often driftless areas of north-west Scotland, and the drift-covered areas of the east and south where the hummocky land-forms, characteristic of recent glaciation, are often well developed. There are many drumlin fields in the Central Valley and in Galloway,

*Table 12.6* Pleistocene succession in Scotland

| Flandrian | | Lake deposits, peat, alluvium, estuarine deposits (carse clays), raised beaches | |
|---|---|---|---|
| Weichselian | Late | Zone III Highland (Loch Lomond) Readvance | Beaches and marine clays (so-called 50 ft) |
| | | Zone II  Allerød interstadial | |
| | | Zone I   Perth Readvance | Beaches and marine clays (so-called 100 ft) |
| | Middle and Early | Aberdeen—Lammermuir Readvance | Marine clays of Aberdeen |
| | | Moray Firth—Strathmore glaciation | |
| Ipswichian | | Weathering in moraineless Buchan | |
| Gippingian | | Greater Highland glaciation Scandinavian glaciation | |
| Middle and Early Pleistocene | | | shore-platforms |

and well-defined end-moraines, e.g. those of the Highland and Perth Readvances, mark retreat stages of the Weichselian. Other moraines, especially those of the Southern Uplands, e.g. the Lammermuir-Stranraer moraines, and those of north-west Scotland, are of dis-puted status.

Although a number of fossiliferous interglacial deposits have been described from Scotland, none show convincing evidence for dividing the glacial sequence into stages, except a recently-discovered peat bed in Shetland.[10] There are, however, some areas where the till sequences are well developed, e.g. Caithness, Aberdeen (fig. 12.15)[71] and the Isle of Lewis, but it is usually not clear how many glacial stages are concerned in the sequences. Table 12.6 shows the sequences in various parts of Scotland.

In many areas, including the Outer Isles, Shetlands[10] and Orkneys, the drifts have been divided into a general glaciation with widespread ground-moraine, and valley stages of glaciation marked by crescentic end-moraines. Various retreat, readvance or standstill phases of the Weichselian have been described, including the Perth-Aberdeen-Lammermuir Readvance, the Perth Readvance and the Highland or Loch Lomond Readvance (fig. 12.3).

In addition to the glacial drifts, Scotland has abundant evidence of relative land/sea-levels changes during the Pleistocene. Late Weichselian and Flandrian raised beaches, and marine clays on the west

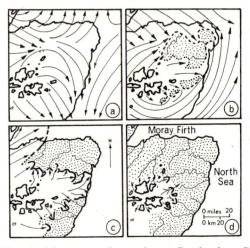

*Fig. 12.15* The glacial sequence in north-east Scotland. a, Greater Highland Glaciation; b, Moray Firth-Strathmore Glaciation; c, Aberdeen Readvance; d, Dinnet Readvance (Synge 1956).

and east coasts, have been correlated with the Late Weichselian and Flandrian pollen zones, so that rates of uplift are to some extent known. The age of the 'preglacial' shore-platforms of the Western Isles are not known.

## IRELAND[40, 72]

Except for small nunatak areas in the south, Ireland was blanketed by ice during maximum glaciation. The ice was mostly of Irish origin but near the east and north-east coasts Irish Sea ice moved inland at various times. Table 12.7 gives the sequence of temperate and glacial stages, and fig. 12.16 the stratigraphy at important sites.

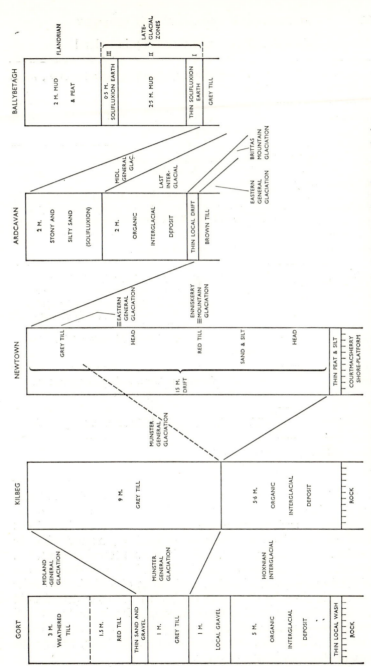

*Fig. 12.16* Important glacial and interglacial sequences in Ireland and their correlation.

*Table 12.7* Pleistocene succession in Ireland

| | | |
|---|---|---|
| Flandrian | Lake deposits, peat, alluvium, estuarine clays, raised beaches | |
| Weichselian Late | Lake deposits of zones I, II and III<br>Inishowen marine deposits | |
| Middle and Early | North Antrim Readvance moraine<br>Kells Readvance moraine<br>Galtrim moraine<br>Southern Irish End-moraine of Midland General Glaciation, Athdown Mountain glaciation, Killumney End-moraine of Lesser Cork-Kerry Glaciation | |
| Ipswichian | Ardcavan interglacial deposit? | |
| Gippingian | Munster General Glaciation | Brittas Mountain Glaciation<br>Greater Cork-Kerry Glaciation<br>(Garryvoe Mountain Glaciation)<br>Eastern General (Ballycroneen) Glaciation<br>Enniskerry Mountain Glaciation |
| | Newtown Head | |
| Hoxnian | Interglacial deposits at Gort, Kilbeg, Baggotstown, Newtown, Courtsmacsherry beach | |
| Lowestoftian | Kildrommin till, erratics in Courtsmacsherry beach | |
| Middle and Early Pleistocene | Killincarrig Crag<br>shore-platforms | |

Apart from the record of a redeposited molluscan fauna of Red Crag type in outwash gravel in Co. Wicklow, little is known of the Pleistocene record prior to a substantial temperate interglacial period correlated on the basis of vegetational history with the Hoxnian. Fossiliferous deposits of this age are found at Gort, Co. Galway, Kilbeg and Newtown, Co. Waterford, and Baggotstown and Kildrommin, Co. Limerick. Indications of a glaciation earlier than this is given by tills under the last two of these deposits. At Newtown, the peat overlies beach material lying in the 'preglacial' shore-platform of the south and east coast of Ireland, and this beach is also correlated with the Hoxnian temperate stage, though the shore-platform itself may be older.

The succeeding glacial stage is the Munster General Glaciation, correlated with the Gippingian glacial stage. Ice movements in this period are shown in fig. 12.17. Three distinct phases are recognised, early and late phases of local glaciation based on upland areas, e.g. Wicklow and Kerry, which sandwich a period of great development of the inland ice and a corresponding Irish Sea ice stream.

The only interglacial site between this glacial stage and the last glacial stage, the Midland General Glaciation, is at Ardcavan, Co. Wexford, where temperate deposits occur in a kettle-hole and are concealed by stony sand, probably a solifluction deposit. The limits and ice flow movements of the Midland General are shown in fig. 12.17. The Southern Irish or Tipperary End-moraine marks the maximum advance. The main continental ice sheet was centred on an ice-shed stretching from Lough Rea in the centre of Ireland through Tyrone to Lough Neagh in the north-east, while local centres of ice dispersal developed in Donegal, Connemara, and the mountains of Munster and Wicklow. In the ice-free areas, corries and block-moraines are found in many mountain groups (e.g. the Knock-mealdowns, Comeraghs, Iveragh and Dingle Peninsulas), and similar features are found in nunatak mountains within the area of the continental ice sheet, e.g. Mountains of Mourne, Slieve League. Outside the glacial limit solifluction deposits are common and stone polygons are also known.

The ice retreat from the Southern Irish End-moraine was accompanied by standstills at the Galtrim moraine, a narrow ridge with feeding eskers, and at the Kells moraine further north, a belt of kame and kettle moraine marking the southern border of a drumlin belt. It has been suggested that this kame and kettle moraine marks a change from orderly retreat to wholesale stagnation of the ice sheet. There appear to be no marked readvance phases except at a very late stage when the Scottish ice sheet advanced over the north-east coast of Ulster, leaving an end-moraine (North Antrim Readvance). A period of marine transgression between this readvance and the main glaciation is recorded by marine clays between the tills in this area.

The North Antrim Readvance may be correlated with zone I of the Late Weichselian. In zone III of this substage no considerable re-advances occur in Ireland as they do in Scotland. Perhaps the corries filled with ice, but no moraines have been related to this zone. On the other hand, solifluction deposits of zone III time are common in kettle-holes of the Midland General Glaciation.

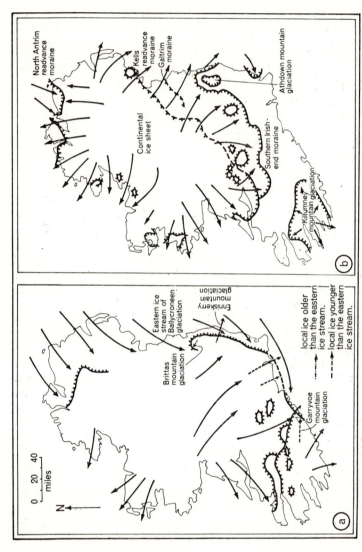

*Fig. 12.17* Ice limits and movements in Ireland. a, Munster general glaciation of Ireland; b, Midland general glaciation of Ireland.

Labels in figure a:

0 20 40 miles
N

Eastern ice stream of Ballycroneen glaciation
Brittas mountain glaciation
Enniskerry mountain glaciation
Garryvoe mountain glaciation

local ice older than the eastern ice stream.
local ice younger than the eastern ice stream.

a

Labels in figure b:

North Antrim readvance moraine
Kells readvance moraine
Galtrim moraine
Continental ice sheet
Southern Irish end moraine
Athdown mountain glaciation
Killarney mountain glaciation

b

## SOUTHERN ENGLAND

Most of southern England lay outside the area of glaciation, but there is much evidence of Pleistocene climatic and sea-level changes, ranging from Lower Pleistocene to the Flandrian. Periglacial climates are recorded by solifluction deposits and patterned ground, and by terrace faunas and floras indicating cold conditions. Temperate stages are recorded by biogenic deposits formed in river-terrace systems or near the sea in response to eustatic sea-level changes. Changes in the relative land/sea-level are recorded by raised beaches and other marine deposits above present sea-level.

The oldest of these marine deposits are sands and gravels (*in situ?*) containing a marine fauna of Red Crag type at Netley Heath in Surrey (183 m O.D.) and Rothamsted, Hertfordshire (131 m O.D.).[17] These have been associated with a high sea-level of about 180 m, of Lower Pleistocene age. At St Erth in Cornwall marine deposits with a rich fauna occur at about 30 m O.D.[41] The age of these is doubtful. They may be Lower or Middle Pleistocene.

The river terrace sequences of the south of England are known in some detail, e.g. those of the Solent and Bournemouth area, the Bristol area, and those of the rivers Medway, Mole and Wey.[95] The most completely known are those of the river Thames.

The terrace sequences of the Thames are shown in fig. 12.18. The Goring Gap, where the Thames breaks through the Chalk escarpment, separates the terrace system of the upper from that of the lower and middle Thames.

In the upper Thames,[3, 53] there are high terraces associated with the northern drift (Combe and Freeland terraces), a lower terrace (Handborough) with temperate fauna correlated with the Hoxnian temperate stage, and then a terrace (Wolvercote), complicated by the presence of a channel in or near it, containing a warm fauna and, above it, a cold flora (late Hoxnian?). The terrace itself is related to the Gippingian glacial stage during which the Midlands Chalky Boulder Clay was laid down to the north of the area. The next lowest terrace (Summertown-Radley) is again a composite terrace, with a cold fauna and flora at the base and a temperate fauna with *Hippopotamus* nearer the top. Probably the cold part dates from the Late Gippingian while the upper temperate part is Ipswichian. Then there are low-level terraces and a buried channel with a cold fauna and flora, of Weichselian age.

In the middle and lower Thames, the sequence is shown in fig. 12.18.[94, 98] Though these two areas are treated together, they differ in that the succession of terraces in the lower Thames area is complicated by increased effects of aggradation, as might be expected nearer the estuary of a large river. The terrace sequence has been divided into three stages. The early (Lower Pleistocene?) stage comprises marine high-level deposits and pebble gravels,[30] antedating the formation of the present valleys, and indicating an early course of the river Thames north eastward (A in fig. 12.19). The terraces of the

*Fig. 12.18* Terrace sequences of the river Thames. a, upper Thames (Sandford 1954); b, middle and lower Thames (Wooldridge 1960). Heights Ordnance Datum (O.D.) on meridian of Slough; C, fauna and/or flora indicating a cold climate; T, fauna indicating a temperate climate.

middle stage form a lower series and often contain quartzites; they indicate an eastward course ($B_1$ fig. 12.19) of the Thames at the time. The diversion south from the early to middle stage may be associated with an ice advance which deposited the Chiltern Drift, or perhaps an early chalky boulder clay.

The terraces of the latest stage follow the present course of the Thames. The oldest (Boyn Hill) is considered to be Hoxnian in age,

while the Taplow Terrace contains a cold fauna and is probably
Gippingian, as is probably the Main Coombe Rock of the lower
Thames. The Upper Floodplain Terrace deposits probably aggraded
in the Ipswichian, and associated with this interglacial are thick
deposits of brickearth at Ilford[87] and Aveley in the lower Thames.
The Lower Floodplain Terrace, the buried channel filling of gravels
and sometimes peat, and the local coombe rocks generally hold a
cold fauna and flora and are of Weichselian age.

Raised beaches and erosion surfaces are known from many areas
of southern England.[98] The best known are those at about 30 m O.D.

*Fig. 12.19* Diversions of the river Thames. A, Pliocene or Lower Pleistocene course; B, course after division south by local Chilterns ice; C, present-day valley following diversion from B by chalky boulder-clay ice. 1,
limits of present-day valley; 2, suggested limits of earlier courses; 3,
southern limit of chalky boulder-clay ice. Localities: B, Beaconsfield;
F, Finchley; G, Goring Gap in the Chilterns; R, Rickmansworth; RI,
Richmond; RU, Ruislip; S, Slough; SA, St Albans; W, Watford; WA,
Ware (Wooldridge 1960).

in Sussex, probably Hoxnian in age, and a younger series at 5 to 8 m,
Ipswichian in age, found in Sussex (plates 8b and 13b) and also traced
to south-west England. In the south-west there is some evidence
for strandlines at 20 m, 7·5 m and 4 m O.D.[44] A shore-platform cut
in rock at a few metres O.D. occurs in north Devon, Cornwall
(fig. 8.4b, plate 13a) and the Scillies. It is thought to be of similar age
to the shore-platform of southern Ireland, and if so, this would

indicate a Hoxnian or older age. If it is Hoxnian, it is difficult to reconcile with the higher sea-levels noted further east for this stage. The question is whether this area is stable. Radiocarbon measurements from Flandrian freshwater estuarine contacts in the area suggest a degree of downwarping to the east has taken place since 6 or 7000 years ago.[12]

In the south-west the shore-platform is overlain by beach gravel, thought to be of Hoxnian age, containing erratics, possibly derived from an early glacial advance (Lowestoftian?) (fig. 12.20). Sections showing till are found on the north coasts of Devon (Fremington Till), Cornwall and the Scillies. The till in places overlies the beach

*Fig. 12.20* Wave-cut shore platform at Godrevy, near St. Ives, Cornwall, typifying a characteristic coastal sequence of south-west England and southern Ireland. a, rock; b, beach gravel; c, sand and pebbles; d, head; e, blown sand and soil (after Stephens and Synge 1966).

gravel and the ice lobe which deposited it (fig. 12.3) is thought to be Gippingian in age.

A few biogenic deposits of Ipswichian age are known in the Solent area at about present sea-levels. They show freshwater and estuarine deposits, and record a change of sea-level which took place in the first half of the Ipswichian.[88]

Periglacial features abound in the south of England. Under the heading of solifluction deposits are included the coombe rock of the Chalk areas, the fan gravels of the limestone areas, the breccias of the shores of the Severn estuary and the block-fields of Dartmoor. Ice-wedge casts and involutions are not uncommon in sections of river gravels and large scale polygonal markings of fossil ice-wedge networks have been described from terrace surfaces. Periglacial aeolian deposits include ventifacts and also wind-blown fractions incorporated into soil horizons, and loess, particularly in Kent and Sussex. The formation of dry valleys in the Chalk may have been assisted by periglacial action, and in east Kent some coombes were cut during zone III of the Late Weichselian.[33]

## SOME GENERAL ASPECTS OF THE PLEISTOCENE

Having described the Pleistocene of the different regions of the British Isles, there remain several topics of wider than regional significance which deserve separate mention.

### Periglacial phenomena

Solifluction processes and patterned ground of recent origin are common in the mountains of the British Isles, and 'fossil' periglacial phenomena have been related to many of the Pleistocene ice advances. For example, the stratigraphical position of ice-wedge casts in East Anglia, indicating former permafrost periods is shown in table 12.8. At each of these times ground ice formed and mean annual temperatures were at a maximum −4°C. The features of Weichselian age are naturally the best known, and are widely distributed in the periglacial area outside the Weichselian ice (fig. 12.21),[79, 90] but they also occur further north, where they are associated with the colder climates of the Middle and Late Weichselian.[21, 96] Solifluction deposits (including head and coombe rock), patterned ground, including unsorted polygon and stripes (plate 10a), and ice-wedge networks (plate 10b), have been reported from many parts of southern Britain. A detailed periglacial stratigraphy for the Weichselian, showing times of permafrost, loess formation and so on, has yet to be worked out. Recent studies of this type in Kent are very promising. They show the sequence in table 12.8.

### Cave deposits

The excavation of cave deposits in various parts of Britain has shown sequences covering parts of the Weichselian, with thermoclastic scree sediments of the colder periods alternating with weathered finer-grained material of the less severe periods. In a few caves the record extends further back through a temperate interglacial stage (Ipswichian) to an earlier cold period (Gippingian).[69]

Table 12.8 Stratigraphical positions of periglacial phenomena in south and east England

| Locality | Feature | Periods of freeze/thaw (F/T), permafrost (P), aeolian acitity (A) | Outline of stratigraphy proving age | Age (non-periglacial intervals in brackets) | Reference (if none given, author's unpublished observations) |
|---|---|---|---|---|---|
| Isle of Thanet, Folkestone, Medway Valley, Kent | chalk detritus (snow or thaw melt-water deposits) coombe cutting | F/T | overlies $C^{14}$ dated soil | Late Weichselian Zone III (Allerød) | |
| | chalk detritus (snow or thaw melt-water deposits) | F/T | overlies $C^{14}$ dated soil | Late Weichselian Zone Ic (Bölling) | Kerney 1963 Kerney 1965 Kerney, Brown and Chandler 1964 |
| | loess | A | | middle Weichselian | |
| | snow melt-water deposits, involutions, solifluction (coombe rock) | F/T | underlie $C^{14}$ dated soil | middle Weichselian | |
| Wretton, Norfolk | ice-wedge casts penetrate involutions | P F/T | overly organic deposits of probable Chelford age | middle Weichselian | |
| | | | | (Ipswichian) | |
| Beetley, Norfolk | ice-wedge cast | P | underlies Ipswichian, penetrates valley outwash | late Gippingian | |
| Ebbsfleet, Kent | solifluction (coombe rock) | F/T | on Chalk, below Ipswichian | Gippingian | Burchell in Zeuner 1959 West, Lambert and Sparks 1964 |
| | | | | (Hoxnian) | |
| W. Runton, Mundesley, Bacton Norfolk | ice-wedge casts, involutions | P F/T | underlie Lowestoftian tills, penetrate Cromerian, associated with arctic plant beds | early Lowestoftian | Donner and West 1958 West and Wilson 1966 |
| | | | | (Cromerian) | |
| W. Runton, Mundesley, Beeston, Norfolk | ice-wedge casts, involutions | P F/T | underlie Cromerian, penetrate Pastonian, associated with arctic plant beds | Beestonian | West and Wilson 1966 |
| | | | | (Pastonian) | |
| Covehithe, Suffolk | involutions | F/T | disturb upper Baventian silts | late Baventian | |
| Beeston, Norfolk | solifluction (coombe rock) | F/T | on Chalk, below Pastonian | Baventian | |

single ice wedges
ice wedge polygons
stone polygons & stripes
chalkland patterns
involutions

limit of Weichselian
ice advance

75 miles

*Fig. 12.21* Distribution of Weichselian periglacial features in Britain.
England and Wales from Williams (1968), Worsley (1966). Scotland from
Sissions (1965). Chalkland patterns refer to the non-sorted stripes and
polygons of Eastern England found on the Chalk

T

*Relative land/sea-level changes*

There is abundant evidence in the British Isles for these changes, but the interpretation of the evidence is difficult, as we have already discussed in Chapter 8. First, there are problems of determining sea-level height from the evidence of a marine or estuarine deposit, and secondly, eustatic effects must be separated from isostatic and tectonic effects. When considering broad changes of relative land/sea-level the first of these difficulties is not so important, but the second always remains. In general, Late Weichselian and Flandrian isostatic uplift formed tilted raised beaches in north-east Ireland, northern England and Scotland, particularly along the shores of the northern part of the Irish Sea. In southern England and southern Ireland there seems little evidence for tilted beaches, except that there has been a recent suggestion of Flandrian down-warping in the south-east.[12] If this is so, then there will obviously be difficulties in the correlation of older high-level beaches along the south coast. The pattern of the suggested Flandrian downwarping corresponds generally with the pattern seen in the Lower Pleistocene, during which there appears to have been high sea-levels in southern England at 120 to 180 m O.D., compared with the considerable depth of Lower Pleistocene shallow-water Crag well below O.D. in East Anglia. Such depression in the south-east is related to the downwarping in the southern part of the North Sea, well known from the Netherlands. In the Lower Pleistocene, more exact measurements of the downwarping, and whether it was accompanied by folding, will have to await more detailed knowledge of the succession.

The shore-platforms of Ireland, Wales, west Scotland and south-west England indicate important times of sea-level standstill, but the correlation with the stratigraphical sequence is uncertain. Often they are overlain by interglacial or Flandrian beach gravels, and there seems at present to be no possibility of dating them, apart from the fact that they are probably mostly Hoxnian or older, as in many sections the overlying gravels are of Hoxnian age.

Interglacial sea-levels have been identified in part but their correlation with sequences of wave-cut platforms and erosion surfaces in southern Britain remains obscure.[85] In the Cromerian of East Anglia the freshwater/estuarine contact occurs near O.D. and estuarine deposits extend to a few metres above O.D. In the Hoxnian, there is evidence of change from freshwater to estuarine deposits near O.D. but marine sediments and raised beaches are known at elevations up to 40 m O.D. In the Ipswichian the freshwater to estuarine transition again occurs near O.D. and beach gravels are known up to about 12 m

*Table 12.9* Pleistocene marine deposits

| | Northern Britain and Ireland (*inside zero isobase for Flandrian beaches*) | Southern Britain and Ireland (*outside zero isobase for Flandrian beaches*) |
|---|---|---|
| Flandrian | ('15 ft') Raised beaches ('Neolithic', '25 ft') | Romano-British silts in alluvial sequences<br>Estuarine clays of Middle Flandrian |
| Late<br>Weichselian | Raised beaches and marine clays of Scotland and Northern Ireland | |
| Ipswichian | | Raised beach at Brighton to 40 ft O.D.<br>Estuarine clays at Selsey and Stone (c. O.D.) |
| Hoxnian | | Marine clays Nar Valley, 19 to 65 ft O.D.<br>Marine clays at Clacton, 9 to 27 ft O.D.<br>Beach gravels in Sussex to 130 ft O.D.<br>Beach gravels in south-west England and Ireland, 10 to 50 ft O.D. |
| Cromerian | | Estuarine deposits 5 to 15 ft O.D. in east Norfolk |
| Pastonian | | Estuarine deposits −5 to 5 ft O.D. in east Norfolk |
| Early Pleistocene | | Crags −160 ft O.D. to O.D. in East Anglia<br>400–600 ft O.D. in south-east England<br>St Erth marine clays 100 ft O.D. |

O.D. The heights mentioned are taken from sites where there is substantial evidence for dating. There are many isolated deposits and wave-cut features which may relate to these periods, but it is as yet impossible to make wide correlations showing sea-level heights at

*Fig. 12.22* Provisional isobases (ft O.D.) for the first postglacial raised shoreline in Scotland (Sissons 1965).

particular times, or even maxima in particular interglacials. Because of the possibilities of downwarping, it is also difficult to make correlations with the classic Mediterranean sequences, though there are suggestions of a correlation of the Ipswichian with the 7·5 m Monastirian II and Hoxnian with the 30 m level.[88] A very detailed discussion of sea level changes in Britain and their relation to the Mediterranean levels can be found in Zeuner's book.[98] Table 12.9 summarises the occurrence of estuarine or marine interglacial deposits, their age and height.

The sea-levels of the glacial stages are unknown, though estimates suggest—100 m O.D. or so. The deep buried channels of the rivers are associated with these low sea-levels. Whether sea-levels rose to around present heights during interstadials is also unknown, though there have been suggestions for this in the Bristol Channel for an interstadial of Weichselian age.[16]

In the Late Weichselian and Flandrian, changes are known in greater detail. There are Late Weichselian tilted beach levels in north-east Ireland and Scotland, including the so-called 100 ft and 50 ft beaches, and some shoreline diagrams have been constructed (fig. 8.6a).[18, 62, 64, 65] In the same area occur tilted lower beaches of Flandrian age (Neolithic and later), including the so-called 25 ft and 15 ft beaches. Isobases for the first postglacial raised beach in Scotland, corresponding to the 25 ft beach, are shown in fig. 12.22.

Outside the zero isobase for the 25 ft beach (fig. 12.23), in the area where eustatic rise is presumably the important controlling factor, submerged Flandrian peats are common and on their age in relation to depth a curve of eustatic rise has been suggested, shown in fig. 12.23. Alluvial sequences from the Somerset Levels and the Fenland show estuarine deposits resulting from Flandrian marine transgressions, and the ages of these are shown in fig. 12.23. Further detailed work in the dating of the transgressions is required to find how apparent eustatic rises have been affected by upwarping and downwarping.

Finally, we should mention that measurements of very recent sea-level change, given by tide-gauge measurements, indicate downwarping in the south of England relative to the north (fig. 8.2).[76]

*Late Weichselian and Flandrian*

Deposits of this age are widespread in the British Isles as lake fillings, peat deposits and alluvium (fig. 12.1). The subdivisions of the Late Weichselian and Flandrian are based on pollen zonation. The three Late Weichselian zones, I, II and III are characterised by a preponderance of non-tree pollen (NAP) and by the absence of thermophilous tree genera. Zone II (Allerød period) shows a temporary amelioration of the climate with higher percentages of arboreal pollen. The lower boundary of the Late Weichselian has not been clearly defined. As there is difficulty in separating Middle from Late Weichselian events on biostratigraphical evidence, it is probable that lithostratigraphical evidence will become basic for this division.

*Fig. 12.23*

a.  Outer limits of the 100 ft raised beach of Scotland (inner circle), and of the 25 ft beach (outer circle) according to Wright (1937). The dot in the Callander region in southern Scotland is the presumed centre of uplift of the 100 ft beach (Donner 1959).

b.  Time curve for the eustatic rise (Godwin, Suggate and Willis 1958).

c.  Age of marine transgressions as shown by estuarine clays intercalated in freshwater deposits, in two areas outside the zero isobase (Fenland and Somerset levels) (West 1963).

The boundary between the Late Weichselian and the Flandrian is taken at the zone III/IV boundary, and zones IV to VIII cover Flandrian time. The main vegetational characters of the pollen zones and their nomenclature is shown in table 12.10. Some of the zone boundaries have been dated by the radiocarbon method, so there is an overall reliable time-scale for the Late Weichselian and Flandrian.

Sediments in closed lakes, sediments formed in relation to changes in relative land/sea-level, and peat, constitute the most widespread deposits of the Late Weichselian and Flandrian. Lakes are typical of the morainic landscape of the Weichselian. In many of the lakes Flandrian sedimentation has been insufficient to fill their basins. The lakes frequently have a characteristic series of Late Weichselian and Flandrian sediments. The Late Weichselian sediments are predominantly inorganic, except for zone II where the biogenic component may be considerable. This predominance of inorganic sediment is associated with a cold climate, when solifluction must have been common. In contrast, the Flandrian sediments are mainly biogenic, either autochthonous or allochthonous. The sediments formed during cultivation periods may have an increased proportion of inorganic sediments derived from the erosion of cleared lands. The changing chemical composition of Flandrian lake sediments has been related to rates of erosion within drainage basins, which itself may be related to climatic change.[39]

River valleys near the coast were filled with alluvial deposits during the Flandrian eustatic rise. Such alluvial areas are extensive, for example, Firth of Forth,[97] Humber, Fenland (fig. 4.4d),[24] Norfolk Broads,[36] Belfast.[97] Typically the alluvial series contain an early freshwater peat, a middle estuarine wedge of clay (Carse Clay of Scotland, Buttery Clay of the Fenland), and an upper peat. There may be an upper estuarine series of later age in some areas, e.g. Romano-British silt of the Fenland. The main clay wedge of the large alluvial areas formed as a result of the transgression of the Flandrian eustatic rise of sea level.

Coastal shingles and sand dunes of Flandrian age are widespread round the coasts.[63] A large group of inland dunes, now largely fixed, is found in Breckland in central East Anglia, where the dune sand is derived from the very sandy facies of the drift.

Raised bog and blanket bog peats are prominent in the landscapes of the western and northern parts of the British Isles.[45] Many raised bogs show the development of *Sphagnum* peats during the middle Flandrian, above earlier lake sediments and fen peats (fig. 4.4b). Bog stratigraphy and recurrence surfaces have been studied in many areas,[31, 78] and some of the latter have been dated by radiocarbon.[25]

Table 12.10 Sequences of main vegetational changes during the Late Weichselian and Flandrian in the British Isles

| Stage | Time based on C$^{14}$ dating | Blytt and Sernander periods | ENGLAND AND WALES | | IRELAND | | SCOTLAND | |
|---|---|---|---|---|---|---|---|---|
| | | | Zone | Characteristics of vegetation | Zone | Characteristics of vegetation | Zone | Characteristics of vegetation |
| Flandrian | 1000 | Sub-Atlantic | VIII modern | | X | Pinus–Fagus | VIII modern | Afforestation |
| | | | VIII | Afforestation | | Afforestation | | |
| | | | | Alnus–Quercus –Betula (–Fagus –Carpinus) | IX | Alnus–Quercus –Betula | | Fagus |
| | A.D. B.C. | | | | | Ulmus decline | | |
| | | Sub-Boreal | | Deforestation | | Deforestation | VIII– VIIb | Alnus–Quercus –Betula |
| | 1000 | | | | | Quercus maximum | | Deforestation |
| | 2000 | | VIIb | Alnus–Quercus –Tilia | VIII | Alnus–Quercus | | |
| | 3000 | | | Ulmus decline | | Ulmus decline | | Ulmus decline |

| Age (years) | Period | | Alnus–Quercus–Ulmus–Tilia | | Alnus–Quercus–Ulmus–Pinus | | Alnus–Quercus–Ulmus | |
|---|---|---|---|---|---|---|---|---|
| 3000 | Flandrian | Atlantic | | | | | | |
| 4000 | | Atlantic | VIIa | *Alnus–Quercus–Ulmus–Tilia* | VII | *Alnus–Quercus–Ulmus–Pinus* | VIIa | *Alnus–Quercus–Ulmus* |
| 5000 | | | | c *Quercus–Ulmus–Tilia* | | c *Pinus* max. | | |
| 6000 | | Boreal | VI | b *Quercus–Ulmus* / a *Ulmus–Corylus* — *Pinus–Corylus* | VI | b *Ulmus* maximum / a *Corylus* maximum — *Corylus–Pinus* | V–VI | *Betula–Pinus–Corylus* |
| 7000 | | | V | *Corylus–Betula–Pinus* | V | *Corylus–Betula* | | |
| 8000 | | Pre-Boreal | IV | *Betula–Pinus*  AP rise | IV | *Betula*  AP rise | IV | *Betula*  AP rise |
| 9000 | Late Weichselian | | III | Park tundra | III | Tundra (Younger *Salix herbacea* period) | III | Tundra (Highland Readvance) — The Zone II Interstadial is best indicated by biogenic sediments compared with the solifluction deposits of Zones I and III |
| | | | II | *Betula* with park tundra | II | Park tundra with *Betula* (Late glacial birch period) | | Tundra |
| 10,000 | | | I | Park tundra | I | Tundra (Older *Salix herbacea* period) | I | (Perth–Aberdeen Readvance) |

Blanket bogs are widely developed in southwestern and northern England,[14] Wales, Scotland and Ireland.[31] Blanket bog formation started in many areas around the beginning of zone VIIa (Atlantic Period) and is associated with increased humidity of climate at that time. Blanket bog peats frequently show buried horizons of tree stumps, often pine, and these have been thought to indicate periods of cessation of growth of the bog surface related to climatic change. A complex sequence of climatic change was put forward for Scotland on such evidence,[37] but it remains to be substantiated. Many areas of blanket bog now suffer from erosion and gullying, which may result from changed climatic conditions, unfavourable hydrological conditions following bog growth and from the prevention of their regeneration by burning or grazing.[14, 73]

Little subaerial denudation has accompanied the deposition of sediments just described. There is good preservation of features of the Weichselian Glaciation and of periglacial patterned ground. Solifluction in the Late Weichselian and hillwash in the late Flandrian may have smoothed the landforms, and in upland regions of steeper river gradients and softer bed rock, incision of rivers may have occurred. Coastal changes have resulted from marine erosion, particularly where soft drift cliffs form the coastline, as in east Yorkshire and East Anglia.

*Dating*

During the Late Weichselian and Flandrian, as well as in the earlier temperate stages, each with their characteristic sequence of vegetational history, pollen analysis has been extensively used as a method of relative dating. In till and terrace sequences geomorphological criteria have often been used as a means to relative dating of a more general sort. Thus base-levels of tills have been used as a criterion of age. As already mentioned, the relative ages of biogenic interglacial deposits may often be determined from their topographical relationships. A detailed relative chronology of the Thames has been attempted based on studies of erosional benches.[98] Relative dating of bones by the fluorine method has been applied to many problems of provenance and relative age.[43]

Of the methods of absolute dating, varve analysis has hardly been used in the British Isles, but radiocarbon dating has been extensively applied to problems of Late Weichselian and Flandrian stratigraphy, vegetational history, changes in relative land/sea-levels and archaeology.[25, 27] Thus there is a time-scale of radiocarbon years as a background for events in this period (table 12.10). But there remain

Table 12.11 Weichselian radiocarbon dates (B.P.)

| Stage | | Dates | | Events |
|---|---|---|---|---|
| Flandrian | Late | III ——— 10250 | | Allerød interstadial |
| | | II ——— 10750 — dates based on a number of assays | | |
| | | I ——— 11950 | | |
| Weichselian | Middle | Colney Heath, Herts | 13560 ± 210 | Q 385 | Cold flora and fauna, peat erratic in Colne Valley gravels |
| | | Barnwell, Cambridge | 19500 ± 650 | Q 590 | Cold flora in Cam Valley terrace |
| | | Sandiway, Cheshire | 28000 ± 1800 | I | Marine molluscs, predate upper till of Cheshire Plain |
| | | Lea Valley, Arctic Bed, Essex | 28000 ± 1500 | Q 25 | Cold flora, peat erratic in Lea Valley gravels |
| | | Coleshill, Warwickshire | 32160 ± 1780 | NPL 55 | Cold faunas and floras associated with Low Terrace of the Tame, Avon No. 2 Terrace, |
| | | Fladbury, Worcs | 38000 ± 700 | GRO 1269 | Main Terrace of Severn—(Upton Warren Interstadial Complex) |
| | | Upton Warren, Worcs | 41900 ± 800 | GRO 1245 | |
| | Early | Chelford, Cheshire | 60800 ± 1500 | GrN 1480 | Boreal coniferous forest, interstadial |
| Ipswichian | | | | | |

very many problems of chronology, in particular the synchroneity of pollen zones, the dating of important events in the history of vegetation and the history of particular genera, and the dating of the course of relative land/sea-level changes. There are also few dates of Weichselian deposits. Table 12.11 gives some of these older dates related to particular Weichselian episodes, but many more are required before there can be reconstruction and correlation of the glacial and periglacial sequences.

### Conclusions

It will be apparent that we have a good general knowledge of the Pleistocene succession in the British Isles. Perhaps it is based on too much detailed stratigraphy of sites and too little mapping. But the former has given the outline succession. For the detail of subdivisions of the stages, especially the glacial stages, much detailed mapping is required. When we consider the doubts about the margins of the Weichselian, and even more so of the older glacial stages, and the doubts about the subdivision of these stages, it is clear that only mapping in relation to the stratigraphy of biogenic deposits within and outside the drift sequence will give the required detail.

Having built up our local succession we should then turn to its correlation with the continent. Table 12.12 summarises the correlations presently suggested, but it should be remembered that even in

*Table 12.12* Correlation with the continent

| Pleistocene | | British Isles | N.W. Europe | |
|---|---|---|---|---|
| | Upper | Flandrian<br>Weichselian<br>Ipswichian<br>Gippingian | Flandrian<br>Weichselian<br>Eemian<br>Saalian | |
| | Middle | Hoxnian<br>Lowestoftian<br>Cromerian<br>Beestonian<br>Pastonian | Holsteinian<br>Elsterian<br>'Cromerian'<br>?<br>? | Menapian<br>Waalian |
| | Lower | Baventian<br>Antian<br>Thurnian<br>Ludhamian | Menapian<br>Waalian<br>Eburonian<br>Tiglian | Eburonian<br>}<br>} Tiglian<br>} |

the classic area of northern Europe, the succession, even of the glacial stages, is not yet clear. For example, the identity of temperate stages in north-east Europe in relation to those of north-west Europe is not clear, the nature of the interval between the Saale and Warthe is not clear, the number of advances within the Saale Glaciation is not clear, and Cromerian and pre-Cromerian stratigraphy is not at all settled, as indicated by the two alternative correlations at the base of the table.

All the more reason that we should not make correlations with the Alps, where the succession is equally or more difficult, and that we should use a local succession based on our own stratigraphical evidence.

# REFERENCES

1 ARKELL, W. J. 1947, *The geology of Oxford*. Oxford: Clarendon Press.

2 BADEN-POWELL, D. F. W. 1948. 'The chalky boulder clays of Norfolk and Suffolk', *Geol. Mag.*, **85**, 279–96.

3 BISHOP, W. W. 1958. 'The Pleistocene geology and geomorphology of three gaps in the Midland Jurassic escarpment', *Phil. Trans. R. Soc.*, B, **241**, 255–305.

4 BOULTON, G. S. and WORSLEY, P. 1965. 'Late Weichselian glaciation in the Cheshire-Shropshire basin', *Nature*, **207**, 704–6.

5 BOSWELL, P. G. H. 1952. 'The Plio-Pleistocene boundary in the east of England', *Proc. Geol. Ass. London*, **63**, 301–12.

6 BOWEN, D. Q. 1966. 'Dating Pleistocene events in south-west Wales', *Nature*, **211**, 475–6.

7 BOYLAN, P. J. 1966. 'The Pleistocene deposits at Kirmington, Lincolnshire', *Mercian Geol.*, **1**, 339–49.

8 BULL, A. J. 1942. 'Pleistocene chronology', *Proc. Geol. Ass. London*, **53**, 1–45.

9 CATT, J. A. and PENNY, C. F. 1966. 'The Pleistocene deposits of Holderness, East Yorkshire', *Proc. Yorks. Geol. Soc.*, **35**, 375–420.

10 CHAPELHOW, R. 1965. 'On glaciation in North Roe, Shetland', *Geogr. J.*, **131**, 60–70.

11 CHARLESWORTH, J. K. 1929. 'The South Wales End Moraine', *Q.J. Geol. Soc. London*, **85**, 335–58.

12 CHURCHILL, D. M. 1965. 'The displacement of deposits formed at sea level, 6,500 years ago in southern Britain', *Quaternaria*, **7**, 239–49.

13 CLAYTON, K. M. 1960. 'The landforms of parts of southern Essex', *Trans. Inst. Br. Geogr.*, No. 28, 55–74.

14 CONWAY, V. M. 1954. 'Stratigraphy and pollen analysis of southern Pennine blanket peats', *J. Ecol.*, **42**, 117–47.

15 COOPE, G. R. and SANDS, C. H. S. 1966. 'Insect faunas of the last

glaciation from the Tame Valley, Warwickshire', *Proc. R. Soc.*, B, **165**, 389–412.

16 COOPE, G. R., SHOTTON, F. W. and STRACHAN, I. 1961. 'A Late Pleistocene fauna and flora from Upton Warren, Worcestershire', *Phil. Trans. R. Soc.* B, **244**, 379–421.

17 DINES, H. G. and CHATWIN, C. P. 1930. 'Pliocene sandstone from Rothamsted (Hertfordshire)', *Summary of Progress, Geol. Surv. G.B. for 1929*, Pt. III, 1–7.

18 DONNER, J. J. 1959. 'The late and post-glacial raised beaches in Scotland', *Ann. Acad. Sci. Fennicae*, Series A III, No. 53.

19 DONNER, J. J. and WEST, R. G. 1958. 'A note on Pleistocene frost structures in the cliff section at Bacton, Norfolk', *Trans. Norfolk Norwich Nat. Soc.*, **18**, 8–9.

20 EASTWOOD, T. 1953. *British Regional Geology—Northern England.* London: H.M.S.O.

21 FITZPATRICK, E. A. 1956. 'An introduction to the periglacial geomorphology of Scotland', *Scottish Geogr. Mag.*, **74**, 28–36.

22 FORBES, E. 1846. 'On the connexion between the distribution of the existing fauna and flora of the British Isles, and the geological changes which have affected their area, especially during the epoch of the Northern Drift', *Mem. Geol. Surv. G.B.*, **1**, 336–432.

23 FUNNELL, B. M. 1961. 'The Palaeogene and Early Pleistocene of Norfolk', *Trans. Norfolk Norwich Nat. Soc.*, **19**, 340–64.

24 GODWIN, H. 1940. 'Studies on the Post-glacial history of British vegetation. III. Fenland pollen diagrams. IV. Post-glacial changes of relative land- and sea-level in the English Fenland', *Phil. Trans. R. Soc.*, B, **230**, 239–303.

25 GODWIN, H. 1960. 'Radiocarbon dating and Quaternary history in Britain', *Proc. R. Soc.*, B, **153**, 287–320.

26 GODWIN, H., SUGGATE, R. P. and WILLIS, E. H. 1958. 'Radiocarbon dating of the eustatic rise in ocean level', *Nature*, **181**, 1518–19.

27 GODWIN, H. and WILLIS, E. H. 1959. 'Radiocarbon dating of the Late-glacial Period in Britain', *Proc. R. Soc.*, B, **150**, 199–215.

28 GREGORY, K. J. 1965. 'Proglacial Lake Eskdale after sixty years', *Trans. Inst. Br. Geogr.*, No. 36, 149–62.

29 HARMER, F. W. 1902. 'A sketch of the later Tertiary history of East Anglia', *Proc. Geol. Ass. London*, **13**, 416–79.

30 HEY, R. W. 1965. 'Highly quartzose pebble gravels in the London Basin', *Proc. Geol. Ass. London*, **76**, 403–20.

31 JESSEN, K. 1949. 'Studies in Late Quaternary deposits and flora-history of Ireland', *Proc. R. Irish Acad.*, **52**, B, 85–290.

32 KELLY, M. R. 1964. 'The Middle Pleistocene of north Birmingham', *Phil. Trans. R. Soc.*, B, **247**, 533–92.

33 KERNEY, M. P. 1963. 'Late-glacial deposits on the Chalk of south-east England', *Phil. Trans. R. Soc.*, B, **246**, 203–54.

34 KERNEY, M. P. 1965. 'Weichselian deposits in the Isle of Thanet, East Kent', *Proc. Geol. Ass. London*, **76**, 269–74.

35 KERNEY, M. P., BROWN, E. H. and CHANDLER, T. J. 1964. 'The Late-glacial and Post-glacial history of the Chalk escarpment near Brook, Kent', *Phil. Trans. R. Soc.*, B, **248**, 135–204.

36 LAMBERT, J. M., JENNINGS, J. N., SMITH, C. T., GREEN, C. and HUTCHINSON, J. N. 1960. *The making of the Broads*. R. Geogr. Soc. Memoir No. 3.

37 LEWIS, F. J. 1907. 'The plant remains in the Scottish peat mosses. Pt. III. The Scottish Highlands and the Shetland Isles', *Phil. Trans. R. Soc. Edin.*, **46**, 33–70.

38 LEXIQUE STRATIGRAPHIQUE INTERNATIONAL, 1963. Fascicule 3a XIII. *Neogene and Pleistocene of England, Wales and Scotland.* Centre National de la Recherche Scientifique.

39 MACKERETH, F. J. H. 1966. 'Some chemical observations on post-glacial lake sediments', *Phil. Trans. R. Soc.*, B, **250**, 165–213.

40 MITCHELL, G. F. 1960. 'The Pleistocene history of the Irish Sea', *Adv. Sci.*, **17**, 313–25.

41 MITCHELL, G. F. 1965. 'The St Erth Beds—an alternative explanation', *Proc. Geol. Ass. London*, **76**, 345–66.

42 NORTH, F. J. 1943. 'Centenary of the glacial theory', *Proc. Geol. Ass. London*, **54**, 1–28.

43 OAKLEY, K. P. and HOSKINS, W. R. 1950. 'New evidence on the antiquity of Piltdown Man', *Nature*, **165**, 379–82.

44 ORME, A. R. 1960. 'The raised beaches and strandlines of South Devon', *Fld Stud.*, **1**, 109–30.

45 OSVALD, H. 1949. 'Notes on the vegetation of British and Irish Mosses', *Acta Phytogeogr. Suecica*, No. 26.

46 PEAKE, D. S. 1961. 'Glacial changes in the Alyn river system and their significance in the glaciology of the north Welsh border', *Q.J. Geol. Soc. London*, **117**, 335–66.

47 PENNY, L. F. 1964. 'A review of the Last Glaciation in Great Britain', *Proc. Yorks. Geol. Soc.*, **34**, 387–411.

48 PIGOTT, C. D. 1962. 'Soil formation and development on the Carboniferous limestone of Derbyshire. I. Parent materials', *J. Ecol.*, **50**, 145–56.

49 POOLE, E. G. and WHITEMAN, A. J. 1961. 'The glacial drifts of the southern part of the Shropshire–Cheshire plain', *Q.J. Geol. Soc., London*, **117**, 91–130.

50 POSNANSKY, M. 1960. 'The Pleistocene succession in the middle Trent basin', *Proc. Geol. Ass. London*, **71**, 285–311.

51 RAISTRICK, A. 1934. 'The correlation of glacial retreat stages across the Pennines', *Proc. Yorks. Geol. Soc.*, **22**, 199–214.

52 REID, C. 1890. *The Pliocene deposits of Britain.* Mem. Geol. Surv. U.K.

53 SANDFORD, K. S. 1954. 'River development and superficial deposits', in *The Oxford Region*, eds. A. F. Martin and R. W. Steel, pp. 21–36. Oxford University Press.

54 SHOTTON, F. W. 1953. 'The Pleistocene deposits of the area between Coventry, Rugby and Leamington, and their bearing upon the topo-

graphic development of the Midlands', *Phil. Trans. R. Soc.* B, **237**, 209–60.

55 SHOTTON, F. W. 1960. 'Large scale patterned ground in the valley of the Worcestershire Avon', *Geol. Mag.* **97**, 404–8.

56 SIEVEKING, G. DE G. 1968. 'Excavations at High Lodge, Mildenhall', *Quaternaria*, in the press.

57 SIMPSON, I. M. and WEST, R. G. 1958. 'On the stratigraphy and palaeo-botany of a late-Pleistocene organic deposit at Chelford, Cheshire', *New Phytol.*, **57**, 239–50.

58 SISSONS, J. B. 1965. Quaternary. In *The Geology of Scotland*, ed. G. Y. Craig, pp. 467–503. Edinburgh: Oliver and Boyd.

59 SMITH, D. B. in Discussion in Catt and Penny 1966.

60 SPARKS, B. W. and WEST, R. G. 1964. 'The drift landforms around Holt, Norfolk', *Trans. Inst. Br. Geogr.*, No. 35, 27–35.

61 SPARKS, B. W. and WEST, R. G. 1965. 'The relief and drift deposits', in *The Cambridge Region 1965*, ed. J. A. Steers. Cambridge University Press.

62 Special number on the vertical displacement of shore-lines in highland Britain. 1966. *Trans. Inst. Br. Geogr.*, No. 39.

63 STEERS, J. A. 1953. *The Sea Coast.* London: Collins.

64 STEPHENS, N. and SYNGE, F. M. 1965. 'Late-Pleistocene shorelines and drift limits in North Donegal', *Proc. R. Irish Acad.*, **64**, B, 131–53.

65 STEPHENS, N. and SYNGE, F. M. 1966. 'Pleistocene shorelines', in *Essays in Geomorphology*, ed. G. H. Dury, pp. 1–51. London: Heinemann.

66 STEVENS, L. A. 1960. 'The interglacial of the Nar Valley, Norfolk', *Q.J. Geol. Soc. London*, **115**, 291–316.

67 STRAW, A. 1958. 'The glacial sequence in Lincolnshire', *East Midland Geogr.*, **1**, 29–40.

68 STRAW, A. 1963. 'The Quaternary evolution of the Lower and Middle Trent', *East Midland Geogr.*, **3**, 171–89.

69 SUTCLIFFE, A. J. and ZEUNER, F. E. 1962. 'Excavations in the Torbryan Caves, Devonshire', *Proc. Devon Archaeol. Explor. Soc.*, **5**, 127–45.

70 SWINNERTON, H. H. and KENT, P. E. 1949. *The geology of Lincoln-shire.* Lincoln: Lincolnshire Naturalists' Union.

71 SYNGE, F. M. 1956. 'The glaciation of North-east Scotland', *Scottish Geogr. Mag.*, **72**, 129–43.

72 SYNGE, F. M. and STEPHENS, N. 1960. 'The Quaternary Period in Ireland—an assessment, 1960', *Irish Geogr.*, **4**, 121–30.

73 TALLIS, J. H. 1964. 'Studies on southern Pennine peats. II. The Pattern of erosion', *J. Ecol.*, **53**, 333–44.

74 TOMLINSON, M. E. 1963. 'The Pleistocene chronology of the Midlands', *Proc. Geol. Ass. London*, **74**, 187–202.

75 TROTTER, F. M. and HOLLINGWORTH, S. E. 1932. 'The glacial sequence in the north of England', *Geol. Mag.*, **69**, 374–80.

76 VALENTIN, H. 1953. 'Present vertical movements of the British Isles', *Geogr. J.*, **119**, 299–305.

77 VALENTIN, H. 1955. 'Die Grenze der letzten Vereisung im Nord-

seeraum', Deutscher Geographentag Hamburg 1955. *Tagungsbericht u. Wiss. Abh.*, 359–66.

78 WALKER, D. and WALKER, P. M. 1961. 'Stratigraphic evidence of regeneration in some Irish bogs', *J. Ecol.*, **49**, 169–85.

79 WATSON, E. 1965. 'Periglacial structures in the Aberystwyth region of central Wales', *Proc. Geol. Ass. London*, **76**, 443–62.

80 WEST, R. G. 1956. 'The Quaternary deposits at Hoxne, Suffolk', *Phil. Trans. R. Soc.*, B, **239**, 265–356.

81 WEST, R. G. 1957. 'Interglacial deposits at Bobbitshole, Ipswich', *Phil. Trans. R. Soc.* B, **241**, 1–31.

82 WEST, R. G. 1961a. 'Vegetational history of the Early Pleistocene of the Royal Society Borehole at Ludham, Norfolk', *Proc. R. Soc.*, B, **155**, 437–53.

83 WEST, R. G. 1961b. 'The glacial and interglacial deposits of Norfolk', *Trans. Norfolk Norwich Nat. Soc.*, **19**, 365–75.

84 WEST, R. G. 1963. 'Problems of the British Quaternary', *Proc. Geol. Ass. London*, **74**, 147–86.

85 WEST, R. G. 1967. 'The Quaternary of the British Isles', in *The Quaternary*, Vol. 2, ed. K. Rankama. New York: Interscience.

86 WEST, R. G. and DONNER, J. J. 1956. 'The glaciations of East Anglia and the East Midlands: a differentiation based on stone orientation measurements of the tills', *Q.J. Geol. Soc. London*, **112**, 69–91.

87 WEST, R. G., LAMBERT, C. A. and SPARKS, B. W. 1964. 'Interglacial deposits at Ilford, Essex', *Phil. Trans. R. Soc.*, B, **247**, 185–212.

88 WEST, R. G. and SPARKS, B. W. 1960. 'Coastal interglacial deposits of the English Channel', *Phil. Trans. R. Soc.*, B, **243**, 95–133.

89 WEST, R. G. and WILSON, D. G. 1966. 'Cromer Forest Bed Series', *Nature*, **209**, 497–8.

90 WILLIAMS, R. B. G. 1964. 'Fossil patterned ground in eastern England', *Biul. Peryglacjalny*, **14**, 337–49.

91 WILLIAMS, R. B. G. 1968. 'The distribution of permafrost in southern England in the last glacial period', in *The periglacial environment: past and present*, ed. T. L. Péwé. Montreal: McGill University Press.

92 WILLS, L. J. 1938. 'The Pleistocene development of the Severn from Bridgnorth to the sea', *Q.J. Geol. Soc. London*, **94**, 161–242.

93 WIRTZ, D. 1953. 'Zur Stratigraphie des Pleistocäns im Westen der Britischen Inseln', *Neues Jb. Geol. u Palaeont.*, **96**, 267–303.

94 WOOLDRIDGE, S. W. 1960. 'The Pleistocene succession in the London Basin', *Proc. Geol. Ass. London*, **71**, 113–29.

95 WOOLDRIDGE, S. W. and LINTON, D. L. 1955. *Structure, surface and drainage in south-east England*. London: Philip.

96 WORSLEY, P. 1966. 'Some Weichselian fossil frost wedges from east Cheshire', *Merc. Geol.*, **1**, 357–65.

97 WRIGHT, W. B. 1937. *The Quaternary Ice Age*. 2nd edn. London: Macmillan.

98 ZEUNER, F. E. 1959. *The Pleistocene Period*. 2nd edn. London: Hutchinson.

# CHAPTER 13

# PLEISTOCENE HISTORY OF THE FLORA AND FAUNA OF THE BRITISH ISLES

## HISTORY OF THE FLORA[45, 70]

**B**EFORE considering in detail the Pleistocene history of the flora, it is necessary to point out the main vegetational changes which occurred during Tertiary time in north-west Europe. Floras with tropical affinities are known from the Lower Tertiary (Palaeocene, Eocene, Oligocene), and these became replaced during the Upper Tertiary (Miocene, Pliocene) by more temperate floras. The plant geographical relationships of these Upper Tertiary floras were very wide, with strong Asian and North American elements. The few Miocene-Pliocene plant-bearing deposits in the British Isles have been little studied and we have to refer to the well-known Pliocene deposits of the Rhine Valley in Germany and the Netherlands.[149] Here the Pliocene flora contains such exotic forest genera as *Carya*

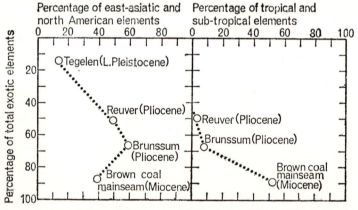

*Fig. 13.1* Comparison of the geographical relationships of Upper Tertiary and Pleistocene macrofloras in the lower Rhine valley (Zagwijn 1959).

*Nyssa, Tsuga, Sequoia* and *Taxodium*. The changes in the exotic elements from this area in Upper Tertiary and Lower Pleistocene time are shown in fig. 13.1.

The change to the Pleistocene in the Netherlands is recorded in the pollen diagram (fig. 13.2) from Meinweg. Forest is replaced by open vegetation with few thermophilous plants, the change taken to indicate the worsening of the climate marking the first cold period (Pretiglian) of the Pleistocene. On the recurrence of temperate conditions during the following interval (Tiglian), many of the exotic genera do not reappear. This reduction of the forest flora was described in detail by C. and E. Reid.[97] They explained the extinction in Europe of many exotic genera as a result of the climatic deterioration forcing temperate genera south. They pointed out that in Europe and western Asia there were barriers to this southward migration in the form of mountains, deserts and seas, while in eastern Asia and North America there were no such continuous barriers. The result was that only the more hardy of the circumboreal Tertiary forest genera remained in Europe, while in eastern Asia and North America the present forest genera survived the Pleistocene climatic deteriorations, and are much more nearly related to their Tertiary precursors.

The extinction in Europe was not entirely accomplished at the very beginning of Pleistocene time. Certain exotic genera persisted into the Early Pleistocene (e.g. *Tsuga, Carya*). But by the beginning of the Middle Pleistocene, the forest genera are those of modern Europe, as are most of the shrub and herbaceous species. So, for

*Table 13.1* Pleistocene occurrence of some species and genera exotic to the native British flora

| Species or genus with present distribution | Stage | | | | | | |
|---|---|---|---|---|---|---|---|
| | *Ludhamian* | *Antian* | *Pastonian* | *Cromerian* | *Hoxnian* | *Ipswichian* | *Flandrian* |
| *Tsuga* (E. Asia, N. America) | + | + | | | | | |
| *Pterocarya* (Caucasus, E. Asia) | + | + | | | + | | |
| *Abies alba* (C. & S. Europe) | | | | + | + | | |
| *Picea abies* (N. & C. Europe) | + | + | + | + | + | | |
| *Najas tenuissima* (N. Europe) | | | + | + | | | |
| *Azolla filiculoides* (N., C. & S. America) | | | + | + | + | | |
| *Salvinia natans* (C. & S. Europe) | | | | + | | + | |

*Fig. 13.2* Pollen diagram from Meinweg, S.E. Netherlands, across the Plio/Pleistocene (Reuverian/Pretiglian) boundary (Zagwijn 1960).

example, the plant species identified from the temperate Cromerian stage are nearly all found in the modern British flora. The Pleistocene occurrence of some species and genera exotic to the native British flora is shown in table 13.1.

Although the record of Miocene and Pliocene deposits with fossil flora in the British Isles is poor, in the Pleistocene there is a good record of fossil floras. Table 13.2 lists important sites with fossil floras. From the stratigraphical point of view most of the floras are well dated, as they are intercalated in the sequence of glacial deposits. The glacial advances, at least in midland England and Ireland, were

*Table 13.2* Localities with fossil floras

| Early Pleistocene | Cromerian | Lowestoftian | Hoxnian | Gippingian | Ipswichian | Early and Middle Weichselian | Late Weichselian | Flandrian | Locality | Reference |
|---|---|---|---|---|---|---|---|---|---|---|
| + | | | | | | | | | Ludham, Norfolk | West 1961a |
| + | | | | | | | | | Easton Bavents, Suffolk | Funnell and West 1962 |
| + | + | + | | | | | | | Norfolk coast | Reid 1899 |
| | + | | | | | | | | Norfolk and Suffolk coast | Duigan 1963 |
| | | | + | + | | | | | Hoxne, Suffolk | West 1956 |
| | | | + | + | | | | | Nechells, Birmingham | Kelly 1964 |
| | | | | + | | | | | Nar Valley, Norfolk | Stevens 1960 |
| | | | | + | | | | | Gort, Co. Galway | Jessen, Farrington and Andersen 1959 |
| | | | + | | | | | | Baggotstown, Co. Limerick | Watts 1964 |
| | | | | | + | | | | Dorchester, Oxfordshire | Duigan 1955 |
| | | | | | + | | | | Ipswich, Suffolk | West 1957 |
| | | | | | + | | | | Selsey, Sussex | West and Sparks 1960 |
| | | | | | + | | | | Ilford, Essex | West, Lambert and Sparks 1964 |
| | | | | | + | | | | Ardcavan, Co. Wexford | Mitchell 1948 |
| | | | | | | + | | | Chelford, Cheshire | Simpson and West 1958 |
| | | | | | | + | | | Upton Warren, Worcs | Coope, Shotton and Strachan 1961 |
| | | | | | | | + | | Cambridge | Lambert, Sparks and Pearson 1962 |
| | | | | | | + | + | + | British Isles | Godwin 1956 |
| | | | | | | + | + | | Lea Valley, Essex | Allison, Godwin and Warren 1952 |
| | | | | | | | + | + | Ireland | Jessen 1949 |
| | | | | | | | + | + | Wales | Seddon 1962 |
| | | | | | | | + | + | Cumberland | Godwin, Walker and Willis 1957 |
| | | | | | | | + | + | Lake District | Pennington 1964 |
| | | | | | | | + | + | Scotland | Donner 1957 |

*Fig. 13.3* Increment graphs for all dated records of plant species in Ireland and in the British Isles, excluding aliens (*sensu* Checklist of British Vascular Plants), hybrids and crop-plants, but including doubtful identifications at species level (17 per cent of the total), and genera for which no species has been recorded up to the time in question. The records for the British Isles begin with the Weichselian (full-glacial), those for Ireland with the Late Weichselian (late-glacial). Above: total numbers of species; below: percentages of the existing flora, taken for this purpose to be 1500 for the British Isles and 1000 for Ireland). Note the high proportion of all records already made for the Late Weichselian, and by the beginning of the Atlantic period in both areas. In the graphs for the British Isles note the increased rate of rise in zones VIIb and VIII, in part at least a consequence of the extension of disforestation and agriculture (Godwin 1956).

not strong enough to remove the older Pleistocene deposits and their contained floras. Naturally the most complete record is from the most recent stage, the Flandrian, where the history of the flora in most parts of the British Isles is known in considerable detail, and can be related to various environmental events, such as changes in sea-level, and man's clearance activities. As we go further back into the Pleistocene, the described fossil floras decrease in number. There are many from the Weichselian glacial stage, fewer of the Ipswichian and Hoxnian temperate stages, fewer still of the Gippingian and Lowestoftian glacial stages, while the few Cromerian and pre-Cromerian floras are confined to coastal regions of East Anglia.

As regards the completeness of the fossil record from the point of view of the native flora, up to 1953[45] over 500 species of vascular plants, say around thirty per cent of the present British flora, had been recorded fossil (fig. 13.3) in Weichselian and Flandrian deposits, and somewhat less (twenty-five per cent) of the Irish flora. Since that time there has been a considerable increase in these figures, though most of the new records merely carry the history of species already known fossil back through the Pleistocene. The fossil vascular flora is naturally the best known, but recent work on the Bryophyte flora, with a large number of species identified fossil, should add much to our knowledge of the history of the British flora. The records of Algae are mostly confined to the Flandrian, where sequences of diatoms have been recorded from a number of lake deposits.[102]

*Early Pleistocene floras*

The pollen floras recorded from the Early Pleistocene Crags (fig. 13.4) are of two types, those with high non-arboreal pollen frequencies and low frequencies of thermophilous trees, representing cold periods, and those with lower non-arboreal pollen frequencies and higher pollen frequencies of thermophilous trees, representing temperate periods.[139] These temperate pollen floras show the presence of mixed coniferous and deciduous forest during two stages, the Ludhamian and the Antian. The genera *Tsuga* and *Pterocarya* are characteristic trees of these times, the former being a 'Tertiary relic', now extinct in Europe, and confined to eastern Asia and North America. The flora of the cold stages, the Thurnian and Baventian, is characterised by the high frequencies of Ericales tetrads, many of which are of *Empetrum-nigrum* type. The vegetation suggested is oceanic heath, and the climate cold in comparison with the forested stages.

Possibly a flora of macroscopic plant remains from Castle Eden,

Co. Durham, is of Early Pleistocene age.[98] It was originally described as being slightly younger than the Reuverian (late Pliocene) stage of the Netherlands, as it had fewer exotic species than that stage, but the plant list, which indicates temperate conditions, gives little help in age determination. The paucity of exotic species and its stratigraphical position below the oldest glacial deposits in the area, suggest an Early Pleistocene age.

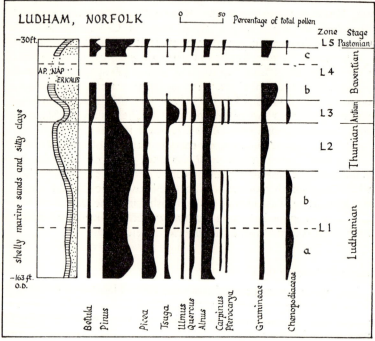

*Fig. 13.4* Schematic pollen diagram through the Crag at Ludham, Norfolk (after West 1961a).

## Glacial floras

In this category we include the fossil floras closely related to glacial or periglacial deposits and showing little or no indication of forested conditions at their time of deposition. The earliest such flora is Baventian in age, from the cold period preceding the Pastonian temperate stage, and there are floras from all the subsequent cold stages (Beestonian, Lowestoftian, Gippingian and Weichselian). The sediments containing the floras are channel or terrace sediments, often of an organic type suggesting sedimentation in shallow transient pools (fig. 13.5b). Reworking of these organic deposits is indicated by their being found as erratics in coarse gravel, formed presumably by the undercutting of meandering channels in a flood-plain environment (fig. 13.5a).

Fig. 13.5 Sections in terraces showing full-glacial organic deposits. a, erratic of detritus mud in Weichselian gravels in the flood plain of the river Colne, Herts. Sketch after photo by P. Evans. b, Weichselian pond deposit in terrace sands and gravels at Wretton, Norfolk, penetrated by an ice-wedge cast and covered by solifluction gravels.

The pollen of these deposits usually shows a small amount of tree or shrub pollen, usually *Salix*, *Betula* (including *B. nana*-type), *Juniperus* and *Pinus*, and much greater frequencies of non-tree pollen, especially sedge and grass pollen, but also varying amounts of the pollen of marsh and aquatic plants (*Filipendula*, *Caltha*), of ruderals and open-habitat plants (*Artemisia*, *Helianthemum*, *Plantago*), and of plants of tall-herb communities (*Polemonium*, *Urtica*, *Sanguisorba*).

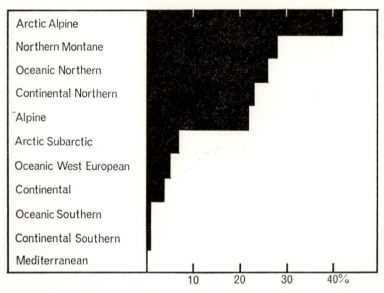

*Fig. 13.6* Diagram showing the relative percentage of various geographical elements in the British Isles flora (Matthews 1955), represented by records in the British Weichselian. Species with wide extra-British range are not included in the analysis (Godwin 1956).

Amongst the macroscopic plant remains (plate 11) there is a mixture of ecological and plant-geographical categories (fig. 13.6), e.g. northern and montane plants, halophytes and other plants now commonly maritime, many widely distributed plants, often now weeds, plants indicative of open habitats and a few species of more southern distribution. A few of the more characteristic species may be mentioned:

Northern and montane plants: *Draba incana*, *Dryas octopetala*, *Salix herbacea*, *Saxifraga oppositifolia* (plate 11a), *Thalictrum alpinum*.

Maritime plants: *Armeria maritima, Atriplex hastata, Plantago maritima, Suaeda maritima.*
Weeds: *Polygonum aviculare, Potentilla anserina, Ranunculus repens.*
Plants of a more southern distribution: *Lemna, Potamogeton crispus, Ranunculus sceleratus.*

There are also suggestions of continentality of climate in the presence of *Hippophaë, Centaurea cyanus* and *Poterium sanguisorba,* and the often considerable frequencies of *Artemisia* pollen. These have been considered to give a steppe-like character to the flora. The scarcity of trees and the variety of herbs in the glacial floras are their two characteristics. The assemblages recorded require an explanation in climatic terms. For a flora and fauna of Weichselian age in Worcestershire, it has been suggested that ameliorating climate and grazing by large herbivores help to explain the mixture of floristic elements and the rarity of trees.[28] At an early Weichselian site in Cambridge a mixture of geographical elements could be related to a deteriorating climate at the beginning of the Weichselian, the more southern plants and molluscs possibly being survivors from interglacial time.[65]

Assuming that there is little or no secondary deposition of plant remains, two facts require explanation: the mixture of cold- and warm-indicating geographical elements and the absence or rarity of trees. It is also relevant that similar plant assemblages are recorded from all the glacial stages. The mixture of species is probably related to the great diversity of microclimates occurring in a periglacial area of lower latitude than the present arctic. Regarding the absence of trees, many periglacial environmental conditions do not favour tree growth and survival, e.g. wind, permafrost, solifluction and waterlogging of soils, as well as the climatic extremes themselves. The explanation may be in a combination of environmental factors rather than in a single biotic factor such as grazing. The repeated occurrence of these glacial floras in the Weichselian (they have been dated by the radiocarbon method at 13560, 19500, 28000, 41900 years B.P.[48]), and in the earlier glacial stages, indicates that this type of flora was essentially that which existed in southern Britain during full-glacial and near full-glacial conditions of the cold stages, and they indicate the considerable extent to which plants, of many differing ecological and geographical categories, were able to survive in this country during these cold stages.

We should also consider here the late-glacial floras, which date from the times of retreat of the successive glaciations, but which precede the afforestation occurring in temperate non-glacial periods.

Such late-glacial episodes are known from the Beestonian, Lowe-stoftian, Gippingian and Weichselian cold stages. These floras are similar to those of the full-glacial periods except that they may show increased percentages of tree (*Betula*) and shrub pollen. For example in the Lowestoftian late-glacial at Hoxne, the remains of *Hippophaë rhamnoides*, the sea buckthorn, are very common. In some late-glacial sequences, e.g. those of the Ipswichian, the pollen spectra remain similar over a period of time, suggesting stable late-glacial conditions. These are followed by rapid vegetational changes leading to interglacial forest vegetation. In other late-glacial sequences, e.g. the Lowestoftian and Weichselian, there are fluctuations of the climate within the sequence. The best-known late-glacial is of course the Late Weichselian, where there is a division into three zones, I, II and III, which appear to be synchronous over north-west Europe. The vegetational sequence is summarised in table 12.10. In general, the vegetation of zones I and III was similar with much open vege-tation and scattered *Betula* copses, which in zone II (Allerød period) expanded somewhat and may have been associated in the south and east with *Pinus*. In more westerly areas oceanic heaths with *Empetrum* were common in the Late Weichselian, but the flora as a whole was still dominated by northern and montane plants. Evidence of a minor oscillation in zone I (the Bølling oscillation of the continent?) has been reported from the north of England.[11] Examples of pollen diagrams covering these Late Weichselian oscillations are shown in figs. 13.10 and 13.15.

*Interstadial floras*

This type of flora, indicating climatic oscillation towards boreal environmental conditions rather than to full interglacial temperate conditions, is rare. The best known is a flora from Chelford of Early Weichselian age ($C^{14}$ age 60,800 years B.P.), from a thin layer of sandy detritus mud within the middle sands of the Cheshire Plain.[111] Here pollen and macroscopic plant remains indicate a cool climate with a *Betula-Pinus-Picea* forest as the dominant local vegetation, similar to a forest-type now found in northern Finland. Pollen spectra of the same kind have been found in Early Weichselian deposits at Wretton in Norfolk.

*Temperate (interglacial) floras*

During the interglacials climatic amelioration proceeded as far as in the Flandrian, and these temperate stages are characterised by the presence of deciduous forest. For the purpose of vegetational comparisons we may include within the term interglacial the present temperate stage—the Flandrian—as its vegetational development so far has been of the same general nature as those of the interglacials. Interglacial deposits have been found at many sites in central and southern England and Ireland (fig. 12.8). They are usually lacustrine deposits associated with glacial deposits or with terrace deposits. They show a sequence of vegetational change, which, at its most complete, comprises four major zones, shown in table 13.3. The zones

*Table 13.3* Zonation of temperate stages of Middle and Late Pleistocene

|  |  |  |  |  | Vegetational aspect |
|---|---|---|---|---|---|
| cold stage | e L | e G | e W |  | early-glacial |
| temperate stage | Cromerian C IV | Hoxnian H IV | Ipswichian I IV | Flandrian | post-temperate |
|  | C III | H III | I III |  | late-temperate |
|  | C II | H II | I II | F II (zones VII, VIII) | early-temperate |
|  | C I | H I | I I | F I (zones IV, V, VI) | pre-temperate |
| cold stage | 1 Be | 1 L | 1 G | 1 W (zones I, II, III) | late-glacial |

e, early; l, late; H, Hoxnian      F, Flandrian
                L, Lowestoftian    W, Weichselian
                C, Cromerian      I, Ipswichian
                Be, Beestonian    G, Gippingian

are defined on pollen assemblages, indicated in subsequent tables, and the changes in these assemblages are associated with the cycle of interglacial environmental change. The detail of the vegetational history of each interglacial differs from that of the others, and these differences therefore provide possibilities of characterising each particular interglacial temperate stage by its vegetational history. But the regional differences of vegetation in any one interglacial are not yet clear, for the reason that interglacial deposits have not so far been widely found or studied.

The vegetational histories of the temperate stages of the Middle and Late Pleistocene are as follows:

*Pastonian.*[145] Deposits of this stage on the Norfolk coast have been insufficiently investigated. The pollen diagrams do, however, show the presence of temperate *Quercus* and *Pinus* woodland, with *Ulmus* and *Carpinus* also well represented. The vegetational history leading to this forest development and the changes associated with its disappearance at the end of the stage are not yet clear.

*Cromerian*.[145] The vegetational history of this temperate stage has again been insufficiently studied. A pollen diagram from the Upper Freshwater Bed at West Runton is shown in fig. 13.7, but it comprises only the first half of the stage, and most of the late-glacial is missing.

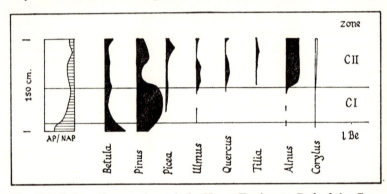

*Fig. 13.7* Pollen diagram through the Upper Freshwater Bed of the Cromerian stage at West Runton, Norfolk (after Duigan 1963). Values expressed as percentages of total tree pollen. Only the first half of the Cromerian temperate stage is recorded in this diagram.

*Table 13.4* Zone characters of the Cromerian stage and related deposits

| early-glacial | e L | High NAP,* few or no thermophilous trees | Arctic Freshwater Bed |
|---|---|---|---|
| post-temperate | C IV | *Pinus, Picea, Betula, Alnus* | Estuarine Bed |
| late-temperate | C III | M.o.f.,* *Carpinus, Abies* | Estuarine Bed |
| early-temperate | C II | M.o.f., High *Ulmus*, low *Corylus* | Upper Freshwater Bed |
| pre-temperate | C I | *Pinus, Betula* | Upper Freshwater Bed |
| late-glacial | 1 Be | High NAP, few or no thermophilous trees | Upper Freshwater Bed |

* NAP, non-arboreal pollen; m.o.f., mixed oak forest.

On the basis of more recent studies of freshwater and estuarine deposits around the Norfolk coast, the outline pollen zonation shown in table 13.4 has been drawn up.

Apart from the pollen record, about 150 species are known macroscopically from the Forest Bed Series.[95] But these were mostly identified many years ago, and their allocation to particular zones is in many cases impossible. The plants are nearly all native to the present flora, amongst the few exotics being *Najas minor*, *Picea abies*, *Abies*, *Trapa natans*, *Azolla filiculoides* and *Salvinia natans*. There are none of the so-called Tertiary-relics. Compared with the succeeding interglacials the Cromerian vegetational history is distinct in the absence or scarcity of *Hippophaë* in the late-glacial zone, the very low frequencies of *Corylus* throughout, the high frequencies of *Ulmus* and scarcity of *Tilia* in zone C II, and the late phase, zone C III, with *Abies* and *Carpinus*.

*Hoxnian*. Several deposits of this age are known in England. Both macroscopic and pollen remains are well known. The flora is very similar to that of the Cromerian in its paucity of exotic genera. A pollen diagram from this interglacial is shown in fig. 13.8, and the sequence of zones is as follows:

*Table 13.5* Zone characters of the Hoxnian stage and related deposits

| early-glacial | e G | High NAP |
|---|---|---|
| post-temperate | H IV | *Pinus*, *Betula*, NAP higher |
| late-temperate | H III | M.o.f., *Abies*, *Carpinus* |
| early-temperate | H II | M.o.f., *Corylus*, *Taxus* |
| pre-temperate | H I | *Betula*, *Pinus* |
| late-glacial | l L | High NAP, *Hippophaë* |

The characters distinguishing this sequence from the others are: the high frequency of *Hippophaë* in zone l L, the abundance of *Tilia* in zone H II, the late rise of *Ulmus* and *Corylus* in zone H II, and the important *Abies* phase in zone H III. The Irish interglacial deposits of Hoxnian age indicate the development of a distinctive type of flora with many evergreens, e.g. *Abies*, *Taxus*, *Rhododendron*, *Ilex* and *Buxus*, after an early phase which resembles the Hoxnian interglacial in England.[57, 135] All of these, except *Rhododendron*, have been found in the English deposits. They indicate a high oceanicity of climate during this temperate stage, perhaps more so than in the Cromerian, Ipswichian, and Flandrian.

An interesting feature of Hoxnian pollen diagrams from East Anglia is a period of deforestation towards the end of zone H II. At

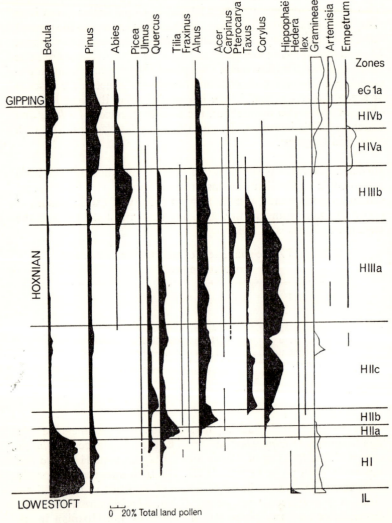

*Fig. 13.8* Pollen diagram from the Hoxnian interglacial lake deposit at Marks Tey, Essex (C. Turner). Values expressed as percentages of total land pollen.

Hoxne Palaeolithic artefacts occur associated with this, but it is impossible to say whether the presence of man caused the deforestation, or the deforestation allowed the incoming of man, or whether other environmental factors were responsible.

*Ipswichian.* Floras of Ipswichian age are known from south and east England, and both macroscopic fossils and pollen have been found. A pollen diagram from the period is shown in fig. 7.4. But there is no

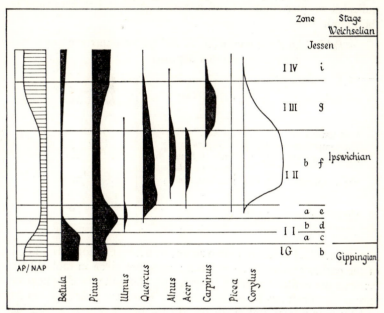

*Fig. 13.9* Composite pollen diagram through the Ipswichian temperate stage, based on a number of sites. Values expressed as percentages of total tree pollen.

one site showing all the vegetational changes of the interglacial; the pollen diagram, fig. 13.9, is therefore compounded from several sites. The zone characters are given in table 13.6.

The characteristics of the Ipswichian vegetational succession are the high frequencies of *Corylus* at the beginning of zone I II; the occurrence of substantial frequencies of *Acer* pollen, the scarcity of *Tilia* pollen, the varied behaviour of the *Alnus* pollen curve, the high frequencies of *Carpinus* pollen in zone I III, and the absence or scarcity of *Abies* and *Picea* throughout the interglacial.

Most of the Ipswichian sites contain abundant macroscopic plant

x

remains (plate 11), including only a few species not now found native, e.g. *Acer monspessulanum*, *Najas minor* (plate 11i), *Pyracantha coccinea*, *Trapa natans*, *Xanthium* and *Salvinia natans*. *Azolla filiculoides* is not found, though frequent in the earlier temperate interglacial stages. The presence of certain water plants, and of seeds of other water plants now rarely fruiting, or rarely found fossil in the Flandrian, in the British Isles, e.g. *Hydrocharis morsus-ranae*, *Lemna minor*, *Najas minor*, *Stratiotes aloides* and *Salvinia natans*, indicates warmer summers and a more continental climate than in the Flandrian.

*Table 13.6* Zone characters of the Ipswichian stage and related deposits

| early-glacial | e W | High NAP | *Equivalent zones of Jessen & Milthers 1928* |
|---|---|---|---|
| post-temperate | I IV | *Pinus*, NAP higher | i |
| late-temperate | I III | *Carpinus* | g |
| early-temperate | I II | M.o.f, *Pinus*, *Acer*, high *Corylus* | e, f |
| pre-temperate | I I | *Betula*, *Pinus* | c, d |
| late-glacial | 1 G | High NAP | b |

*Flandrian*. The Flandrian pollen zones, equivalent to zones II and III of the earlier temperate interglacial stages, are given in table 12.10. As with the earlier temperate stages, they show the development of temperate deciduous forests, but this development is brought to an end by man's interference. In the British Isles a widely applicable zonation after zone VIIb has not been established because of the local regional differences of vegetational history, mainly arising from the variability of man's activities in different areas. Such difficulties have been made apparent by the multitude of studies of Flandrian vegetation history. In the earlier pollen zones, too, similar problems of correlation are also appearing. The application of radiocarbon dating to these problems of the synchroneity of zones and subzones should clarify these difficulties.

The Flandrian vegetation sequence differs from those of the interglacial times by the early very abundant frequencies of *Corylus* pollen (zone V), the occurrence of *Tilia*, *Carpinus* and *Fagus* in the temperate forest, and the absence of *Picea* and *Abies*. Some examples of Flandrian pollen diagrams are shown in figs. 13.10 to 13.16. These

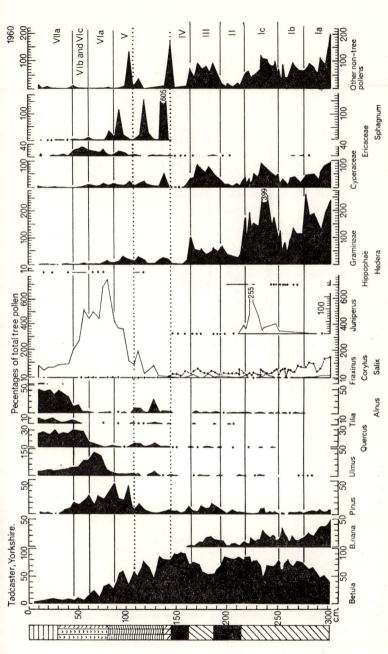

*Fig. 13.10* Pollen diagram from a lake infilling at Tadcaster, Yorkshire. All values expressed as percentages of total tree pollen (Bartley 1962).

**Fig. 13.11** Tree pollen diagram at Hockham Mere in the north of the Breckland of East Anglia. At the 340 cm level the strong decline of the *Ulmus* curve indicates the boundary between zones VIIa and VIIb. The pollen-zones are fairly characteristic for East Anglia but zone VIII is difficult to recognise in the absence of *Fagus* (Godwin 1956).

pollen diagrams show the principal Flandrian pollen zones, as found in eastern England (fig. 13.11), North Wales (fig. 13.12), Lake District (fig. 13.13), Cumberland (fig. 13.14), Scotland (fig. 13.15), and Western Ireland (fig. 13.16). These diagrams are from different regions, different elevations and different sediment types; their general uniformity demonstrates the usefulness of a system of pollen zonation. In the Cumberland diagram (fig. 13.14) a series of radio-carbon dates gives a time scale to the sequence.

Table 12.10 gives the main characteristics of the pollen zones in various parts of the British Isles. Zone IV (Pre-Boreal period) covers the time when birch, mostly *Betula pubescens* in Ireland, but both *B. pubescens* and *B. verrucosa* in Britain, established closed forests. In zone V, pine became an important forest tree in the south and east of the British Isles, and remained so in zone VI; in Ireland it displaced birch at a later time, in zone VI. Zone VI has been subdivided on the basis of changes in the pollen frequencies of the mixed oak forest trees. Both zones V and VI, constituting the Boreal period, show high frequencies of *Corylus* pollen. There is evidence that towards the end of the Boreal there was a period of dryness as seen, for example, in lowered lake levels at this time. The Boreal-Atlantic transition (B.A.T.) is the zone VI/VII boundary. At this time the climate apparently became much more oceanic and the change is marked in pollen diagrams by the decrease of *Pinus* pollen frequencies and increase of *Alnus* frequencies. Corresponding with this change is the development of ombrogenous blanket bog in upland areas and ombrogenous raised bogs in lowland areas. The climatic optimum of the Flandrian (average temperatures some 2°C warmer) is thought to have occurred in late Boreal/early Atlantic times. *Ulmus* (probably mostly *U. glabra*) is an important tree in the Atlantic mixed oak forest, and a sharp decline in its pollen frequencies marks the end of the Atlantic and the opening of the Sub-Boreal period. This decline is taken as the boundary between zones VIIa and VIIb.[112] There has been much discussion about the cause of this decline—whether it is of climatic origin or whether it is partly the effect of the agricultural activities of Neolithic man, which start to be of widespread occurrence around this time. There is also a possibility that disease may have contributed. A widespread synchroneity of the elm decline, demonstrated by radiocarbon dating, would be an argument for a controlling climatic cause of the decline, but although a degree of synchroneity has been demonstrated in north-west Europe, it is not close enough to make this conclusion certain.[46] The elm decline is usually accompanied by an increase in the pollen of herbs, in particular of *Plantago lanceolata*, which is an

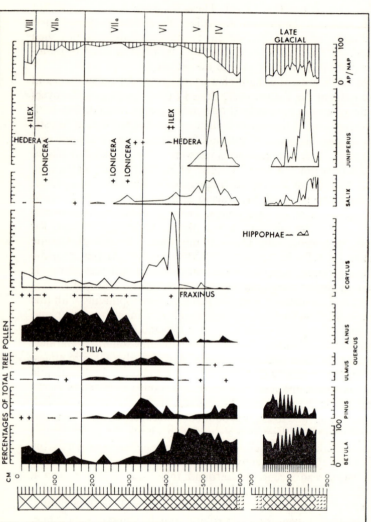

*Fig. 13.12* Tree pollen diagram from lake infilling in the Nant Ffrancon Valley, N. Wales. The curves shown black comprise the total on which percentages are calculated. The ratio AP/NAP shows the changing proportions of arboreal pollen (representing forest) and non-arboreal pollen (representing other vegetation) through the Late Weichselian and Flandrian (Seddon 1962)

important indicator of open ground, and these changes are taken to indicate forest clearance associated with Neolithic activity. Figure 13.17 shows a typical elm decline and associated clearance phenomena in northern Ireland.

The process of deforestation continued in zones VIIb and VIII or their equivalents. The boundary between these zones is more obscure than the earlier zone boundaries. In general, there are tendencies indicating climatic deterioration at the zone boundary between VIIb and VIII, as shown by the increases in *Betula* pollen and the decreases of *Tilia*, *Hedera* and *Ilex* pollen which have usually been taken to indicate these boundaries. The climate appears to have taken a turn towards wetter conditions, as bog stratigraphy indicates fresh growth of *Sphagnum* peats after earlier drier conditions in the Sub-Boreal when growth was slow or had ceased. Such fresh growth gives rise to the recurrence surfaces already mentioned in Chapter 10. The radiocarbon dates of these surfaces around the VIIb/VIII boundary vary between 450–900 B.C., an age near the supposed age (600 B.C.) of Weber's classical *Grenzhorizont* at the opening of the Sub-Atlantic period.[45] But the climatic changes at this time and later, as indicated by vegetational changes, are much confused by local anthropogenic effects. The introduction of various crop plants at Neolithic and later times becomes more and more noticeable. Both wheat and barley were cultivated from Neolithic times on, and rye and oats became important in Romano-British times.

## Some aspects of the history of the flora

*Comparisons of the floras of temperate stages.* The changes in the fossil assemblages of plants already described must now be considered from a more general environmental point of view. In the pre-Weichselian temperate floras it is difficult to make out a more than general environmental picture from the vegetational changes, partly because of the small number of sites studied, but also because the physiographic background is to a large extent unknown. When we come to consider what are the possible causes for the differing vegetational histories of the temperate stages, we are unable to distinguish the effects of the following possible factors:[141]

1. The distances from our area of glacial refuges where species might have survived.
2. The differences in the rates of movement of different species.
3. The roles of competition, succession, and soil maturation in vegetational change.

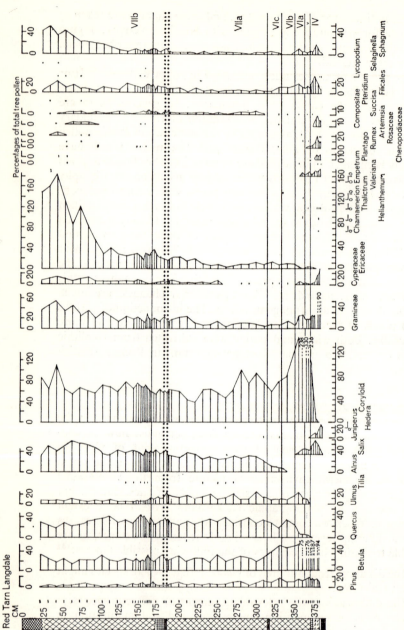

*Fig. 13.13* Pollen diagram from Red Tarn, Langdale, Lake District (1700 ft O.D.). The dotted lines indicate the horizon, just below the *Ulmus* decline, where sudden fluctuations in pollen curves suggest inwash of soil containing pollen (Pennington 1964).

*Fig. 13.14* Pollen diagram from Scaleby Moss, Cumberland. Values expressed as percentages of total tree pollen. Radiocarbon dates at zone boundaries are shown on the diagram (Godwin, Walker and Willis 1957).

*Fig. 13.15* Tree pollen diagram from lake infilling at Drymen, Stirlingshire, Scotland. Only a simple zonation is possible (Donner 1957).

4. Possible barriers to plant movements, e.g. high sea-levels.
5. The effects of climate.

First, factors connected with the distances of the glacial refuges of the plants from England and the rates of migration of different species. If the climatic amelioration at the beginning of a temperate stage is more rapid than the rate of migration, this rate and the distance of the glacial refuge will affect the time of appearance of, say, the mixed oak forest trees in the temperate stage. Difficulties in

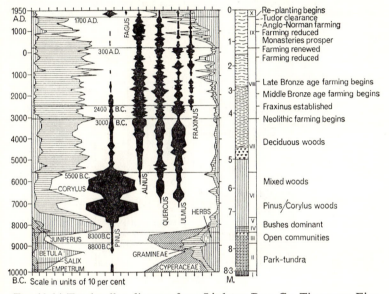

*Fig. 13.16* Total pollen diagram from Littleton Bog, Co. Tipperary, Eire. Stratigraphy, pollen zonation and notes are on the right of the diagram (Mitchell 1965).

interpreting the differences in the pollen diagrams resulting from this kind of factor arise because often we do not know the species concerned in the pollen diagrams, and because we know little of the biological factors determining the rate of migration. In the absence of palaeobotanical evidence of glacial floras in refuge areas it is difficult to suggest the positions of these areas, though some information may be gained about the direction of migration from a comparison of pollen diagrams of the same age over a large area.

In the early-temperate substages *Ulmus* and *Quercus* are the first of the thermophilous trees to appear in the temperate stages, including the Flandrian. *Alnus* and *Corylus* appear at variable times.

FALLAHOGY TD. Co. LONDONDERRY.

Fig. 13.17 Pollen diagram from the bog at Fallahogy, Co. Londonderry, N. Ireland. Values expressed as percentage of total tree pollen, including *Corylus*, but with totals of *Betula*, *Pinus*, *Alnus* and *Corylus* divided by

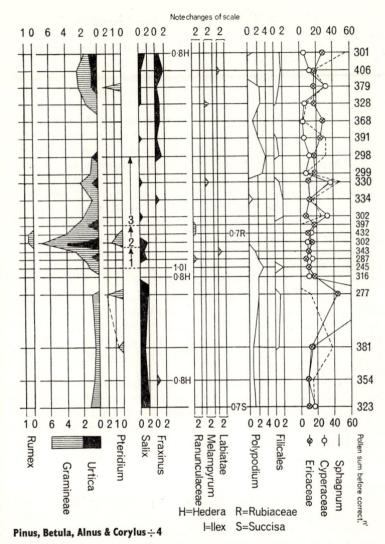

Note changes of scale

Pinus, Betula, Alnus & Corylus ÷ 4

H=Hedera  R=Rubiaceae
I=Ilex  S=Succisa

4 before calculation. The numbers 1, 2 and 3 in the centre of the diagram refer to phases of clearance (1), farming (2) and regeneration (3). Radiocarbon ages on the left (Smith and Willis 1962).

*Corylus* also behaves differently in the different temperate stages and the Flandrian. Nuts ascribed to *C. avellana* have been found in all the temperate stages, so it is probably with this species that we are concerned. Possibly the differing *Corylus* curves result from the behaviour of the species in competition with the mixed oak forest trees, following a different time of arrival of the species. In the earlier temperate stages, *Corylus* expands late, well into the mixed oak forest zone, and is not very well represented in the pollen diagrams. In the Ipswichian, *Corylus* expands to high percentages with the mixed oak forest. Perhaps this early spread is related to the incomplete forest cover suggested by pollen diagrams. In the Flandrian, *Corylus* appears in quantity before the mixed oak forest and the pollen frequencies expand to high values before the mixed oak forest becomes dominant. As mentioned above, these differences might be a reflection of the differing distances of the glacial refuges of *Corylus* during the successive glaciations. But it is also possible that ecological preferences, or some other properties of the species affecting its competition with the mixed oak forest trees, have changed during the long period of time involved.

In the case of forest trees appearing later in the temperate stages, other considerations arise in the interpretation of the differences between them. The conifers of the late-temperate substages are replacing the mixed oak forest trees, either as a result of climatic change, or possibly as a successional change following soil changes as the temperate stage proceeds.

The second kind of factor to be considered is that concerning barriers to migration of plants into Britain, in particular, the effects of sea-level changes in the temperate stages. During the glacial periods, with sea-levels perhaps 100 m lower than at present, Britain must have been joined to the continent by a wide isthmus, and Ireland to Britain by at least a narrow isthmus in the north. Fig. 13.18 shows the submarine contours around the British Isles. In the Flandrian, and in each temperate stage, Britain would be cut off by a eustatic rise in sea-level as the ice melted, providing that the land bridge across the Straits of Dover was flooded. The time of the rise in sea-level in relation to the development of the vegetation is obviously of importance in determining the course of its development. In the Flandrian, the rising sea-level seems to have cut off Britain from the continent at some time during the Boreal period (zone VI). As an example of the effect on plant distribution of isolation by a rising sea-level, we may mention the two trees, *Tilia* and *Fagus*, present in England but not native in Ireland. Perhaps these trees were prevented from further spread to Ireland by the rising

Flandrian sea-level. In the Ipswichian there is evidence that sea-level rose above its present height in the early-temperate substage, zone III, relatively earlier than in the Flandrian. It is possible that this early rise may account for the differences between the continental and English Ipswichian interglacial pollen diagrams, e.g. the apparent lack of *Tilia* and *Picea* in England though it is common on the

*Fig. 13.18* Submarine contours around the British Isles.

continent in this interglacial. On the other hand, in the Hoxnian, there is some evidence that the rise above present sea-level was much later, late in the early-temperate substage, or in the late-temperate substage, and this may account for the similarity of the late-temperate substage vegetation in England and on the continent, with both *Abies* and *Picea* as prominent conifers. An alternative explanation for the similarity is that a land bridge with the continent existed in this interglacial, the Straits of Dover being fully cut in the subsequent glaciation.

The sea-level changes of the older interglacials, however, are difficult to reconstruct, since tectonic changes have considerably affected the North Sea area.

Lastly, there is climate as a factor determining the differences in the interglacial vegetational successions. It is difficult to distinguish the effects of climate in detail. The arrival and spread of species are not necessarily correlated with climatic change. If the rate of climatic change is faster than the rate of migration of the plants, the presence of a species gives a 'minimum' value for climate. As we have seen, the vegetational succession can obviously be determined by factors other than climatic change. Where the vegetation type shown by the pollen diagrams remains stable, general indications of climate, e.g. degree of oceanicity or continentality, may be inferred. Where the disappearance of species can be correlated with climatic amelioration or deterioration we may obtain some indication of the nature of the climatic change.

The climatic differences between the temperate stages are difficult to infer. For example, the Ipswichian shows a very different pollen diagram from the other interglacials and from the Flandrian, with high percentages of *Carpinus* pollen and much pollen of *Acer*, in part *A. monspessulanum*, fruits of which are found in the deposits concerned. Both these plants have a continental distribution and their abundance might be thought to indicate a climate more continental than that of the Flandrian or of the Hoxnian. In the latter, *Alnus*, *Hedera* and *Ilex* are all very well represented, perhaps an indication of a more oceanic climate than in the Ipswichian Interglacial where these plants are not common. But the differences between the Ipswichian and Hoxnian pollen diagrams might be due to accidents of distribution and the effect of barriers to migration. It will be seen that it is difficult to disentangle the real climatic significance of the differences between the vegetational histories reflected in the pollen diagrams.

*Weichselian and Flandrian: theories of the origin of the flora.* When we come to consider the Weichselian and Flandrian, however, we have a much better picture of the general physiographic conditions under which the vegetational changes took place, and we have much more detail of the history of the flora.

Here we should consider the history of biogeographical thought about the origin of the British flora, as it is in respect of the Weichselian and Flandrian floras that most discussion has taken place.[33] Edward Forbes[40] in his classic essay of 1846 put forward the idea that five different geographical components in the British flora (and fauna) were the result of successive migrations into the British Isles under different climatic conditions at several distinct points of time and that gradual changes ensued as climatic changes occurred. He envisaged that the Lusitanian element was settled in Ireland in pre-glacial times, that the atlantic (south-west England) element and the more continental element of south-east England were probably also of preglacial 'migratory' origin, that the glacial (arctic-alpine) element appeared during the glacial epoch, and that the widespread Germanic element was received after the glacial epoch.

At a later date there was much discussion over the problem of 'perglacial' survival. Clement Reid in 1899 suggested that during the maximum glaciation the flora was nearly exterminated, only arctic plants survived in the south, and temperate species were entirely lost.[96] Wilmott maintained that species of local distribution survived in their local areas during glaciation.[146] Thus the peculiar Teesdale flora[90] would represent a nunatak flora which survived glaciation in that area. However, with our now increased knowledge of the history of the flora, it is clear that no generalisations on these lines can be made. Each species has its own particular history. Some survived glaciation in the British Isles, some are restricted and local because their habitat area was reduced by the forest spread in the Flandrian, while others may be now restricted by reason of narrow climatic tolerances or by man's interference with the balance of environment.[91]

We should now briefly consider the course of Late Weichselian and Flandrian vegetation change in relation to the present British flora. Godwin calculated that about half of the British flora was present in the British Isles in the Weichselian.[45] We know most about the Late Weichselian and at this time the flora, as we have seen, was a very varied one, mainly herbaceous, in which occurred many species now known as weeds and ruderals. During the Flandrian, forest was established, open habitats became rare, and there was an expansion in range of the woodland ground flora and thermophilous species. In zone VII, the extension of mires, soil changes towards podsolisation, and cultivation effects reduced forest.[36] In upland areas 'montane' species (e.g. *Armeria*, *Juniperus*) disappeared as a result of peat growth.[127] Many Late Weichselian relics survived these changes in steep and hilly areas, particularly where the rocks were calcareous, where trees found difficulty in growing, where grazing was an unimportant factor and where mire growth could not take place. The Flandrian vegetational changes produced a greater extinction of Late Weichselian species in Ireland (e.g. *Betula nana*) than in Britain, perhaps because such environments were much rarer, slopes gentler, and mires more widespread.

Y

In Neolithic and post-Neolithic times, zone VIIb and onwards, there developed much diversity of vegetation. Deforestation was accompanied by a rapid spread of weeds and ruderals, a diminution of the woodland flora and development of scrub, and widespread cultivation resulted in the introduction of both alien crop plants and alien weeds. Peat erosion started in the Pennines at the zone

Fig. 13.19 Clearance types at six bog sites. The sequences are dated by radiocarbon (Turner 1965).

VIIa/b boundary, and continued into historic times.[128] Temporary and extensive clearances have been distinguished by respectively low and high pollen frequencies of grasses. Pastoral activities have been distinguished from arable, the former showing high frequencies of *Plantago* and *Pteridium* pollen, and the latter with marked frequencies of *Artemisia*, Compositae, *Rumex*, Chenopodiaceae and Ranunculaceae pollen.[130] Fig. 13.19 shows the distribution of these agricultural activities, recognised by pollen frequency changes, in respect of six sites in Britain.

*The Irish flora.* The history of the Irish flora, in particular that of the so-called Lusitanian and North American elements, has long aroused interest. The flora is small (around 1260 species) compared with that of Britain (around 2200 species), and the area is of course much smaller than Britain, and has a less continental climate. It has already been pointed out that many British species must owe their absence in Ireland to the barrier of the Irish sea, for example, *Tilia cordata, Fagus sylvatica, Carpinus betulus, Paris quadrifolia.*

The species in the Lusitanian (L) and North American (N.A.) elements cannot be treated in groups. Rather they each have a separate history. Some frost-tolerant species e.g. *Eriocaulon septangulare* (N.A.), *Erica mackaiana* (L), may have survived in Ireland or in the north-west of the British Isles during the glacials. *E. septangulare* has been found fossil in the Hoxnian in Ireland. Both the fossil and living Irish species appear similar to each other, but distinct from the North American species, which suggests a disjunction of a former wider circumboreal distribution and slight speciation. Other species, frost-sensitive, e.g. *Arbutus unedo* (L), probably immigrated in the early Flandrian, while there is a possibility that some whose distribution is now seen to be expanding, may be introductions, e.g. *Juncus tenuis* (N.A.). There are a few Irish calcicolous species, of wide continental distribution, but not in Britain, e.g. *Inula salicina* and *Euphrasia salisburgensis*, and here the peculiar distribution type may result from extinction in Britain as a result of the later Flandrian environmental changes and destruction of habitats.

*Conclusions.* Even with the huge amount of data we have on the history of British flora, there are still very many gaps in our knowledge. There is yet no synthesis possible of the history of particular plant communities in the Weichselian or Flandrian, of the history of particular vegetation types on particular soil types, or much knowledge of how the plant lists can be segregated into their component communities. Neither are we able to carry interpretations of pollen diagrams far enough because of absence of data on recent pollen rain originating from vegetation types similar to those we believe were present in the Pleistocene. Rates of immigration and expansion of particular genera are also largely unknown, but here refined use of radiocarbon dating may give a lot of information. Because of our detailed knowledge which has already accumulated, and the comparatively small size of the British Isles and its isolated position in relation to the continent, there is every promise that progress can be made on these problems.

## HISTORY OF THE FAUNA

Forbes's essay on the history of the British flora and fauna has already been mentioned; his interpretation of the history of the faunal migrations was identical to that of the flora migrations already described. Scharff[105] continued along the lines mapped out by Forbes. As a contrast, Beirne's study of the history of the British fauna, dealing with the living fauna, is largely based on ecological, taxonomic and zoogeographical evidence.[12] Whereas we have a very rich record of plant fossils in the Pleistocene, which gives a substantial basis for reconstructing the history of the flora, it is not yet possible to reconstruct the faunal history in the same detail; the difficulties have been that many of the old records of fossils require re-study and placing in the stratigraphical scheme. Non-marine molluscs and insects are two exceptions here, for these groups are being actively studied in close relation to stratigraphical sequences. On the other hand, the Pleistocene vertebrates, subject to monographic study in the last century, require thorough revision and stratigraphical treatment.

### Foraminifera, Crustacea, Bryozoa

The most extensive records of Foraminifera are from the East Anglian Crag. A study of foraminiferal populations from boreholes and sections in the Crag has given indications of climatic and habitat change during Crag deposition and of the time of disappearance of certain Pliocene-relic forms.[42] In general two faunas are found; a Red Crag type with Pliocene-relic genera (*Pararotalia*, and the Lituolid genera *Dorothia* and *Gaudryina*), and a much poorer Icenian fauna. At the Neutral Farm pit, Butley, there is some evidence for cold conditions in the presence of *Elphidiella orbiculare* but the Red Crag type of fauna found in the Crag (Ludham Crag) at the base of the Ludham borehole, has warmer indications, based on a rich fauna including genera of the Anomalininae, Lituolidae, Rotaliidae, and Elphidiidae.

The Icenian Crags, represented at outcrop and above the Ludham Crag in the Ludham borehole, have a much more restricted fauna, in the same way that the Icenian mollusc fauna is also restricted compared with the older faunas, and the tests of the Foraminifera are generally thinner than those of the older Crags. Pliocene-relic forms are no longer found, *Elphidiella* is abundant, the Anomalininae are only represented by *Cibicides lobatulus*, and '*Rotalia*' *beccarii* is common at certain levels. The frequency of these three genera varies much in the Icenian Crag and it appears that in the warmer episodes *Cibicides* and *Rotalia* are abundant, with *Elphidiella* less conspicuous, while in the cold episodes *Elphidiella* is most abundant and the other two genera are much reduced in frequency. The species of *Elphidiella* are cold-tolerant, *E. orbiculare* and *E. cf. bartletti* in particular indicating cold conditons. The colder faunas are associated with the Thurnian, Baventian (both in the Ludham borehole), and are found in the Weybourne Crag of Sidestrand (Baventian?). The warmer faunas occur in the Antian of the Ludham borehole and in the Norwich Crag of Bramerton and the Chillesford Clay.

Foraminifera have also been recorded from the marine Cromerian (*Leda-myalis* bed), and also from the Corton Sands, where they are believed to be largely derived from earlier formations.[68, 140] Faunas have been recorded from the Hoxnian,[10] Ipswichian[7] and Flandrian,[69] but no detailed studies have been made of faunal successions in the Middle and Late Pleistocene.

Few studies of Pleistocene Ostracoda have been made, though these fossils are widespread in both the cold and temperate stages. A fauna of Middle Weichselian age, including a species of brackish water has been described from Upton Warren, Worcs.[28] A freshwater notostracan, *Lepidurus arcticus*, with a circumpolar distribution in northern latitudes, has been found in Weichselian and Middle Pleistocene deposits in association with floras of late- or full-glacial type. Studies of Cladocera in Late Weichselian and Flandrian lake

*Table 13.7* Localities with fossil Foraminifera, Crustacea, Bryozoa

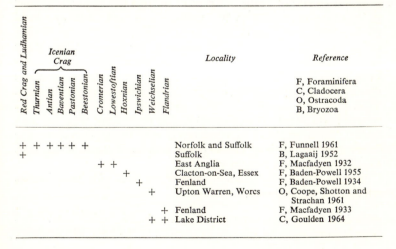

| Red Crag and Ludhamian | Thurnian | Antian | Baventian | Pastonian | Beestonian | Cromerian | Lowestoftian | Hoxnian | Ipswichian | Weichselian | Flandrian | Locality | Reference |
|---|---|---|---|---|---|---|---|---|---|---|---|---|---|
| + | + | + | + | + | + | | | | | | | Norfolk and Suffolk | F, Funnell 1961 |
| + | | | | | | | | | | | | Suffolk | B, Lagaaij 1952 |
| | | | | + | + | | | | | | | East Anglia | F, Macfadyen 1932 |
| | | | | | | + | | | | | | Clacton-on-Sea, Essex | F, Baden-Powell 1955 |
| | | | | | | | + | | | | | Fenland | F, Baden-Powell 1934 |
| | | | | | | | | | + | | | Upton Warren, Worcs | O, Coope, Shotton and Strachan 1961 |
| | | | | | | | | | | + | | Fenland | F, Macfadyen 1933 |
| | | | | | | | | | | + | + | Lake District | C, Goulden 1964 |

sediments in the Lake District have shown that these animals undergo frequency changes associated with climatic history and limnological conditions.[50] The Bryozoa of the Crag have been discussed in relation to the Plio-Pleistocene Bryozoa of the Netherlands, but again no detailed evidence of faunal changes is available.[64]

*Insects*[108]

The study of insect faunas has been one of the most interesting recent developments in Pleistocene research. Many faunas of different age have been studied (Table 13.8) in close relation to stratigraphy, and conclusions have been drawn about climatic conditions and the relation of the faunas to the contemporary vegetation. Of the insect skeletal fragments found fossil, most are coleopteran, both aquatic and terrestrial species, but larval heads and jaws of Diptera (Chironomids in particular) and Trichoptera are also sometimes common. Most remains are identifiable to living species, at least in the Late Pleistocene faunas which have been most frequently studied, and some even in Cromerian faunas. A very small number appear to be extinct, for example a scarab beetle (*Aphodius* sp.) with a distinctive head tubercle, not known living. There is no palaeontological evidence so far for any marked evolution of insects in the Middle and Late Pleistocene.[108]

Distributions of living species are known quite well, especially in Scandinavia, so it has proved possible to interpret climatic and vegetational conditions on the basis of the constitution of insect faunas. In the Weichselian, it often appears that both northern and southern species of beetle are present in the same fauna, a parallel to the situation found with Weichselian floras, and probably related to the effects of shifting climates and to the probability that Weichselian environmental conditions cannot today be paralleled. Many species identified are not British today, and these exotic species occur both in cold and temperate stages; in the former, northern European species occur, in the latter, central or southern European species. Thus it is now possible to envisage changing insect populations related to the Pleistocene climatic changes in the same way, and with similar biogeographical significance, as with the plant record. The relation of the two is of course close, because of the food relations existing between the two groups.

We can now briefly mention some of the sites with insect faunas which have been studied.

*Hoxnian.* A very good sequence of insect remains, mainly beetles, has been isolated from the interglacial deposit at Nechells, Birmingham, covering Lowestoftian late-glacial and much of Hoxnian times.[109] The fauna of about seventy species and many more genera is essentially a British one with only three non-British species named, two of which have disjunct distributions in southern Europe (a weevil and a species of *Platypus*). Other weevil species were abundant enough to allow their frequency to be correlated with the pollen frequency of their food plant, e.g. *Rhynchaenus quercus* and *Quercus*. The fauna indicates that at the optimum of the interglacial, climatic conditions were not greatly different from the present climate in the same region.

*Ipswichian.* Insect faunas from three Ipswichian sites have been studied.[27, 87] Several species have a distinctly southern or continental distribution in Europe, some exotic to the present British fauna, e.g. *Oodes gracilis*, a ground beetle of reedswamp habitat. A climate with summer temperatures distinctly warmer than that at present is thus indicated, a similar conclusion to that resulting from vegetational studies.

*Weichselian.* A small Early Weichselian fauna is known in Cambridge from terrace deposits with plant remains indicating Early

*Table 13.8* Localities with fossil insect faunas

| Hoxnian | Ipswichian | Early and Middle Weichselian | Late Weichselian | Flandrian | Locality | Reference |
|---|---|---|---|---|---|---|
| + | | | | | Nechells, Birmingham | Shotton and Osborne 1965 |
| | + | | | | Selsey, Sussex | Pearson 1963 |
| | + | | | | Trafalgar Sq., London | Coope 1965 |
| | + | | | | Bobbitshole, Ipswich | Coope 1965 |
| | | + | | | Sidgwick Ave., Cambridge | Lambert, Pearson and Sparks 1963 |
| | | + | | | Chelford, Cheshire | Coope 1959 |
| | | + | | | Upton Warren, Worcs | Coope, Shotton and Strachan 1961 |
| | | + | | | Fladbury, Worcs | Coope 1962 |
| | | | + | | Colney Heath, Herts | Pearson 1962 a |
| | | | + | | St Bees, Cumberland | Pearson 1962 b |
| | | | | + | Shustoke, Warwickshire | Kelly and Osborne 1964 |
| | | | | + | General | Osborne 1965 |

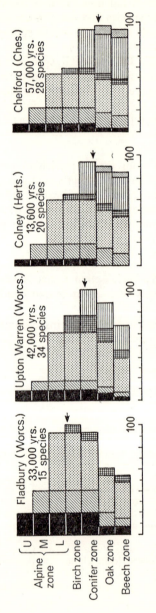

*Fig. 13.20* The distribution of carabid beetles from four Weichselian sites in England. The histograms show the percentage of the list of fossil carabids occurring in each of the present vegetational zones of Fennoscandia. The arrows mark the inferred vegetation equivalent at the fossil site. Chelford is seen to have the least severe environment (interstadial) and Fladbury the most severe (full-glacial?) (Shotton 1962).

Weichselian open vegetation.[65] The list gives no clear climatic indication towards warmth or cold, but contains halophilous species, as
does the flora. The interstadial organic deposit at Chelford, Cheshire,
contains a large fauna of about a hundred species and genera.[25]
A distinct thermophilous element is absent, and there is a collection
of species of a more northern type including three exotic species now
found in Scandinavia and the mountains of central Europe. Many
species are associated nowadays with coniferous or birch forest in
south Finland (fig. 13.20), e.g. the phytophagous pine weevil *Hylobius
abietis*, and these indications of the interstadial vegetation compare
closely with the flora list from the same site. The climate prevalent
at the time has been compared with the cool continental climate of
Finland between latitude 60° to 64° north.

The full-glacial faunas, such as that from Fladbury ($C^{14}$ age
38,000 B.P.), are very different.[26] This fauna indicates open almost
treeless vegetation in the region, and contains about fifty species. Of
these, eleven are exotic to the present British fauna, e.g. the beetles
*Diachila artica*, *Amara torrida*, and eight in Britain are only found
in the north. All except one are found today north of the Arctic
circle. Fig. 13.20 shows how the carabid species from Fladbury are
at present distributed in the vegetation zones of Fennoscandia, and
from this a climate with July mean temperature of about 11°C,
5·5°C lower than present, has been suggested. A similar comparison
is made in fig. 13.20 between the Upton Warren fauna ($C^{14}$ age
41,900 B.P.) and the vegetation zones of Fennoscandia indicating
slightly more temperate conditions than the Fladbury fauna. This
fauna is very large, about 190 species and genera.[28] Seventy-eight
per cent of the species are living in the area today, nine per cent are
restricted to north Britain or the mountains of Wales and thirteen
per cent are exotic to the present British fauna and mostly occur
in northern Europe. Other species are more southern and there is
a small continental element. Here we have an example of the very
different types of present geographical distribution present in one
fauna. Another interesting point is that although the carabid species
are mostly common in the conifer zone of Fennoscandia, few remains
of trees were found at the site. It is not clear whether these properties
of the fauna (and flora) result from rapid amelioration of climate
and resulting overlapping of distributions or from other climatic
factors, or from biotic factors, such as grazing by bison reducing
tree cover.

Another fauna, of Late Weichselian age, comes from Colney
Heath, Herts ($C^{14}$ age 13,560 B.P.);[85] the Fennoscandian distribution
of the carabid element of this fauna is shown in fig. 13.20. Forty-

seven species were recorded, including both northern and southern species, but again the flora from this site shows the vegetation to have been open, though the Fennoscandian correlation is with the conifer zone. Distributions mapped in fig. 13.21 of three Late Weichselian species from Corstorphine, near Edinburgh, show how ranges

*Fig. 13.21* Present distributions of three beetle species in Late Weichselian deposits at Corstorphine, Edinburgh (Coope 1965). *Barynotus squamosus* ||| , *Diachila arctica* \\\ , *Chlaenius costulatus* /// .

have changed since Late Weichselian time. It has been suggested that late-glacial climatic indications of cold continental type permitted the existence of *Chlaenius*, and of *Diachila* where the habitat was more exposed, but the western species of *Barynotus* was nocturnal and avoided the summer's day heat of a continental climate.[27]

*Flandrian.* A study of insect faunas from two horizons of alluvium at Shustoke, Warwickshire,[59] one near the zone VIIa/b boundary ($C^{14}$ age 4830 B.P.), the other about 400 years old, showed the predominance of a fauna characteristic of deciduous woodland at the first level, and a great increase in the latter fauna of insects living in open habitats. Weeds of cultivated ground are the food plants of some of the phytophagous beetles of this latter horizon. In the same way that some species of the full- and late-glacial flora again become widespread on deforestation in the Flandrian, so it appears that some beetle species (e.g. the carabid beetle *Agonum mulleri*) which are found in full- or late-glacial deposits are now associated with man's clearance activities.[87]

### Non-marine molluscs

These have been found very commonly in Pleistocene deposits in the British Isles. Much early descriptive work was done in the period up to 1950;[60] since that time more detailed quantitative studies have been made, especially in south and east England, and these have led to important conclusions regarding the environmental significance of the faunas.[118]

To judge by numbers of extinct species, it appears that some evolution has occurred in the Pleistocene. In the Cromer Forest Bed Series about twenty-one per cent of the species recorded appear to be extinct, in the Hoxnian about seventeen per cent, Ipswichian about fifteen per cent, and Early Flandrian about five per cent.[119] But these figures are taken from total faunal lists for each temperate stage, and there are great variations from site to site, so that the figures are less significant than they appear. A few species appear to be confined to particular stages, e.g. *Nematurella runtoniana* to the Cromerian, and *Valvata antiqua* and *Viviparus diluvianus* to the Hoxnian, but such conclusions are based on studies of few sites. In the Flandrian, presence of certain species indicates Roman and later times, e.g. *Helix pomatia* and *H. aspersa*, while an abundance of others e.g. *Lauria anglica*, *Vertigo angustior*, indicates an early Flandrian age.

Assemblages have been found to be indicative of particular types of climate. Cold faunas show a dominance of a few species in great numbers, temperate faunas a larger number of species, many of which occur abundantly. The cold 'loess-type' fauna contains abundant *Pupilla muscorum*, and also *Columella columella* (plate 16a), *Vertigo parcedentata*, *Pisidium obtusale lapponicum* and *P. vincentianum*. Species characteristic of temperate stages include *Corbicula fluminalis*, now in the Nile area and Asia west of India, and *Belgrandia marginata* (plate 16b), a southern European species, and also several extinct species, e.g. *Theodoxus serratiliniformis* and *Helicella crayfordensis*.

Deposits older than the Lowestoftian have not been systematically studied recently. Molluscan faunas of Lowestoftian and later age are mentioned in table 13.9. The late Lowestoftian fauna at Hoxne, nearly all freshwater species, is a nondescript one with no positive indications of climate.[116] The Hoxnian fauna at Swanscombe is a larger one, of nearly a hundred species and genera;[18] here a number of distinct faunas occur—a mainly freshwater one in the Lower Gravel, a marsh fauna in the Lower Loam, and again a mainly freshwater one in the Middle Gravels. Woodland species occur in the Loam and Middle Gravels, as do calcareous grassland species. The Middle Gravels fauna is characterised by the presence of species

*Table 13.9* Localities with fossil non-marine mollusc faunas

| Lowestoftian | Hoxnian | Gippingian | Ipswichian | Early and Middle Weichselian | Late Weichselian | Flandrian | Locality | Reference |
|---|---|---|---|---|---|---|---|---|
| + | + | | | | | | Hoxne, Suffolk | Sparks 1956 |
| | + | | | | | | Swanscombe, Kent | Castell 1964 |
| | | + | | | | | Thriplow, Cambs | Sparks 1957 |
| | | | + | + | | | Summary of many sites | Sparks 1964 |
| | | | | + | | | Upton Warren, Worcs | Coope, Shotton and Strachan 1961 |
| | | | | | + | + | Kent | Kerney 1963 |
| | | | | | | + | Apethorpe, Northants | Sparks and Lambert 1961 |
| | | | | | | + | General | Sparks 1962 |

described as 'Rhenish', including *Corbicula fluminalis*, *Valvata antiqua* and *Belgrandia marginata*.

A fauna of Gipping age has been found in tjaele gravels at Thriplow, Cambs.[117] It is very similar to the loess-type fauna, with a combination of dry and wet-loving species and abundant *Pupilla muscorum*. *Columella columella*, an indicator of cold conditions, is also present. This type of fauna is also common in Weichselian terrace deposits e.g. at the well-known sites of Barnwell Station, Cambridge and Ponders End, Herts.

Many Ipswichian faunas have been described in detail.[120] 125 species are known from this temperate stage. There is a steep rise in the number of species in zone I I, a maximum in zone I II, and a slow decline after this (fig. 7.2). Many southern species occur in zones I II and I III, e.g. *Corbicula fluminalis, Belgrandia marginata, Potamida littoralis* (plate 16c); their entry and expansion in number have been correlated with vegetational changes. On the whole the land molluscs first occur at a later time than the freshwater species, probably because dispersal of freshwater species is more easily accomplished by natural agents. Many of the southern species appear to survive well into the later part of the stage and even into the early part of the Weichselian. The Ipswichian fauna as a whole is not fundamentally different from the Flandrian, but it includes a number of species of central and south-east Europe (*Ena montana, Helicella striata*), a southern group (*Belgrandia marginata, Corbicula fluminalis*) and a south-west European group (*Potamida littoralis*). On the other hand, the Flandrian contains some central and south European species, but more species with oceanic, Mediterranean-oceanic, central and south-west European distribution types. Thus there is an indication, as with the plants, of a more continental type of climate in the Ipswichian than in the Flandrian.

The Weichselian faunas include those from terrace deposits and those from chalky sludge deposits in south-east England. The former are usually of a tolerant type, with no clear climatic indications, or of the 'loess-type' already mentioned, such as those of the Flood Plain terrace at Ponder's End in the Lea valley. Freshwater faunas of Middle Weichselian age at Upton Warren, Worcs, have *Pisidium vincentianum* and *P. obtusale lapponicum*, indicating cold conditions.[28] At this site there is some suggestion of water salinity dwarfing *Lymnaea peregra* and *Planorbis laevis*.

Late Weichselian faunas, predominantly of land molluscs, are well known from Kent.[61] Twenty-one species have been recorded. The affinities of the fauna are alpine rather than arctic. Several geographical elements are present; a very tolerant group, two arctic-alpine species (*Columella columella* and *Vertigo genesii*), southern Scandinavia and European species, west European species not in the Scandinavian mainland (*Abide secale*), and a species now known only in the Scandinavian mountains and from maritime habitats in north-west Europe (*Catinella arenaria*). Here we have similar variance of distribution types as with plants and insects, and presence of species whose distribution scarcely overlaps today, e.g. *Columella columella* and *Hygromia hispida*. A similar mixture of xerophilous and hygrophilous species is seen in the earlier Weichselian faunas. It has been suggested that with colder average temperatures, too rapid evaporation of ground moisture is prevented, and this allows the growth of species which would normally avoid such places. In zone I of the Late Weichselian the fauna is mainly of hardy Holarctic species, dry land species of open habitats; in zone II (Allerød) the assemblages increase in variety, indicating diversification of habitats, and thermophilous species spread. In zone III, the same fauna survives in spite of the climatic deterioration manifested by frost-heaving and frost-shattering of the Chalk. Some evidence, e.g. the frequency of hygrophilous species, points to an increased dampness in this zone compared with zone I, and perhaps the temperatures did not return to zone I severity.

The early Flandrian faunas show the continuance of the open grassland element, and a number of common European species appear at this time (*Helix nemoralis, Discus rotundatus*). In later Flandrian times *Pomatias elegans* becomes abundant on the Chalk and is characteristic of the warm part of the Flandrian. Many species appear about Romano-British times and later, e.g. *Helicella gigaxii, Monacha cantiana*. The effects of cultivation on the mollusc habitats must have diversified them and is presumably a major cause of the late spread of many species, especially the xerophilous land snails.

## Marine molluscs

There are abundant records of marine molluscs throughout the Pleistocene (table 13.10), in particular from the marine Early Pleisto-

*Table 13.10* Localities with fossil marine molluscs

| Red Crag and Ludhamian | Antian | Pastonian | Beestonian | Cromerian | Lowestoftian | Hoxnian | Ipswichian | Weichselian | Flandrian | Locality | Reference |
|---|---|---|---|---|---|---|---|---|---|---|---|
| + | + | + | + | + | | | | | | General | Reid 1890; Wood 1848–1882; Harmer 1914–25 |
| + | + | + | + | | | | | | | Norfolk | Norton 1967 |
| | + | | | | | | | | | Easton Bavents, Suffolk | Funnell and West 1962 |
| | | | | | + | | | | | Corton, Suffolk | Baden-Powell 1950 |
| | | | | | | + | | | | Clacton-on-Sea, Essex | Baden-Powell 1955 |
| | | | | | | | + | | | Fenland | Baden-Powell 1934 |
| | | | | | | | | + | | Cheshire Plain | Thompson and Worsley 1966 |
| | | | | | | | | + | | Scotland | Jamieson 1865 |
| | | | | | | | | + | + | North-east Ireland | Praeger 1896 |
| | | | | | | | | | + | General | Baden-Powell 1927 |
| | | | | | | | | | + | North-west Scotland | Baden-Powell 1937 |

*Icenian Crag* spans the Antian and Pastonian columns.

cene of East Anglia, but also from marine transgression deposits of the temperate stages and from sands closely associated with till sequences. There has been much discussion with faunas of the last type over the question of whether the faunas are *in situ* or derived. There was much early work on fossil marine molluscs, especially the systematics, in the nineteenth[147] and early twentieth centuries.[51] A more quantitative and ecological approach has more recently been applied to the faunas.[82]

Three properties of the changing mollusc faunas of the Pleistocene have been studied, times of extinction of species, times of arrival of new species, and the changes in climate suggested by percentages of northern and southern forms. By the time of the Middle Pleistocene interglacials there are only a few species which have since become

*Table 13.11* Distribution of marine Gastropoda in the Crags
(Boswell 1952)

|  | northern % | southern % | not known living % | total no. of species |
|---|---|---|---|---|
| Icenian | 26 | 0 | 28 | 98 |
| Butleyan | 21 | 2 | 40 | 163 |
| Red Crag Newbournian | 12 | 7 | 53 | 226 |
| Waltonian | 16 | 11 | 48 | 352 |
| Coralline Crag (Pliocene) | 4 | 12 | 57 | 303 |

extinct e.g. *Tellina obliqua* in the Ipswichian fauna. Thus a major time of extinction was after Icenian Crag times, and before the Hoxnian temperate stage. Several species have been recognised as first appearing at particular times, e.g. *Chlamys varia* in the Corton Sands, *Tellina tenuis* in the Ipswichian. Table 13.11 shows some of the trends which have been revealed by analysis of gasteropod faunas of Early and Middle Pleistocene age.

Several hundred species have been recorded from the Crags. The sequence of Crags determined by Harmer has already been referred to in Chapter 12. As with the Foraminifera, it appears that the Pleistocene Crag sequence is conveniently divisible into Red Crag, older or partly coeval with the Ludhamian, and the Icenian Crag, containing faunas of ages varying between the Antian and Cromerian. The Red Crag fauna is a rich one of several hundred species, with a marked percentage of northern species, the Crag itself being a shallow water shore deposit of landlocked bays or inlets. In contrast, the Icenian faunas appear to have lived in a more open and shallow sea, and are much impoverished, with about a hundred and fifty species, only forty of which are common. The shells are commonly thinner and more fragile than those of the Red Crag, perhaps an indication of decreased salinity. Characteristic species include *Littorina littorea, Rissoa semicostata, Leda oblongoides, Cardium edule, Astarte borealis, Scrobicularia piperata,* and *Mactra subtruncata.* The Icenian type of fauna is found at Easton Bavents[43] in the Antian stage, and at Bramerton and Chillesford in later temperate parts of

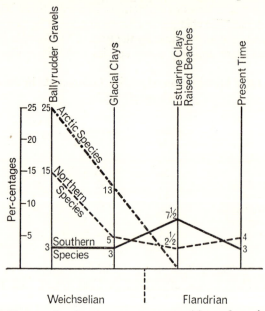

*Fig. 13.22* Changes in the percentage composition of marine mollusc faunas in north-east Ireland, showing the evidence for the climatic optimum in raised beach ('Neolithic') times (after Praeger 1896).

the Early Pleistocene and lower Middle Pleistocene. The fauna with *Leda myalis, Mya truncata* and *Astarte borealis,* at W. Runton, Norfolk, belongs to the marine transgression deposits of the Cromerian stage. Where the climatic conditions are more severe, e.g. in the Baventian basal stone bed at Sheringham, Norfolk, the Icenian fauna is much reduced and a prominent member is *Macoma balthica,* which characterises the so-called Weybourne Crag, once thought to be a specific horizon in Crag stratigraphy, but more probably of wider age limits.

A rich fauna from the Corton Sands in the Lowestoft area has been the subject of much controversy over whether it is wholly, partly or not derived.[140] The subject is still an open one, but the fauna is interesting in being intermediate in type between that of the Crag and that of the present day, with a small number of extinct species, some cold indicators and some warm indicators.

A fauna from the Hoxnian deposits at Clacton-on-Sea, Essex, is of a modern intertidal type,[10] and those from gravels thought to be associated with marine transgression of the Ipswichian, e.g. at Selsey, Sussex and the March Gravels of Fenland, are again modern in aspect.[7] Faunas also occur in Weichselian sands and gravels, as in the Cheshire Plain[129] and east Lincolnshire, but these shells are most likely to be derived from Ipswichian interglacial marine sediments or even perhaps partly from interstadial marine sediments, as suggested by a radiocarbon date of 28,000 B.P. from two shells of *Nucella lapillus* from fluvioglacial sands in the Cheshire Plain. Late Weichselian marine clays with a restricted mollusc fauna which includes arctic species (*Portlandia arctica*, *Pecten groenlandica*, *Astarte borealis*) have been found associated with the so-called 100-ft late-glacial sea in Scotland around the Clyde and near Edinburgh.[55]

Flandrian faunas are of modern type, but there is evidence that distributions have changed during this time; in particular, that ranges were extended during the warmer part of the Flandrian. For example, in north-east Ireland several species absent in the existing fauna are present in the mid-Flandrian estuarine clays and raised beaches, including *Tapes decussatus*, *Thracia pubescens* and *Rissoa albella*. In fact this difference between modern and mid-Flandrian faunas in north-east Ireland was the basis for the postulation of the climatic optimum by R. L. Praeger and it is graphically represented in fig. 13.22.[92]

*Vertebrates*

Although there is a large body of evidence concerning the Pleistocene vertebrate fauna, rarely are fossils found abundantly enough or in sufficiently continuous stratigraphical series to make possible detailed reconstruction of faunal history. Many of the past finds are difficult to relate to the geological sequence and many genera (*Elephas* in particular) have not been studied systematically for a considerable time.

There are records of fishes, reptiles, amphibians and birds throughout the Pleistocene. Several species of bird have been discovered in Weichselian and Flandrian cave deposits and from Flandrian peats.[15] But most attention has been paid to the mammal faunas, particularly

z

the land mammals. British Pleistocene mammals have been mono-graphed in considerable detail,[1, 31, 32, 99] but in many instances the finds have been recorded with insufficient stratigraphical data; con-sequently their provenance, age and ecological relations are in doubt. An example is the long list of species from the Cromer Forest Bed Series.[81] This sequence covers a number of climatic changes, and the stratigraphical context of each find is not often recorded. The process of faunal change and the nature of the faunal assemblages are therefore not very clear.

Evolution and extinction, or change in distribution patterns, have led to some species or genera having a limited range within the Pleistocene, and this is the basis for the use of faunal stage names in Pleistocene stratigraphy; for example, the Villafranchian faunal stage of the Early Pleistocene, which contains a number of species common to the late Tertiary.[63] In British faunal stratigraphy such stages have not been defined, except that the pre-Cromerian faunas have a Villafranchian aspect. Superimposed on the gradual faunal change resulting from evolution and extinction there are the changes related to climatic and vegetational changes. Thus in the Middle and Upper Pleistocene occur faunas characteristic of the interglacials (*Elephas* (*Palaeoloxodon*) *antiquus*, *Rhinoceros* (*Dicerorhinus*) *kirchbergensis* (*merckii*), *Hippopotamus*), and of the glacials (*Elephas* (*Mammuthus*) *primigenius*, *Rhinoceros tichorhinus* (*Tichorhinus antiquitatis*), *Rangifer tarandus*).

Of the temperate species, some are thought to be characteristic of woodland, others of steppe, or more open habitats,[151] and there is some support for this in their association with plant remains indicat-ing such environmental types.

Table 13.12 lists mammal faunas from the various Pleistocene stages, and, based on these lists, it is possible to outline a history of the mammal fauna.

The Cromerian and older faunas[122] are characterised by a Villafranchian element, more strongly represented in the Red and Icenian Crags, including *Elephas* (*Archidiskodon*) *meridionalis*, *Equus stenonis*, *Rhinoceros* (*Dicerorhinus*) *etruscus*, *Cervus* (*Euctenoceros*) *ctenoides*, *Cervus* (*E.*) *falconeri*, *Libralces gallicus* and *Mimomys plio-caenicus*. There are also a large number of extinct cetacean species associated with this period. There is a diversification of species within genera, including at least four types of elephant (*E. meridion-alis*, *E. antiquus*, *E.* cf. *trogontherii* and *E.* cf. *primigenius*), fifteen species of deer, and a number of species of the extinct vole *Mimomys*.[53] Unfortunately it is not yet possible to relate faunal changes in the Early Pleistocene with the known stages, but it appears that the

Villafranchian element is well represented in the Pastonian, because the rich fauna of the shelly crag of east Runton is thought to be of this age. But this faunal element is greatly reduced in the Cromerian. Two interesting records from this part of the Middle Pleistocene in Norfolk are a glutton (*Gulo luscus*) probably from the Pastonian, and a suslik (*Spermophilus*), a mainly steppe genus, from the early Lowestoftian (Arctic Freshwater Bed).

By the time of the Hoxnian, the Villafranchian element has been very much reduced or lost. Thus *Elephas meridionalis* and *Rhinoceros*

*Table 13.12* Localities with fossil vertebrate faunas

| Red Crag and Ludhamian | Icenian Crag | | | Cromerian | Hoxnian | Gippingian | Ipswichian | Weichselian | Flandrian | Locality | Reference |
|---|---|---|---|---|---|---|---|---|---|---|---|
| | Antian | Pastonian | Beestonian | | | | | | | | |
| + | + | + | + | + | | | | | | Norfolk and Suffolk | Newton 1891, Spencer 1964 |
| | + | + | + | | | | | | | Norfolk | Azzaroli 1953 (deer) |
| | | | | | + | | + | | | Swanscombe, Kent and Lower Thames | Sutcliffe 1964 |
| | | | | | + | + | + | | | Upper Thames | Sandford 1925 (elephants) |
| | | | | | + | + | + | + | | Lower Thames | King and Oakley 1936 |
| | | | | | | + | + | + | + | Torbryan Caves, Devon | Sutcliffe and Zeuner 1962 |
| | | | | | | | | + | | Pin Hole Cave, Derbys | Armstrong 1931 |
| | | | | | | | | | + | Star Carr, Yorks | Fraser and King 1954 |

*etruscus* have been lost. A species of *Mimomys* survives, but *Microtus* and *Arvicola*, first appearing in Cromerian, are well represented. Faunas of Hoxnian age are well known from the Thames valley, particularly from Swanscombe.[124] Here a fauna of many woodland species (*Elephas antiquus*, *Rhinoceros kirchbergensis*, *Sus*, *Cervus clactoniana*) is found in the Lower Gravels, together with a Clactonian industry, and above this in the Middle Gravels there are indications of increasing openness in the vegetation, with *Bos primigenius* and *Equus caballus* showing an increase in abundance.

In the Ipswichian similar woodland faunas are found, but *Hippopotamus*, thought to be absent in the Hoxnian, is also present.[124] In the Thames valley such Ipswichian faunas are found in London

(Trafalgar Square), Ilford and Aveley. The first named site is apparently earlier than the last two and contains a different fauna with no *Equus* or *Elephas primigenius*. At Ilford, in the late part of the interglacial, the palaeobotanical evidence shows open vegetational conditions; two species of elephant are present, *E. antiquus* and an early form of *E. primigenius*, together with *Bison*, *Equus* and two species of *Rhinoceros*, *R. kirchbergensis* and *R. hemitoechus*. The former is thought to be a woodland species, the latter a species of open steppe-like vegetation. In fact *R. hemitoechus* is more abundant than *R. kirchbergensis*, so that the vegetational evidence appears to support the difference between the two species. In the same way *E. antiquus*, the woodland form, is outnumbered by *E. primigenius*, a species of open vegetation. At Aveley, Essex, *E. primigenius* appears at the time when the forest opens out in the latter half of the interglacial. This fossil is a form of *Elephas primigenius*, related to the closely similar true *E. primigenius* of the Weichselian.

Of the faunas from the cold stages, several examples are known from the Gippingian, and many more from the Weichselian.[62] They are characterised by the presence of *Elephas primigenius*, *Rhinoceros tichorhinus*, *Rangifer tarandus*, with, less commonly, *Megaceros giganteus*,[76] *Ovibos moschatus*,[110] *Microtus nivalis*, *Lemmus lemmus*, and *Dicrostonyx henseli*. Sometimes *Equus caballus* and *Bison* are present, perhaps indicating conditions towards steppe rather than tundra. The mixture of steppe and tundra animals is characteristic of cold stage faunas. But a tundra species of *Bison* has been recorded in the Late Weichselian of the continent,[34] and studies of such remains from this country are necessary before closer ecological interpretation can be made.

The characteristic large mammals of the interglacials are not found in the Flandrian and the fauna is reduced to the fauna we know today, apart from recent extinctions from the British Isles, such as the wolf *Canis lupus* and the beaver *Castor fiber*.[30, 41, 115] Other species, such as *Cervus elaphus*, have undergone reduction in size since Late Weichselian time.[67]

Regarding the smaller British land mammals, present distribution patterns have been used to interpret the history of the fauna in Weichselian and Flandrian time. Species now common to Britain and Ireland, e.g. *Sorex minutus* and *Sciurus vulgaris*, are thought to have spread before Ireland was isolated by the rising Flandrian sea-level, while others found only in Britain, e.g. *Talpa europea*, *Sorex araneus*, were prevented from further spread to Ireland by the rising sea-level.[104] Particular problems are the presence of the common European vole *Microtus arvalis* in Orkney and Guernsey, though absent in the rest of the British Isles and the subspecies of *Microtus agrestis* in the Hebrides and mainland of Scotland. There are conflicting views about whether the peculiar geographical distributions of these species and subspecies are a result of speciation after introduction or after isolation following natural migration. There is insufficient fossil evidence to decide the matter.[29]

*Man.* Apart from finds of *Homo sapiens* in the Flandrian, two occurrences of *Homo* remains in older Pleistocene deposits deserve mention. One is the skull from the terrace gravels of the 100 ft Boyn Hill Terrace of the Lower Thames at Swanscombe, Kent,[84] associated with an Acheulian industry. This skull, found in 1935, is believed to be similar to the Steinheim skull, showing *H. sapiens* characters but with a Neanderthaloid bent (*H. sapiens steinheimensis*). The other is the find published in 1912 of a jaw and cranial fragments at Piltdown, Sussex, in terrace gravels either Middle or Late Pleistocene in age. The discovery resulted in much discussion on their significance in the evolution of man, and the remains were ascribed to *Eoanthropus dawsoni*. In 1953, following fluorine tests on these remains, it was demonstrated that the Piltdown skull was a forgery.[136]

Much more is known concerning the relation of man's artefacts to the Pleistocene succession, and a brief relation of the main industries and cultures to the Pleistocene sequence is given in table 13.13. The table emphasises the richness of the area and the completeness of the record. Eoliths, regarded by some as artefacts, have been recorded from the Early Pleistocene Crags. It is not until the Middle Pleistocene that the first well-defined industries occur. Artefacts of the Clactonian flake industry and the Acheulian hand-axe industry occur in deposits of Hoxnian age, proved by pollen analysis of lake sediments. Acheulian artefacts are more frequently found in river terrace gravels, and may be reworked into later terraces. Thus Acheulian artefacts have been found in gravels correlated with the Hoxnian, Gippingian and Ipswichian stages. Levalloisian artefacts occur in the Gippingian stage, in the Lower Thames area beyond the ice margin of the time. The Lower Palaeolithic sites appear to be settlements by lakes or rivers and they are mainly known from the southeast of England. The first cave industries occur in the Upper Palaeolithic, in the Pennines and in north Wales. These industries appear to be Weichselian in age but their exact correlation with the substages of the Weichselian remains in doubt.

The Mesolithic and later stages spread over Britain and into Ireland. The sites are usually open, often by lakes in the Mesolithic, and on raised beaches e.g. the so-called Neolithic raised beach of

*Table 13.13* The archaeological sequence related to stratigraphy

| Stage (time-scale not linear) | Industry/culture | Locality example (with radiocarbon dates B.P.) | Reference | Archaeological stage | General reference |
|---|---|---|---|---|---|
| VIII | Romano-British Iron Age A, B (La Tène), C Late Bronze Age | Trackway, Shapwick, Somerset (2642) | Godwin 1960b | Romano-British Iron Age Late | Richmond 1964 Hodson 1964 |
| VIIb | Urn Food vessel Beaker Chambered-tomb Windmill Hill | Avebury, Wilts (4530) | | Middle Bronze Age Early Neolithic | Longworth 1961 Devizes Museum 1964 Piggott 1954 Clark and Godwin 1962 Watts 1960 |
| Flandrian VIIa | Larnian-Obanian Horsham Sauveterrian-type | Oban, Argyllshire Co. Dublin (4260) Oakhanger, Hants (6300) Stump Cross, Yorks (6500) | Clark 1956 Mitchell 1949 Movius 1953 Rankine *et al* 1960 Walker 1956 | Mesolithic | Clark 1936 Rankine 1956 Wainwright 1963 |
| VI | Maglemosian Cresswellian Larnian | Shippea Hill, Cambs. Brandesburton, Yorks Cresswell Crags, Derbyshire (7602) Co. Londonderry (7680) Thatcham, Berks (9840) | Clark 1955 Clark and Godwin 1956 Armstrong 1956 Mitchell 1955 Wymer and Churchill 1962 | | Bohmers 1956 |
| IV and V | Protomaglemosian | Seamer, Yorks (9557) | Clark 1954 | | |

| Stage | Industry | Site | Reference | Palaeolithic | |
|---|---|---|---|---|---|
| Weichselian — L | Late-Magdalenian | Aveline's Hole, Somerset<br>Kent's Cavern, Devon | Garrod 1926<br>Garrod 1926 | Upper Palaeolithic | McBurney 1959<br>Garrod 1926 |
| Weichselian — M | 'Proto-Solutrean/Aurignacian' | Vale of Clwyd Caves, N. Wales<br>Kent's Cavern, Devon | Hicks 1888<br>Garrod 1926 | | |
| Weichselian — E | Mousterian | Oldbury, Kent | B.A. Rept 1891 | | |
| Ipswichian | 'Levalloisian' | Brundon, Suffolk | Moir and Hopwood 1939 | | Burkitt 1955 |
| Gippingian | Baker's Hole Levalloisian | Northfleet, Kent | Smith 1911 | | Roe 1964 |
| | Acheulian | Hoxne, Suffolk (zone IId)<br>Swanscombe, Kent | West and McBurney 1955<br>Ovey 1964 | Lower Palaeolithic | |
| Hoxnian | Clactonian | Clacton-on-Sea, Essex<br>Swanscombe, Kent | Warren 1951<br>Ovey 1964 | | |
| Lowestoftian | derived Abbevillian | Sidestrand, Norfolk | Moir 1923 | | |
| Cromerian | | | | | |
| Early Pleistocene | Crag eoliths | | Moir 1927 | | |

north-east Ireland and south-west Scotland. Artefacts of most of the
Flandrian industries occur in biogenic deposits so that their dating
by the radiocarbon method and by pollen analysis has been possible
in considerable detail.

## CONCLUSIONS

We have been concerned mainly with the fossil evidence for the
history of the flora and fauna of the British Isles, and it will now be
of interest to make comparisons between, and general observations
on, the histories of different groups as deduced from the fossils. The
total change we see in any group in the Pleistocene is the net result
of environmental changes acting in conjunction with evolution of
species. Our knowledge of evolution of species is based on the harder
parts of the organisms only. Concerning the history of the flora, a
few 'Tertiary relic' living genera are known in the Early Pleistocene,
but by Cromerian times, the flora appears to be largely of modern
European species. With the land vertebrates, the Early Pleistocene
Villafranchian element just survives into the Cromerian, but even
then the faunas younger than this are not of modern species, but
characteristically contain modern genera with extinct species. An
exception is *Cervus elaphus*, one of the oldest modern species and
known in the lower Middle Pleistocene. With the marine molluscs,
the number of extinct species is reduced at the Plio–Pleistocene
boundary and again at the Red Crag–Icenian Crag boundary.
Following Cromerian times very few extinct species are found. A
similar change in the foraminiferal fauna takes place at the Red
Crag–Icenian Crag boundary, and both these changes are probably
related not only to climatic change but also to the isolation of the
North Sea from the Atlantic by uplift of the southern part of the
Red Crag area, as indicated by Red Crag at high levels (at 400 to
600 feet O.D.) in south-east England (Netley Heath, Rothamsted).
There is little or no evidence concerning the history of the insects
or non-marine molluscs in the Early Pleistocene. In the Middle and
Late Pleistocene, the floras and faunas chiefly contain modern
species, except that the land vertebrates show high percentages of
extinct species of modern genera or genera closely related to modern
genera. Considering the gross climatic and other environmental
changes of these times, it is surprising that so little evidence of
evolution or extinction is seen in the lists of fossil plants and animals,
apart from the vertebrates.

But changes of distribution which modern species have undergone
are evident. Such changes in distribution have presumably in the first

place resulted from climatic change, and secondly from geographical barriers to species movement. In the British Isles relative land/sea-level changes must have played an important part in permitting or hindering movements. In the case of the Flandrian, where the rise in sea-level is quite well known, it is possible to explain certain plant and animal distributions as being a result of isolation by rising sea-level, for example, the absence of *Tilia*, *Carpinus*, and *Talpa* from Ireland. The relative numbers of species of land mammals in west Europe (167), Britain (41) and Ireland (21) is a result of this isolation, and the flora shows a similar trend. During the glaciations at times of low sea-level, Britain was certainly connected with the continent, and indeed the Weichselian and Gippingian faunas of Britain and the continent are similar. Ireland too has a limited Weichselian fauna with *Megaceros* and *Rangifer tarandus*, so land connections are indicated in that glacial stage, but earlier cold faunas in Ireland are not certainly known,[104] and there is some doubt about earlier land connections. The history of the Irish fauna and flora previous to the Weichselian poses interesting biogeographical questions. If isolation was the rule, then the survival of the Hoxnian floras through earlier glaciations may be possible, and this would suggest the Irish flora in Hoxnian times was a survival from an early western European oceanic flora, possibly of late Tertiary age.

In Britain, there is also the question of isolation during the inter-glacials. In Cromerian and Hoxnian times, it is highly probable that land connections existed, because of the similarity of faunas and floras across the channel. Perhaps this land connection was brought into existence by the Early Pleistocene uplift already referred to, for the Pliocene shell beds of Kent (Lenham Beds) and East Anglia (Coralline Crag) have strong southern affinities, suggesting junction of North Sea and the Atlantic. In the Ipswichian faunal comparisons[107] (e.g. *Hippopotamus* on both sides of the Channel) indicate a land connection with the continent, but the vegetational history is certainly very different from that on the continent, particularly in the absence of the late zone f (zone I III) expansion of *Tilia* and the absence of the *Picea* zone (h) of Jessen and Milthers. But perhaps there are climatic or edaphic or other reasons for such differences.

Such geological problems as these are presented by a consideration of the fossil evidence, as well as the problems of a biological nature. Of prime interest is the nature of the response to climatic change by species; questions of speciation, biotype formation and extinction, and rates of change of distribution area. It may be possible in future to relate fossil evidence to other lines of evidence concerning the history of the flora and fauna, such as the study of present distributions, and cytogenetic studies of biotypes and the ecological amplitudes of biotypes. It is only in this way that there will be more understanding of the nature of the changes in the fauna and flora which are so evident in the Pleistocene.

# REFERENCES

1 ADAMS, A. L. 1877–81. 'Monograph on the British fossil elephants', *Mon. Palaeontogr. Soc.*

2 ALLISON, J., GODWIN, H. and WARREN, S. H. 1952. 'Late-glacial deposits at Nazeing in the Lea Valley, north London', *Phil. Trans. R. Soc.*, B, **236**, 169–240.

3 ARMSTRONG, A. L. 1931. 'Excavations in the Pin Hole Cave, Cresswell Crags, Derbyshire', *Proc. Prehist. Soc. E. Anglia*, **6**, 330–4.

4 ARMSTRONG, A. L. 1956. 'Palaeolithic, Neolithic and Bronze Ages', in *Sheffield and its region*. Sheffield: British Association for the Advancement of Science.

5 AZZAROLI, A. 1953. 'The deer of the Weybourne Crag and Forest Bed of Norfolk', *Bull. Br. Mus. Geology*, **2**, 3–96.

6 BADEN-POWELL, D. F. W. 1927. 'On the present climatic equivalent of British raised beach Mollusca', *Geol. Mag.*, **64**, 433–8.

7 BADEN-POWELL, D. F. W. 1934. 'On the marine gravels at March, Cambridgeshire', *Geol. Mag.*, **71**, 193–219.

8 BADEN-POWELL, D. F. W. 1937. 'On a marine Holocene fauna in north-western Scotland', *J. Anim. Ecol.*, **6**, 273–83.

9 BADEN-POWELL, D. F. W. 1950. 'Field meeting in the Lowestoft district', *Proc. Geol. Ass. London*, **61**, 191–7.

10 BADEN-POWELL, D. F. W. 1955. 'Report on the marine fauna of the Clacton channels', *Q.J. Geol. Soc. London*, **111**, 301–4.

11 BARTLEY, D. D. 1962. 'The stratigraphy and pollen analysis of lake deposits near Tadcaster, Yorkshire', *New Phytol.*, **61**, 277–87.

12 BEIRNE, B. P. 1952. *The origin and history of the British fauna.* London: Methuen.

13 BOHMERS, A. 1956. 'A preliminary report on the statistical analysis of the Younger Palaeolithic of north-western Europe', *Palaeohistoria*, **5**, 7–38.

14 BOSWELL, P. G. H. 1952. 'The Plio-Pleistocene boundary in the east of England', *Proc. Geol. Ass. London*, **63**, 301–12.

15 BRAMWELL, D. 1960. 'Some research into bird distribution in Britain during the Late-glacial and Post-glacial periods', *Bird Rept. Merseyside Nat. Ass.*, 1959–60, 51–8.

16 BRITISH ASSOCIATION REPORT. 1891. Excavations at Oldbury Hill, Ightham, Kent. pp. 353–4.

17 BURKITT, M. C. 1955. *The Old Stone Age*. Cambridge: Bowes and Bowes.

18 CASTELL, C. P. 1964. 'The non-marine Mollusca', Ch. 8 in Ovey 1964.

19 CLARK, J. G. D. 1936. *The Mesolithic settlement of Northern Europe.* Cambridge University Press.

20 CLARK, J. G. D. 1954. *Excavations at Star Carr.* Cambridge University Press.

21 CLARK, J. G. D. 1955. 'A Microlithic Industry from the Cambridgeshire Fenland and other industries of Sauveterrian affirmities from Britain', *Proc. Prehist. Soc.*, **21**, 3–20.

22 CLARK, J. G. D. 1956. 'Notes on the Obanian with special reference to antler and bone work', *Proc. Soc. Antiqu. Scotland*, **22**, 91–106.

23 CLARK, J. G. D. and GODWIN, H. 1956. 'A Maglemosian site at Brandesburton, Holderness, Yorkshire', *Proc. Prehist. Soc.*, **22**, 6–22.

24 CLARK, J. G. D. and GODWIN, H. 1962. 'The Neolithic in the Cambridgeshire Fens', *Antiquity*, **36**, 10–23.

25 COOPE, G. R. 1959. 'A late-Pleistocene insect fauna from Chelford, Cheshire', *Proc. R. Soc.*, B, **151**, 70–86.

26 COOPE, G. R. 1962. 'A Pleistocene Coleopterous fauna with arctic affinities from Fladbury, Worcestershire', *Q.J. Geol. Soc. Lond.*, **118**, 103–23.

27 COOPE, G. R. 1965. 'Fossil insect faunas from Late Quaternary deposits in Britain', *Adv. Sci.*, **21**, 564–75.

28 COOPE, G. R., SHOTTON, F. W. and STRACHAN, I. 1961. 'A Late Pleistocene fauna and flora from Upton Warren, Worcestershire', *Phil. Trans. R. Soc.*, B, **244**, 379–421.

29 CORBET, G. B. 1961. 'Origin of the British insular races of small mammals and of the "Lusitanian" fauna', *Nature*, **191**, 1037–40.

30 CORBET, G. B. 1964. *The identification of British Mammals.* London: British Museum (Nat. Hist.).

31 DAWKINS, W. B. 1869. 'On the distribution of the British Post-glacial Mammals', *Q.J. Geol. Soc. London*, **25**, 192–217.

32 DAWKINS, W. B. and SANFORD, W. A. 1866–87. 'The British Pleistocene Mammalia', *Mon. Palaeontogr. Soc.*

33 DEEVEY, E. S. 1949. 'Biogeography of the Pleistocene', *Bull. Geol. Soc. Am.*, **60**, 1315–1416.

34 DEGERBØL, M. 1964. 'Some remarks on late- and post-glacial vertebrate fauna and its ecological relations in northern Europe', *J. Anim. Ecol.*, **33** (Supplement), 71–85.

35 DEVIZES MUSEUM. 1964. *Guide Catalogue of the Neolithic and Bronze Age collections in Devizes Museum.* Devizes.

36 Discussion on the development of habitats in the Post-Glacial. 1965. *Proc. R. Soc.*, B, **161**, 293–375.

37 DONNER, J. J. 1957. 'The geology and vegetation of Late-glacial retreat stages in Scotland', *Trans. R. Soc. Edin.*, **63**, 221–64.

38 DUIGAN, S. L. 1955. 'Plant remains from the gravels of the Summertown-Radley Terrace near Dorchester, Oxfordshire', *Q.J. Geol. Soc. London*, **111**, 225–38.

39 DUIGAN, S. L. 1963. 'Pollen analyses of the Cromer Forest Bed Series in East Anglia', *Phil. Trans. R. Soc.*, B, **246**, 149–202.

40 FORBES, E. 1846. 'On the connexion between the distribution of the existing fauna and flora of the British Isles, and the geological changes which have affected their area, especially during the epoch of the Northern Drift', *Mem. Geol. Surv. G.B.*, **1**, 336–432.

41 FRASER, F. C. and KING, J. E. 1954. 'Faunal remains', in J. G. D. Clark. *Excavations at Star Carr*, pp. 70–95. Cambridge University Press.

42 FUNNELL, B. M. 1961. 'The Palaeogene and Early Pleistocene of Norfolk', *Trans. Norfolk Norwich Nat. Soc.*, **19**, 340–64.

43 FUNNELL, B. M. and WEST, R. G. 1962. 'The Early Pleistocene of Easton Bavents', *Q.J. Geol. Soc. London*, **118**, 125–41.

44 GARROD, D. 1926. *The Upper Palaeolithic Age in Britain*. Oxford: Clarendon Press.

45 GODWIN, H. 1956. *History of the British Flora*. Cambridge University Press.

46 GODWIN, H. 1960a. 'Radiocarbon dating and Quaternary history in Britain', *Proc. R. Soc.*, B, **153**, 287–320.

47 GODWIN, H. 1960b. 'Prehistoric wooden trackways of the Somerset levels: their construction, age and relation to climatic change', *Proc. Prehist. Soc.*, **26**, 1–36.

48 GODWIN, H. 1964. 'Late-Weichselian conditions in south-eastern Britain: organic deposits at Colney Heath, Herts', *Proc. R. Soc.*, B, **160**, 258–75.

49 GODWIN, H., WALKER, D. and WILLIS, E. H. 1957. 'Radiocarbon dating and post-glacial vegetational history: Scaleby Moss', *Proc. R. Soc.*, B, **147**, 352–66.

50 GOULDEN, C. E. 1964. 'The history of the Cladoceran fauna of Esthwaite Water (England) and its limnological significance', *Arch. Hydrobiol.*, **60**, 1–52.

51 HARMER, F. W. 1914–1925. 'The Pliocene Mollusca of Great Britain', *Mon. Palaeontogr. Soc.*

52 HICKS, H. 1888. 'On the Cae Gwyn Cave, North Wales', *Q.J. Geol. Soc. London*, **44**, 561–77.

53 HINTON, M. A. C. 1926. *Monograph of the voles and lemmings (Microtinae)*. London: British Museum (Natural History).

54 HODSON, F. R. 1964. 'Cultural grouping within the British pre-Roman Iron Age', *Proc. Prehist. Soc.*, **30**, 99–110.

55 JAMIESON, T. F. 1865. 'On the history of the last geological changes in Scotland', *Q.J. Geol. Soc. London*, **21**, 161–203.

56 JESSEN, K. 1949. 'Studies in Late Quaternary deposits and flora-history of Ireland', *Proc. R. Ir. Acad.*, **52** B, 85–290.

57 JESSEN, K., FARRINGTON, A. and ANDERSEN, S. J. 1959. 'The interglacial deposit near Gort, Co. Galway, Ireland', *Proc. R. Ir. Acad.*, **60** B, 1–77.

58 KELLY, M. R. 1964. 'The Middle Pleistocene of north Birmingham', *Phil. Trans. R. Soc.*, B, **247**, 533–92.

59 KELLY, M. R. and OSBORNE, P. J. 1964. 'Two faunas and floras from

the alluvium at Shustoke, Warwickshire', *Proc. Linn. Soc. London*, **176**, 37–65.

60 KENNARD, A. S. and WOODWARD, B. B. 1922. 'The post-Pliocene non-marine Mollusca of the east of England', *Proc. Geol. Ass. London*, **33**, 104–42.

61 KERNEY, M. P. 1963. 'Late-glacial deposits on the Chalk of south-east England', *Phil. Trans. R. Soc.*, B, **246**, 203–54.

62 KING, W. B. R. and OAKLEY, K. P. 1936. 'The Pleistocene succession in the lower parts of the Thames Valley', *Proc. Prehist. Soc.*, 1936, 52–76.

63 KURTEN, B. 1963. 'Villafranchian faunal evolution', *Soc. Sci. Fenn. Comment. Biol.*, **26**, No. 3.

64 LAGAAIJ, R. 1952. 'The Pliocene Bryozoa of the Low Countries', *Med. Geol. Sticht.*, Ser. C, V, No. 5.

65 LAMBERT, C. A., PEARSON, R. G. and SPARKS, B. W. 1962. 'Pleistocene deposits from Sidgwick Avenue, Cambridge', *Proc. Linn. Soc. London*, **174**, 13–29.

66 LONGWORTH, I. H. 1961. 'The origin and development of the primary series in the Collared Urn tradition in England and Wales', *Proc. Prehist. Soc.*, **27**, 263–93.

67 LOWE, V. P. W. 1961. 'A discussion on the history, present status and future conservation of the Red Deer (*Cervus elaphus* L.) in Scotland', *Terre et la vie*, **108**, 9–40.

68 MACFADYEN, W. A. 1932. 'Foraminifera from some late Pliocene and glacial deposits of East Anglia', *Geol. Mag.*, **69**, 481–97.

69 MACFADYEN, W. A. 1933. 'The Foraminifera of the Fenland clays at St. Germans, near King's Lynn', *Geol. Mag.*, **70**, 182–91.

70 MATTHEWS, J. R. 1955. *Origin and distribution of the British Flora.* London: Hutchinson.

71 MCBURNEY, C. M. B. 1959. 'Report on the first season's fieldwork on British Upper Palaeolithic Cave deposits', *Proc. Prehist. Soc.*, **25**, 260–9.

72 MITCHELL, G. F. 1948. 'Two inter-glacial deposits in south-east Ireland', *Proc. R. Ir. Acad.*, **52** B, 1–14.

73 MITCHELL, G. F. 1949. 'The "Larnian" culture: a review', *J. R. Soc. Antiqu. Ireland*, **79**, 170–81.

74 MITCHELL, G. F. 1955. 'The Mesolithic site at Toome Bay, Co. Londonderry', *Ulster J. Arch.*, **18**, 1–16.

75 MITCHELL, G. F. 1965. 'Littleton Bog, Tipperary: an Irish vegetational record', *Geol. Soc. Am.* Special Paper No. 84, 1–16.

76 MITCHELL, G. F. and PARKES, H. M. 1949. 'The Giant Deer in Ireland', *Proc. R. Ir. Acad.*, **52** B, 291–314.

77 MOIR, J. R. 1923. 'An early palaeolith from the Cromer Till at Sidestrand', *Antiqu. J.*, **3**, 135–7.

78 MOIR, J. R. 1927. *The antiquity of man in East Anglia.* Cambridge University Press.

79 MOIR, J. R. and HOPWOOD, A. T. 1939. 'Excavations at Brundon, Suffolk (1935–37)', *Proc. Prehist. Soc.*, **5**, 1–32.

80 MOVIUS, H. L. 1953. 'Curran Point, Larne, County Antrim: the type site of the Irish Mesolithic', *Proc. R. Ir. Acad.*, **56** C, 1–195.

81 NEWTON, E. T. 1891. *The Vertebrata of the Pliocene deposits of Britain.* Mem. Geol. Surv. U.K.

82 NORTON, P. E. P. 1967. 'Marine Mollusca in the Early Pleistocene of Sidestrand, Bramerton, and the Royal Society borehole at Ludham, Norfolk', *Phil. Trans. R. Soc.*, B, **253**, 161–200.

83 OSBORNE, P. J. 1965. 'The effect of forest clearance on the distribution of the British insect fauna', *Proc. 12th Int. Congress Ent. (London)*, 454–5.

84 OVEY, C. D. 1964. *The Swanscombe Skull. A survey of research on a Pleistocene site*, ed. C. D. Ovey. Royal Anthropological Institute, Occasional Memoir No. 20.

85 PEARSON, R. G. 1962a. 'The Coleoptera from a detritus deposit of full-glacial age at Colney Heath, near St Albans', *Proc. Linn. Soc. London*, **173**, 37–55.

86 PEARSON, R. G. 1962b. 'The Coleoptera from a Late-glacial deposit at St. Bees, West Cumberland', *J. Anim. Ecol.*, **31**, 129–50.

87 PEARSON, R. G. 1963. 'Coleopteran associations in the British Isles during the Late Quaternary Period', *Biol. Rev.*, **38**, 334–63.

88 PENNINGTON, W. 1964. 'Pollen analyses from the deposits of six upland tarns in the Lake District', *Phil. Trans. R. Soc.*, B, **248**, 205–44.

89 PIGGOTT, S. 1954. *The Neolithic cultures of the British Isles.* Cambridge University Press.

90 PIGOTT, C. D. 1956. 'The vegetation of upper Teesdale in the north Pennines', *J. Ecol.*, **44**, 545–86.

91 PIGOTT, C. D. and WALTERS, S. M. 1954. 'On the interpretation of the discontinuous distributions shown by certain British species of open habitats', *J. Ecol.*, **42**, 95–116.

92 PRAEGER, R. L. 1896. 'Report upon the raised beaches of the northeast of Ireland, with special reference to their fauna', *Proc. R. Ir. Acad.*, **4**, (3rd series), 30–54.

93 RANKINE, W. F. 1956. 'The Mesolithic of southern England', *Surrey Arch. Soc.*, Research Paper No. 4.

94 RANKINE, W. F., RANKINE, W. M. and DIMBLEBY, G. W. 1960. 'Further excavations at a Mesolithic site at Oakhanger, Selbourne, Hants', *Proc. Prehist. Soc.*, **26**, 246–62.

95 REID, C. 1890. *The Pliocene deposits of Britain.* Mem. Geol. Surv. U.K.

96 REID, C. 1899. *The origin of the British Flora.* London: Dulau.

97 REID, C. and E. M. 1915. 'The Pliocene floras of the Dutch-Prussian border', *Med. Rijksopsporing v. Delfstoffen*, No. 6.

98 REID, E. M. 1920. 'Two preglacial floras from Castle Eden', *Q.J. Geol. Soc. London*, **76**, 104–44.

99 REYNOLDS, S. H. 1902–12. 'A monograph of the British Pleistocene Mammalia', *Mon. Palaeontogr. Soc.*

100 RICHMOND, I. A. 1964. *Roman Britain.* 2nd edn. London: Penguin.

101 ROE, D. A. 1964. 'The British Lower and Middle Palaeolithic: some problems, methods of study and preliminary results', *Proc. Prehist. Soc.*, **30**, 245–67.

102 ROUND, F. E. 1961. 'The diatoms of a core from Esthwaite Water', *New Phytol.*, **60**, 43–59.

103 SANDFORD, K. S. 1925. 'The fossil elephants of the upper Thames basin', *Q.J. Geol. Soc. London*, **81**, 62–86.

104 SAVAGE, R. J. G. 1966. 'Irish Pleistocene mammals', *Ir. Nat. J.*, **15**, 117–30.

105 SCHARFF, R. F. 1907. *European animals: their geological history and geographical distribution.* London: Constable.

106 SEDDON, B. 1962. 'Late-glacial deposits at Llyn Dwythwch and Nant Ffrancon, Caernarvonshire', *Phil. Trans. R. Soc.*, B, **244**, 459–81.

107 SHOTTON, F. W. 1962. 'The physical background of Britain in the Pleistocene', *Adv. Sci.*, **19**, 1–14.

108 SHOTTON, F. W. 1965. 'Movements of insect populations in the British Pleistocene', *Geol. Soc. Am.* Special Paper No. 84, 17–33.

109 SHOTTON, F. W. and OSBORNE, P. J. 1965. 'The fauna of the Hoxnian interglacial deposits of Nechells, Birmingham', *Phil. Trans. R. Soc.*, B, **248**, 353–78.

110 SIMONS, J. W. 1962. 'New records of Musk Ox from Plumstead, Kent and Cosgrove, Northants', *Lond. Nat.*, No. 41, 42–53.

111 SIMPSON, I. M. and WEST, R. G. 1958. 'On the stratigraphy and palaeobotany of a late-Pleistocene organic deposit at Chelford, Cheshire', *New Phytol.*, **57**, 239–50.

112 SMITH, A. G. 1961. 'The Atlantic—Sub-boreal transition', *Proc. Linn. Soc. London*, **172**, 38–49.

113 SMITH, A. G. and WILLIS, E. H. 1962. 'Radiocarbon dating of the Fallahogy Landnam phase', *Ulster J. Archaeol.*, **24–5**, 16–24.

114 SMITH, R. A. 1911. 'A Palaeolithic industry at Northfleet, Kent', *Archaeologia*, **62**, 515–32.

115 SOUTHERN, H. N. 1964. *The handbook of British Mammals.* Oxford, Blackwell.

116 SPARKS, B. W. 1956. 'The non-marine Mollusca of the Hoxne Interglacial', Appendix, in West 1956.

117 SPARKS, B. W. 1957. 'The tjaele gravel near Thriplow, Cambridgeshire', *Geol. Mag.*, **94**, 194–200.

118 SPARKS, B. W. 1961. 'The ecological interpretation of Quaternary non-marine Mollusca', *Proc. Linn. Soc. London*, **172**, 71–80.

119 SPARKS, B. W. 1962. 'Non-marine Mollusca and archaeology', in *Science and Archaeology*, ed. D. R. Brothwell and E. S. Higgs. London: Thames and Hudson.

120 SPARKS, B. W. 1964. 'The distribution of non-marine Mollusca in the last Interglacial in south-east England', *Proc. Malac. Soc. London*, **36**, 7–25.

121 SPARKS, B. W. and LAMBERT, C. A. 1961. 'The post-glacial deposits at Apethorpe, Northamptonshire', *Proc. Malac. Soc. London*, **34**, 302–15.

122 SPENCER, H. E. P. 1964. 'The contemporary Mammalian fossils of the Crags', *Trans. Suffolk. Nat. Soc.*, **12**, 333–44.

123 STEVENS, L. A. 1960. 'The interglacial of the Nar Valley', *Q.J. Geol. Soc. London*, **115**, 291–316.

124 SUTCLIFFE, A. J. 1964. 'The mammalian fauna', Ch. 9 in Ovey 1964.

125 SUTCLIFFE, A. J. and ZEUNER, F. E. 1962. 'Excavations in the Torbryan Caves, Devonshire. 1. Tornewton Cave', *Proc. Devon Arch. Expl. Soc.*, **5**, 127–45.

126 SYLVESTER-BRADLEY, P. C. 1963. 'Post-Tertiary Speciation in Europe', *Nature*, **199**, 126–30.

127 TALLIS, J. H. 1964a. 'The pre-peat vegetation of the southern Pennines', *New Phytol.*, **63**, 363–73.

128 TALLIS, J. H. 1964b. 'Studies on southern Pennine peats. II. The pattern of erosion', *J. Ecol.*, **52**, 333–44.

129 THOMPSON, D. B. and WORSLEY, P. 1966. 'A late Pleistocene marine molluscan fauna from the drifts of the Cheshire Plain', *Geol. J.*, **5**, 197–207.

130 TURNER, J. 1965. 'A contribution to the history of forest clearance', *Proc. R. Soc.*, B, **161**, 343–53.

131 WAINWRIGHT, G. J. 1963. 'A reinterpretation of the Microlithic industries of Wales', *Proc. Prehist. Soc.*, **29**, 99–132.

132 WALKER, D. 1956. 'A site at Stump Cross, near Grassington, Yorkshire, and the age of the Pennine Microlithic industry', *Proc. Prehist. Soc.*, **22**, 23–8.

133 WARREN, S. H. 1951. 'The Clacton flint industry; a new interpretation', *Proc. Geol. Ass. London*, **62**, 107–35.

134 WATTS, W. A. 1960. 'C-14 dating and the Neolithic in Ireland', *Antiquity*, **34**, 111–16.

135 WATTS, W. A. 1964. 'Interglacial deposits at Baggotstown, near Bruff. Co. Limerick', *Proc. R. Ir. Acad.*, **63**, B, 167–89.

136 WEINER, J. S., OAKLEY, K. P. and LE GROS CLARK, W. E. 1953. 'The solution of the Piltdown problem', *Bull. Br. Mus. Geology*, **2**, 139–46.

137 WEST, R. G. 1956. 'The Quaternary deposits at Hoxne, Suffolk', *Phil. Trans. R. Soc.*, B, **239**, 265–356.

138 WEST, R. G. 1957. 'Interglacial deposits at Bobbitshole, Ipswich', *Phil. Trans. R. Soc.*, B, **241**, 1–31.

139 WEST, R. G. 1961a. 'Vegetational history of the Early Pleistocene of the Royal Society Borehole at Ludham, Norfolk', *Proc. R. Soc.*, B, **155**, 437–53.

140 WEST, R. G. 1961b. 'The glacial and interglacial deposits of Norfolk', *Trans. Norfolk Norwich Nat. Soc.*, **19**, 365–75.

141 WEST, R. G. 1961c. 'Interglacial and interstadial vegetation in England', *Proc. Linn. Soc. London*, **172**, 81–9.

142 WEST, R. G., LAMBERT, C. A. and SPARKS, B. W. 1964. 'Interglacial deposits at Ilford, Essex', *Phil. Trans. R. Soc.*, B, **247**, 185–212.

143 WEST, R. G. and MCBURNEY, C. M. B. 1955. 'The Quaternary deposits

at Hoxne, Suffolk, and their archaeology', *Proc. Prehist. Soc.*, **20,** 131–54.

144  WEST, R. G. and SPARKS, B. W. 1960. 'Coastal interglacial deposits of the English Channel', *Phil. Trans. R. Soc.*, B, **243,** 95–133.

145  WEST, R. G. and WILSON, D. G. 1966. 'Cromer Forest Bed Series', *Nature*, **209,** 497–8.

146  WILMOTT, A. J. 1935. 'Evidence in favour of survival of the British Flora in glacial times', in Discussion on the origin and relationship of the British Flora. *Proc. R. Soc.*, B, **118,** 197–241.

147  WOOD, S. V. 1848–1882. 'A monograph of the Crag Mollusca', *Mon. Palaeontogr. Soc.*

148  WYMER, J. and CHURCHILL, D. M. 1962. 'Excavations at the Maglemosian sites at Thatcham, Berkshire, England. The stratigraphy of the Mesolithic sites III and IV at Thatcham, Berkshire, England', *Proc. Prehist. Soc.*, **28,** 329–70.

149  ZAGWIJN, W. H. 1959. 'Zur stratigraphischen und pollenanalytischen Gliederung der Pliozänen ablagerungen im Roertal-Graben und Venloer Graben der Niederlande', *Fortschr. Geol. Rheinld. u. Westf.*, **4,** 5–26.

150  ZAGWIJN, W. H. 1960. 'Aspects of the Pliocene and Early Pleistocene vegetation in the Netherlands', *Med. Geol. Sticht.*, series C III, **1,** No. 5.

151  ZEUNER, F. E. 1959. *The Pleistocene Period.* 2nd edn. London: Hutchinson.

*Appendix 1*

# METHODS OF ISOLATING AND COUNTING FOSSILS

## EXTRACTION OF THE SMALLER MACROSCOPIC FOSSILS (SEEDS, FRUITS, MOLLUSCA, SMALL VERTEBRATES)

*Method 1*

Break up the lumps of material along the bedding planes and pick out any leaves or large moss stems. Put small lumps of material into a pudding basin and cover with 10 per cent $HNO_3$, or 5 per cent NaOH; the NaOH tends to soften plant tissue, but is better for breaking down some muds. Leave in a fume chamber for at least 24 hours, and stir occasionally until all the lumps have broken down.

Remove any seeds or other fossils which have floated to the top and put a small amount of the broken-down sediment, say 20 ml, on a sieve (100 mesh to the inch), and wash with a spray of water, stirring or agitating the sediment until the washing water becomes clear. If there is coarse detritus it may be necessary to use a coarser sieve (about 35 mesh to the inch) above the fine one, and then to examine the material in two fractions.

Tip the coarse fraction on to a soup plate, add water and use a fine paint brush to lift out seeds and other identifiable remains. Put the finer fraction into a smaller dish and extract the seeds under a low-power binocular microscope (about ×6).

Collect the identifiable remains on damp filter paper in a Petri dish or partially sort them into 4-part paint palettes, or similar dishes, in water and cover with a Petri dish. Surface patterns of the remains are often best seen while they are drying out after wetting with alcohol. But the remains should be kept either dry or wet, as alternate wetting and drying tends to damage them.

When the remains have been identified, they should be stored in small tubes in a glycerine, alcohol and formalin or thymol mixture, and labelled with glass writing ink.

*Method 2*

This method for the extraction of shells, fruits, seeds and small bones is abridged from the detailed account by Sparks.[7]

To break down sands and silts only gentle washing may be necessary, but a compacted sediment may need soaking in dilute NaOH, KOH or Calgon. When the matrix is broken down the residue is dried and sifted dry into fractions of over 2 mm, 1–2 mm, $\frac{1}{2}$–1 mm, and $\frac{1}{4}$–$\frac{1}{2}$ mm. The largest grade is sorted on a black glass plate, the next two by sprinkling the material thinly on a lined porcelain plate and systematically scanned with a low-power binocular microscope. All identifiable remains can be picked out with a moistened brush. The $\frac{1}{4}$–$\frac{1}{2}$ mm grade is examined for very small seeds, *Chara* oospores and the tests of Foraminifera.

The fruits, seeds, etc., should be kept dry, since alternate wetting and drying tends to damage them. They can be conveniently stored dry in glass tubes.

### EXTRACTION OF INSECTS[3]

In predominantly inorganic sediments such as sands and silts, the material is first broken down (as above) then washed through a series of sieves, and the residues sorted under a low-power binocular microscope. It is found that most beetle remains are in the fractions retained by sieves of 50 mesh to the inch or less. In biogenic sediments such as felted peats, it is best to split the material along the bedding planes and pick out insect remains. Associated fragments of the same individual can be found in this way, but it has also been demonstrated that there may be a subjective bias to the advantage of the more obvious and larger insects.

### EXTRACTION OF FORAMINIFERA (AND OSTRACODS)

Numerous methods of extraction of Foraminifera and ostracods from different types of sediment have been devised, details of which can be found in text books of micropalaeontology. For unconsolidated clastic sediments commonly encountered in the Pleistocene simple methods are usually sufficient. A useful summary of the factors to be considered in the sampling, preparation and investigation of Pleistocene Foraminifera is given by Feyling-Hanssen.[6] The following account has been very kindly provided by Dr B. M. Funnell.

The quantity of original sediment required to yield a few hundred Foraminifera is very variable. In sparsely fossiliferous sediments up to 2 kg may be desirable, whereas in highly fossiliferous sediments

10 gm will suffice. In general, however, 100 gm is often found to be a convenient amount to prepare, although larger samples may be collected to provide a reserve of material in case of need.

*Dispersion and cleaning.* The sediment to be prepared should be thoroughly dried and if it is clayey broken up into fragments of not more than 1 ml in size. It is then dropped into a beaker containing a hot solution of sodium carbonate, and gently boiled for ten minutes—longer if the lumps of clay have not dispersed by then. It can be stirred with a glass rod to assist dispersion but care should be taken not to crush the Foraminifera against the bottom of the beaker with the end of the rod. If the clay is tenacious and does not disperse easily it is probably more straightforward to decant the clay already dispersed, dry out the residue and start again rather than to continue boiling and stirring. An alternative method of dispersion for dense clays is to immerse the broken up dry clay in a dilute (5 per cent) solution of hydrogen peroxide. The effervescence produced is rather variable, depending on the state of oxidation and organic content of the clay, and delicate tests may be damaged by the slightly acid reaction.

*Sieving.* The dispersed sediment is sieved wet through a 240 mesh ($65\mu$ opening) sieve, flushing out gently with running water. This sieve retains all sand-size particles including Foraminifera, allowing silt and clay to pass through. Some Foraminifera, particularly immature individuals, are smaller than $65\mu$, but their systematic study is impracticable. Indeed, it is customary to make routine observations only on the Foraminifera retained by a 120 mesh ($125\mu$ opening) sieve, the 125 to $65\mu$ fraction being reserved for special study of rare forms, immature individuals, and so on. The maximum size of Foraminifera varies between different environments but for the Pleistocene of north-west Europe only rare individuals exceed $1000\mu$ (1 mm).

*Picking.* After sieving, the sediment retained on the sieves is dried and spread on a small (10 cm square or less) tray with a black ground divided into a grid. It is examined systematically under incident illumination with a low-power binocular microscope at magnifications of ×20 or ×40, and the Foraminifera removed to a standard slide on the end of a '00' or '000' sable brush moistened with water (the amount of moistening required can only be learned with practice —it should be remembered that the brush may dry out relatively quickly under the heat of the incident illuminator). Some investigators prefer to divide the residue into separate fractions, e.g. 1000–500$\mu$, 500–250$\mu$ and 250–125$\mu$ for picking: this avoids the necessity for frequent magnification changes, and scanning is made easier when all the particles are more or less the same size. If the original sediment was a relatively pure clay a high proportion of the residue being examined will consist of microfossils; if it was sandy they will be scattered amongst mineral grains. A concentration of the chambered tests of Foraminifera and of paired ostracod values can be effected by completely drying out the residue (using alcohol if necessary) and floating on the heavy liquid, carbon tetrachloride. In general mineral grains sink and the air-filled Foraminifera float and can be decanted. However the proportion of shell to chamber space is high in some Foraminifera and the chambers may be infilled with authigenic minerals, notably pyrites and glauconite, after deposition, causing some Foraminifera to sink; the method cannot therefore be relied upon to give a quantitative yield.

*Mounting.* The standard slide used for Foraminifera consists of a recessed black card cell, with a glass cover of the same size as a standard microscope slide. The cell is either single and circular (c.1 cm diameter) for types or single species, or rectangular (c. 4 × 2 cm) and divided into 60 or 100 subdivisions for assemblages. The black base of the cell (with its subdivisions) is frequently photographic paper with an emulsion surface. Foraminifera will adhere to this satisfactorily for most laboratory purposes by placing them in position wet and allowing them to dry without disturbance. If the surface is not adhesive a *small* amount of gum tragacanth, preferably incorporating some mould preventative (e.g. thymol), may be applied. In either case it should be possible to remove the Foraminifera easily at a later date by application of a little water at the end of a sable brush. Difficulties in removal may be experienced if the specimen is allowed to adhere by a flat or slightly concave surface. Examination for purposes of identification requires magnifications up to the limit of the low-power binocular microscope, i.e. around ×200.

### EXTRACTION OF MARINE MOLLUSCS

Take a sample of about 300 gm. If there is much clay, wet with water and cover with 100 volumes hydrogen peroxide solution in a pudding basin. The mixture may boil if too little water is added at the beginning. Organic matter is destroyed, so pollen or plant macroscopic samples required should be removed previously.

The sample is then washed through sieves of the following mesh numbers: $3\frac{1}{2}$, 7, 20, 40, 80. This can conveniently be done by placing the sample in the coarsest sieve, agitating it in a bucket of water until separation is as complete as possible, then washing the material remaining on the sieve with a jet of water into the bucket. The sieve and its contents are then dried in an oven. This procedure is repeated with the remaining four sieves, by pouring the contents of the bucket through the second sieve into another bucket, and so on. The dried sieve contents are then assembled in a column and shaken to complete the separation.

The contents of each sieve are tipped into a 9 inch Petri dish and examined systematically under a low-power binocular microscope and fragments and whole shells are picked out with a sable brush, identified and recorded.

In counting, a gasteropod shell with an apex, or one lacking so little of the apex that the remainder cannot be identified alone, is counted as one individual. A lamellibranch fragment with a hinge, or so much of hinge that the remainder cannot be identified alone, is counted as half an individual.

Specimens can be stored in cavity slides with a black background or in tubes.

### POLLEN ANALYSIS

The following procedures are used in the Sub-department of Quaternary Research at Cambridge. A much fuller discussion of methods and problems is given by Faegri and Iversen,[5] Erdtman,[4] and Brown.[2]

Samples for pollen analysis are chemically treated to remove the organic and inorganic material which obscures the pollen. Since not all samples need every treatment, it is useful to prepare temporary mounts in glycerine after each process for each different type of sediment, to check how the preparation is proceeding. Samples are washed and centrifuged between each treatment. 50 ml Pyrex or polypropylene centrifuge tubes are most commonly used, but for fresh pollen or samples which do not settle well after centrifuging, 10 or 15 ml size tubes are better. The hydrofluoric acid (HF) treatment slightly dissolves Pyrex glass.

Samples in 50 ml tubes should be centrifuged for about 4 minutes at c. 2000 r.p.m.; those in 10–15 ml tubes for 1–2 minutes. Balance alternate pairs of tubes before each centrifugation. After each chemical treatment add water and stir well. Balance the tube, centrifuge, and then carefully pour off in one movement the supernatant liquid.

It is advisable to wear rubber gloves while handling HF. HF burns should be treated as soon as possible at hospital by an injection of 10 per cent calcium gluconate under the coagulum of the burn. An ampoule of calcium gluconate should be kept in the laboratory for taking to the hospital.

### Breaking up sediments

*Muds and clays*. Put a small amount of the sample on a watch glass and add dilute HCl. If effervescence occurs put about 2 gm in a beaker with 7 per cent HCl. Stir and add more HCl until effervescence ceases. Froth may be dispersed with acetone or alcohol. Filter as for peats.

*Peats*. Put 1 to 2 gm of the peaty sample in a boiling tube with about 20 ml of 10 per cent NaOH or 5 per cent KOH. (This removes unsaturated soil colloids.) Break up with a glass rod. Leave in a bath with boiling water until the sample is thoroughly broken down and no lumps remain (10 minutes to 1 hour).

Filter through a fine steel gauze (100 mesh to the inch) into a centrifuge tube.

Wash the sediment towards the middle of the gauze with running water. Invert and wash the sediment into a Petri dish. Keep this residue in water for subsequent examination.

Centrifuge and decant. The supernatant liquid will be very dark if much humic material is present.

Wash, centrifuge and decant. Wash and centrifuge again if necessary, i.e. if the supernatant is not fairly clear.

### Oxidation (*for the removal of lignin*)

Pollen is easily destroyed by oxidation so the reaction should be stopped with water as soon as the sample is bleached.

Add 8 ml glacial acetic acid and 4·5 ml sodium chlorate (a saturated solution is c. 100 gm to 200 ml water). Stir with a glass rod and add 1 ml concentrated $H_2SO_4$ drop by drop. Cover the tube with a glass ball or watch glass and leave it in a fume chamber until the supernatant becomes yellow or orange. Although muds and clays may be safe when left for 12 to 16 hours, peats may oxidise in a few minutes. Slow oxidation can be accelerated by adding one or more drops of concentrated hydrochloric acid.

Centrifuge and decant.

If the sample contains coarse sand, add water, stir, and decant into a small beaker. Rinse out the centrifuge tube and decant the sample back again. Centrifuge and decant.

*Treatment of siliceous samples*

A chemical method is given here, but flotation and gravity separation methods are also used.

Transfer about ½ ml of the material into a 10 ml copper, nickel or platinum crucible. Use a little 7 per cent HCl if necessary.

Add HF (40 to 60 per cent) until the crucible is about two-thirds full.

Gently boil for 2 or 3 minutes, on a sand bath or clay triangle, in a fume chamber.

When the mixture has cooled a little, pour it (using nickel tongs) into a small beaker containing about 20 ml of 7 per cent HCl, then tip this mixture into a centrifuge tube and cover it.

Centrifuge and decant.

Wash, centrifuge and decant. If sample contains clay or silt omit this washing, and carry on with the next.

Without boiling, heat with 7 per cent HCl to remove colloidal silicon dioxide and silicofluorides.

Centrifuge while hot and decant.

Add a few drops of dilute NaOH to the next washing water, centrifuge and decant.

Examine with the aid of a microscope; if clumps of inorganic material remain, repeat with further hot HCl.


*Acetolysis* (Acid hydrolysis of the cellulose)

This stage may be omitted if there is very little cellulose in the sample.

Add 10 ml glacial acetic acid, stir, and carefully add ½ ml concentrated $H_2SO_4$.

Leave in a bath of boiling water for half an hour and stir the sample occasionally.

Centrifuge, and wash twice. To the first washing water add a few drops of dilute NaOH.


*Erdtman's Acetolysis*

Erdtman's acetolysis is an effective method of removing organic material which cannot otherwise be destroyed. If rapid oxidation is used, it should not precede this acetolysis or the grains may become very swollen. Badly-preserved pollen may be destroyed or swollen beyond recognition. Well-preserved grains are slightly enlarged and become yellow or brown. Staining may be omitted if preferred.

Use 10 or 15 ml tubes and dehydrate the sample by centrifuging with glacial acetic acid, and then decant.

Prepare the acetolysis mixture by adding 1 ml of concentrated $H_2SO_4$ to 9 ml of acetic anhydride. Thoroughly mix in a measuring cylinder with a glass rod.

Add the acetolysis fluid, put a glass rod in each tube and place the tubes in a water bath at a temperature below 70°C.

Heat the water bath to 100°C and leave tubes there for 1 to 2 minutes. Stir the contents two or three times while heating, but take care that the water does not boil into the tubes.

Balance with the acetolysis fluid or with glacial acetic acid, centrifuge for 1 or 2 minutes and decant.

Wash with glacial acetic acid, centrifuge and decant.

Wash and centrifuge twice with water. Add a few drops of dilute sodium hydroxide to the first washing.


*Preparation of pollen mounts* (*washing, staining and mounting*)

*Glycerine jelly.* The mounts are permanent, and the mounting medium gels. Grains cannot be moved about on the slide unless it is heated first.

Pour off all supernatant liquid, carefully invert tube and drain over filter paper.

Add twice the bulk of glycerine jelly stained with safranin, stir well and warm for half a minute.

Prepare up to 5 slides for each sample, with large thin coverslips e.g. 2 inch $\times$ $\frac{7}{8}$ inch, No. 0.

Use a pipette or glass rod to streak out the material on to a slide, and gently lower the coverslip. If necessary leave the slide on a hot plate to spread the jelly evenly.

Label with glass-writing ink.

N.B. Examine with a microscope one slide prepared from each sample to see if further dilution with glycerine jelly is needed. If organic material clumps and obscures the pollen, gentle movement of the coverslip may help to disperse it.


*Silicone Oil.*[1] A liquid mounting medium of high viscosity. The slides are permanent. Dehydration is necessary before staining and mounting.

Wash with a few drops of water and 96 per cent alcohol. Centrifuge and decant.

Wash with 99 per cent alcohol and stain with fuchsin if desired. Centrifuge and decant.

Wash with benzene. Centrifuge and decant.

Add c. 1 ml benzene, transfer to small tube, add silicone oil

BB

(viscosity 2000 centistokes or more), leave to evaporate for about 24 hours. The tubes may be stored in this state.

Add silicone oil to give suitable concentration of pollen grains, but as little as possible. Place the contents of the tube on a slide, cover with ⅝ inch square No. 0 coverslip.

## Preparation of pollen reference slides

Take the stamens of the flower concerned, grind in a mortar, wash through a fine sieve with a jet of alcohol into a 10 or 15 ml centrifuge tube, and centrifuge. Then treat with either a 10 minute acetolysis or by Erdtman's acetolysis. Wash twice and prepare slides with ⅝ inch square No. 0 coverslips. Mount as above.

## Pollen counting

A high-power binocular microscope with a mechanical stage is used for the analyses. Magnifications of at least × 300 are required for routine counting, but for closer examination of grains, × 1000 is also essential. This entails the use of an oil immersion lens with a high numerical aperture (1.3). The most convenient immersion oil is anisol, which can be easily removed from slides and lenses. Phase-contrast equipment is also desirable, as this type of microscopy gives greater detail of pollen grain morphology, and keys to modern pollen types may be based on phase-contrast observations.

The procedure for counting is to traverse the width of the slide at standard intervals, not less than 1½ field diameters apart. As the pollen may be unevenly distributed on the slide, it is important to traverse the whole width of the slide and space the traverses at intervals over the length of the slide. A note is kept of the number of traverses, as this gives a rough idea of pollen frequency on the slide.

Each grain encountered during the traverses is identified and recorded on a form with the main pollen types already printed on it. The traverses are continued till the total number required is achieved. The positions of unidentified grains are carefully recorded by ringing them with ink or recording the mechanical stage reading. These grains should be identified as nearly as possible after the count has been made.

### DIATOM ANALYSIS

The following account has been very kindly provided by Dr G. H. Evans.

*Extraction and mounting*

Place a small quantity (e.g. about 0·1 gm dry weight) of the sample in a small conical flask.

Add a few drops of 30 per cent hydrogen peroxide to break up the sample.

Add 10 ml normal potassium dichromate and mix thoroughly.

Add slowly 20 ml of concentrated $H_2SO_4$ and allow to stand for half an hour. Oxidation of organic matter occurs.

Wash and centrifuge the flask contents till the supernatant is clear.

Place the contents of the centrifuge tube in a 50 ml measuring cylinder and add distilled water to 50 ml. Shake thoroughly.

Transfer a drop of the suspension to a coverslip and allow to dry at room temperature.

Prepare a slide by placing a crystal of Mikrops 163 mountant (Refractive Index 1.63) on it and melting in an oven at c. 110°C.

Invert the slide on to the coverslip, place in the oven at c. 110°C. and allow the mountant to spread across the slide.


*Counting*

The procedure is similar to that used in pollen analysis. A count of 600 to 1000 valves per horizon has been used as a basis for percentage frequency calculations.

## REFERENCES

1 ANDERSEN, S. T. 1960. 'Silicone oil as a mounting medium for pollen grains', *Danm. Geol. Unders.*, IV Raekke, **4**, No 1.

2 BROWN, C. A. 1960. *Palynological techniques.* Baton Rouge.

3 COOPE, G. R. 1961. 'On the study of glacial and interglacial insect faunas', *Proc. Linn. Soc. London*, **172**, 62–5.

4 ERDTMAN, G. 1943. *An introduction to pollen analysis.* Waltham, Mass.: Chronica Botanica.

5 FAEGRI, K. and IVERSEN, J. 1964. *Textbook of pollen analysis.* 2nd edn. Oxford: Blackwell.

6 FEYLING-HANSSEN, R. W. 1964. 'Foraminifera in late Quaternary deposits from the Oslofjord area', *Norges Geol. Unders.*, No. 225.

7 SPARKS, B. W. 1961. 'The ecological interpretation of non-marine mollusca', *Proc. Linn. Soc. London*, **172**, 71–80.

# LACQUER METHOD OF TREATING SECTIONS[1]

The following account includes notes which have been very kindly provided by Dr W. H. Zagwijn of the Geological Survey of the Netherlands.

The exposure should be cleaned very thoroughly and left at a near vertical angle, at about 70 to 80°. The surface should be neither completely dry nor wet, so that the right weather should be chosen for the purpose. If it is too wet the surface may be dried by a blowlamp. A horizontal gully is made along the top of the section near its edge. A mixture of lacquer (polyvinyl acetate) and thinner (acetone) is then made in proportions about 3 : 1 and poured into the gully. It overflows down the section. Add more mixture in the gully till the whole cleaned surface has been covered. About 2 kg of the mixture will cover 1 sq m of the section. A less dilute mixture is required with sands than with clays.

An alternative method, suitable for greater heights of section, is to spray the mixture on to the surface, then paint less dilute mixture over this.

The lacquer should be left to dry for a day, then, in order to strengthen the lacquer film, gauze is laid on the lacquer surface and incorporated by painting on undiluted lacquer. This should then be left to dry for another day, when the whole may be peeled off the section. The lacquer sheet with the adherent sediment may then be glued to hardboard and permanently framed if necessary. A thin film of the sediments is thus permanently preserved.

## REFERENCE

1 VOIGT, E. 1949. 'Die Anwendung der Lackfilm-Methode bei der Bergung geologischer und bodenkundlicher Profile', *Mitt. Geol. Staatsinst. Hamburg*, **19**, 111–29.

# INDEX

*(An asterisk refers to a text-figure)*